The Master Plant

The Master Plant

Tobacco in Lowland South America

Edited by
Andrew Russell and Elizabeth Rahman

Bloomsbury Academic
An imprint of Bloomsbury Publishing Plc

B L O O M S B U R Y

LONDON • OXFORD • NEW YORK • NEW DELHI • SYDNEY

Bloomsbury Academic
An imprint of Bloomsbury Publishing Plc

50 Bedford Square
London
WC1B 3DP
UK

1385 Broadway
New York
NY 10018
USA

www.bloomsbury.com

BLOOMSBURY and the Diana logo are trademarks of Bloomsbury Publishing Plc

First published 2015
Paperback edition first published 2016

British Library Cataloguing-in-Publication Data
A catalogue record for this book is available from the British Library.

ISBN: HB: 978-1-47258-754-1
PB: 978-1-350-00739-0
ePDF: 978-1-47258-755-8
ePub: 978-1-47258-756-5

Library of Congress Cataloging-in-Publication Data
The master plant : tobacco in lowland South America /
edited by Andrew Russell and Elizabeth Rahman.
pages cm
ISBN 978-1-4725-8754-1 (hardback) – ISBN 978-1-4725-8755-8 (epdf) –
ISBN 978-1-4725-8756-5 (epub) 1. Tobacco–South America–History.
2. Tobacco–Social aspects–South America. 3. South America–Social life
and customs. I. Russell, Andrew, 1958- editor. II. Rahman, Elizabeth, editor.
GT3021.S68M37 2015
394.1'4–dc23
2014037314

Typeset by Integra Software Services Pvt. Ltd.

This book is dedicated to Jane, Ben and Euan and to Syeed, Olivia, Carlos, Sasha and Sofia, with love.

Contents

List of Illustrations

List of Tables

Contributors

Bernd Brabec de Mori received his PhD in ethnomusicology from the University of Vienna. He conducted fieldwork in the Western Amazon for five years and since then has been working at the audiovisual archive *Phonogrammarchiv* of the Austrian Academy of Sciences, at the Centre for Systematic Musicology in Graz. He is currently employed as senior scientist at the Institute of Ethnomusicology at the University of Music and Performing Arts, Graz. His publications address the complex of music, healing and cosmologies among indigenous groups in the Western Amazon as well as ethnohistory and the ontology of sound perception. He recently edited *The Human and Non-Human in Lowland South American Indigenous Music*, a special issue of the British journal *Ethnomusicology Forum* (2013).

Renzo S. Duin trained in the four-field Anthropology Department of the University of Florida, and has held teaching and research positions at the University of Florida (USA) and Leiden University (the Netherlands). He is also a research associate of the University of Oxford (UK). Since 2009, Duin has been a research fellow of the Dutch National Science Foundation (NWO) based at Leiden University. He was the principle investigator and team leader of the NWO-Veni research project 'Beauty and the Feast' (2010-2014). His research is focused on socio-political landscapes, the transformation of local identities, and historical ecology in Guiana.

Juan Alvaro Echeverri received his PhD in anthropology from the New School for Social Research (New York). He is currently an associate professor of the Amazonia Campus of the Universidad Nacional de Colombia. He is a specialist in native Amazonian indigenous populations, with work and research experience since the 1980s in the Putumayo, Caraparana, Igaraparana, Caqueta and Amazon Rivers. He has conducted research in social anthropology, ethnohistory, traditional knowledge, linguistic documentation and revitalization, indigenous education, indigenous territories and ethnobotany. Publications include *Cool Tobacco, Sweet Coca: Teachings of an Indian Sage from the Colombian Amazon* (Themis Books).

Paolo Fortis is a lecturer at Durham University. He has been conducting research with Guna people in Panama since 1999 focusing on cosmology, visual arts, ecology, notions of the person and alterity. His publications include several articles and book chapters and a monograph entitled *Kuna Art and Shamanism: an Ethnographic Approach* (University of Texas Press).

Françoise Barbira Freedman has worked as a medical anthropologist at the University of Cambridge since she received her PhD in Social Anthropology in

1979. She has done extensive longitudinal field research In Western Amazonia on shamanism, medicinal plant use, maternal and child health and indigenous resurgence. She also directs two outreach projects derived from her academic research, Birthlight, a registered UK charity and Ampika, a spin-out company from the University of Cambridge.

Peter Gow is a professor at the University of St Andrews. Publications include *An Amazonian Myth and its History* (Oxford University Press) and *Of Mixed Blood – Kinship and History in Peruvian Amazonia* (Clarendon Press).

Nicholas C. Kawa is an assistant professor in the Department of Anthropology at Ball State University. His research focuses primarily on human relationships to soils and plants with specific interest in Amazonian agrobiodiversity and its management. He has published in such journals as *Current Anthropology*, *Anthropology Today*, *Human Ecology*, *Human Organization* and *Economic Botany*. He is also author of the forthcoming book *Amazonia in the Anthropocene* (University of Texas Press).

Augusto Oyuela-Caycedo is an associate professor at the University of Florida. He focuses on the relationship between humans and the natural environment, particularly the impact of Amerindian societies on diverse ecologies of northwestern South America. The problem is approached firstly in terms of the historical ecology of the upper Amazon and northern Andes; secondly, by emphasizing the role of ideology in human relations with the environment; and lastly, by focusing on the history of archaeology and anthropology in Latin America.

Elizabeth Rahman is based at the University of Oxford, trained in social anthropology at the LSE and social and medical anthropology at Oxford. Elizabeth specializes in hands-on, indigenous and applied techniques that cultivate mindfulness in diverse (environmental and climatic) milieux. Her doctoral research, entitled *Made by Artful Practice: Reproduction, Health and the Perinatal Period among Xié River Dwellers of Northwestern Brazil*, considers the repertoire of hands-on perinatal techniques used by the Amazonian Warekena and how these are used to make particular types of adept and healthy people. Forthcoming publications include a book chapter entitled 'Intergenerational mythscapes and infant care in northwestern Amazonia' in *Reproductive Cultures: Kinship, Social Practice and Inter-Generational Transmission* (K. Qureshi and S. Pooley (eds), Berghahn Books).

Alejandro Reig is a post-doctoral associate at the University of Oxford. He has carried out research in the Venezuelan Amazon since the early 1990s, engaged with several Venezuelan institutions, including the National Science Museum, the Centre for Tropical Health Research CAICET and Fundación La Salle de Ciencias Naturales. His doctoral research on Yanomami landscape and place-making was undertaken between 2007 and 2011 in the Upper Ocamo basin. Publications include 'The Orinoco headwaters expedition as a turning point in the development of external territorializations of the Venezuelan Amazon' in *Cambridge Anthropology*; and 'Vivencia de las identidades regionales, etnicidad y espacio cultural', in Cunill Grau, ed., *Geo Venezuela, Volume 8, Geografía Cultural* (Fundación Polar).

Andrew Russell is a reader in the Department of Anthropology, Durham University where he convenes the Anthropology of Health Research Group and teaches public health anthropology. His textbook for medical students *The Social Basis of Medicine* (Oxford: Wiley-Blackwell) won the British Medical Association's student textbook of the year award in 2010. He has also (with Elisa Sobo and Mary Thompson) edited *Contraception Across Cultures: Technologies, Choices, Constraints* (Berg) and, with Iain Edgar, *The Anthropology of Welfare* (Routledge).

Juan Pablo Sarmiento Barletti is a lecturer in Social Anthropology at Durham University. He has also taught at the University of St Andrews. Sarmiento Barletti has been working among different groups of Ashaninka people in Peruvian Amazonia since 2007. His forthcoming book, *The Pursuit of Well-being in an Amazonian Village* (Berghahn) centres on Ashaninka people's *kametsa asaiki* ('living well') as a joint project of reconciliation in the wake of the Peruvian internal war and of political resistance in response to the impositions of the Peruvian State's extractive agenda. Sarmiento Barletti is affiliated to the Centre for Amerindian, Latin American and Caribbean Studies at the University of St Andrews and to the Instituto de Estudios Peruanos in Lima, Peru.

Robin Wright is professor at the University of Florida and author of the acclaimed *Mysteries of the Jaguar Shamans: Ancient Knowledge of the Baniwa Maliiri* (University of Nebraska Press).

Foreword

From Gift of the Deities to Scourge among Humans

Robin Wright

> *The Indians say that this smoke is very wholesome for clearing and consuming superfluous humours of the brain. Moreover, if taken in this manner it satisfies hunger and thirst for some time. They also commonly use it if they have to discuss some matters among themselves: they draw in the smoke and then speak…*
>
> Thevet (1575)[1]

It is a great satisfaction to write the Foreword to this volume, an outstanding work that presents a valuable complement to Wilbert's pioneering *Tobacco and Shamanism in South America* (1987). Wilbert's work provided a comprehensive ethnographic survey of the uses of tobacco in nearly three hundred Indian societies in South America. His in-depth ethnographies of the Warao in the Orinoco delta fleshed-out the survey with detailed interpretations of tobacco use and shamanism, cosmology and ecology. Lévi-Strauss' *Mythologiques*, especially 'From Honey to Ashes', likewise analyses variations of tobacco myths from South and North American native societies.

This volume focuses on native cultures primarily of the South American lowlands and more especially, in western Amazonia (with Fortis' final chapter, on the Guna in Panama, offering fruitful comparisons). It makes significant advances by incorporating multiple temporal and spatial dimensions into the analyses. Firstly, it summarizes what is known from the archaeological record of the *longue durée* diffusion of Nicotiana species on the South American continent, the extraordinary diversity in forms of use and preparation and the variety of paraphernalia associated with consumption. Each chapter adds important ethnographic perspectives on tobacco use among specific peoples. In Gow's study, tobacco is analysed synchronically among related Arawakan cultures, as an element that may or may not combine with the psychoactive *ayahuasca* through complex processes of 'structural diffusion'. Further north, tobacco and the psychoactive *pariká* (various *Virola* species) combine as basic elements of Arawakan shamanism and sorcery, while *yagé* and tobacco are more characteristic of eastern-Tukanoan shamanic practice. It is such in-depth synchronic analyses engaged with historical diffusion processes that offer original perspectives on shamanic combinations of sacred plants in ritual practices.

The political-economic history of tobacco 'ideologies' in Barbira Freedman's study of over four centuries of colonization in the upper Amazon provides the context for a comprehensive perspective on shamanic practices in history, animistic cosmologies and pharmacology. Such multi-level approaches hold great potential as they 'address both local and scientific understandings of transformative actions within animistic ontologies' (Barbira Freedman, this volume).

Several chapters favour a micro-focus on the semiotics of tobacco in body and person-shaping, especially in passage and healing rites. Shamanic tobacco-blowing is the medium par excellence for transmitting powerful healing agencies onto a person, a state of being, *materia medica*, or environmental conditions. It is the privileged spiritual means through which harmonious conviviality and sociality are created and renewed.

Tobacco has most certainly stimulated human creativity in discovering as many possible ways of utilizing its properties to form and bind social relations: Yanomami wads of rolled-up leaves tucked in the lower lip are shared between ceremonial partners; the Bora and Witoto paste of tobacco mixed with salt is based in a tradition that is an integral 'part of the patterns of production and consumption of substances and of the production of bodies and persons' (Echeverri, this volume); Tukanoan peoples of the Uaupés insert long and thick cigars in forked and decorated wooden holders during ceremonies that recreate the migratory trajectory of their ancestors.

Among indigenous inhabitants of lowland South America tobacco is widely perceived to promote well-being, conviviality and shared relationships among humans and non-humans, humans and their ancestors, humans and the spirit-worlds. Examples abound in this volume to confirm the intimate connections between tobacco use and spirituality.

In both in South and North America (the latter, understandably, not covered in this book), tobacco is a medium through which prayers are offered to the deities, through which sacred words are embodied in and empower subjects and through which bonds of sociality are created and renewed. Divisiveness, conflict and anger are cooled and calmed; sweet-smelling smoke produced by mixtures of tobacco with a wide variety of aromatic leaves induce a desired state of healing and harmony.

My own research was among the Baníwa of northwest Amazonia. According to Baníwa traditions, tobacco was a gift from the spirit-owners: in primordial times, the Creator went to visit the House of Grandfather Tobacco, *Dthemaferi*, to request some tobacco to smoke. The elder Grandfather gave him dried tobacco leaves, but the Creator replied he wanted some green plants to put in his garden. The old *Dthemaferi* instructed the Creator to return home, for he would deliver the tobacco that night. Characteristically, in Baníwa stories, spirit-owners of natural elements deliver their gifts in mysterious ways. As the Creator's children waited for the visitor, during the night they felt a gust of wind blow and saw a fireball descending from the sky. It was *Dthemaferi* who informed the children that he would leave some seeds outside the back of the longhouse. Next morning, the Creator asked the children if a visitor had come during the night, and they looked out back to marvel at the fields of fresh green tobacco plants that had burst into bloom. The gift of tobacco plants was then given to all future generations. From the tobacco leaves, people make the sweet-tasting, smooth and cooling smoke that 'makes our souls content'.

Among Baníwa elders, tobacco was generally used in moderation. The elders would make one cigar rolled in *tauari* tree bark and tied together with a strip of the bark. One cigar would last them the whole day, they would not smoke it all at once, but rather a few puffs at a time, then put it out, hold it behind one ear, or in a pocket, and continue with their activities until the next pause for a few more puffs. Tobacco in this context was used as much to take away hunger as to socialize, or simply to pause and reflect.

In their ancestral emergence stories, the Baníwa primordial shaman blew sacred tobacco smoke over the umbilical cords of the very first ancestors to protect them from any harm. The umbilicus unites all generations to their ancestral sources. Each ancestor received its own spirit-names for sacred tobacco. The same sacred tobacco is invoked in post-birth chants which elders perform for newborn children and their families; when they search for the ancestral names to bestow upon the newborn; and when they initiate young children into adulthood. In the last-mentioned, chanters perform the most elaborate 'thought-journeys', done since the beginning of the world, in which their souls travel along the paths of sacred place-names created by tobacco smoke, departing from the centre of the world, voyaging by leaps and bounds through the ancestral spirit-world to all known 'ends' of the world to leave sacred music. Once they have completed the cycle of journeys, they return along the sun's path to the centre of the world bringing back the sacred tobacco. These tobacco voyages protect initiates from harmful spirits, leaving their bodies strong and resistant to pain and sickness.

Among northern Arawak, tobacco dries the small bodies of newborns from their 'leaky' state, making their bodies firm (Rahman, this volume), regulating their body temperatures. Without that regulatory action, facilitated by tobacco-blowing, babies would lose their body shapes, dissolving into watery beings, or – as myth tells – an assemblage of animist others. This process of body-shaping depends on a balance in which tobacco smoke plays a key role throughout early life.

Among the Baníwa, *pajés* never perform healing rites without their cigars (frequently made from commercially produced cords of tobacco which are considered stronger than home-grown plants). The shamans' cigar complements the psychoactive *pariká* snuff (*Virola anadenanthera*), called the 'blood of the Sickness Owner', a resinous exudate from the inner bark of the *Virola* which is boiled down to a reddish-brown crystalline snuff. This 'blood' is blown with a powerful blast of air through a long eagle-bone tube from the mouth of one shaman to the nostril of another, in the same way the Yanomami do with their *epena*. The *pariká* 'opens' their vision, 'shows' them the Other world, at which point the tobacco cigar is raised to the sky in order to encounter the jaguar-shaman-spirits. The primordial *pajé*, addressed as *padzu* ('Father'), is the 'owner' of sacred tobacco and *pariká* and will guide the *pajé*s in their search for the lost souls of the sick. In the celestial world, all the jaguar-shaman spirits from time immemorial dwell in villages of *pariká* and tobacco; their smoke forms the clouds that *pajés* must sweep away to get better vision.

So much more could be said about tobacco as the 'primary shamanic plant of the New World' (Pendell 2010: 32). While this volume is focused primarily on western Amazonian use, it provides a basis for extending comparisons to Central and North America and even the traditional cultures of Tibet (Berounský 2013). For example, some Mayan, Incan and Aztec carvings show ceremonial tobacco use. What better-known example from North America is there than of tobacco in the sacred pipe? The sacred pipe is the centre of traditional Native American spirituality.

The pipe is used for prayers and healing; its design has changed little over the centuries. Only tobacco or traditional red willow is smoked in it. Tobacco is the most widely used plant in Native North American rituals: tobacco ties are made as offerings and prayers tied to the centre-pole in the Sun Dance of the Plains; pinches of tobacco are sprinkled or put down on the ground as offerings to the spirit owners of places in the natural world.

'Clearly tobacco was a plant of enormous ritual potency and enormously variable use, but behind all the variety of uses was the idea that tobacco had the power to put one into a spiritually exalted state which was necessary even for secular enterprises. Because of its power it made a particularly appropriate gift to the spirits and means of addressing them.' (Springer 1981: 219, cited in Lyon, 1998: 336)

As with all the bountiful resources the natural world produced in the Americas, tobacco became vulnerable to the avarice and greed of powerful foreign interest groups. So, when colonization of the Americas began, the ancient traditions of the 'master plant' became the target of wealth-seeking agriculturalists. By the end of the seventeenth century, the seeds of two of the most difficult social problems that we still face today – tobacco abuse and slavery – had become firmly rooted in American soil. The use of tobacco products would continue to grow steadily from their humble beginnings, through the mass marketing of cigarettes in the twentieth century, until its growth was somewhat abated by the realization of the health risks inherent in tobacco consumption. Tobacco abuse is toxic, a fact that was well-known to native cultures long before industrial agriculture dominated its production. And, growing beside the tobacco plants, almost from the beginning, was slavery, another of the great poisons of our civilization. Many of the chapters in this volume eloquently speak to the adaptations and dilemmas by Amazonian indigenous peoples when faced by these perversions of the 'Master Plant'.

Note

1. André Thevet was a French Franciscan missionary (1502–1590) working among the Tupinamba Indians of the South American coast in what is now Brazil.

Acknowledgements

The symposium at which some of the papers in this volume were first presented and discussed was held in Durham in July 2013. We are grateful to those contributors who were able to be present at the symposium for their fine company, comments and insights both during the event and over the course of this project. We are grateful to Durham University's Wolfson Research Institute for Health and Wellbeing for a small grant which funded the attendance of participants at the symposium and to the University's Santander mobility grant fund which supported the attendance of Juan Alvaro Echeverri. Andrew Russell held a Leverhulme Trust Research Fellowship during 2014 which expedited some of the editing work. Mark Nesbitt and Caroline Cornish at the National Herbarium, Kew, were very helpful in giving us access to their collections and encouraging their use. We are grateful to Luci Attala and the conference, Botanical Ontologies, held in Oxford in May 2014, and to Danilo Paiva Ramos, for pointing out some of the insights into tobacco intelligence outlined in the Introduction. Finally it is clear from the chapters that follow what an immense debt of gratitude all authors owe to their Amerindian friends and interlocutors, too numerous to mention, whose unique insights fill the pages of *The Master Plant*.

The editors and publisher gratefully acknowledge the permissions granted to reproduce copyright material in this book. Utah Press, Johannes Wilbert and Noel Diaz are thanked for the reproduction of Figure I.1. Figure I.2 is reproduced with kind permission of Stephen Hugh-Jones, Fernando Santos-Granero and the University of Arizona Press. Thanks are given to the Royal Botanic Gardens, Kew for permission to reproduce the photo of the object appearing in Figure I.3. R. S. Lewis and Springer-Verlag Press are thanked for permission granted to reproduce Table 1.1. Figure 4.2 is reproduced with the kind permission of the Collection Ethnomedicine, Medical University Vienna. Thanks go to O.L. Montenegro for Figures 5.1 and 5.4. Oscar Román Muruy is thanked for his drawing which appears in Figure 5.3. Finally, thanks are given to the Pitt Rivers Museum for allowing us to produce the photo of the object appearing in Figure 7.2. Every effort has been made to trace copyright holders and to obtain their permission for the use of copyright material. The publisher apologizes for any errors or omissions in the above list and would be grateful if notified of any corrections that should be incorporated in future reprints or editions of this book.

Andrew Russell and Elizabeth Rahman

Introduction: The Changing Landscape of Tobacco Use in Lowland South America

Andrew Russell and Elizabeth Rahman

Introduction

The effects of the global spread of tobacco and its associated products are well documented, but relatively little recent attention has been paid to traditional modes of tobacco use among indigenous groups in what is its historical source area, lowland South America. The ways in which tobacco is viewed and used in this region are, cosmologically speaking, poles apart from the ways in which tobacco has been exploited by the forces of corporate and state-sponsored global capitalism, conditions which have proved so devastating for long-term human health and well-being.[1] The people who are the primary focus of this book often have a different perspective on tobacco. Our aim is to articulate some of these viewpoints, with the suggestion that their consideration might encourage new ways of thinking about the problems that commercially exploited tobacco has created in terms of human health and well-being.

Tobacco consumption around the world has increased exponentially since European explorers first observed its use and transported seeds of the plant from indigenous communities in the Americas in the sixteenth century.[2] Today, there are an estimated 1 billion regular tobacco users worldwide, consuming (apart from other tobacco products) an estimated 6 trillion cigarettes per year (WHO 2011a: 17). Tobacco has come to occupy a prominent place in public health discourse, both nationally and internationally. Headline statements include 'the world's greatest cause of preventable death' (Kohrman and Benson 2011: 329) and that 'one in every two life-long smokers is killed by tobacco and most smokers lose many years of active life' (ASH 2008: 1). The prospect is that smoking will cause 1 billion deaths in the twenty-first century – around 70–80 per cent in low- and middle-income countries (WHO 2011b). In response to the increasing volume of tobacco consumption and the widely acknowledged health dangers, the world's first World Health Organization-mediated treaty, the Framework Convention on Tobacco Control (WHO 2003), has been established as a response to such a global threat. Much of the impetus for its success and ongoing development of this treaty has come from countries of the 'global South' as they seek redress against the machinations of the overweening power of the transnational tobacco industry (Russell et al. 2014).

The role of tobacco among indigenous populations in lowland South America provides some fascinating comparisons and contrasts with its status in other parts of the world. In this Introduction, we review the scholarship that has preceded this book and the different frameworks that can be used to understand the place of tobacco among indigenous groups in lowland South America from whence its status as a 'master plant' derives. These include ethnographic knowledge about the diverse uses of tobacco (in the context, sometimes, of other psychoactive drugs) as well as key developments in anthropological theory and emergent public health responses to indigenous forms of tobacco use. Our book fills an important gap in the literature about what has become a transnationally exploited commodity and serves to portray this controversial plant in a more complex way, as an agent of both enlightenment and destruction.

Tobacco as a 'master plant'

Tobacco is often described as a 'master plant' by indigenous users in lowland South America, a status that seems intrinsically related to its potent toxicity and role in shamanism. Goodman (1993) comments on the ubiquity of narcotic plants used for shamanic purposes among indigenous societies in both North and South America, with at least 130 plants that could be categorized as hallucinogenic. In order to achieve the altered states of consciousness necessary for shamanic journeying to occur, a range of plants may be used. Datura, mescal, peyote, coca, *parikā*[3] and *ayahuasca* (or *yagé*, produced from the vine *Banisteriopsis caapi*) are some of the most well-known South American narcotics and stimulants in this regard.[4] What Goodman points out, however, is that 'when one looks more carefully at what plants shamans actually used, one discovers a most remarkable phenomenon: regardless of location, the one plant used more than any other was tobacco. *Virtually every Amerindian society knew tobacco*' (1993: 24 [our emphasis]).

Given its ubiquity, the relative lack of scholarly attention to tobacco in lowland South American studies is remarkable. Miller talks of 'the humility of things' by which he means the ability of something like tobacco to 'fade out of focus and remain peripheral to our vision and yet determinant of our behaviour and identity' (2005: 5).[5] It may be that the very ubiquity and long history of tobacco use in lowland South America has led to the naïve assumption that tobacco in Amazonia was 'just there', 'so ancient as to be virtually meaningless at the level of concrete ethnohistorical and ethnographic data' (Gow, this volume). Tobacco continues to litter contemporary ethnography, but it has rarely formed the focus of any concrete study or analysis.

Another reason for the relative paucity of detailed studies may be the 'show stopping' presence of one major work on the topic, namely Wilbert's (1987) book, *Tobacco and Shamanism in South America*. This work combines anthropology, history, botany and pharmacology in a widely referenced *tour de force*. Wilbert pulled together pretty much all that was known about the subject at the time of publication – its bibliography alone constitutes 77 of its 294 pages, and much of the information it contains remains salient today. In *Tobacco and Shamanism*, he looks first at the botany of the wild and cultivated genus Nicotiana. He points out that forty-six of the sixty-four species identified are found in the Americas, thirty-seven of these in South America, thus making it highly likely that lowland South America is the progenitor of tobacco worldwide.[6] The commercial tobacco now used in most cigarettes, *Nicotiana tabacum*, is one of two cultivated species. The other, *N. rustica*, 'hardier and richer in narcotic properties' (1987: 6), has spread far beyond the tropical and subtropical belt.

Wilbert emphasizes the tremendous diversity of methods for tobacco use in South America. This diversity (along with linguistic evidence) suggests a long history of regional engagement with tobacco and its by-products. Chewing, drinking tobacco juice, licking, snuffing, smoking and its use in enemas – all are meticulously described and discussed in their multifaceted diversity, along with the paraphernalia associated with each. One striking observation is of a Yaruro shaman who 'in the course of an all-night performance ... was observed to have consumed forty-two industrial cigarettes and about one hundred native cigars' (1987: 85). Wilbert also addresses the common scenario of outsourced tobacco: 'For the Warao of the Orinoco Delta [the group among which Wilbert himself had conducted fieldwork] tobacco is of utmost cultural significance despite the fact that they cannot grow it in their swampy habitat but rely on its importation from the island of Trinidad and from regions adjacent to the Orinoco Delta' (1987: 83). Many other groups in addition to the Warao use tobacco that has been imported either to supplement, or instead of, the locally grown product.

Wilbert also looks at pharmacological aspects of tobacco use, its active ingredients and the modes by which these are absorbed, distributed and metabolized within the body. In his view, the physiological and psychological effects of tobacco (at least, of the species consumed by the respective groups in the quantities that they do) confirmed rather than shaped the 'basic tenets of shamanic ideology' (1987: 148).[7] He suggests that shamanism preceded tobacco use, with South American hunter and gatherer groups relying 'on endogenous and ascetic techniques of mystic ecstasy rather than on drug-induced trance' (1987: 149). The use of tobacco for shamanic purposes apparently developed only among horticultural peoples.[8] Since horticulture in lowland South America has a history of at least 8,000 years, the diffusion of *N. rustica* and *N. tabacum* as cultigens, presumably for their hallucinogenic properties, must likewise be 'of considerable antiquity' (1987: 150).

Wilbert continues his theme of how the botany and biochemistry of tobacco provides empirical, experiential support for a number of shamanic practices (including initiations, near- and actual-death experiences and other ordeals). Those using tobacco for these purposes are categorized by the umbrella term 'tobacco shaman', by which he means 'the religious practitioner who uses tobacco, whether exclusively or not, to be ordained, to officiate, and to achieve altered states of consciousness'

(150, fn1). The frequent presence of Nicotiana species on recently disturbed ground such as graves has, Wilbert suggests, led to Amerindians 'etiologically identifying the plant with the ancestors and with ancestral deified shamans' (1987: 151), a fact also elucidated by myth. Butt-Colson's (1977: 53) account of a tobacco which the Akawaio call 'tiger tobacco' (*kumeli*) is also mentioned. Because its mottled leaves resemble a jaguar's markings, shamans are said to smoke it order to summon a type of jaguar spirit.[9]

Among other themes that seem near universal in their applicability across the Amazon region (albeit in varying proportions and different cosmological contexts) are the blowing of tobacco smoke (or tobacco spit), tobacco as shamanic food (and, by sublimation, a sacramental food of the gods or spirits), the analgesic properties of tobacco in creating shamanic insensitivity to heat and pain, the ingestion of tobacco products to contact the spirit world, and shape-shifting to become were-animals (particularly jaguars) – combative champions against 'evil spirits, sorcerers, sterility, sickness and death' (Butt-Colson 1977: 192). The chemical action of nicotine as an insecticide also leads to the use of tobacco as a fumigant for maize, fish and cassava (Butt-Colson 1977: 152), as a poultice against ticks and sand fleas and, by extension, for cleansing and curing and as a more general elixir for human vitality (Butt-Colson 1977: 154). Its analgesic properties are used to treat toothache (Butt-Colson 1977: 189).

The definitive quality of Wilbert's work may have contributed to a sense that tobacco in South America had been dealt with and that there remained nothing more to be said about it. Twenty-five years later, Barbira Freedman observed 'tobacco has received comparatively little attention in recent anthropological research on Amazonian shamanism' (2002: 136). It would be churlish to criticize Wilbert's monumental tome, but its approach is largely ethnological rather than ethnographic, concerned more with mapping than with meaning. In revisiting this topic nearly thirty years after the publication of Wilbert's book, we can see various ways in which the ethnographic record, aspects of anthropological thinking and the wider political-economic landscape have developed meanwhile. We shall go on to consider these issues and their implications for how we apprehend the 'master plant' today.

But why 'Master'? Barbira Freeman (2010) demonstrates a pairing of plants among the Lamista Quechua into females and males, with each belonging to a different cosmological domain (female plants to the water domain and male plants to the upland forest). Tobacco is considered 'the male catalyst that enhances the effects of all other shamanic plants' and is the 'father of all plants' according to Lamista Quechua shamans, 'a male consort to the "mother spirits" of all shamanic plants' (Barbira Freeman 2010: 151). In choosing the title of this book, however, we are not subscribing to an essentialized 'male' view of tobacco. Londoño Sulkin found 'differences between clans and language groups concerning the gender of tobacco itself: for some, the sweat-*cum*-seminal substance of the Grandfather of Tobacco was the origin of the Land of the Centre, of rivers, and eventually, of people. For others, the tobacco deity was the Mother upon whose shoulder the creator god created the land and placed it. In the myths of at least one Muniane clan... the creator deity made the first man out of tobacco paste and other substances, and brought him to life by blowing tobacco breath on him' (2012: 97–98). The Spanish translation of our title would necessarily be feminine, namely, 'La planta maestra', which resonates with Shakespeare's 20th sonnet 'Hast thou, the master-mistress[10] of my soul... ' (Echeverri, personal communication).

The androgyny implied in the Spanish and Shakespearean versions of 'master' is reflected in the androgyny Barbira Freedman suggests shamans need to acquire 'for the purpose of engineering balance between the polarized domains of the male/ female, water/sky, this world, the underworld and the underwater world' (2012: 173). Following Wilbert's observation that, while women may know shamanism and most shamanic crafts, 'I have known but few practicing female shamans and am aware of none who were ecstatics who were initiated, like male shamans, by resorting to tobacco (nicotine) as a medium of trance' (Wilbert 1987: 22), Barbira Freedman reflects on 'the paradox that in Amazonia women are often declared to have innate shamanic abilities, yet the large majority of shamans are male' (2010: 135).

Some scholars might consider the basis of the 'tobacco shamans = male' paradox to lie in the social and political dimensions of gender relations, but Barbira Freedman argues it is the result of cosmological epistemologies (2010: 149). Such a suggestion is easily grounded in regional ethnographies, since the bodies of women are seen as highly transformational in their reproductive potential, whereas men need to seek out such possibilities through shamanry (cf. McCallum 2001: 17). For women, combined shamanic and reproductive capacities may simply be too potent for a human person – that is, for a person who can also live well with her kin – to achieve with any degree of equanimity. This would explain why most female shamans tend to be sterile or over reproductive age, and are thus those who no longer draw on menstruation and their procreative potential as a source of transformation. For Viveiros de Castro, however, 'tobacco is a masculine plant important in shamanism, but women prepare the cigarettes for their husbands, hold the cigars of shamans in trance, and also smoke' (1992: 45), while for Londoño Sulkin, it is significant that 'tobacco, the quintessential constitutive substance of humanity, was transmitted via male lines only.... People of the Centre also tended to attribute to tobacco virtues they particularly valued in men' (2012: 97).

Tobacco epistemologies

Subsequent work on tobacco in lowland South America has tended to focus more on the relationship of tobacco to what McCallum (1996) calls 'ethno-epistemologies' (indigenous theories of knowledge). These investigations require approaches that are different and in many ways more diverse and complex methodologically, semantically and idiomatically, than the ethnological mapping of people's behaviour. For a start, we may need to forego cherished linguistic distinctions and the ways they categorize the world as we know it. Hugh-Jones, for example, queries the tripartite division of 'food', 'drugs' and 'medicines' which he says is historically quite recent and confined to non-Islamic industrial societies in which ' "drugs" are opposed to "medicines" supplied legally by doctors and chemists to specified individuals and used for supposedly beneficial and non-recreational purposes; on the other hand, they are opposed to "foods" which have to do with "nutrition" or "feeding" rather than with "curing". "Foods" and "medicines" are used, "drugs" are "ab-used" ' (2007: 48). Yet these are analytical categories which, in other contexts, 'might more profitably be discussed together' (2007: 48). As a case in point, Hugh-Jones considers the northwestern Amazonian Barasana, noting the implicit distinctions they make between 'foods' (principally meat, fish, chilli sauce and manioc bread), 'non-foods' (coca, tobacco and manioc drink) and 'snacks'. Ritual settings are marked by additional 'non-foods' – *yagé*, tobacco snuff and manioc beer. Among the Barasana tobacco snuff, cigars, coca and *yagé* constitute nurturing substances or spirit-foods, without the moral and political overtones of 'drug'. The Yamomami, meanwhile, put tobacco into a 'food' rather than 'non-food' category (Reig, this volume).

Tobacco and the experience of multinatural bodies

Tobacco is seen as a shaper and transformer of persons. This reflects Vilaça's view that for many lowland South American groups, bodies are 'chronically unstable' (2005), determined largely by external influences. As McCallum, writing about the Cashinahua, explains, the body 'is the place in which social and supernatural processes coalesce and is made by others in a constant flow involving nutrition, abstention, the application of medicines, body painting, baptismal rituals, and formal training' (1996: 352). Tobacco offers a vital means for the 'cooling, drying and firming-hardening' of young bodies (Rahman, this volume), making them less likely to inadvertently slip out of their human bodily form and take on a different one. Sometimes, the plant may be specifically chosen in order that some of its properties may be transferred to tobacco users – for example, the consumption of tobacco juice by a breast-feeding mother as a way of establishing the shamanic agency of her child (Santos-Granero 2012: 197).

In northwestern Amazonia, tobacco used in conjunction with ritual chants serves to 'cook the rawness' (as does sacred chilli pepper), 'dry the danger' and protect against 'the wasting sickness'. It sweetens initiates by removing their wetness as well as their saliva (Wright 1993: 9; 16; 17; 18). These are common Amerindian idioms used to talk about the effects of tobacco, as is the 'laboured breathing of intoxication', which is linked to a sense of lightness (Viveiros de Castro 1992: 220; 131) as well as the production of phlegm (e.g. Goldman 2004: 313; see Brabec de Mori, this volume).[11] Among 'People of the Centre', words breathed into tobacco paste become the power whereby Witoto hunters may be successful in obtaining game (Echeverri 1996). Alertness and vigilance are also desirable characteristics associated with the plant, as are a range of other characteristics which are perhaps most vividly articulated as morally imbuing among the Muinane (Londoño Sulkin 2012: 100). The effects of tobacco thus fit with a schema of personal virtues, upheld and reproduced thanks to the application of plants, thereby demonstrating the way in which species manifest 'the affects and capacities of a diversity of other living beings', including those of the tobacco spirits (Santos-Granero 2009a: 7).[12]

This fluidity of the body reflects a broader epistemological theme in lowland South America which has been characterized as its 'multinaturalism'. In contrast to the 'multiculturalism' which characterizes Western Enlightenment and post-Enlightenment thought – constituted by the sense of a universal 'nature' but multiple 'cultures' (Viveiros de Castro 2012: 46), the multinatural perspective posits a universal 'culture' but a multiplicity of 'natures'. However, 'culture' in this 'cosmological perspectivist' view of the universe is not quite the same as 'culture' in conventional Western conceptions of the term. Instead, it is akin to a 'soul substance' (cf. Rivière 1999) that is found in diverse ranges of what may be counted as 'human' forms. As Vilaça (2005: 448) summarizes it, 'in Amazonia … humanity is not restricted to what we conceive as human beings: animals and spirits may also be human, which means that humanity is above all a position to be continually defined'.

Tobacco and agency

Thanks to their relationships with auxiliary spirits, shamans act as brokers between this and other worlds. They are persons who, with the ingestion of tobacco in hallucinogenic quantities, can traverse time and space and travel in both (da Cunha 1998). Sometimes as they do so, shamans transform into other corporeal forms. At once worldly and otherworldly, shamans act as translators, world-makers (Overing 1990) and prophets in new worlds (Hill and Wright 1988). Their dangerous but necessary 'acts of crossing' empower them, both at home and away (Luedke and West 2006). Da Cunha gives the example of a Kaxinawá (Cashinahua) shaman called Carlos, living in the capital of Acre province, who combines Yawanaua, Katukina do Gregorio and Tarauaca techniques with those of Umbanda, learnt in the cities of Belem and Manaus (1998: 15). Another Cashinahua shaman, Inkamuru, travelled to the thriving metropolis of São Paulo in order to learn techniques of acupuncture (McCallum, personal communication). In these contexts, it is perhaps not surprising that the shaman's food – tobacco – 'is a two-way converter between life and death, and a commutator between domains' (Viveiros de Castro 1992: 220). Tobacco, like the shaman himself, finds its place within a network of relations with the outside.

For this to happen, the practitioner needs to establish a relationship with the tobacco plant. This is usually premised on a set of behavioural and dietary proscriptions such as those followed by initiate shamans among the Araweté. These initiates 'eat tobacco' (i.e. smoke it) as what Viveiros de Castro calls an 'anti-food'[13] which also takes away their hunger (1992: 131; 219).[14] In order to develop other ways of seeing-knowing, Araweté men gather for collective smoking sessions, where they become 'killed by tobacco' and faint and convulse from intoxication and are said to 'die' (1992: 131). Initiates become 'diaphanous' (*mo-kyaho*), 'smooth' (*mo-kawo*) and 'lightweight' (*mo-wewe*, 1992: 131), qualities that render the connection between body and soul more pliable, allowing shamans to experience, commune with or transform into other beings (1992: 195). The resultant dreams, visions, or thought-streams are then subject to interpretation by shamans, who poetically describe and attempt to decipher their frequently uncertain hallucinogenic perceptions (da Cunha 1998: 13).[15] This instructive capacity is shared by other 'master plants' (or 'plants which have mothers', above). Such plants have the ability to teach their users about the cosmos, developing complex relationships with them that command respect from their associates. Working with these plants, shamans' apprentices can see entities and, with practice, perceive them to be 'the owners of things', that is, as other beings who 'own' and care for still other beings in asymmetrical relations of power (Viveiros de Castro 1992: 8; 131; also see Kopenawa 2013). Tobacco then facilitates people's complex cosmological perceptions, allowing them to see other beings as persons and, sometimes, persons as beings.

More recent work has looked at the 'dark side' of shamanism. Brabec de Mori (this volume) points out that benevolent shamanic healing and malignant sorcery are two sides of the same coin since success in curing involves casting the problem back to its originator (i.e. the sorcerer). Dark and light shamans use their tobacco breath to harm and heal respectively (Whitehead and Wright 2004). Wilbert describes the appearance of a Warao *hoarotu* ('dark shaman') during his night visits, noting 'their paling yellow chests, tremulous hands, black lips, and furring tongues ... fusty body odor and pronounced halitosis' (Wilbert 2004: 37). These less attractive characteristics of prolonged nicotine use combine with their fetid living places and habit of smoking cigars made of curdled human blood to create a much feared and deadly persona. *Hoarotu* contrast, Wilbert opines, with the 'light shaman' or *bahanarotu*, those who 'smoke or suck' (Wilbert 2004: 25).

For shamans, tobacco can be both an animating agent that brings artisanal objects to life, and a special food for their non-human auxiliaries. Santos-Granero writes that tobacco smoke, together with an offering of manioc beer and coca juice, activates the 'subjectivity and generative powers' (2009a: 15) of Yanesha panpipes. He reports barely noticing that each time a panpipe owner tried one, he blew tobacco smoke – as well as his coca-perfumed breath – into it (2009b: 114). Shamans similarly activate jaguar stones 'by blowing smoke on them and reciting some magical chants' (2009b: 116). Among the Urarina, Walker details how otherwise predatory beings must be captured and then tamed: 'a shaman immediately blows tobacco smoke on the bowl and places it at the foot of the Brugmansia tree … where its cooperation is gradually enlisted through forms of ritual dialogue'. He goes on to describe how the spirit is cared for at home and asked to serve his owner obediently, 'to respect his family and not to cause them harm, and to share its knowledge with him' (2009a: 92). Tobacco is thus used to maintain and establish relationships of mastery over other beings.[16]

We should not forget that several central Brazilian 'drug-averse' societies, such as certain Gé groups, have no tradition of tobacco or any other form of ritual drug consumption. Amongst them the importance of blowing indicates that preoccupations with the vitality inherent in breath and breathing might be an even more ancient and pan-South American phenomenon than the tobacco which, in smoked form, is its manifestation (Hill 2009b; Hill and Chaumeil 2011). In the Munducuru tobacco myth, even the Mother of Tobacco, who created tobacco smoke *sui generis* and carried it in a calabash from which she periodically sucked her vital sustenance, died as soon as she ran out of the life-giving smoke (Kruse 1951: 918). Even in the absence of tobacco, other substances are smoked that do not contain nicotine but which are still referred to as cigarettes, including the rolling papers themselves (e.g. Wilbert 1987: 85). Thus the ability to elucidate breath and blowing, of which Butt-Colson's work among the Akawaio (1956) is the single most comprehensive ethnographic work of its kind, appears as one of the most salient aspects of tobacco smoking.

In addition to healing and sorcery, shamans may also be called upon to blow tobacco smoke over crops as a form of protection (e.g. Wilbert 1987: 79), and to carry out rituals as part of the wider practice of weather shamanism that may involve 'blowing against the wind', 'chanting to the rain' and 'dancing away the clouds' (Wilbert 1996, 2004).[17] Shamans, however, do tend to care for and cultivate their tobacco,[18] and unlike staple crops, tobacco is predominantly cared for by men. Wilbert notes the careful attention paid to ensure that tobacco plants have sufficient light, drainage, and pest removal (Wilbert 1987: 8).[19] On the other hand, rather than 'growing their own', many shamans obtain their tobacco from other indigenous groups (and commercial sources, in increasing quantities) and many have never had direct contact with tobacco cultivation.

As well as the shamanic agency they facilitate and produce, tobacco plants – from a phytological perspective – also have their own, independent, agency. For example, botanical research has established that tobacco plants exude a sticky scent which is attractive both to lizards and their caterpillar prey, thereby displaying a rather complex tactic of self-preservation (Stork et al. 2011). Further, one of the most multifarious examples of light perception has been recorded in *N. longiflora*, which uses the perception of far-red light in order to predict the growth patterns of its neighbours, and to begin growth responses which lessen shading (Trewavas 2003).[20] This reveals tobacco as complex type of being, displaying what Ballaré terms 'illuminated behaviour' (2009). Karban et al. (2000) demonstrated increased resistance to insect herbivores in wild *N. attenuata* plants situated next to clipped sagebrush compared to those growing next to unclipped controls.[21]

Tobacco and myth

Wilbert has gone on to say more about the mythic apparatus associated with tobacco (2004). He describes the cosmic centre of the Warao light shamans as an egg-shaped house (the self-contained cosmos) built by the Tobacco Spirit (a swallow-tailed kite, *Elanoides forficatus*, fathered by the avian God of Origin) (see Figure I.1).

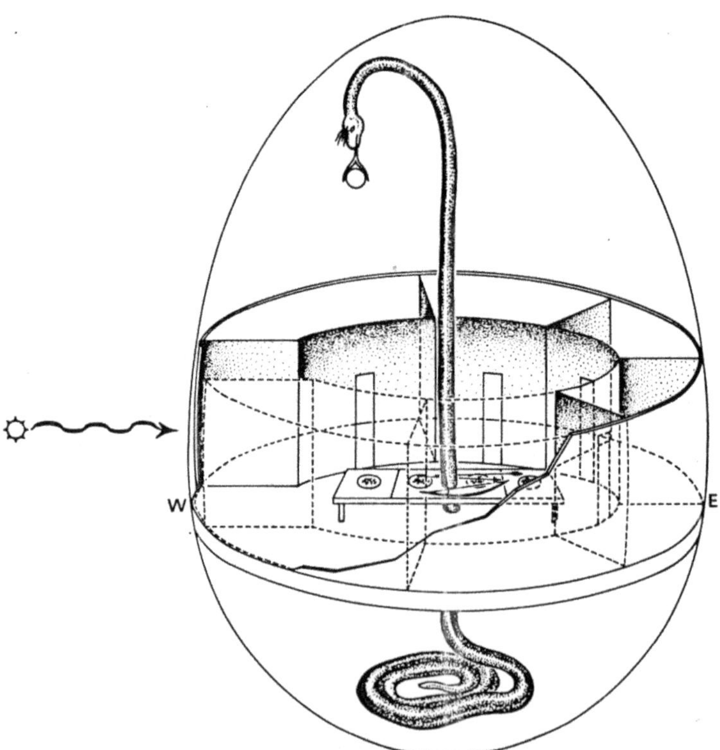

Figure I.1 Zenithal house of the Tobacco Spirit (drawing by Noel Diaz, from Wilbert 2004: 26). Image reproduced with the kind permission of Johannes Wilbert and Utah University Press.

The house, its contents and residents are made from the thickened smoke of flowering tobacco plants that border both sides of a rope bridge (also made from smoke) that links the house to the apex of the world. The original light shaman now lives in the Tobacco Spirit's house where his wife changed from a bee to a frigate bird (*Fregata magnificens*) to become a white female shaman specializing in curing nicotinic seizures. Four insects living in the house periodically 'gather around a gambling table on which they move specific counters to invade each other's spaces according to an arrow dice cast by the Spirit of Tobacco…. Depending on which gambler wins, someone will live or die on earth' (2004: 26).

Among the Arawakan Wakuénai of northwestern Amazonia, Hill describes how during birth and initiation rituals: 'thick clouds of [tobacco] smoke transfer the chant-owner's poetic vocal sounds into the sensual realms of vision, touch, taste, and smell' (1993: 126). Wakuénai *málikai* chants employ a musical and sensory repertoire that evokes myth and during which ancestral tobacco names are 'chased after', 'searched for' and 'heaped up'. Myth elucidates how the culture-hero Nhiaperikuli, at the mythic centre of the Hipana raids, pulls out all the people known by the Wakuénai. Nhiaperikuli confers them with rank according to their sequence of emergence from a large hole in the Hipana rapids and bestows land, the sounds of their tobacco namesakes and sacred chilli pepper upon them. The first to emerge are the whites, indicating their relative power as the eldest brother (see variations of this emergence story among the Hohodene and Walipere-Dakenai of the Aiary River). They are followed by the Wakuénai sibs and then other regional ethnicities. The litany then involves searching for tobacco names. While the Wakuénai find names for their sibs, the whites are too numerous to be named, so their names are simply 'heaped up in a pile'. As such, despite their influence, they lack ancestral names and hence the power that comes from the tobacco spirits (1993: 111).

Another important aspect of indigenous mythology relating to tobacco concerns its role in the creation of landscapes. The Baníwa regard the headwaters of the Solimões River as one among several places from which they bring back tobacco (Wright 1993: 14). They consider tobacco smoke to have widened the course of the Içana River, with the wind-borne smoke creating its twisted path (Garnelo 2007). An itinerary of these topographic features is provided through ritual chants which maintain their prominence in Baníwa collective memory (see chapter 4 of Wright 2013; also see 'the tobacco *garapés*', Meira 1996: 180). Reig (this volume) recalls that Yanomami myths actualized in agricultural practices connect tobacco to the transformation and human impregnation of landscapes.

For the Tukanonan people, tobacco has an even more progenitive role. Grandfather of the Universe tries but fails to create people by blowing cigar smoke over a gourd of sweet *kana* berries (*Sabicea amazonensis*) (Hugh-Jones 2009). Grandmother of the Universe therefore takes over, blowing more smoke and spells on the gourd, which produces seven 'Universe People' (Hugh-Jones 2009: 36–38; see Figure I.2) who between them encapsulate all elements of the known Universe.

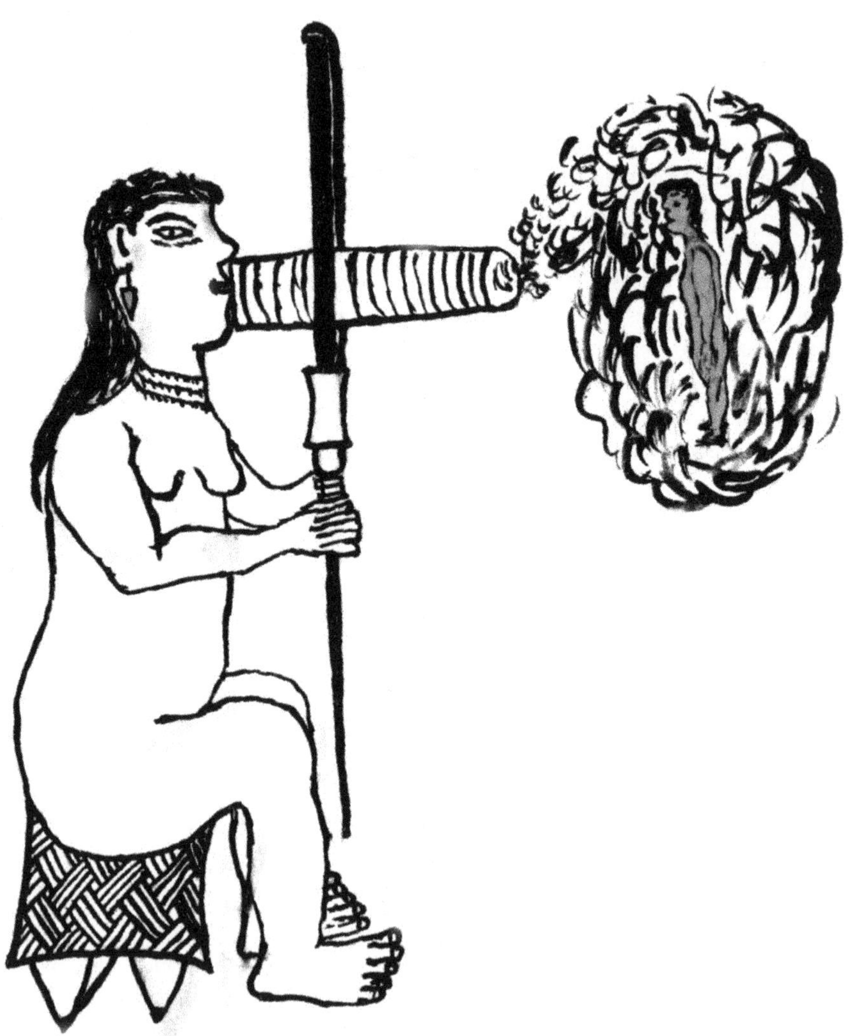

Figure I.2 Grandmother of the Universe creating the *Umuari Masa* or Universe People.[22] (Drawing by Feliciano Lana in Panlõn Kumuand Kenhiri, appearing in Hugh-Jones 2009: 38. Image reproduced with permission of F. Santos-Granero and S. Hugh-Jones and the University of Arizona Press.)

The chapters in this book

Hugh-Jones argues against making 'overly hasty generalizations about Amazonia and Amazonians' (2009: 35), and others caution against giving an impression of cultural homogeneity or of making sweeping generalizations that take us 'away from the nitty-gritty of indigenous real life' (Ramos 2012: 482). The chapters in this book are written either by social anthropologists or researchers in related disciplines, all of whom have had plenty of first-hand experience of the nitty-gritty of life in lowland South America. The key methodological contribution made by social anthropology is ethnography, the long-term study and writing about what has traditionally been a single small community or communities but which now has expanded in scope to include virtually any aspect of social life within or across the global world system. The strengths of this approach lie in its descriptive richness and its ability to generate in-depth understanding based on a position that might be termed 'embedded' (Lewis and Russell 2011). This enables the disaggregation of general terms such as 'Amerindian' or 'Amazonian' and the fine-grained, nuanced appreciation of the heterogeneity within and between groups. The weakness of ethnography, of course, lies in its lack of generalizability and the danger of regarding groups as indigenous isolates. Multi-sited ethnography, such as that provided by Brabec de Mori in his use of Iskobakebo, Yine, Ashaninka and Shipibo songs (this volume), goes some way towards enabling comparisons to be made across 'ethnic' and linguistic boundaries.

The book is divided into three parts. Part One commences by considering the variation in how indigenous peoples in lowland South America have used tobacco through time. Oyuela-Caycedo and Kawa present a 'deep history' of tobacco that introduces us to its origins, which extend back to the initial domestication of diverse wild plants in the Nightshade family (Solanaceae). They suggest that we should remain cognizant of the diverse functions tobacco has played in the region as well as its myriad forms of consumption and associated cultural materials. They also discuss the rise of tobacco as a valuable commodity during the colonial period, exploring its impact on both the regional and global economic systems. By looking at new techniques for recovering archaeobotanical remains while also examining human societies' attitudes towards plants through time, the authors present a new framework for understanding both the origins of tobacco and contemporary variation in how it is used.

In Chapter Two, Peter Gow compares the use of tobacco by two Maipuran-speaking peoples of southwestern Amazonia, the Piro-Manchineri (Piro) people and their eastern neighbours the Apurinã. His main concern is with a major change in the use of tobacco by the former since the nineteenth century, and he uses data from their neighbours the Apurinã (also known as the Hypuriná and Ipurina, among other terms) in order to better understand the Piro in their regional context. Gow originally intended to explore the incorporation of *ayahuasca* into earlier shamanic uses of tobacco. However, as he began to explore the data further, a much more complex and hitherto unappreciated system of tobacco use began to emerge. Gow uses an anthropological method known as controlled comparison to find out why one group (the Piro) adopted tobacco smoking while it was apparently rejected by the Apurinã, who continue to use snuff. To do this he focuses on the material accoutrements involved, namely snuff tubes and the emergent use of pipes. This, he argues, is not the result of ad hoc borrowings or non-borrowings by two socially and linguistically neighbouring peoples, but the result of 'structuralist diffusion', a neglected form of explanation. In tracing the shifts in methods, modes, devices and orifices used to ingest tobacco, Gow provides evidence of the endless dialectics between systems in a constant process of transformation. It is significant, in similar vein, that the Piro have adopted *ayahuasca* shamanry[23] while the Apurinã reject it, despite being surrounded by enthusiastic non-indigenous users of *ayahuasca*.

Barbira Freedman's chapter takes the vantage point of another group, the Keshwa Lamas of the Peruvian upper Amazon. They, like the Piro, have been instrumental in the development of *ayahuasca* shamanism since the eighteenth century. Developing further Wilbert's arguments for the primacy of tobacco use in indigenous shamanism, she uses a combination of historical and ethnographic sources to show the continuity of tobacco use as well as its increasing reach via the more generic forms of non-indigenous shamanic medicine that evolved in colonial contact points in Western Amazonia. The use of tobacco smoke blown on patients' bodies for the treatment of illness has been documented in South America since the sixteenth century, both in and outside the Amazon region. Like Gow, she considers how relatively neglected both tobacco use and the 'tobacco path' as an adjunct to *ayahuasca* shamanism, have been in the anthropological literature on Western Amazonia. She sees the recent expansion of *ayahuasca* tourism as inseparable from a renewed use of local varieties of *N. tabacum*, smoked in pipes rather than as cigars, and of specific uses of tobacco juice for shamanic treatments not only in Amazonia but wherever *ayahuasca* healing has been exported.

The 'shifting perspectives' of Part Two pays tribute to Viveiros de Castro's work on perspectivism in considering the place of tobacco in a multinatural environment. A series of tobacco songs, or rather magical songs related to the use of tobacco, are analysed by Brabec de Mori in Chapter Four in order to underline the fundamental historical importance of tobacco in the Ucayali valley of the Peruvian lowlands. Here tobacco is a medium of communication and transformation shared between human and non-human entities, the progenitor and carrier of healing, sorcery and even love magic. The songs are not always sung out loud – the words can simply be whistled or thought, but concentration and focus is usually required. The songs' power lies in the way in which tobacco, song and physician become one (encapsulated in the Shipibo word *kano*, 'world-in-the-song'). The tobacco smoke carries the manifest power of the words (and the physician using them) through space into the spirit's world. Likewise songs from the spirit world can manifest themselves as powerful entities in this world (e.g. as thunder). There is a reciprocal relationship of tobacco with warfare and sorcery as well as with curing and illness, which makes its role more morally ambiguous in the contemporary world. The more commercially oriented use of *ayahuasca* seems detached from such reciprocity and represents the 'good side' of what is probably a Christian dichotomy. Meanwhile the touristic potential of *ayahuasca*-based 'shamanism' makes it an attractive commercial proposition for younger Shipibo. The chapter ends with an *ayahuasca* healer complaining about Brabec de Mori's use of tobacco as 'an addictive drug'. The concept of 'addiction' is totally at odds with traditional Shipibo attitudes to tobacco and was probably assimilated while travelling outside Peru providing *ayahuasca* sessions for westerners. These myriad factors help to explain the decline of tobacco-oriented magic and the loss of its evocative songs.

Juan Alvaro Echeverri describes and analyses the uses and meaning of tobacco among the Witoto and neighbouring groups of southeastern Colombia, collectively known as 'People of the Centre'. The main form of tobacco consumption found here consists of licking it in the form of a paste. The information presented in this paper derives from the author's own experience and information from two elders: Kɨneraɨ (Hipólito Candre), an Ocaina-Witoto man who lived by the Igaraparaná River, and Enokakuiodo (Oscar Román-Jitdutjaaño), who lives in the Middle Caquetá region. Echeverri commences by considering the indigenous belief that a man must use tobacco if he is to know the tobacco spirit. However, Kɨneraɨ's advice to Echeverri was that he should moderate his smoking habit in favour of tobacco paste. After describing the technical processes of heating and cooling involved in making the paste, Echeverri discusses the symbolism inherent in its two constituents: tobacco juice (menstrual blood) and ash salt (semen). He goes on to consider the relationship of these and other substances (e.g. chilli sauce, meat, coca, cassava bread, and non-meat foods) along the two axes of what he calls 'culinary space': one that addresses relationships of seasoning (in the way that, for example, salt is the seasoning of tobacco paste) and one that concerns how meat and non-meat foods are combined (for instance, coca in combination with tobacco). He compares the opposition of dry tobacco and moist honey, as posited by Lévi-Strauss in his analysis of myths surrounding smoked and inhaled tobacco, with the opposition of dry salt and moist tobacco in the case of tobacco paste. He suggests that with the change in product a transformation of structural oppositions has taken place. Echeverri concludes by suggesting that the heating and cooling involved in making tobacco paste has the effect of transcending the culinary space and helps to define tobacco's dual character as both a hazard and a healing agent.

Part Two concludes with Elizabeth Rahman's chapter on tobacco's place in the formation of the infant, based on fieldwork conducted in northwest Amazonia between 2010 and 2011 along the Rio Xié, a small tributary of Brazil's Rio Negro. During fieldwork Rahman was struck by how much tobacco smoke and spell-blowing was used in perinatal care. Tobacco smoke blowing was frequently employed as both a preventative and a curative measure for the neonatal family. She explains how tobacco smoke-blown-blessings – *umutauari* – form part of a repertoire of techniques used to guide the emergence of the hot (*saku*), limp and humid neonate (*taina piranga* – literally 'red child') into more (but not exclusively) cool, firm (*santo*) and dry (*otipáua*, fluid-free) social and personal states. Tobacco smoke, among other virtues which are discussed in this chapter, affords a coolness and dryness that mediates the volatile state of extreme and leaky dampness that babies are in. These actions facilitate the growing engagement of the child with the others who care for him or her. Rahman suggests that tobacco-spell-blowing induces a specific 'somatic mode of attention', and that the primary effect of tobacco blessings is to direct and reorient the participant's attention to the present moment. As such, tobacco smoke blessings can be seen as a mindfulness-generating technique. She argues that a consideration of indigenous 'mindful' techniques enables us to understand the potency of tobacco use in Amazonian healing practices in terms that are closest to local aetiologies and pathologies, and articulates this with regard to the health-promoting benefits of mindfulness recognized in the biomedical literature. She also suggests that early exposure to tobacco smoke and other sensory stimuli in ritualized contexts encourages an efficacious response to later shamanic interventions. Elucidating the 'pragmatic efficacy of aesthetic forms', Rahman provides us with a means of considering efficacy that moves beyond the importance of symbolism, placebos and psychosomatics; and concludes by suggesting tobacco's importance in lubricating relations with others.

Relationships are changing, but so is the broader political-economic environment, which is the primary focus of Part Three. In Chapter Seven Renzo Duin considers the place of commercial cigarettes and *pïjai tamï ale* among the Wayana in northern Amazonia. In a 1964 TV broadcast, *Voyage sans Passeport*, an actor hands out commercial cigarettes from a boxed packet to a handful of indigenous Wayana men in the upper Maroni River region, on the frontier of French Guiana and Suriname. He lights the cigarettes and a young Wayana boy intensely smokes a commercial cigarette. The voice-over claims that 'Indians start smoking early'. Some young Wayana boys learn how to smoke cigarettes, inhale, and blow out clouds of tobacco smoke as a result of their father's wishes that they might one day become shamans (*pïjai*). Commercial cigarettes have not replaced the traditional long cigarettes (*tamï ale*) used by *pïjai*, however. *Tamï ale* and some used cigarettes with charm leaves were both collected by the ethnologist Audrey Butt-Colson in 1964. *Tamï ale* are made from tobacco leaves (*Nicotiana* spp.) rolled inside thin sheets of an inner tree bark (*okalat*; *Couratari guianensis*, see Figure I.3) and are still used by *pïjai* despite the introduction of commercial cigarettes.

Duin describes how during fieldwork in 1998 he suffered sunstroke (or so he thought), and in order to feel better went to lie in his hammock. The Wayana people, deeply concerned, concluded that '*sisi je*' (the mother sun) had poisoned his head. One of the Wayana standing by his hammock asked for a packet of commercial cigarettes which Duin happened to have in his backpack. After sunset a *pïjai* arrived to visit him, the commercial cigarettes requested earlier having been used as an

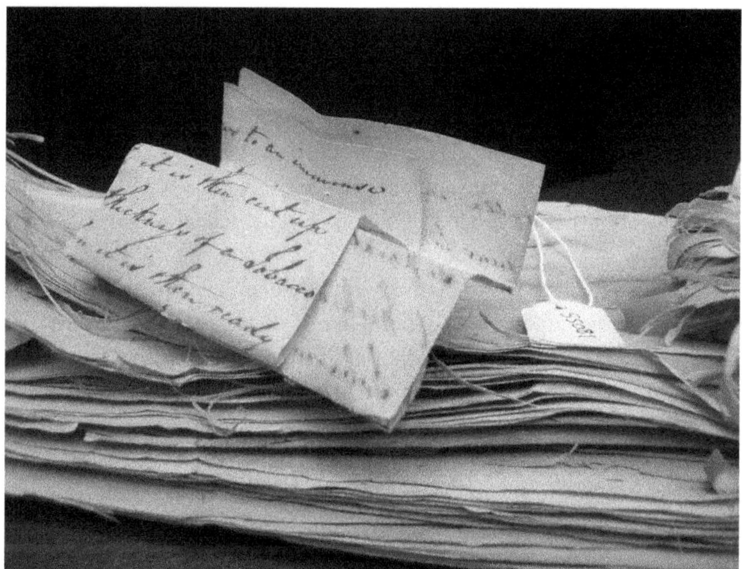

Figure I.3 The bark of *Couratari guianensis*, used throughout South America as rolling papers. Object number EBC 00000. Image reproduced courtesy of Economic Botany Collection, Royal Botanic Gardens, Kew. (Photograph by Elizabeth Rahman.)

invitational gift. The *pïjai*, though, had brought *tamï ale* for curative purposes and, during his years of fieldwork and living among the Wayana, Duin witnessed *tamï ale* being used in curing rituals on several occasions. Commercial cigarettes were rarely used in these contexts and were considered less powerful. He also observed younger Wayana occasionally smoking commercial cigarettes, a recreational use of tobacco that was not perceived as a shamanic act. He argues that the traditional role of the *tamï ale*, using locally grown tobacco, has not been rearticulated or replaced by commercial cigarettes, nor has it affected the role of the *pïjai*. Commercial cigarettes reflect a desire for 'Western modernity', but their quality and power are almost always trumped by traditional *tamï ale*.

Alejandro Reig takes a similarly ethnographic approach to tobacco use and exchange among a group of Yanomami villages in the Ocamo basin of the Venezuelan Amazon, making use of myths about tobacco and other foodstuffs to illuminate the role of these staples in the creation of what he calls 'landscapes of desire' in inter-group sociality. The Yanomami provide an example of a world in which tobacco is not used in rituals but is the object of everyday pleasurable consumption, and as such it forms a central thread in the weft of social life, and he suggests that it should be looked at together with other stimulants central to Yanomami sociality. It appears in mediations with both the outside and the inside, including the initial sharing of substances with visitors, where it seems to perform an immediate welcoming procedure of 'making kin out of the other' (Vilaça 2002). Tobacco wads circulate between kin inside the village, but there is also pressure to give it away or else have it stolen, from those with less gifted gardens (and gardeners). Tobacco craving configures a libidinised relation with places, and its scarcity may lead to downriver people travelling to upriver villages, or to upriver interfluvial people visiting other villages when their harvest is finished. Among the myths that account for the different staples given to people by the ancestors, that of the origin of tobacco stages a connection between need, landscape and a nameless but driving desire. Like the Wayana studied by Duin, many downriver Yanomami in permanent contact with national society have substituted the traditional practice of sucking the tobacco wad with commercial cigarette smoking, but this does not appear to have disrupted traditional usage. Following Londoño Sulkin's proposition that the 'Amazonian package' involves both the 'sharing of substances' and the 'incorporation of otherness', it is the latter which seems to be intensified in the use of tobacco by the Yanomami. It is interesting to reflect on the similarities between these approaches and how people embedded deep in late capitalism might use cigarettes, a notion well documented in current anthropological literature.

Juan Pablo Sarmiento Barletti steps away from the prevalent analyses of the use of tobacco in ritual practice among indigenous Amazonians in Chapter Nine. Instead, he looks at the less explicitly 'mystical' everyday functions of the plant by discussing the various roles tobacco plays in the contemporary social lives of two different groups of Ashaninka people in Peruvian Amazonia. Groups around the Ene River have renewed dedication to planting tobacco as part of a much larger reconciliatory effort in the wake of the Peruvian internal war (1980–2000). In this context tobacco becomes a tool through which the Ashaninka seek to mend with the earth and spirits that were broken during the war years. Sarmiento Barletti then moves onto to look at the everyday uses of tobacco in the form of commercial cigarettes among those living by in the Bajo Urubamba River area. He proposes (like Duin and Reig) that cigarettes are one of the objects used to define what it means to be both 'Peruvian' and a 'civilised' indigenous person. These two different uses of tobacco by people within the same society demonstrate how the plant, in its different forms, is key to understanding indigenous Amazonian notions of wellbeing.

Paolo Fortis attends to the tobacco smoking practices of the Guna ('Kuna') people of the San Blas Archipelago of Panama in Chapter Ten. He considers the association between tobacco and fermented ('bitter') and unfermented ('sweet') *chicha* (beer), an analysis which emerged from the careful analysis of Guna explanations of their curing rituals. Drinking sweet *chicha* is an important form of conviviality and in the daily effort of making bodies; but bitter *chicha* provokes drunkenness and is mainly consumed in contexts where the presence of others – non-kinspeople or spirits – is key. Fortis argues that tobacco smoke corresponds to the sweet *chicha* of the *nudsugana* – auxiliary spirits – while tobacco ashes are the bitter *chicha* of the *bonigana* – animal spirits. Fortis analyses this tobacco and *chicha* nexus in the context of demographic growth over the past 100 years or so. The growing population has led to a lack of space on the San Blas islands for Guna villages to split in response to internal conflict as they once did. In consequence, he argues, it is possible to trace a link between the metaphysical projection of violence and animosity in the everyday life of Guna people, the proliferation of ritual specializations, and the increasing consumption of commercial cigarettes and pipes.

The chapters of this book provide original reflections supported by both long-term and recent ethnographic, archaeological and historical research on tobacco. Translations from indigenous languages are the authors own, as are chapter photos, unless otherwise stated. In their sum, they reflect on and incorporate the themes of musicality, mythology, animist spirits, cultivation, exchange and power, healing and efficacy and wellbeing at the local level and within global networks and nation states. It opens up new vistas for further exploration concerning this remarkable plant.

Conclusions and implications

Welcome, then, to a book which places indigenous cosmological, ethnobotanical and pharmacological perspectives against a backdrop of the increasing power of national and transnational tobacco industries. Its chapters offer some fascinating comparisons and contrasts with the ways in which tobacco is viewed, used and abused elsewhere in the world.

While the purpose of this book, and perhaps its greatest strength, is to explore the meaning and metaphysics of tobacco rather than questions of utility and intervention, the landscape of contemporary tobacco use in lowland South America is clearly changing rapidly. National and global tobacco industries have continued their transformation of the economic landscape of tobacco in many parts of the region, increasing the spread of commercially produced tobacco products (Stebbins 2001). Of course, the trade in tobacco between groups is nothing new and may well have been an important part of pre-colonial interethnic exchanges. However, with their increased availability and ease of use, cigarettes imported from elsewhere enable the potentially constant use of tobacco in casual everyday rather than, or as well as, formal ritual contexts. It would be irresponsible to ignore the increasingly clear evidence of tobacco's potential for harm, particularly when consumed in this 'fast food' fashion as products of the 'harm industries' (Benson and Kirsch 2010) which are in its thrall. Yet the focus of the tobacco control movement on the frequently nefarious activities of the transglobal tobacco corporations has meant that indigenous cultivation and use of tobacco has stayed largely 'beneath the radar' of contemporary concerns.

There is little collected data on tobacco consumption and health effects among the peoples we are considering in lowland South America. National data for the countries concerned – Venezuela, Guyana, Brazil, Colombia, Peru and Panama – do not disaggregate into regions and ethnic groups, assuming such information could be readily collected. In the Amazon Basin there are still plenty of infectious and non-infectious diseases which at population level are likely to mask the effects of any increased morbidity and mortality due to the increased and more regular use of commercially produced tobacco. There is, however, evidence that public health messages are reaching the ground, albeit subject to local interpretations that conflict with public health agenda. For instance, Xié dwellers with whom Rahman worked asked whether it was true that tobacco affected their ability to get an erection, a notion probably heard from visiting nurses and one otherwise contradicted by the widespread association they made between tobacco and virility. Both Echeverri and Brabec de Mori (this volume) note the infiltration – and interpretation – of messages such as 'tobacco kills'.

Meanwhile discussions within tobacco control are also moving on from crude, total abstinence messages towards greater consideration of the potential for 'harm reduction' strategies, although these remain controversial (Hastings et al. 2012; McNeill and Munafò 2013). Along with the prospect of substituting cigarettes for alternative nicotine-containing products, a renewed interest in mindfulness both as a feature of reduced tobacco dependence and in stop smoking programmes (e.g. Vidrine et al. 2009; Brewer et al. 2011) has been developing.[24] Rahman (this volume) suggests that the mindfulness associated with tobacco healing in lowland South America is an activity nurtured in childhood. Understanding first and judging later would seem to be the way forward.

Health promotion initiatives around tobacco among the indigenous groups living in the Americas aim to canvas these more nuanced understandings of tobacco use and abuse. Stimulants may be used in different ways and with more caution in their source origin, than when newly transposed and classified as 'drugs'.[25] With this in mind, Alderete et al. (2010: 37) are optimistic that 'indigenous worldviews that support respect and reverence for [the] ritual use of tobacco can be integrated into smoking prevention programs'. The distinction Daley et al. (2006) make between sacred and recreational tobacco use in North American populations is mirrored in an example from Amazonia when Rosengren, writing about the Matsigenka, argues 'an important distinction must be made … between the tobacco that is locally cultivated and the industrially produced cigarettes that can be bought from local traders'. The former, he says, is for sharing with the spirits and its consumption is limited to ritual events; the latter is 'consumed for the mere pleasure of the smokers'. 'Today practically all men smoke cigarettes when they have an opportunity. In contrast, the everyday consumption of locally produced tobacco is largely limited to senior men, who take it either as a finely grained snuff that is blown up the nose through tubes or ingested as a viscous 'syrup' known as *seri opatsa* (literally "tobacco's turbid water") which is generally acknowledged to be so strong that only grown men can take it' (2006: 809). This might be a step forward in terms of health promotion work, but the relationship between 'ritual' and 'everyday', 'spiritual' (or 'sacred') and 'recreational', or 'indigenous' and 'commercial' are divisions frequently blurred.[26]

Finally we should consider the metaphysical nature of tobacco as spirit in many parts of lowland South America, something which was transmogrified in the transatlantic and transcultural shipment of the plant from 'New World' to 'Old'. Now tobacco companies are starting to market brands such as 'Natural American Spirit' ('100 per cent additive free natural tobacco'). The 'Santa Fe Natural Tobacco Company' which produces this brand was purchased by RJ Reynolds Company in 2001, becoming a division of Reynolds American (42 per cent owned by British American Tobacco) in 2001. They are cashing in on the concept of 'spirit', as well as that of 'natural' (McDaniel and Malone 2007); other companies are developing what they argue is 'organic' and 'additive-free' tobacco. However, the respect that goes with the cosmology of Wilbert's 'house of the tobacco spirit' is completely lacking in these profit-motivated language games and in terms of the health studies conducted thus far, the risks of long-term use of 'additive-free' tobacco compared to the tobacco found in 'normal' cigarettes can be compared to the choice between jumping from a 12th floor and a 13th floor window. If we are serious about reducing the health impacts of tobacco worldwide, maybe those working in tobacco control should consider the potential for refashioning tobacco, the 'master plant', as a 'master spirit' that is in need of greater respect and, perhaps, exorcism? This book presents a more dualistic – and certainly more nuanced – perspective on this controversial plant, presenting it as an agent of both enlightenment and destruction. Ultimately, it could be argued, the historical and contemporary failure of the rest of the world to acknowledge the power and respect accorded tobacco among many indigenous groups in lowland South America has enabled the 'master plant' to master us all.

Notes

1. For authoritative accounts of the transformation of tobacco from plant to late industrial capitalist commodity, see Goodman (1993); Brandt (2007) and Proctor (2011).
2. The first known printed reference to tobacco comes from the Spanish explorer Oviedo y Valdes who in 1535 reported on the Caquetio of what is now northern Venezuela 'There is in the country an herb which they call *tabaco*, which is a kind of plant, the stalk of which is as tall as the chest of a man' (Wilbert 1987: 11).
3. 'Pariká is a crystalline powder made from the blood-red exudates of the inner bark of *Virola theidora* and *Ananenanthera peregrina* trees found in the northwest Amazon region. Its active chemical principle is DMT (dymethyltriptamine). The more experienced pajés [shamans] sometimes use a mixture of pariká and another hallucinogen known as *caapi* (*Banisteriopsis caapi*)' (Wright 2013: 26).
4. Traditional forms of tobacco use generally involve very large quantities of tobacco and may reach hallucinogenic quantities. This use of tobacco is generally restricted to some men on certain occasions. Commercially produced tobacco on

the other hand, is designed for more constant, low-level use, and is chemically engineered to enhance its addictive properties (e.g. Land et al. 2014).

5. Santos-Granero suggests 'the Amerindian fascination with animals and the emphasis on people in recent theories of native Amazonian political economies have conspired to make the world of objects somewhat invisible' (2009a: 1).
6. Feinhandler et al. (1979) dispute this, arguing that because tobacco is also native to Australia and the southwest Pacific it could have originated elsewhere.
7. Wilbert is struck by the fact that 'among Europeans and their descendants elsewhere it [tobacco] became a habit and an addiction but played no role in religion. But after tobacco reached Siberia, probably also in the latter part of the sixteenth century or at the latest in the seventeenth century, it is astonishing how quickly the tribesmen adapted it to shamanism, thus recapturing for it the religious meaning that it has always had for the American Indians' (Wasson 1968: 332 in Wilbert 1972: 56fn).
8. Some Gé and other non-Tupí horticulturalists in eastern and southern Brazil are largely 'drug-free' in their shamanic practices (Wilbert 1987: 104).
9. This is an inaccuracy on Wilbert's part as Butt-Colson actually says the Akawaio shaman drinks tobacco juice.
10. 'Master' also translates as S. *dueña(o)*, S. *ama(o)*, and as 'owner' in English.
11. Phlegm recurs in other tobacco references. Gow (personal communication) notes that, for the San Martín (i.e. Lamista) Quechua, phlegm resides in the shaman's stomach and is the source of knowledge that tobacco 'pulls up' as a rattling cough into his/her throat as s/he smokes. In Piro, it is called *yowuma koslewatachri*, which also means 'magnet'. It is generated by drinking *ayahuasca* and *toé*, but not apparently by tobacco, which activates or potentializes this.
12. Young (2005) for example, records how much the Pitjantjatjara of Western Australia, appreciate wild tobacco (*mingkulpa* – probably *N. excelsior or N. gossei*) for its rich greenness and strong odour.
13. 'Anti-food' is Viveiros de Castro's equivalent to Hugh-Jones' 'non-food' (above).
14. Many Shipibo and mestizo fishermen and hunters smoke and chew tobacco in order 'not to feel hunger'. Somehow, here, tobacco is 'food', because it 'feeds' the chewer – although not in the sense of nutrition. Those people who do this often are described as very thin but at the same time strong, because they eat little (which resembles the 'diet' for shamanic growth, Brabec de Mori, personal communication).
15. Londoño-Sulkin (2012: 84) notes that among the Colombian 'People of the Centre', one indigenous friend, Emanuel, cites 'forest tobacco' (*Virola multinervia*) as the cause of strong hallucinations that inspired him to build a new longhouse, together with his more practical reason of crowding in an overly smoky environment. Other groups see the plants themselves as a source of divinatory information.
16. For more on the Amerindian category of master or 'owner', see Fausto (2008).
17. Among the Baníwa, tobacco séances by the celestial deities literally create clouds of smoke (Wright 2013: 81; 175) and the jaguar shamans sing to sweep them away ('brush away').

18. Wilbert (1987: 89) observes that among the Carib of Surinam (Cariña) 'to make the tobacco strong, the ribs and the leaves are punctured with a sting-ray barb.'
19. Such is the devastation on tobacco plants wrought by the caterpillar *Manduca sexta*, that the Yanomam (a subgroup of the Yanomami) sometimes refer to tobacco as 'caterpillar's vegetable food' (Albert in Wilbert and Simoneau 1990: 335, fn 361). Among the northwestern Hupd'äh, shamans who also feed off this plant are seen to metamorphose in the same way as their caterpillar counterparts (Ramos 2013).
20. Trewavas (2003) pulls together a number of botanical studies evincing plants' awareness and active responses to a wide range of environmental factors, including touch, gravity, light, sound and chemical stimulation. Plants appear to assimilate knowledge in doing so and this comes to constitute part of their life history.
21. Tobacco plants near the clipped sagebrush increased their levels of what is possibly a defensive enzyme (polyphenol oxidase) in response to an airborne signal (methyl jasmonate) released by the sagebrush.
22. Seated on a ceremonial stool and smoking a cigar in her cigar holder, Grandmother Universe makes a new being appear – the Grandson of the Universe, creator of light, of the layers of the universe, and of humanity.
23. 'Shamanry' refers to the specific work of the shaman, the most gifted intermediary in the animist cosmos; 'shamanism' refers to the complex of esoteric animist knowledge or worldview, sometimes also shared with non-shamans.
24. See also http://www.nydailynews.com/life-style/health/mindfulness-app-smokers-quit-article-1.1372697.
25. For example, see McGonigle (2013) on *khat* (*Catha edulis*) chewing; Tomlinson (2007) on drinking *kava* (*Piper methysticum*).
26. For example, Alderete et al. (2010: 29) point out that in the Andean Pachamama ceremony, 'cigarettes have replaced tobacco leaves as offerings'. Both Gow and Fortis (this volume) query the ability to easily distinguish between religious/ritual and recreational tobacco use.

Part I
Tobacco in Ecological and Historical Contexts

1

A Deep History of Tobacco in Lowland South America

Augusto Oyuela-Caycedo and Nicholas C. Kawa

The white man took the ritually used tobacco of the Indian and made it one of the first great crops of overseas commerce.

Carl Sauer [1937] (2009: 282–283)

Introduction

This chapter traces the origins of tobacco use and its variation in Lowland South America. It begins by examining new evidence on the origins of several species in the genus Nicotiana and follows their dispersal across South America. It then mines the archaeological and ethnographic records to explore variation in indigenous tobacco consumption and the cultural materials associated with it. The second half of the chapter describes tobacco's rise as a valuable commodity during the colonial period, providing observations made by visiting scholars and scientists. Turning attention to present-day rural communities of Brazilian Amazonia, an examination is provided of tobacco production on anthropogenic soils[1] characteristic of archaeological sites, thus linking contemporary tobacco cultivation to the extended history of Amerindian settlement and horticultural practice. By synthesizing archaeological and botanical findings while also examining human societies' consumptive and productive relationships to tobacco through time, this chapter seeks to illuminate the deep history[2] of tobacco.

The origins of tobacco

Tobacco is derived exclusively from plants of the genus Nicotiana, established by Linnaeus in 1753, and recognized as one of the largest genera within the family Solanaceae (Knapp et al. 2004; Olmstead et al. 2008). The genus was initially divided into 3 subgenera (Table 1.1), 14 sections and 60 species (Goodspeed 1954). A recent DNA sequence study revised the genus, adding several new species to extend the total to 76 while also organizing the genus into 13 sections (Knapp et al. 2004). Several species are recognized as endemic to Australia along with one found in Africa (Goodspeed 1954: 8), and recent DNA studies support this view (Knapp et al. 2004). But while species of Nicotiana exist in various parts of the globe, more than half of them are endemic to South America (54 per cent of all species; Table 1.2) and it is here that humanity's relationship to tobacco originates.

Table 1.1 Nicotiana species, natural distribution and number of chromosomes (where known).

Section/species	Natural geographical distribution	N
***Nicotiana* Section *Paniculatae* Goodspeed**		
Nicotiana benavidesii Goodspeed	Peru	12
Nicotiana cordifolia Philippi	Chile (Juan Fernandez Islands)	12
Nicotiana cutleri D'Arcy	S Bolivia	12
Nicotiana knightiana Goodspeed	Peru (S Coast)	12
Nicotiana paniculata L.	W Peru	12
Nicotiana raimondii J.F. Macbride	Peru, Bolivia	12
Nicotiana solanifolia Walpers	Chile (N Coast)	12
***Nicotiana* Section *Rusticae* Don**		
Nicotiana rustica L.	Ecuador, Peru, NW Bolivia	24
***Nicotiana* Section *Tomentosae* Goodspeed**		
Nicotiana kawakamii Y. Ohashi	Bolivia	12
Nicotiana otophora Grisebach	Bolivia, NW Argentina	12
Nicotiana setchellii Goodspeed	N Peru	12
Nicotiana tomentosa Ruiz and Pavon	S and C Peru, W Bolivia	12
Nicotiana tomentosiformis Goodspeed	Bolivia	12
***Nicotiana* Section *Nicotiana* Don**		
Nicotiana tabacum L.	Bolivia, Paraguay, Peru	24
***Nicotiana* Section *Undulatae* Goodspeed**		
Nicotiana arentsii Goodspeed	Peru, Bolivia	24
Nicotiana glutinosa L.	Peru, S Ecuador	12
Nicotiana thyrsiflora Bitter ex Goodspeed	N Peru	12
Nicotiana undulata Ruiz and Pavon	Peru, Bolivia, N Argentina	12
Nicotiana wigandioides Koch and Fintelman	Bolivia	12

(Continued)

Section/species	Natural geographical distribution	N
***Nicotiana* Section *Trigonophyllae* Goodspeed**		
Nicotiana obtusifolia M. Martens & Galeotti	SW United States, Mexico	12
Nicotiana palmeri A. Gray	SW United States, Mexico	12
***Nicotiana* Section *Sylvestres* Knapp**		
Nicotiana sylvestris Spegazzini and Comes	Bolivia, NW Argentina	12
***Nicotiana* Section *Alatae* Goodspeed**		
Nicotiana alata Link and Otto	Uruguay, Brazil, Paraguay, Argentina	9
Nicotiana azambujae L.B. Smith & Downs	S Brazil	?
Nicotiana bonariensis Lehmann	SE Brazil, Uruquay, Argentina	9
Nicotiana forgetiana Hemsley	SE Brazil	9
Nicotiana langsdorffii Weinmann	Brazil, Paraguay, Argentina	9
Nicotiana longiflora Cavanilles	Bolivia, Brazil, Paraguay, Uruguay, Argentina	9
Nicotiana mutabilis Stehmann & Samir	Brazil	9
Nicotiana plumbaginifolia Viviani	Peru, Bolivia, Argentina, Paraguay, Brazil	10
***Nicotiana* Section *Repandae* Goodspeed**		
Nicotiana nudicaulis S. Watson	NE Mexico	24
Nicotiana repanda Willdenow ex Lehmann	S United States, N Mexico	24
Nicotiana stocktonii Brandegee	Mexico (Revillagigedo Islands)	24
Nicotiana nesophila Johnston	Mexico (Revillagigedo Islands)	24
***Nicotiana* Section *Noctiflorae* Goodspeed**		
Nicotiana acaulis Spegazzini	Argentina	12
Nicotiana ameghinoi Spegazzini	Argentina	12
Nicotiana glauca Graham	Bolivia, N. Argentina	12
Nicotiana noctiflora Hooker	Argentina, Chile	12
Nicotiana paa Martinez Crovedo	N Argentina	12
Nicotiana petunioides (Grisebach) Millan	Argentina, Chile	12
***Nicotiana* Section *Petunioides* Don**		
Nicotiana acuminata (Graham) Hooker	Chile, Andes Mountains of Argentina	12
Nicotiana attenuata Torrey ex S. Watson	W United States, NW Mexico	12
Nicotiana corymbosa Remy	Chile, Argentina	12
Nicotiana linearis Phillipi	Argentina, Chile	12

(Continued)

Section/species	Natural geographical distribution	N
Nicotiana longibracteata Philippi	Andes Mts. of N Argentina and Chile	12
Nicotiana miersii Remy	Chile	12
Nicotiana pauciflora Remy	Chile	12
Nicotiana spegazzinii Millan	Argentina	12
***Nicotiana* Section *Polydicliae* Don**		
Nicotiana clevelandii A. Gray	SW United States, NW Mexico	24
Nicotiana quadrivalvis Pursh	W United States	24
Nicotiana Section *Suaveolentes* Goodspeed		
Nicotiana africana Merxmuller and Buttler	Namibia	23
Nicotiana amplexicaulis Burbidge	E Australia	18
Nicotiana benthamiana Domin	NC and NW Australia	19
Nicotiana burbidgeae Symon	S Australia	21
Nicotiana cavicola Burbidge	W Australia	23
Nicotiana debneyi Domin	E Australia	24
Nicotiana excelsior J.M. Black	Australia	19
Nicotiana exigua H.-M. Wheeler	SE Australia	16
Nicotiana fragrans Hooker	South Pacific Islands	24
Nicotiana goodspeedii Wheeler	S Australia	20
Nicotiana gossei Domin	C Australia	18
Nicotiana hesperis Burbridge	Australia	21
Nicotiana heterantha Kenneally & Symon	W Australia	24
Nicotiana ingulba J.M. Black	Australia	20
Nicotiana maritima Wheeler	S Australia	16
Nicotiana megalosiphon VanHeurck & Mueller	E Australia	20
Nicotiana occidentalis Wheeler	Australia	21
Nicotiana rosulata (S. Moore) Domin	Australia	20
Nicotiana rotundifolia Lindley	SW Australia	22
Nicotiana simulans Burbidge	Australia	20
Nicotiana stenocarpa H.-M. Wheeler	Australia	20
Nicotiana suaveolens Lehmann	SE Australia	16
Nicotiana truncata Symon	W Australia	?
Nicotiana umbratica Burbidge	W Australia	23
Nicotiana velutina Wheeler	Australia	16
Nicotiana wuttkei Clarkson & Symon	NE Australia	16

Source: Lewis (2011): 187–188; based on section classification of Knapp et al. (2004).

Table 1.2 Natural distribution of Nicotiana species in the world.

Area of natural distribution	Percentage of *Nicotiana* species
Lowland Andes area of Ecuador, Peru, Bolivia, Chile, Argentina	43.4
Humid areas of Paraguay, Brazil, Northern Argentina, Uruguay	10.5
North America	11.8
Africa (Namibia)	1.3
Australia and South Pacific Islands	32.9

Source: Lewis (2011): 187–188; based on section classification of Knapp et al. (2004).

The alkaloid nicotine is what has long drawn human attention to Nicotiana, although not all of the species in the genus produce nicotine and can thus be considered 'tobacco-producers'. About a dozen Nicotiana species were used by South America peoples, but eventually two species stood out as the principal cultigens after the European conquest: *Nicotiana rustica* and *Nicotiana tabacum* (Wilbert 1987: 4). The wild ancestors of *N. rustica* and *N. tabacum* are believed to have originated in the highland Andes, either in Ecuador, Peru, Bolivia or northwest Argentina (Goodspeed 1954: 353; Goodspeed 1961). The ancestral parent of *N. tabacum* is *Nicotiana sylvestris*, which is found in northwest Argentina and Bolivia (Lewis 2011: 189), and which likely hybridized with *Nicotiana tomentosiformis* (from Bolivia), or possibly *Nicotiana otophora*. The second most used species by indigenous people of the Americas is *N. rustica*, which has an origin somewhere in the eastern Andes, either in southwest Ecuador, Southern Peru or Northern Bolivia. Its ancestral plants are believed to be *Nicotiana paniculata* and *Nicotiana undulate*, both of which very likely evolved in north-central Peru. *N. rustica* exhibits higher concentrations of nicotine than *N. tabacum* and for this reason it is preferred by shamans for inducing altered states of consciousness (Winter 2000a: 103–108). *N. tabacum*, on the other hand, was recognized by the English for its pleasant smoke, which favoured its quick adoption by Europeans during the colonial period, eventually spreading across the globe (Norton 2008).

While the area of origin for *N. tabacum* is fairly clear, DNA studies point out other problems in relation to our understanding of its domestication. In fact, there appears to be contradictory evidence, and some geneticists suggest that the polyploidy condition of *N. tabacum* developed a long time before humans came into contact with the plant, perhaps by as much as hundreds of thousands of years. Some genetic studies estimate the origin of *N. tabacum* as early as 6 million years ago (Okamuro and Goldberg 1985), while others suggest an origin of 200,000 years ago (Kovarik et al. 2008). Both of these estimates strongly contrast with the scenarios proposed by archaeologists who suggest an origin between 6,000 and 10,000 years ago. These latter estimates are based on the logic that increasing selection for a higher content of nicotine ($C_{10}H_{14}N_2$) drove early human selection, and that is why the strong preference for *N. rustica* (2.47 per cent nicotine) and *N. tabacum* (1.23 per cent nicotine) can be seen in South America (see Winter 2000c: 321–322). How do we reconcile the difference between the genetic and archaeological dating? The implications of this difference are significant because if geneticists are correct, then the most widely used species of the Nicotiana genus (*N. tabacum* and *N. rustica*) did not undergo a process of domestication but simply benefitted from the dispersion by humans outside their original range. While several species of tobacco were likely to have been used by hunter-gatherers for inducing hallucinations and/or for important curing activities, the dispersion of Nicotiana appears to be tied more broadly to the development of horticulture and the spread of other tropical domesticated plants as proposed by Wilbert (1987: 4).

In a review by Winter (2000a), it is explained that four species of Nicotiana were cultivated in North America *(N. bigerlovii* var. *quarivalvis*, *N.* var. *multivalvis*, *N. attenuate* and *N. rustica)*. The evidence indicates that tobacco was associated with the horticultural complex of corn, beans and squash along with sunflowers somewhere around the beginning of the Christian era but reached a broader use around 900 to 1000 AD. Evidence of *N. attenuate* is found in the Anasazi archaeological context in pre-Pueblo archaeological sites in New Mexico, Colorado and Arizona that date to around 300 to 400 AD. However, the earliest evidence of *N. attenuate* comes from a Late Archaic Site near Tucson, Arizona that dates from 387 to 205 BC (calibrated carbon dates, Winter 2000a).

In terms of archaeological findings, the largest problem area is South America where evidence is sorely lacking. This is partly because few South American archaeologists use flotation techniques that would allow for the recovery of carbonized seeds. For this reason, very few findings of Nicotiana are reported. In one rare case, preserved leaves of *N. glauca* were recovered inside a cranium that was used as an offering found in the Valley of Chavina, Peru. It dates to about 450 ± 70 AD. Other examples of Nicotiana appeared in a Tiahuanco burial inside bundles associated with *Ilex guayusa* with three radiocarbon dates of AD 355 ± 200, AD 375 ± 100, AD 1120 ± 100, but the individual species were not identified (Wassén 1972). There have also been finds of wild specimens of Nicotiana from the archaeological sites of Caral and Mina Perdida and the valley of Lurín in coastal Peru, dating around 2200–1200 BC (Chevalier 2013: 104–105, 109). Still others are reported in Bolivia at the Chiripa site, during the formative period (1500–100 BC), but once again the individual species were not identified (Whitehead 2006: 269). At Kala Uyuni, a site near Chiripa and very close in time period, the presence of *N. cf. undulate* has been reported (Moore et al. 2010: 183–184; Bruno 2014: 136). Lastly, in the upper Mantaro of Peru seeds of Nicotiana species have been found in association with the Wanka II (1300–1470 AD) and Wanka III (1470–1532) periods (Earle 1987: 83–84).

In southern regions of South America, especially in the Chaco region, a great diversity of pipes is found in the archaeological record. This includes single pipes and double-barrelled pipes made of bone, ceramic, stone and other materials. These pipes actually produce some of the best evidence of the early use of tobacco, but the exact species of Nicotiana utilized are not known because only nicotine residues have been identified from the archaeological materials. Through analysis using gas chromatography coupled with mass spectrometry, different archaeological artefacts found at the Early Ceramic period site at La Granja in central Chile (500–1000 AD) offer evidence of nicotine in pipes, bowls and small mortars and pestles. Evidence of carbonized seeds of the species *N. corymbosa* has also been found in a cave dating to the Early Ceramic period at the Las Morrenas 1 site in the Andes of central Chile (Planella et al. 2012; Echevarría et al. 2014). In the Atacama regions, evidence of nicotine in the hair of several mummies from Late Formative (ca. 100 BC–400 AD) and Middle (400–950 AD) has been reported as well (Echeverría and Niemeyer 2012).

Based on the natural distribution of Nicotiana species, South America's importance to the dispersion of nicotine plants is clear. After all, more than half of all the species originate in two areas: the central lowland Andes and adjacent foothills (Ecuador, Peru, northern Chile, Bolivia and northwest Argentina) with 43.3 per cent of the Nicotiana species and the lowland humid environments of the Mojos and the Pantanal with another 10.5 per cent of the species (Table 1.2). Of the 33 species found in the former area, most of them were used for what were probably medicinal purposes by local populations. However, the preferred medicinal species, *N. rustica*, spread from the arid environments of Peru, Ecuador, and the Bolivian Lowlands to the north, and it is speculated that hunter-gatherers are responsible for this species' dispersion northward out of the Andes into Central America and Mexico and the rest of North America before agriculture was established (Winter 2000c: 324–325). The desert species of North America appear to have followed a similar route from south to north during the Pleistocene before the arrival of humans to the Americas. However, many of those species disappeared from parts of Central America during the Holocene due to increased humidity. In contrast, *N. tabacum* moved eastwards into the lowlands of Bolivia, Peru, Brazil and the Paraguayuan Pantanal as well as the humid forests of the Amazon where it is better adapted than *N. rustica* (Winter 2000c: 325–326).

Variation in tobacco use

There is great variation in how indigenous people of Lowland South America have used tobacco through time. It is not possible, however, to reconstruct the social history of its use due to the lack of archaeological evidence available. Nonetheless, Nordenskiöld et al. (1919: 91–93) made an early attempt by constructing maps of the distribution of tobacco pipes as well as by detailing the ethnographic distribution of tobacco smoking. Later, Johannes Wilbert (1987: 9–132) developed a more systematic approach that looked at the geographical distribution and ethnic consumption of tobacco. In Wilbert's classic study, he pointed out that in order to access tobacco's intoxicating nicotine, indigenous groups developed techniques of chewing, drinking, licking, and snuffing. Some even developed tobacco enemas as has been described among the Achuar in Ecuador as well as in Pre-Columbian Mesoamerica societies (Robicsek et al. 1978: 22–23; Schultes and Raffaut 1990: 432–436). And, of course, the technique of smoking tobacco was also developed, which today is the most widespread form of tobacco consumption among Amerindians in South America (Wilbert 1987: 124).

Smoking in pipes was very common in the Chaco region and this is supported by archaeological evidence that extends deep into prehistoric times. In Amazonia, however, pipe smoking appears to have been limited to a few select areas, including the Araguaia River, the Marañon-Huallaga-Ucayali region, and northern Colombia (Nordenskiold 1919: 91–93; Wilbert 1987: 121–123). Smoking cigarettes or cigars, on other hand, was a more widespread technique at the time of European contact. However, it seems that the context of its use was often ceremonial, related to ritualistic curing with smoke and/or the clearing of malevolent deities and spirits from places. Recreational use of tobacco in the form of cigars or cigarettes most likely expanded following the arrival of the Spanish and Portuguese and the subsequent commodification of tobacco (Wilbert 1987: 124; observed also by Sauer in the opening quotation to this chapter).

Aside from smoking, there are other forms of tobacco consumption that are more restricted in their use. In northwestern Amazonia, for example, one way of consuming tobacco is the sucking of tobacco juice (*ambíl*). The consumption of *ambíl* is common among the Chibcha speaking groups of Northern Colombia, such as the Kogui and Ijka, as well in the Predio Putumayo region (between the regions of Caquetá and Putumayo). It is also found among the Witotos, Boras, the Yukunas of the Miriti-Parana River, and the Apaporis groups. *Ambíl* paste is made by extracting juice from tobacco leaves boiled in water until they produce a paste, which is then mixed with potassium salts extracted by percolation from the ashes of some plants (Echeverri et al. 2001 and this volume). The paste has a strong smell of ammonia and is consumed in low doses because of its heavily concentrated amounts of nicotine. In northwest Amazonia, *ambíl* is simply licked, at any point where the individual is sucking coca powder or does not have coca powder in the mouth. The Kaggaba or Kogui use it by spreading the paste on their teeth to create a protective layer against the corrosive acidity of the shell lime used with coca leaf powder. Part of this difference is because the former groups use the less acidic ashes from Cecropia leaves in combination with coca powder. In both cases the *ambíl* is stored in a small calabash or any other small container that is easy to seal. In the case of the Witoto, they use the hollowed fruit of the *Theobroma bicolor* (a wild relative of cacao), which helps to flavour the *ambíl* (Schultes and Raffauf 1990: 435).

The use of tobacco snuff today is very restricted in Native South America and is largely associated with areas where coca is consumed in powder form rather than

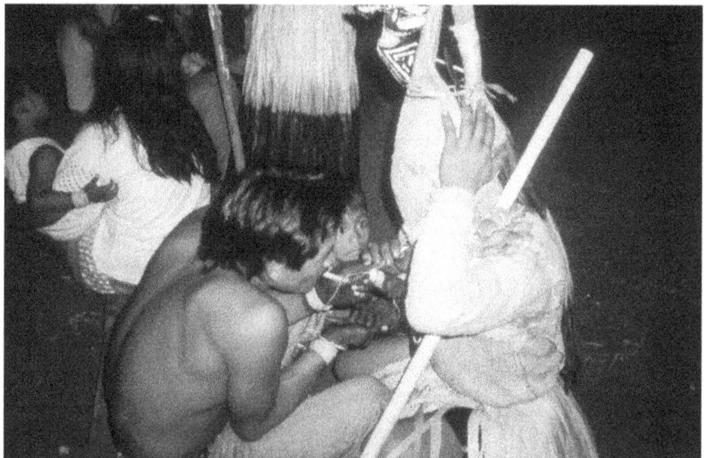

Figure 1.1 Insufflating tobacco snuff into the noses of participants during the Peach Palm Festival, Caqueta River, Comeyafu, Pedrera, Colombia. (Photograph by Augusto Oyuela-Caycedo.)

chewed in leaf form as is customarily seen in the Peruvian Andes. Tobacco snuffing also occurs in ritual activities. During the peach palm festival among groups living near the Caquetá River in the Colombian Amazon (Figure 1.1), tobacco smoke is ritualistically blown to clear the area of any negative spirits that may harm visiting dancers, and snuff is shared among the dancers themselves. During the peach palm dance, there is a simulated attack performed by the visitors who wear masked dresses and carry a large wooden phallus that represents *To'ry*, the spirit of the forest. In order to calm the *To'ry*, the host who is attacked while observing the spectacle must simulate the manual masturbation of the forest spirit by stroking the phallus with his fingers. The masked dancer then partially removes his mask, allowing the host to see him, at which point they exchange tobacco snuff, blowing the fine powder into each other's noses using the bones of a bird (Plate 1.1). After that, the host and dancer become friends (Schultes and Raffauf 1990: 434–435; Oyuela-Caycedo 2004).

As discussed in the archaeological record, many contemporary indigenous groups do not consume tobacco alone but rather in combination with one or several other plants. Prance (1972) reports that the Jamamadis in Brazilian Amazonia use a mixture of tobacco and cacao ash (Theobroma *subincanum*) for the snuff (*shinã*), which they suck into their nostrils through a small pipe made from a hollow monkey leg bone. The Jamamadis insist that the snuff is ineffective without the Theobroma bark ash and they never take pure tobacco snuff. The Denis call their snuff by practically the same name as the Jamamadis (*tsinã*) (Prance 1972) and a similar practice can also be found among the Witoto (Schultes and Raffauf 1990: 433). Tobacco is also consumed along with *ayahuasca* in western Amazonia societies where it is used to protect individuals in healing ceremonies as is reported among the Shuar, for example (Bennett 1992).

Table 1.3 Predominant areas of tobacco consumption techniques in the twentieth century. Compiled from Wilbert (1987): 22–24, 42, 67–77, 125–131.

Technique	Material culture	Area centre in South America	Example of ethnic group	Number of groups
Licking (*Ambíl*)	Small calabash	1. Sierra Nevada de Santa Marta (northern Colombia)	Kogui, Ijka, Sanka (Chibcha speakers)	16
	Camera film container	2. Area between Putumayo and Caqueta River drainage (Colombian Amazon)	Huitoto, Bora, Muinane, Miraña, Andoque	
Chewing		1. upper Amazon	Ticuna, Omagua, Cocama, Shipibo	56
		2. Peru, Paraguay, Northern Argentina	Toba, Abipon	
		3. Orinoco River (Venezuela)	Panare	
Snuffing	Palms seed container	1. Colombian Amazon: Caqueta river and Putumayo	Yukuna	53
	Snail shell Bird bone tubes	2. upper Amazon River: Upper Ucayali river, Peru; Upper Purus (western Brazil)	Shipibo, Campa, Machigenga	
		3. Machado river (Mina de Gerais, western Brazil)	Munde,Tuparí, Kepikiriwát.	
Drinking		1. upper Amazon, Peru	Zaparo, Shipibo	64
		2. Guiana shield	Warao, Cariña, Macushi.	
Smoking	Cigarette holders	1. upper Amazon: Ucayali, Huayaga rivers, Javary, Caqueta, Putumayo rivers	Cocama, Omagua, Witoto, Zaparo, Shipibo, Machigenga	233
	Cigarettes, pipes	2. Chaco region (Northern Argentina; Paraguay; Mato Grosso, Brazil) and Bolivia	Mataco, Chorote, Maca, Toba, Mbaya	
		3. Moxos, Upper Mamore and Guapore River drainage	Chiriguano, Chiquito	
		4. Between the Xingu and upper tributaries of the Tapajos (Brazil)	Carajá, Kalapalo, Bororo	
		5. Rivers of the Guyana Shield, Orinoco River (Venezuela, northern Brazil)	Trio, Wayana, Waiwiai, Macushi	

What can we learn from the spatial distribution of different techniques of tobacco consumption (Table 1.3)? One interpretation derived from the data of Johannes Wilbert (1987) is that the only places where divergent techniques co-exist is in the Eastern Andes of Peru and Ecuador, the region of southwest Bolivia, northern Chile and Argentina, as well as Paraguay and southwest Brazil. These areas overlap with the origins of *N. rustica* and *N. tabacum*, thus favouring the hypothesis that these were the places where the ritual use of tobacco originated, from whence it spread north towards Mesoamerica and North America in the case of *N. rustica* and east towards the Amazon in the case of *N. tabacum*. It seems likely that the use of *N. tabacum* in Amazonia also enters later with the dispersion of other cultigens such as manioc. And, it appears that few indigenous communities used tobacco simply for recreation. Where such a tendency is present, it is often the consequence of tobacco's commercialization, born out of the history of colonization.

Colonial tobacco: From speciality to staple

During the colonial period, tobacco quickly circulated throughout the regional and global economic system. The rise of global tobacco was inextricably linked to its rapid adoption in Europe, and later Asia and Africa. In sixteenth- and seventeenth-century Europe, the medicinal properties of tobacco were emphasized by early-adopters. Its green leaves were used as a topical application on sores and wounds, its oil was used against headaches, and its smoke was said to help those 'subject to catarrhs, rheums, and pains' (Chamberlayne 1682). It was also recognized for its ability to stave off hunger and thirst (Goodman 1993: 44–45). However, some scholars have argued that this medicinal argument is often overblown, ignoring the seductive novelty of the act of smoking as well as the pleasure produced by nicotine (Nater 2006: 93; Norton 2008: 8–9). Tobacco's association with royalty and nobility thanks in part to Jean Nicot,[3] the French ambassador to Portugal who had sent seeds and plants to the French Royal Court, helped to further legitimate tobacco's place in Europe (Goodman 1993: 47–48). But perhaps in the end, it was tobacco's great variability in application and use that made it such a success. Not long after its arrival to Europe at the end of the fifteenth century, it swept through the Iberian Peninsula, England, Belgium and the Netherlands before it eventually gained acceptance across the continent (Goodman 1993: 47–48).

In the seventeenth century, tobacco (*N. tabacum*) cultivation in the Americas expanded rapidly in response to European demand, and Brazil became the world's largest producer. Especially in the northeastern states of Bahia, Pernambuco and Maranhão, tobacco emerged as one of Brazil's primary high-value exports, along with cotton, sugar and sugar cane rum (Bakewell 2010: 441). In 1639, the city of Salvador da Bahia went as far as to prohibit the planting of tobacco due to fear that the little land available to grow food for the local population would be overtaken by the cash crop (Bakewell 2010: 441; see also Schwartz 1996: 84–93).[4] By the late seventeenth and early eighteenth centuries, it became a common form of payment for slaves in Africa and was even considered more profitable than sugar (Boxer 1962: 151; See also Russell-Wood 1998: 140–141). André Antonil, the pseudonym of an Italian Jesuit living in Brazil, commented in 1711: 'Changing from a speciality to a staple crop, today only the thousands of rolls [of tobacco] that the fleets take are sufficient to satisfy the appetites of all nations. This is not just in Europe, but also in other parts of the world, where they order it in spite of its high cost' (Antonil 2012: 138). Antonil remarked further, 'Because of the large quantities of tobacco consumed in all the cities and towns, not even today do the rulers of Europe have a business with a higher income' (Antonil 2012: 138).

Tobacco in Colonial Brazil was exported 'in roll' or snuff but never in leaf form (Boxer 1962: 151). The first harvest of leaves was considered 'the best, the strongest, and longest lasting' (Antonil 2012: 132). Such high quality tobacco was exported from Brazil to Portugal, which then sometimes went on to Goa and Portuguese India (Russell-Wood 1998: 140). The Portuguese Crown ordered that third grade tobacco be exported to West Africa, although first and second-grade quality tobacco often made it there as well, much to the chagrin of the Portuguese King Dom João VI (Russell-Wood 1998: 141). In fact, a large contraband trade of tobacco developed in Brazil and the Caribbean, creating a considerable headache for colonial powers that taxed its production in the New World. Despite the many attempts to impose greater control on the flow of tobacco out of the Americas, a significant portion of it was trafficked by smugglers.

Unlike sugar production, tobacco cultivation in colonial Brazil was initially small scale, with tobacco producers working with 'only a few slaves each' and occasionally curing the tobacco themselves (Boxer 1962: 151). However, tobacco later played an important role in heightening the demand for slave imports as it became more and more profitable (Schwartz 1996: 92), as the Bahian example attests. The historian Stuart Schwartz explains, 'Small-scale peasant production and slave-based agriculture were no longer two distinct alternatives, but rather two related processes in which the tendency for slavery to expand predominated' (Schwartz 1996: 92). In the late colonial period, Schwartz notes that in the state of Bahia, for example, about 20,000 Africans arrived between 1786 and 1790, but in the following five year period that number ballooned to 34,000 (p. 72). By the period of 1826–1830, nearly 10,000 slaves were arriving per year (Schwartz 1996: 72).

In the early settlement of eastern Amazonia and the province of Grão Para, the plantation system of tobacco production was implemented. This was mostly geared towards the internal market in Brazil as tobacco's consumption became widespread, usually consumed as snuff, but also commonly chewed and smoked. Despite the growing demand for tobacco in colonial Brazil, the eastern Amazonian plantations largely failed due to a constellation of factors from the high price of African labour to the spread of epidemic diseases (Gomes 2002: 471). Scant information can be found on the cultivation of tobacco in colonial *vilas* of central and western Amazonia at this time, but based on later accounts, it is reasonable to assume that it was fairly commonplace. Missionaries motivated colonial expansion in the Portuguese Amazon through collecting expeditions for uncultivated spices, which began as early as the mid-seventeenth century (Roller 2010). To finance mission activities, the missionaries often tended small plantations of cacao and other valuable crops like tobacco while encouraging or coercing their new converts to collect spices (e.g. wild clove and sarsaparilla) in the *sertão* or backlands (Walker 2009b: 546–547).

By the mid-nineteenth century, numerous foreign scientists and visitors passed through the Amazon region, commenting on the presence of tobacco in fields and small home gardens. Some Confederate families that left the United States following the American Civil War even established farms outside of the Amazonian city of Santarém where they planted tobacco, along with corn, cotton and sugarcane (Smith 1879: 144; Harter 1985: 30). Many of the Confederates situated their plantations on soils that were known in Brazilian Amazonia as '*terra preta do índio*' or Indian Black Earth. Whether they initially realized it or not, the Confederates had begun farming on old Amerindian villages. Herbert Smith, a visiting geologist to the Confederate community, commented on the dark soils upon which they grew tobacco: 'It [tobacco] is cultivated on the rich black lands along the edge of these bluffs ... All along this side of the Tapajós ... [which] must have been lined with these villages, for the black land is continuous, and at many points pottery and stone implements cover the ground like shells on a surf-washed beach' (1879: 238; also cited in Denevan 2001: 105).

Other visitors from this period noted the widespread presence of tobacco cultivation in the Amazon region, including US Naval officers William Lewis Herndon and Lardner Gibbon who descended the Madeira River in 1852 while conducting a survey of the region. They claimed that tobacco produced in central Amazonia was the best in Brazil and that it was traded to the Atlantic Coast along with cacao, sarsaparilla, coffee and Brazil nuts (Herndon and Gibbon 1854: 311). Alfred Russel Wallace, while travelling along the Rio Negro a few years earlier, also took extensive notes on tobacco cultivation, processing, and production during the tobacco-picking season:

> Tobacco is sown thickly on a small patch of ground, and the young plants are then set in rows, just as we do cabbages .... When they show any inclination to flower, the buds are nipped off; and as soon as the leaves have reached their full size, they are gathered in strong wicker baskets, and are laid out in the house or a shed, on poles supported by uprights from the floor to the ceiling. In a few days they dry, and during

> the hot days become quite crisp; but the moisture of the night softens them, and early in the morning they are flaccid. When they are judged sufficiently dry, every leaf must have the strong fibrous midrib taken out of it. For this purpose all the household – men, women, and children – are called up at four in the morning, and are set to work tearing out the midrib, before the heat of the day makes the leaves too brittle to allow of the operation. A few of the best leaves are sometimes selected to make cigars, but the whole is generally manufactured into rolls of two or four pounds each. When the tobacco is good, or has, as they term it, 'much honey in it', it will cut as smooth and solid as a piece of Spanish liquorice, and can be bent double without cracking. (Wallace 1895: 126–127)

The value of tobacco to the livelihoods of rural people was also noted by Franz Keller, who was commissioned by the Minister of Public Works of Rio de Janeiro in 1867 to assess the feasibility of a railroad project along the Madeira River. In the appendix of his book *The Amazon and Madeira Rivers*, he writes: 'they [native people] subsist chiefly by the preparation of India-rubber, the collection of Para nuts, and other fruit of the forests, and on the produce of small cacao and tobacco plantations' (Keller 1875: 208). From these brief accounts, it is clear that Amazonian tobacco was no longer a speciality crop that was cultivated and produced strictly for localized consumption. Instead it had become swept up into the broader flow of commodities that defined the colonial period and that would forever change the region.

Tobacco use and production in rural Amazonia today

Despite being a major global commodity that is often produced in large-scale monocrop plantations today, small-scale tobacco production in rural Amazonia continues to persist. In the municipality of Borba in Amazonas state, Brazil, some smallholder farmers continue to grow tobacco on the fertile anthropogenic soils known as *terra preta do índio*, just as American Confederates had done in the mid-nineteenth century (Kawa 2016). The soils, which typically hold rich concentrations of organic matter and soil macronutrients, have been shown to be the product of long-term indigenous settlement and management during the pre-Columbian era (Kawa and Oyuela-Caycedo 2008). Because of the unique characteristics of *terra preta* soils, many contemporary farmers seek them out for the production of nutrient-demanding or pH-sensitive crops (Glaser et al. 2003; Kawa et al. 2011). Tobacco, for example, thrives in *terra preta* since its yields are considerably hindered by soil acidity (Abruña-Rodríguez et al. 1970). The soils also remain important examples of the long-enduring impacts of human management on the Amazonian landscape linked to early horticultural production, especially for the cultivation of valuable regional crops like tobacco.

Figure 1.2 Tobacco plants under cultivation in the rich anthropogenic soils known in the Brazilian Amazon as *terra preta do índio*. (Photograph by Nicholas C. Kawa.)

Figure 1.3 Tobacco leaves hanging to dry in an open-air palm thatch house in Borba, Amazonas, Brazil. (Photograph by Nicholas C. Kawa.)

Figure 1.4 Seu Jorge pauses to drink his coffee while winding a roll of tobacco with thick string. (Photograph by Nicholas C. Kawa.)

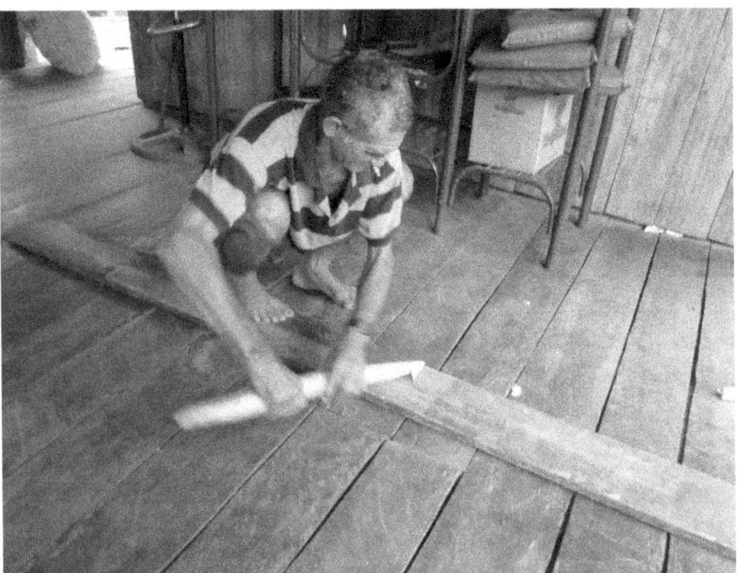

Figure 1.5 To preserve his roll of tobacco Seu Jorge wraps it in the latex of an Amazonian rubber tree that he has dried out on a wooden plank. (Photograph by Nicholas C. Kawa.)

In the community of Vila Gomes on the Madeira River, Seu Jorge, the community president still cultivates his own tobacco in the dark *terra preta* soils (Figure 1.2). Upon harvest, the tobacco is hung to dry in his house (Figure 1.3). After the midribs of the leaves are removed, the dried tobacco is rolled into large cylindrical rolls, usually a few feet in length. As in the past, it is tightened with cord, which is later removed when the roll is sufficiently compressed (Figure 1.4). The end product is wrapped with natural rubber to preserve it (Figure 1.5). The tobacco is then typically shaved off one end with a knife as it is progressively used. Bates described this same form of production in Borba more than a 100 years ago:

> The best tobacco in Brazil is grown in the neighborhood of Borba, on the Madeira, where the soil is a rich black loam.... It [tobacco] is made up into slender rolls, an inch and a half in diameter and six feet in length, tapering at each end. When the leaves are gathered and partially dried, layers of them, after the mid-ribs are plucked out, are placed on a mat and rolled up into the required shape. This is done by the women and children, who also manage the planting, weeding, and gathering of the tobacco. The process of tightening the rolls is a long and heavy task, and can be done only by men. The cords used for this purpose are of very great strength. (Bates 1873: 163)

Today, tobacco cultivated in the region is typically smoked in hand-rolled cigarettes. It is also common for individuals to purchase pouches of loose tobacco, which is rolled into cigarettes with available notebook paper. Yet with expanding availability of industrially-produced cigarettes, more and more rural Amazonians are opting for this more convenient form, and small-scale production of tobacco is becoming increasingly rare.

Despite the changing nature of tobacco production and its use, even in non-indigenous riverine communities it continues to be an important medicinal and healing plant. Stingray wounds and snakebites suffered by riverine inhabitants are treated with tobacco, sometimes mixed with other more recently introduced consumer items such as toothpaste (Kawa pers. obs.). Tobacco's connection to the supernatural realm also remains firmly in place. Rural Amazonians sometimes leave offerings of tobacco behind while hunting in the woods. These are offerings made to *curupira*, one of the masters of game (*mãe do mato*) that looks after forest animals (Reichel-Dolmatoff 1976; Smith 1996). A pinch of tobacco can be left in the crook of a tree to appease the *curupira* and dissuade it from disorienting the hunting party or placing a hex on one of its members. Similarly, in Afro-descendant *Quilombo* communities in the northeastern state of Bahia where artisanal tobacco cultivation continues today, fishermen and mollusc collectors leave offerings of tobacco behind for '*vovó do mangue*', the grandmother of the mangrove. Although tobacco is often divorced from its spiritual and ritualized context in everyday urban contexts, many notable exceptions exist, including its use in Afro-Brazilian religions like Candomblé (e.g. Voeks 1997) and contemporary *ayahuasca* ceremonies (e.g. Beyer 2009). It is quite clear that commodification has not diminished the importance of tobacco in such ritual contexts.

Conclusions

Tobacco and the various plants of the genus Nicotiana that produce it have a complex history in lowland South America. This brief examination of tobacco's history illuminates the importance for understanding how the diversity of species of Nicotiana shaped its early use, including the tendency towards the selection of plants with high nicotine content. It is very likely that hunter-gathers of the eastern Andes first utilized tobacco, spreading several species to the north of the continent while early horticulturalists expanded tobacco's distribution towards Amazonia and the humid lowlands. The high variation in the patterning and spatial distribution of techniques in tobacco use seem to correlate with distribution of Nicotiana species in the eastern Andes and into the lowlands. However, a lack of archaeological data on tobacco in South America continues to raise questions. Nonetheless, advances made in North American archaeology reveal broad usage of Nicotiana species, including several beyond those best known for their selection by humans, primarily *N. rustica* and *N. tabacum.*

The colonial period led to the commodification of tobacco, and Amazonia played a role in its production for the global economy from early on. Despite this, tobacco continued to hold strong ties to Amazonia's indigenous past as it was cultivated in enriched anthropogenic soils characteristic of Amerindian settlement sites, which are still used – for indigenous and non-indigenous populations alike – for tobacco production today. In this manner, tobacco cultivation in Amazonia still reflects some of its deep history derived from indigenous peoples of the region, remaining both a sacred plant and a staple crop.

Notes

1. Anthropogenic soils are the product of long-term deposition of organic waste and vegetative charcoal by human populations, in this case during the pre-Columbian era. For further description of the processes by which human habitation led to the formation of these soils in Amazonia, see Schmidt and Heckenberger (2009).
2. Here we draw from Shyrock and Lord Smailes' edited volume in presenting a temporally deep history of human relations to tobacco in both biological and cultural terms.
3. The word 'nicotine' and tobacco's genus 'Nicotiana' both derive from his last name.
4. This was a problem in Virginia as well and many suffered from famine due to the near complete dedication to the cultivation of tobacco and lack of attention to food crops (Mann 2011: 87, 96–97).

2

Methods of Tobacco Use among Two Arawakan-Speaking Peoples in Southwestern Amazonia: A Case Study of Structural Diffusion

Peter Gow

This chapter concerns the use of tobacco by two Arawakan-speaking peoples of southwestern Amazonia, the Piro (Yine) people of the Urubamba River in Peru and their eastern neighbours the Apurinã on the Purús River in Brazil. These two peoples speak very closely related languages, but their uses of tobacco have become increasing divergent since the middle of the nineteenth century. I shall argue this is undoubtedly due to a dramatic change in shamanic practices among the Piro which has not been experienced by the Apurinã.

It is important to address the ontogenetic pathway by which I formulated the question addressed here. In 1994, I proposed that the hallucinogen *ayahuasca* is a relatively recent addition to the pharmacological and shamanic systems of many indigenous peoples in southwestern Amazonia, a position that has since received growing support from other researchers (e.g. Brabec de Mori 2011; Barbira Freedman, this volume). The spread of *ayahuasca* seems to be connected to the expansion of the rubber extraction industry in the late nineteenth century: this pattern is fairly clear for Peru and fully demonstrable for Brazil. It therefore raises an important phenomenon that has been severely downplayed in recent anthropological work, namely diffusion. Two recent articles by Manuela Carneiro da Cunha address this old problem in a new way. The first directly addresses the socio-cosmological mechanisms that underlie the spread of *ayahuasca* into western Brazil (1998), while the second bears the eloquent title, 'Um difusionismo estrutural existe?' [Does structuralist diffusion exist?] (2009). Both articles are revolutionary applications of Lévi-Strauss' neglected canonical formula – or double twist – to address concrete ethnohistorical and ethnographic data. The present essay addresses these same topics from the point of view of tobacco.

If the use of *ayahuasca* is demonstrably novel in southwestern Amazonia, the product of a recent diffusion from further north, the use of tobacco is clearly very much older. This paper originally intended to explore the extent to which *ayahuasca* use inserted itself into earlier shamanic uses of tobacco as a psychoactive throughout the region.

However, as I began to explore the data, a much more complex system of tobacco use began to emerge, in a series of complex transformations that anticipated the later adoption of *ayahuasca* by certain peoples and not by others. The adoption or not of *ayahuasca* within a general field of diffusion depended, I discovered to my amazement, on prior transformations in the use of tobacco. I had naively assumed that tobacco use in southwestern Amazonia was 'just there', so ancient as to be virtually meaningless at the level of concrete ethnohistorical and ethnographic data. I was simply wrong.

The methodological and analytical problems that emerged as I proceeded with my enquiry were enormous. How to express clearly the genuine complexity of what I was finding? I decided to activate a tried-and-tested anthropological method – controlled comparison. Here, I compare the uses of tobacco by two indigenous peoples, the Piro and the Apurinã. These peoples speak 'sister' languages in the sense that their languages are more closely related to each other than to any others, and they almost certainly formed a single language community in the not too remote past. While the putative shared mode of tobacco use of this ancestral community is unknown, the available historical and ethnographic data allow us to track their uses of tobacco from the mid-nineteenth century to the present and, as importantly, the contexts of tobacco use. The present chapter uses the controlled comparison of these two peoples as a window into the topic for a much larger region of southwestern Amazonia.

A transformational group of instruments for the use of tobacco

The present paper is a response to Wilbert's remarkable and apparently exhaustive *Tobacco and Shamanism in South America* (1987). In it, Wilbert shows both the tight connection between tobacco use and shamanism for the continent and the remarkable diversity of uses. My argument (which mirrors comments about Wilbert's concern with 'mapping' rather than 'meaning' in the Introduction, this volume) is that while Wilbert's book represents a considerable advance in our understanding of tobacco use in South America, its underlying categorization of the topic by methods of use is unnecessarily functionalist. This effectively obscures other levels of order and in particular, structural levels of order in the properly Lévi-Straussian sense of 'structural', in the data he presents. Here, I shift attention from Wilbert's 'methods of tobacco use' to another field that he thoroughly documents but which does not constitute a core organizing principle of his analysis, the instruments used for tobacco (1987: 9–132).

Consider three illustrations of a variety of instruments for tobacco use by Piro and Apurinã people (Figures 2.1, 2.2, 2.3 and 2.4). Figures 2.1 and 2.2 illustrate objects collected by Ehrenreich in the late nineteenth century which are currently in the Museu Nacional in Rio de Janeiro. The black resin collars are pressed against the nose in use. Figures 2.3 and 2.4 illustrate objects collected in 1907, currently in the Peabody Museum. Figure 2.4 actually illustrates a Conibo pipe, but Farabee makes it clear that the Piro use identical pipe forms – examples can be seen in the Peabody Museum collection. The four figures are not to scale.

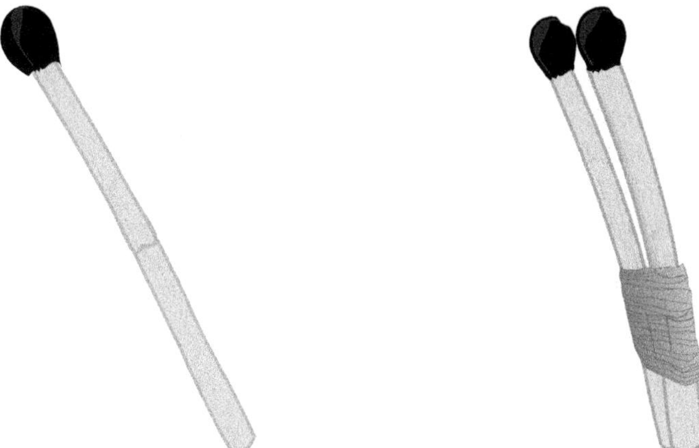

Figure 2.1 Single Apurinã snuff tube. (Redrawn from Schiel 2004: 181.)

Figure 2.2 Double Apurinã snuff tube. (Redrawn from Schiel 2004: 181.)

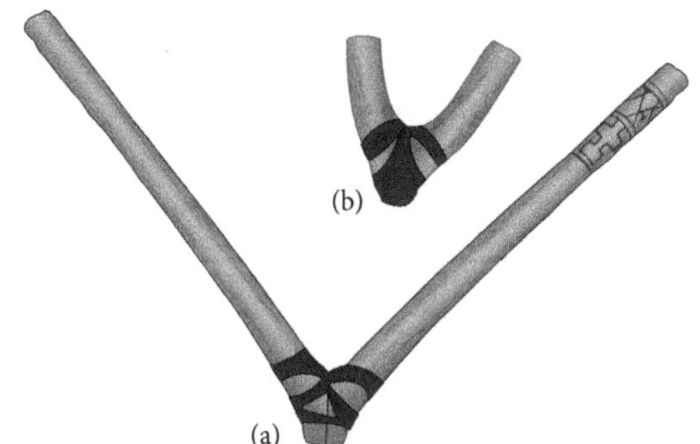

Figure 2.3 Large and small Piro snuff tubes. (Source: Farabee 1922: 58.)

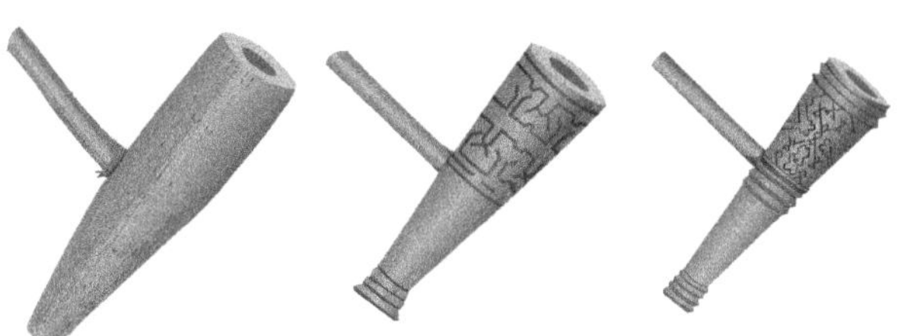

Figure 2.4 Conibo elbow pipes. (Source: Farabee 1922: 81.)

At first sight, a standard Apurinã snuff tube (Figure 2.1) does not look much like the standard Piro elbow pipe represented in Figure 2.4. At most, the two objects share one common element, a narrow tube usually formed of animal bone, but they are directed at two quite distinct modes of use of tobacco in Wilbert's terms: the former the nasal inhalation of tobacco snuff, the latter the buccal inhalation of tobacco smoke. But if we consider the 'doubled' Apurinã snuff tube (Figure 2.2) and the large and small Piro snuff tubes (Figure 2.3), the problem seems to change. Here we find a logical progression of plastic forms from the single Apurinã snuff tube to the doubled Apurinã snuff tube, then to the Piro snuff tubes, and finally to the Piro elbow pipe (Table 2.1).

Table 2.1 The logical progression of Apurinã and Piro instruments for tobacco use.

Single Apurinã snuff tube (Figure 2.1)	Double Apurinã snuff tube (Figure 2.2)	Piro snuff tubes (large and small) (Figure 2.3)	Piro elbow pipe (Figure 2.4)

The progression of plastic forms shown in Table 2.1 is, I think, reasonably compelling *as a logical progression of plastic forms* (also see Thompson 1945). Table 2.1 makes no claims about historical sequence or about technological complexity. It is based instead on an entirely synchronic analysis which does not, as I will show, refer to any real period in the history of the manufacture and usage of these instruments. That said, I believe it would be impossible to arrange the four elements of Table 2.1 in any other transformational sequence *at the level of plastic form*. The present paper shows that this logical transformation of plastic forms is underpinned by rich ethnographic and ethnohistorical data on the Piro and Apurinã people, which strongly suggest that it is a real transformational group. As such, it can be used to interrogate the potential for other levels of structural order, understood as systems in a state of transformation (see Gow 2001), in the data discussed by Wilbert.

The uses of tobacco by Urubamba Piro people from 1980 to 2008

I must admit that it never occurred to me to record non-shamanic uses of tobacco by indigenous people on the Bajo Urubamba during my initial fieldwork from 1980 to 1982. Smoking tobacco, I assumed, was simply what people did. There was no adult, to my knowledge, who did not smoke tobacco, although how much they smoked, what they smoked, and in what circumstances they smoked was very variable. To establish the actual pattern of tobacco use at that period, I would have to engage in a serious review of my photographs from the time, rather than my field notes. In marked contrast, it would be very easy to describe the patterns of consumption of alcohol. Who did and who did not drink fermented beer, and especially commercial cane alcohol, was common knowledge and commonly discussed. The same was true of those who did or did not drink the hallucinogen *ayahuasca*. The consumption of tobacco by smoking was, as the linguists say, unmarked.

In the 1980s, the smoking of tobacco followed a gradient from what we might call the purely 'recreational' to the markedly 'shamanic', although like Fortis (this volume) I am not entirely happy with these categories. By 'recreational' smoking, I mean smoking in an everyday or festive social situation. In this mode, smoking, usually of commercial cigarettes (*finos* or *de la fábrica*), was invariably done in a group, even if the group numbered only two. Solitary smoking tended to take place in situations characterized by the efficaciousness of the smoke – not on the smoker as such but on another being. An example of this would be smoking to repel biting insects. Slightly more marked than this was smoking to repel *kamchine*, 'demons'. This was done in a variety of situations, but most often at night in the village or by the river, or at any time while in the forest: in these times and places, 'the demons are looking'. 'Demons' are repelled by tobacco smoke, as are forest game animals, such that hunters did not smoke while hunting. In such situations of demonic attentiveness, the smoker might simply smoke, or they might blow the tobacco smoke on themselves, or on others, usually small children (cf. Rahman, this volume; Echeverri, this volume). When tobacco was smoked in a pipe by a trained shaman, the activity necessarily engaged his or her shamanic knowledge. The lowest level of shamanic action was precisely this form of smoking, with the blowing of tobacco on to the body of a sick person, accompanied by massaging the blown-upon body part, as the next step up. In such sessions, the shamans might even suck the blown-upon body part, the next step up again. Women often took mildly sick babies and small children to shamans who were engaged in their nightly smoking in order to have these treatments. More serious curing sessions involved the consumption of *ayahuasca*, which was the pre-condition for the shamanic sucking of internal pathogens: the consumption of *ayahuasca*, and hence sucking, necessarily involved smoking with a pipe. The only shamanic activity that did not involve smoking tobacco was the use of *gayapa* (local Spanish: *toé*; Lat. Brugmansia spp.), an infusion drunk in order to cure or reactivate shamanic knowledge.

The shamanic gradients of tobacco use were accompanied by a gradient between factory-produced commercial cigarettes, *cigarros finos* or *cigarros de la fábrica*, which dominated the recreational pole, to *mapacho*, locally produced and cured tobacco which had been tempered with various forest herbs (also see Baribira Freedman, this volume). The least markedly shamanic form of *mapacho* smoking was smoking of hand-rolled cigarettes, while the most markedly shamanic was when a shaman smoked *mapacho* in his or her pipe (which itself had been boiled in herbs like *toé*) during an *ayahuasca* curing ceremony. Interestingly, the difference between factory cigarettes and *mapacho* had nothing to do with commerce as such. Little, if any, *mapacho* was locally produced, although the technique was known, but was instead bought from the same traders who sold factory cigarettes. The main difference was that factory cigarettes were *fino*, 'fine' or 'refined' (in both senses) and *suave*, 'smooth, weak', while *mapacho* was *del monte*, 'of the forest' and *fuerte*, 'strong'.

My hesitancy about the analytical distinction between 'recreational' and 'shamanic' uses of tobacco reflects a genuine chromaticism, in the Lévi-Straussian sense, in local tobacco use. While I have never seen anyone smoking a shamanic pipe while actively engaged in drinking in a manioc beer festival, *mapacho* tobacco in the form of hand-rolled cigarettes was an acceptable, if undesirable, substitute for factory cigarettes in 'recreational' settings. Equally, factory cigarettes were an acceptable, if undesirable, substitute for *mapacho* tobacco in more 'shamanic' settings. I have never seen a shaman use factory cigarettes as a substitute for *mapacho* smoked in a pipe during an *ayahuasca* curing session, but it was common to see young women blow the 'recreational' smoke of factory cigarettes onto their infant children during manioc beer festivals.

Central to Piro people's understanding of, and use of, tobacco was the concept of *gimru*, the product of the verb *gimeta*, 'to induce *gimru*'. In Spanish, *gimru* is usually translated by Piro people as *mareación* or *borrachera*, and we might initially translate these into English as 'dizziness' and 'drunkenness'. These English translations are laden with largely negative values that are unfitting to the original Spanish or Piro. A more accurate translation of *gimru* would be 'altered state', in both the positive and negative senses. These 'altered states' compare with everyday states of health and contentment in being the product of external agents impinging on the person (see Gow 2013).

In relation to 'altered states', the 'recreational' use of tobacco during manioc beer festivals was explicitly tied to alertness. Manioc beer causes sleepiness, especially at night, and smoking tobacco wakes you up. This is the mildest form of tobacco *gimru*. The most intensified form of tobacco *gimru* occurs during *ayahuasca* curing sessions, where the smoke is used both to activate and 'calm down' the powerful 'mother' of the hallucinogen, and to transmit the shaman's potent breath in both blowing and sucking. Unfortunately, as I have said, it never really occurred to me to ask people specifically about tobacco *gimru*, and little was said about it.

In terms of *gimru*, there were two divergent paths. The first path was that of alcohol *gimru*, which we can think of as recreational even although this state is important for ritual purposes. Getting drunk on alcohol eliminates *paachi*, 'shame' and hence leads to *meyiwlu*, 'festive spirit, having a good time': it is primarily directed towards other humans. As I have described, tobacco *gimru* was used here to extend people's resistance to sleep. The second path is that directed at non-humans. This is drug *gimru*. Here tobacco *gimru* is the first step, followed by the *gimru* of hallucinogens such as *ayahuasca*, and culminating in the *gimru* of *toé*. While tobacco *gimru* is primarily protective and activating, the *gimru* of hallucinogens reveals powerful non-humans in their 'human' forms and hence allows communication with them. Alcohol *gimru* and drug *gimru* are rigidly separated by Piro people, although discussed by them in almost identical terms: the former intensifies everyday human sociability by de-activating shame, while the latter allows humans to enhance their human sociability with beings that are, in everyday contexts, non-human. Tobacco *gimru*, with its protective and activating qualities, was the only practical connection between these two paths of altered states. Arguably, tobacco smoking, with its continuum between the recreational and the shamanic, was the generative template around which the divergence of the two paths was organized.

My account here, while focused on my main fieldwork in the 1980s, would have to be modified to account for changes during my most recent period of fieldwork in 2008. By that year, smoking tobacco had become more problematic. While most people continued to smoke in the manner discussed above, a significant minority did not smoke at all, and the reason that they gave was that 'smoking is bad for you' or that 'smoking kills' – messages that they voiced openly and vehemently. Piro people have increasing contact with social agents keen to spread the message of 'healthier life-styles' and who often pathologize their everyday practices. They also talked about cancer, which has come to be more commonly diagnosed by traditional healers. Perhaps more importantly, they had come to see themselves as increasingly living in an industrially toxic environment due to the activities of the Camisea Gas Project further upriver. Until 2008, Piro people generally considered tobacco to be a good thing and remained highly resistant to external medical advice that they considered foolish. Equally, in 2008, shamans still used tobacco, and people would ask me for tobacco for that purpose. What I think was happening was that non-shamanic 'recreational' tobacco use was being rejected, at least by some people.

Piro tobacco use in historical perspective

Referring to his travels down the Urubamba and Ucayali rivers in 1845, Marcoy writes of the Antis [Machiguenga] that the men habitually carry 'snuff-taking instruments consisting of two bits of reed, each a little over an inch long, or of the arm-bones (*humeri*) of an ape joined together with black wax at an acute angle' (1875: 484). In a footnote he adds:

> With the assistance of this *little* apparatus, the snuff-taker may himself provision his nostrils, but the *large* apparatus, each tube of which is more than six inches long, cannot be used without the help of a comrade, who introduces one of the tubes into each nostril of the snuff-taker in turn. The operation is of course undertaken turn and turn about, and the active rôle of the *insuffleur* [blower] is exchanged by each of the two individuals for that of the *insufflé* [blowee]. Snuff is used by the Antis [Machiguenga] as a preservative or as a remedy against colds, which they apt to

> take after a bath, and that often proves fatal to them, rather than as a real pleasure. This custom, even though constantly practised among the Chontaquiros [Piro] and Conibos, ceases beyond the territory of these Indians, where the elevation of the territory renders unnecessary the use of green tobacco against the rheums of the brain. (1875: 484)

Marcoy makes no mention of smoking tobacco or of pipes nor do pipes figure in his drawings of Piro material culture. While not certain, it seems that Piro people did not smoke tobacco at that period.

One possible confirmation of the absence of tobacco-smoking among Piro people at the time of Marcoy's visit is the absence of any words for the technologies of smoking that are not clearly recent loanwords. Marcoy clearly recorded a word for tobacco, *nictiti* (unrecognizable[1]) but no word for pipe. The current Piro word for 'elbow pipe', *kashimpo*, is clearly a loanword from Peruvian Amazonian Spanish *cashimbo*, which in turn seems to be of Cocama and /or Brazilian Portuguese origin. That said, Piro does have the word *monxita*, 'to smoke tobacco', which is not apparently a loanword from any other language.

The Franciscan priest Sabaté spent a considerable time with the Piro in 1874 and 1875. In an account of shamanic initiation, he notes that the candidate retreats to the forest where he diets strictly, smoking tobacco a lot. Although how the candidate smoked the tobacco is not described, a later passage asserts that shamans smoked tobacco in pipes (1925: 659). He also describes the considerable use of tobacco snuff by Piro people. He continues:

> To take the snuff they have two tubes of leg bones of a very large bird that is found in the Ucayali, called *Tuyuyo*[2], the hollowed out bones of which, which we can call tubes, would be in length fifteen centimeters the one and thirty five centimetres the other and they are joined together by one of their ends, forming an angle. The small tube is filled well with snuff, and its end is placed in the nose of the savage who must receive it: then another savage puts the end of the long tube in his mouth and blows as hard as he can, thus making the snuff enter the other's nose, like a projectile shot with great force. (1925: 665–666)

Sabaté continues:

> Aside from the above described apparatus that, in order to take the tobacco cannot be used without the help of a blower, there are other much smaller ones of the same form and the same system, with the difference that the same person can be the one who takes the snuff and the one who blows. (1925: 666)

Fry reports Piro people, in 1886, smoking tobacco in 'unusual *Simitapos* (*pipas* [pipes]), made of palm nut and bull horn, which is a precious possession for them…' (1889: 52). Fry's observation here is important, since *simitapo* is the earliest recorded Piro word for 'pipe'. In a more general account, he notes the use of tobacco snuff, and of snuff tubes made from the wing and leg bones of birds (1889: 70). The pipes described by Fry are as enigmatic in form as they are in name. While palm nuts might make decent bowls for a pipe, I know of no local examples of their use for such a purpose. Further, bull horn seems a strange and inconvenient material for a pipe stem, given that the hollow part of the horn is very wide. As we have seen, the form of the pipes described by Fry does not correspond to Piro pipes recorded later by Farabee, but it does resemble somewhat Tessmann's account of a kind of Lamista pipe from the 1920s. After noting that the Lamista of the Huallaga River mainly smoke tobacco in cigar form, Tessmann writes:

> In addition, there is the tobacco pipe = *šimitápo* (literally 'mouth cover', from *tapa* in Spanish), made from wood or the fruit of *Mauritia* [palm] into which is inserted a hollow bone. (1999: 130)

Fry's comment that these pipes were 'a precious possession' for their Piro owners strongly suggests that they were trade goods, rather than locally produced, a hypothesis perhaps confirmed by the use of the exotic material of bull horn. In the mid-1880s, the growing rubber extraction industry was drawing rubber workers from the Huallaga valley into Piro territory, and it is likely that pipes of Huallaga origin were highly desirable to Piro people.

Tessmann's evidence would also seem to point to the origin of the word *simitapo*, which is absent from all the other records of the Piro language I have consulted. The Lamista word recorded by Tessmann is very close to the Piro word recorded by Fry: indeed, it may even have been identical, given the difficulty that erudite Spanish speakers have with hearing/rendering the /š/ phone.[3]

Farabee visited a Piro community on the Manú River in 1907, and reported the following:

> They grow tobacco, which they smoke in large wooden pipes with short wooden handles like those of the Conebo .... Tobacco is also used for making snuff, which is taken through the nostrils. When the tobacco is dry, they hold it over the fire in a leaf until it is very crisp: it is then pulverized in the palm of the hand, and taken by means of the colipa, a V-shaped instrument made of the two leg bones of a heron .... The end of one bone is decorated so that it may be distinguished from the other. The snuff is placed in the decorated end, while the other end is placed in the nose, and an assistant blows the snuff with a sharp puff into the nostril. Sometimes the arms of the V are made so short, that while one end is placed in the mouth, the other reaches the nostril and allows the operator to do his own blowing. (1922: 56–57)

Matteson, describing the situation among Piro people in the late 1940s and early 1950s, writes:

> Tobacco is used, as far as I have been able to observe, exclusively for superstitious purposes. The juice of the cashew fruit is mixed with wine, and with this mixture

> the leaves of tobacco are sprinkled before being rolled.[4] Also the bark of a certain tree called 'tobacco mixer' is powdered and mixed with tobacco. The pipe which the witch doctor smokes has a bowl about five inches long, carved in the form of a cone from black palm wood. The stem is a monkey's leg bone, about the same length as the bowl. (1954: 75)

The 'tobacco mixer' is *yiri yapjeru* (*tabaco caspi*). Matteson also notes that 'after the witch doctor has drunk *ayahuasca*, he drinks tobacco juice' (1954: 75). This is the only reference to tobacco juice for Piro people, and I know of no Piro word for it. Matteson makes no reference to either tobacco snuff or to tobacco snuff tubes, although words for the latter do appear in her Piro-English vocabulary published in 1965.

In my own fieldwork with Piro people, from 1980 onwards, no spontaneous mention was ever made of either tobacco snuff or of the tubes. This was true even though such a dramatic shift in practice would seem ideally suited to mark the differences, regularly commented on, between the ways of the 'ancient people' and of the 'nowadays people', which was central to how Piro people understood historical change (Gow 1991). At most, in 2008, Sara Fasabi told me that her maternal grandfather, Maximiliano Gordon, used to put tobacco into his ears, nose and mouth when he went fishing at night, 'to scare away demons'. I did not think to enquire what form this tobacco took, although I did notice its 'oddness' as a procedure: as noted, from my experience from 1980 onwards, Piro people would have achieved this effect simply by smoking tobacco. It is likely that Sara's comments reflected the contemporary incipient shift in Piro people's understandings of tobacco, its uses and effects: away from festive uses towards strictly shamanic uses.

These historical data show both the complexity of methods of tobacco use by Piro people, and the abandonment of tobacco snuff and its paraphernalia since the mid-nineteenth century. There is also the strong probability that the smoking of tobacco was taken up by the Piro in the latter half of that century; there seems to have been a rise in non-shamanic use of tobacco smoking over the twentieth century, and then the beginnings of a decline in this century.

Apurinã tobacco use in parallel historical perspective

Quite fortuitously, we can track the parallel changes in Apurinã tobacco use over the same period, and in almost as great detail, as those among their close linguistic relatives to the west. The English geographer William Chandless published one of the earliest descriptions of the Apurinã people, based on his visit in 1864. He wrote:

> The Hypurinás ... are fond of snuff, which they inhale through a narrow bone from the palm of the hand; their snuff-boxes are made of snail-shells, the mouth of the

> snail-shell being stopped with a piece of cockle-shell, and a small tube fixed in the top of the shell to pour out the snuff. 'Ipadú' (coca) is still more indispensable, and they are seldom seen without a lump of it in their cheeks. (1866: 98)

The later accounts of Ehrenreich from 1888–1889 and of Steere from 1901 are very similar. Ehrenreich (1948) reports that the use of cigars and pipes had only recently been introduced, noting:

> Tobacco leaves are initially dried on a clay plate placed on hot coals; following this, they are wedged into a piece of wood, exposing them to the heat until they are completely dry. After this, they are ground up in a fruit shell and mixed with the ashes of certain trees (of which *abakitíri* and *okotanta* are mentioned).... When they want to take the snuff, they pour it onto a leaf or the palm of the hand, sniffing it into the nose with the aid of small bird bones sometimes united in pairs. (1948: 115)

He continues:

> The reaction is very strong. With eyes swimming with tears, and amid sneezings and coughings, the individual who has just taken snuff retreats to his hammock, where he remains lying for a several minutes, with his face transfigured. (1948: 115)

He also quotes Chandless on the use of coca, which he evidently did not see himself.

Ehrenreich goes on to provide considerable data on Apurinã shamanry (*entitxi*, 'shaman'), and their uses of poisons, *mynty*, for sorcery (1948: 124–125). The shamanic initiation consisted of a shaman vomiting – through an unspecified use of tobacco – one or more small quartz stones which the candidate then swallows. The candidate then diets in the forest for three months, eating certain leaves, until he has a vision of the 'Big Jaguar', who either kills him or makes him a shaman. Curing consisted of sucking the same small stones out of the body of the patient, which are then absorbed into his own body. Apart from the initial step in initiation, Ehrenreich does not mention the use of tobacco in shamanic curing, except in the context of a technique of shamanry for destroying meteors, in which the shaman enters a trance using snuff. Given that he witnessed a curing ritual, the absence of tobacco use in this context is probably not an oversight.

In a discussion of changes in Apurinã material culture between the time of Ehrenreich and his own fieldwork in the late twentieth century, Facundes notes that many material forms have disappeared. He writes, 'even the inhaler... is now different, having only one bone tube (which can sometimes be replaced by a hollow pen)' (2000: 21). This shift is confirmed by Schiel (Figures 2.1 and 2.2). Of course, Ehrenreich never argued that the double snuff tube was the only form at the time of his research, but rather that the single and double tubes co-existed.

One of the most striking features of Schiel's account is the remarkable continuity in shamanic practices between Ehrenrenreich's account from the late nineteenth century and her own observations in the twenty-first. The underlying cosmology seems unchanged, and Apurinã have neither adopted *ayahuasca* nor *ayahuasquero* shamanry. At most, Schiel observes, some shamans are involved in the local *ayahuasca*-based *Santo Daime* religion, in order to better understand what they 'should and should not do', but there is no evidence that they have adopted *ayahuasca* for use in shamanry. The key contemporary Apurinã shamanic pychoactives are tobacco snuff and coca. Whether this was true in the late nineteenth century is not entirely clear, but the basic rejection of *ayahuasca* is.

Transforming appetites for 'altered states'

The historical review of Piro tobacco use suggests a continuous process of change for these people, but one also marked by a significant discontinuity, the complete abandonment of tobacco snuff and its attendant paraphernalia and methods of use, and the consequent shift to smoking. There is no evidence that the actual historical change was sudden, since what we see instead seems to have been a gradual decline in the use of tobacco snuff and a gradual increase in the use of tobacco smoking. The two methods of use overlapped for a considerable period, with one gradually replacing the other. But there was no technical overlap between the two methods. Tobacco was either consumed as snuff or as smoke, and there are no obvious chromatic gradients between the two methods of use.

An obvious difference between tobacco as snuff and tobacco as smoke is the intensity of the resultant *gimru*, 'altered state'. Sabaté report of tobacco snuff use among the Piro (above) noted,

> ... it frequently gets the savages drunk and produces in them morbid effects due to the large amount of *nicotine* absorbed. (1925: 666)

Nothing in my own ethnographic experience of Piro tobacco use comes anywhere near to this. Indeed, Piro people were careful, when smoking *mapacho*, to avoid inhaling the smoke into the lungs, and they warned neophytes such as me against doing so. The intense dizziness and nausea that resulted from inhaling *mapacho* smoke was considered undesirable. However, the very similar state (at least to me) of intense dizziness and nausea produced by drinking *ayahuasca* was revered.

One of the most interesting observations of Piro use of tobacco is Fry's account of the *simitapo* pipes. This is the first account of Piro people combining the use of tobacco with the drinking of manioc beer in a festive context. As noted, during my fieldwork, the drinking of alcohol and smoking were closely connected, at least until 2008. As I also noted above, the *gimru* of smoked tobacco is much less intense than that of blown tobacco snuff. In the 1880s, Piro people were beginning to have regular access to distilled alcohols, such as brandy and *cashasa* (cane alcohol), which obviously generate a much faster and more intense alcohol *gimru*. Unlike manioc beer, distilled alcohol is both fully in the possession of men and distributed by them. It seems plausible then to argue that the shift from the use of tobacco as snuff to tobacco smoking was mediated by shifting patterns of the consumption of alcohol.

As noted, however, in the 1870s, Piro shamans were already clearly smoking tobacco in pipes, both during initiation and in some curing rituals. If my analysis here is correct, then the shift from tobacco snuff blowing to tobacco smoking was initiated within the ambit of shamanry, then spread out to the 'recreational' use of tobacco in drinking contexts. In the second half of the nineteenth century, Piro shamanry does not seem to have been marked by strong *gimru* except during initiation. Sabaté states that shamans had three forms of curing: by blowing, by sucking and by songs. The third form referred to a complex collective ritual during which the shaman 'conjured' (Piro: *yokmentalewata*) various celestial powerful beings, who then performed the cure.

What is most surprising about the historical data on the Piro is that the adoption of *ayahuasca* seems to have played no immediate part in this shift in modes of tobacco use. As noted at the outset, I embarked on the present analysis convinced that it would have. However, the earliest observations of *ayahuasca* use among Piro people date to the 1940s and 1950s, while the earliest mentions of its use in Piro oral tradition (excluding mythic narratives) date to the 1910s. Weiss, based on his meticulous reading of the historical archive on the neighbouring Ashaninka people, records the first mention of *ayahuasca* use by these people to be Samanez and Ocampo's report of its use for divinatory purposes in 1884 (1975: 476) Therefore Piro people would certainly have known about *ayahuasca* use by the 1880s, but their adoption of it as a shamanic technique was much later, perhaps even as late as the 1930s. Indeed, the earliest oral testimony of *ayahuasca* use among Piro people is divinatory rather than for curing shamanry.

In the burgeoning literature on Peruvian Amazonian *ayahuasquero* shamanry, there is a very tight, and apparently indissoluble, linkage between the smoking of tobacco in special pipes and the shamanic ingestion of *ayahuasca*. This is exactly what I found among Piro people during my fieldwork from 1980 onwards. However, we do not find this tight linkage in earlier phases of Piro tobacco use and shamanry, but instead a series of phases in the adoption of the various elements of *ayahuasquero* shamanry, of which *ayahuasca* itself was not the initial one. The present analysis, however provisional, suggests that the initial shift by Piro people from tobacco snuff to tobacco smoking was associated with the adoption of tobacco smoking itself as a shamanic technique rather than the introduction of *ayahuasca*.

In relation to my comparison between the Piro and the Apurinã, discussion of the latter people can be brief. For the Apurinã, there is no evidence of a major shift in tobacco use since the mid-nineteenth century to the present. The available literature is silent on the fate of the 'recently introduced' cigarette- and pipe-smoking mentioned by Ehrenreich but from Schiel's account, smoking certainly does not seem to have been integrated into either festive or shamanic tobacco use to any extent. There is definitely an important role played by distilled alcohol, to which the Apurinã attribute a massive increase in intra-community violence, village fissioning and population dispersal (Facundes 2000; Schiel 2004). The adoption of a distilled alcohol 'altered state' is a major change, especially given that Apurinã 'beers' are either unfermented or only weakly fermented, but the 'drunkenness' of alcohol and of tobacco snuff seems to have been maintained as rigidly separate. And of course, as noted, the Apurinã have not adopted *ayahuasca* at all, except for those people who have adopted the *Santo Daime* religion from their non-indigenous neighbours.

The Piro shift to pipes

Returning to the transformational group of the plastic forms of Apurinã and Piro instruments for tobacco use discussed at the outset, we can now see that the structural relations underlying this group are linked to a whole series of other contrasts: between tobacco snuff and tobacco smoke, between the nasal and the buccal, between strong and weak 'drunkenness', and so on. As I noted, Wilbert's very methodology led him to obscure the transformational group of Apurinã and Piro instruments for tobacco use precisely because he sorted them by 'methods of use': snuff tubes are for snuff, pipes are for smoking. These two methods of use, while clearly referring to the same cultivated plant and access to its psychoactive properties, are thence taken as simply different rather than different in the structuralist sense of defining a meaningful system of sensible properties.

In plastic form, if not in method of use, the Piro snuff tubes are much closer to the Piro 'elbow pipes' than either is to the Apurinã snuff tubes, whether single or double, although the latter form is 'on the way' to the Piro forms. Indeed, the plastic forms of the Piro snuff tubes and the Ucayali 'elbow pipes' are remarkably close. In the elbow pipe, one of its elements, the bowl, is consistently much larger, often very much larger, than the other element, the stem. This corresponds to the length difference noted by Sabaté for the Piro large snuff tubes. Equally, only the bowl of the elbow pipe is ever decorated with design, never the stem: this corresponds to the differentiation by design noted by Farabee. These two differentiations correspond to each other: the larger/decorated side of the snuff tube, correlated with the pipe bowl, is consistently the end filled with snuff and used by the blower; while the smaller/undecorated side is that used by the blowee. This allows us to hypothesize that the smoker of an elbow pipe corresponds to the blowee of the Piro snuff tube. Table 2.2 shows some of these transformations.

Table 2.2 The transformations of Apurinã and Piro tobacco use.

Plastic form	**Single Apurinã snuff tube**	**Double Apurinã snuff tube**	**Piro snuff tubes (large and small)**	**Ucayali elbow pipe**
Tobacco form	Snuff	Snuff	Snuff	Smoke
Organ(s) of use	Nasal inhalation	Nasal inhalation	Buccal to nasal insufflation	Buccal inhalation

Table 2.2 shows, I think, a real transformational group, whereby the gradual (chromatic) transformations of the plastic forms coordinates with a dramatic (discrete) shift in the form of tobacco used, from snuff to smoke. Within the transformational group, the shift from tobacco as snuff to tobacco as smoke occurs between its third and fourth terms: that is, the difference between the first and second elements, the single and the double Apurinã snuff tubes, corresponds at once to an apparently minimal technical difference (inhalation into each nostril sequentially or simultaneously), while the difference between the third and fourth terms, Piro snuff tubes and Piro pipes, corresponds to a major technical difference (snuff versus smoke).[5]

Table 2.2 does however make clear a potential structural 'pre-condition' for the transformational shift from snuff to smoking within this system: the practice of insufflation and its attendant organs of use. As Wilbert makes clear, insufflation of snuff and of tobacco smoke is not rare in South America, but self-administered buccal-to-nasal insufflation seems to be unique to the Ucayali area and some neighbouring peoples. This suggests that buccal-to-nasal insufflation is contrastively meaningful in this system and forms a mediating transformational pathway between snuff inhalation and smoking. That is, the system does not allow a direct shift from tobacco snuff nasal inhalation to tobacco smoke buccal inhalation but rather demands the mediation of a buccal-to-nasal insufflation of tobacco snuff.

Confirmation of this transformational system comes from a peculiar detail of Apurinã ethnography. Schiel records an Apurinã myth, in which the main character, Awããĩ, in order to pass the chief of the *javari* palms, is told by his canoe to take snuff. The myth continues: 'Awããĩ threw (*jogou*) snuff into his mouth and inhaled it into his nostril in order to pass by' (2004: 253). Schiel comments on this myth that this is how, Apurinã people say, the ancient shamans (*pajés antigos*) took snuff, 'by the nostril and by the mouth'. This claim corresponds to no known historical evidence or observed practice for the Apurinã. Buccal consumption of tobacco is far from rare in South America and indeed is seen in Piro tobacco smoking, but Wilbert records no examples where tobacco snuff of the form historically attested for Apurinã people is consumed by mouth and indeed it is difficult to imagine how this would work. Further, the historical record shows that the function of a buccally absorbed psychoactive plant was, and is, already occupied for these people by coca. That said, this buccal-absorption of snuff, even if historically non-existent and technically improbable, is an immanent logical possibility within both the Apurinã and wider systems of tobacco use.

The present analysis suggests that the specific form of Piro and other Ucayali snuff tubes constitute a logical 'zone of transition' between Ucayali 'elbow pipes' and Purús-style snuff tubes. Again, my argument here is at the synchronic level of an empirical system rather than its diachronic features. I certainly do not think that the single Apurinã snuff tube historically evolved into the Ucayali elbow pipe or that tobacco smoking in this area evolved out of tobacco snuffing. Instead, I think that methods of tobacco use, instruments of tobacco use and organs of tobacco use, likely to be of highly disparate historical origins, are constantly being elaborated into specific local structural systems that are always aware of their neighbouring systems and seeking to establish transformational mediations between systems, both internally and externally.

One thing that I hope the present analysis shows is that the interior and exterior mediations of transformational systems are never isolated from each other, but are in constant dialectical relation. To put this concretely for the present case, Piro people did not simply borrow or adopt the Ucayali elbow pipe and tobacco smoking from their northern neighbours from the middle of the nineteenth century onwards but rather the elbow pipe was already immanently present in the plastic forms and modes of organ use of their snuff tubes. By contrast, the Apurinã either had no contact with elbow pipes historically or completely rejected them: from both personal observation and the available literature, the canonical mode of smoking in the Brazilian state of Acre, both recreationally and ritualistically, is cigar/cigarette smoking. That said, the Apurinã do seem in the late nineteenth century to have flirted with the plastic form of Ucayali-style snuff tubes in their double snuff tubes, only to abandon this possibility later on. We might say that successful borrowing of an alien technique of tobacco use depends on structural sympathies in the existing system and that unsuccessful borrowing happens when such corresponding structural complexity is absent.

Conclusion

Manuela Carneiro da Cunha asked, 'Does structuralist diffusion exist?' Her reply was that it does, and I emphatically agree. The present essay has been based on the controlled comparison between two peoples speaking very closely related languages. The method has, I hope, proven persuasive, but it must also be abandoned as an end in itself. It points outwards to something as yet unknown. In the conclusion to *The Gender of the Gift*, Marilyn Strathern notes how her reanalysis of Melanesian ethnography, which is rooted in constantly iterated comparison,

> …underlines the failure of a comparative method whose persuasion rests in elucidating a repetition of instances. That arithmetic – based on the plurality of

> units – has disappeared. Here we have varieties of or versions of a 'single' instance. These societies hold their conventions in common. I would draw an analogy. In the same way that one might wish to comprehend capitalist organisation as it developed historically in Europe, so one needs to inject a real history into our comprehension of Melanesian gift economies. The history itself may be irrecoverable, but we surely know enough about historical processes to recognise a series of connected events. (1988: 341)

The adoption of tobacco smoking by the Piro and its apparent rejection by the Apurinã are not *ad hoc* borrowings or non-borrowings by two neighbouring peoples speaking closely related languages, but complex transformations within systems of transformations that are aware of each other at some level. Following from the work of Lévi-Strauss in the *Mythologiques*, we are relatively familiar with this approach with regard to myth, but Lévi-Strauss never considered it to be restricted solely to mythology. The present analysis shows that very similar processes are occurring in the uses of tobacco, in their methods, their instruments and even in the bodily orifices used to consume it. Ethnographically attested practices, such as self-administered buccal-to-nasal insufflation of snuff, cease to be quaint curiosities, and gain their place in a vast system of transformations that are occurring in real time.

Acknowledgements

I thank the various funding bodies that provided the wherewithal to do the research. I thank Elizabeth Rahman and Andrew Russell for their very generous invitation to think these new thoughts, and to the participants at the symposium 'The Changing Landscape of Tobacco Use in Lowland South America', and many others, for their comments. My deepest gratitude is to Claude Lévi-Strauss, for his teachings, for his forbearance and for a mysterious little gesture that set my mind to work.

Notes

1. Possibly *nikchitu*, 'supernatural food'?
2. The *tuyuyo*, or *tuyuyu*, is the jabirú stork (Lat: *Jabiru mycteria*; Piro: *yawuro*), a bird of some importance in Piro cosmology (see Gow 2001).
3. Tessmann (1999) shows a pattern of two words for pipe in the indigenous languages of the former Jesuit and Franciscan missions of the Amazon, Marañon, Huallaga and Bajo Ucayali rivers: they are either variants of *cashimbo* or of *šimitápo*.
4. Wilbert (1987) interprets this as evidence of cigar-use among Piro people, but it is clearly a description of the standard method of making *mapacho*.
5. The inspiration for this analysis is Lévi-Strauss' famous canonical formula or double twist, which takes the form: $fx(a) : fy(b) \simeq fx(b) : fa\text{–}1(y)$.

3

Tobacco and Shamanic Agency in the upper Amazon: Historical and Contemporary Perspectives

Françoise Barbira Freedman

Introduction

The transformation of indigenous shamanic practice through the colonization of Amazonia did remarkably little to modify local ritual uses of tobacco. The reasons are threefold: tobacco smoking, as the main curing tool of shamans, was conflated with licit uses of tobacco in the colonial period; the contribution of the phytochemistry of Nicotiana species to the centrality of tobacco in shamanic plant medicine; and the way in which the specialized path of tobacco shamans, although displaced by the less demanding path of *ayahuasca* shamans in the nineteenth to twentieth centuries, has fostered the conservation of varied modes of tobacco consumption among both indigenous and urban non-Indian shamans. Moreover, despite the discouragement of tobacco use in public health discourse and practice, the development and spread of *ayahuasca* shamanism has contributed to a revival of traditional cultivation, curing and modes of consumption of tobacco.

In the last two decades the expansion of Amazonian anthropology and new studies of shamanism and psychotropic plants in South America have prompted further questions about tobacco use in the context of the wider historical and contemporary political economy of the region. In this chapter, my ethnographic focus is the area of the ancient province of Maynas across the upper Amazon regions of Peru and Ecuador, which was the target of early Spanish colonization and a space of ethnic and cultural miscegenation through colonial and postcolonial times. While Steward (1949: 595–605) dismisses the groups along the upper and middle Huallaga River as 'culturally assimilated', there is a paradox in that their symbolic economy, centred on shamanic plant medicine and tobacco use, has proved remarkably resilient through the centuries. How did the interrelation between external and internal factors in the historical transformation of shamanism in this dense frontier zone create this resilience? Are there specific patterns of change and resistance related to tobacco use? If so, what explanations can be suggested to account for them?

I seek answers to these questions primarily in ethnography, not only because historical sources related to tobacco use in the upper Amazon are scant but also with an intention, as an anthropologist, to centre my analysis in the explanatory potential of participant observation, supplemented by additional data drawn from other ethnographies as well as from botany, pharmacology and accessible historical documents. Notes compiled over thirty-five years of longitudinal research with the Keshwa Lamas allow a more detailed discussion of recent changes. The Keshwa Lamas is the name they have agreed to use for themselves as an endonym in the recent process of forming native communities while retaining their ancient name 'Jakwash' for esoteric uses. In this chapter, I prefer to use endonyms for all the groups I mention. I also indicate words which are Quechua by 'Q.', 'S.' for Spanish words, and 'Q.S.' or 'S.Q.' for hybrid terms used locally in both languages.

The term shaman is accepted in the general anthropological literature and in Amazonia (see Introduction, this volume). Shamans are defined by their control of spirit helpers in the forest as cosmos, their embodied practice of 'journeying' in the cosmos on behalf of their patients and their ambivalence as insiders/outsiders in their communities. While the latter are the specialists, I argue that Amerindians in general might better be thought of as more or less 'shaman' along a continuum of agency that ranges from ordinary male adults to outsiders who are sometimes attributed with extraordinary powers. Like shamanism, tobacco use is not barred to women in principle, but in practice, most shamans are men and most uses of tobacco apply to men, to a lesser extent to post-menopausal women and very rarely to women of reproductive age (Barbira Freedman 2010).

Amerindian shamanism has undergone many historical changes as it was repressed by colonial and subsequently republican authorities over four centuries. Rather than an ongoing flow of information from indigenous practitioners to urban folk healers, there is increasing evidence that both shamans of mixed blood (*Mestizos*) and 'white' shamans (*Blancos*, i.e. non-indigenous persons) have contributed to the syncretic evolution of plant-based shamanic medicine. Known as *vegetalismo* in Peru, this is the main source of informal health care in the region. Comparable syncretic systems of plant medicine developed simultaneously in the foothills of the Andes in Ecuador, Colombia and Bolivia. In these four countries, bordering on western Amazonia and characterized by a variety of microclimates and biodiversity-rich ecological niches, Andean and Amazonian Amerindians interrelated and experimented with the domestication, cultivation and use of a large number of plants, notably coca, tobacco and cacao (Zeder et al. 2006; Pickergill 2007).

The Keshwa Lamas are a mixed aggregate of forest and Andean people who became constituted as a distinctive ethnic minority around the colonial frontier town of Lamas in the Peruvian upper Amazon (founded in 1656). Quechua, the lingua franca of colonization imposed upon pacified forest people, has remained a dominant idiom of shamanic curing in chants, spells and nomenclatures, long after Quechua has ceased to be spoken in the region, although it is still spoken among four relatively large Forest Quechua minorities in Peru and Ecuador. Within the colonial Province of Maynas, the ancestors of the Keshwa Lamas as pacified Indians (Q. *runa*) interacted in various ways with the rebel, wild, forest peoples (Q. *auka*, enemies) who now constitute the native communities of the Awajún, Achuar and Shawi. The Tupi ancestors of the Cocama stood apart in the Jesuit missions of the lower Huallaga.

There is a consensus among palaeobotanists and botanists that *Nicotiana tabacum* and *Nicotiana rustica*, the two species selected for worldwide consumption out of the more than 64 established species in the genus Nicotiana (45 of which are indigenous to the American continent) were first domesticated on the eastern slopes of the central Andes of Peru[1]. While *N. tabacum* is the dominant species for commercial production worldwide, *N. rustica*, whose nicotine content is higher in a rougher black tobacco, is still grown for domestic consumption in Amazonia and in some other parts of the world (Russia, China, Vietnam). Both species are used in Amazonian shamanism, but *N. rustica* was and still is the main source of tobacco traded among shamans in the upper Amazon. Wilbert's assertion that: 'Paleo-Indian shamans relied on endogenous and ascetic techniques of mystic ecstasy rather than on drug-induced trance' in a 'drug-free shamanic ideology' (1987: 149), cannot be easily proved or disproved given the antiquity of the dispersal of wild Nicotianas and the widespread use of domesticated species over 8,000 years in the Americas. At the time of the Spanish Conquest the majority of people practicing horticulture in Amazonia used either or both Nicotianas, an association defended by Steward in 1949.

Early chroniclers observed the mixing of tobacco and coca in Andean snuffs, and there is some archaeological evidence of this practice, albeit limited.[2] The Quechua term for tobacco (Q. *sairi*) refers not just to tobacco but to other aromatic leaves that are smoked, which is also the Bororo concept (Lévi-Strauss 1992: 105). Snuff tablets and pipes have also been found in archaeological sites across the continent.[3] The sharp contrasts Wilbert draws between wild Nicotianas and cultigens, and between an ancient drug-free shamanism and a more recent use of stimulants are questionable. However, his point that 'the extraordinary power of this agent of diffusion is evident in the rather strikingly similar *tobacco ideology of American Indians* [my italics] that coincides with the limits of tobacco distribution in the New World' (1987: 202) continues to deserve attention. In this chapter, I use ethnographic material from the upper Amazon to elucidate the tenets of this ideology that, I argue, underpin shamanic practice in Amazonia.

The historical continuum of economic, recreational and ritual uses of tobacco

Given the rapid spread of tobacco consumption among Europeans in the sixteenth century, it can be assumed that the first Spanish men to reach the upper Amazon, whether they were explorers, soldiers or missionaries, already had knowledge of tobacco. Even the Inquisition's condemnation of tobacco did not deter the Spanish Catholic clergy from smoking and snuffing, while King James's *Counterblaste to Tobacco* (1604) seems to have spread rather than decreased its use.[4] The Spanish followed previous trade routes used by the Inca and other Andeans before them. The paths linking the Huallaga River to the Chachapoya empire that ruled over the lowest eastern slopes of the Andes, now abundant in archaeological finds, indicate that this particular entry point into the Amazonian floodplain was both a boundary and a space for exchange between highland and lowland people for at least two millennia before the Spanish Conquest. The mention of a tobacco processing workshop in the seventeenth century in the ambit of the Franciscan mission, alongside cotton weaving workshops (S. *obrajes*) indexes a long continuity of cultivation in the hot plain selected for the production of export tobacco near the junction between the Mayo and Huallaga rivers.[5]

In the upper Amazon, tobacco, together with coca and curare poison, was probably exported down river on balsa rafts in the way that it still is today and up to the highlands by foot.

The art of curing tobacco continues to be transmitted among the Keshwa Lamas as a special skill, since every tobacco has a different taste and aroma according to both the growing area, the mix of species and varieties used, the aromatic plants that may be added (cinnamon bark – *Cinnamomum zeylanicum*, wild marjoram – *Origanum majorana*) and the curing mode (with honey from different kinds of bees[6]). The aim is to obtain a strong but 'sweet' (Q. *mishki puru*) tobacco that retains its moisture yet can be kept dry for pipe smoking, particularly during the rainy season. The addition of 'wild tobacco' (Q. *sacha tabaku*, S. *tabaco del monte*) – wild Nicotianas such as *N. glauca* and *N. alata*, other plants that are not botanically related to the genus Nicotiana and cultivated Nicotiana escapees from gardens found in former garden sites in forest areas, said to be the tobacco of forest spirits and jaguars, adds power to tobacco mixtures prepared by shamans. *N. rustica* is preferred for tobacco juice as it triggers more visions and dreams but *N. tabacum* is also grown. Some contemporary Keshwa Lamas shamans paradoxically confer higher prestige and value to *N. tabacum* as the 'true' tobacco (S.Q. *la planta legítima*). Shamans grow their tobacco plants in marked off areas of family gardens or in their own gardens. There is a strict gendered division of labour in the cultivation and processing of plants since menstruating women need to keep away from tobacco plants.

However, like the Warao (Wilbert 1987: 179), the Keshwa Lamas rely mostly on trade tobacco in rolls that they buy from specialized non-Indian producers and then prepare for their personal use, sometimes curing it again. The elaboration of tobacco rolls (S. *masos*), with bundles air-dried, cured leaves compressed with stone or wooden presses before being circled into rolls with strips of Tahuari bark (the name given to *Couratari tauary*, *Couratari guianensis* or to *Terra Firme* varieties of *Cariniana* spp.) appears to have been adopted by non-indigenous producers for some time. In the 1970s, Keshwa Lamas shamans wishing to visit partners for exchange of shamanic knowledge took tobacco rolls with them as the most valued item of barter with other shamans in the lowlands. The enduring circulation of similar rolls from Acre to Pernambuco in Brazil indicates that this may have been a widespread way of preparing, storing and trading tobacco in Amazonia.

In 2014, most of the tobacco sold in the Tarapoto and Iquitos markets for shamanic use, in the form of rolls or ready-made cigars and cigarettes, is produced by specialized growers around the tobacco plantations and Tarapoto factory, *N. rustica* rolls and most commonly locally ready-made cigarettes (S.Q. *mapachos*, 'dirties')[7] rolled in rough commercial paper, can be bought in 10s, 50s or 100s in markets or corner shops in small towns of the Peruvian upper Amazon. Simultaneously, it is now possible to purchase manufactured cigarettes, either Peruvian or imported, in most places.

Until imported Virginia tobacco reached the upper Amazon on steamboats in the form of '*finos*' (fine cigarettes made with *N. tabacum*) as a prestige trade item for recreational use, only local variations in tobacco curing created differential value. In 1861, high duties for imports in Pará as port of entry to the Amazon in Brazil include US tobacco, while listed exports of Amazonian tobacco through Pará in 1867[8] are minimal compared to cacao and Brazil nuts. With the advent of imported and then nationally manufactured cigarettes in packets, new contrasts have been established in the social sharing of commercial cigarettes between '*finos*', '*puros*' (Cuban-style cigars either imported or produced locally) and '*mapachos*' (above). For recreational use in social gatherings and feasts, the Keshwa Lamas prefer to use commercial brands: Winston (strong) and Hamilton (suave) are ranked first and second, while imported Malboro cigarettes are rated highest when they can be obtained. Cigarettes are shared by indigenous men in circles of relatives and friends, and rarely extended to women. Women serve their home made maize or manioc beer, and older men control the distribution of alcohol and tobacco among family groups. Smoking is discouraged among women although older Keshwa Lamas women smoke local tobacco and shamans continue to use both home grown or trade tobacco rolls in all aspects of their practice, only using commercial cigarettes when no other tobacco is available to them.

Like other aspects of their culture such as dress and food, the historical consumption of tobacco among Keshwa Lamas and *Mestizo* men can be interpreted as following a series of temporal diacritical contrasts that serve to reinforce ethnic categories and the control of local production and trade by colonists of Spanish and mixed origin. These contrasts were sometimes linked to introduced technologies, such as the cultivation of sugar cane and its processing in sugar mills introduced in the Jesuit missions of the Huallaga in the early eighteenth century. The use of rum for medicinal plant macerates and of cane syrup for curing tobacco facilitated control in non-Indian hands. These distinctions evolved in time as markers of boundary maintenance between forest people (*Indios*) and the dominant urban culture linked to colonizing powers in the historical extractive political economy of Amazonia. Under the cover of these superficial distinctions, the ritual uses of tobacco were blurred through socially approved forms of consumption. Two such rituals from the colonial period are funeral wakes (S. *velorios*) and ritual wakes (S.Q. *veladas*), the latter arranged to celebrate Catholic saints' icons. Both are associated with the world of ancestors and with the transformation of souls, and are overtly Christian social occasions but effectively stage practices and beliefs related to shamanism. They reflect Lévi-Strauss' point that 'in South America the act of smoking is essentially social; while at the same time it establishes communication between mankind and the supernatural world' (1992: 105). Cigarettes, passed around circles of men that include non-Indian ritual kinsmen (S. *compadres*) who are also contractors and traders (S.Q. *patrón*), are associated with symbolic meanings and practices that the non-Indians either ignore or see as superstitions. Tessman (1930) and Karsten (1926)'s comments about the recreational use of tobacco among upper Amazon indigenous peoples as a result of colonization are thus only partly valid. Purely recreational use among *Mestizos* continues to contrast with the more ritually marked use of tobacco in native communities. In social meetings some native men now decline smoking commercial cigarettes not just due to the influence of Protestant churches but also to a greater awareness of the toxic effects of cigarettes.

Diacritical distinctions also extend to modes of medicinal plant use in relation to tobacco. Water-based medicinal preparations are still used in a continuum from household care to specialist shamanic curing, but their potentiation by tobacco smoke differentiates shamanic from non-shamanic medicines. While some indigenous shamans use tobacco with herbs macerated in alcohol, this is more prevalent among urban shamans who identify themselves as non-Indians. Tobacco thus serves as a distinctive marker between mundane health maintenance by householders and the more specialized therapeutic care of mostly male shamans.

Following the expulsion of the Jesuits from Peru in 1767,[9] *Mestizo*s as colonists seeking capital accumulation through trade with Indians took over some of the existing relations of barter among Indians and established new ones, without totally destroying the indigenous networks of exchange in the upper Amazon. In this way, besides controlling the shift from locally produced to imported cotton cloth and Virginia cigarette tobacco between the eighteenth and the nineteenth century, *Mestizo*s as traders (who counted shamans among them) began to move downstream and create settlements along rivers outside the early colonial frontier towns. They took shamanism with them as medicine, as a legitimized defence against sorcery attacks from their Indian labour force and also as a counter-hegemonic ideology, particularly if they had had their lives saved by native shamans through the use of psychotropic plants. Access to shamanic apprenticeships has typically been open to outsiders in many parts of Amazonia, possibly on account of the importance of relations of exchange in Amazonian shamanism (Barbira Freedman 2014). The rubber boom intensified colonization and the settling of both traders and displaced labourers with new opportunities for miscegenation and exchange. Ethnographic accounts indicate that the generation of *Mestizo shamans* immediately following the rubber boom used tobacco in their shamanic practice, in some cases as a specialization (Luna 1986) while spreading the modes of tobacco use drawn from the colonial shamanic system of the upper Amazon, principally drinking and smoking.

In the nineteenth century, urban *Mestizo*s turned shamans labelled themselves as *vegetalistas*, plant medicine doctors, to emphasize their therapeutic use of plant medicines (S.Q. *el vegetal*) in contradistinction with ambivalent healer-sorcerers prosecuted by the Catholic Church and the nascent hegemony of medicine and science in the Amazon region associated with the currents of modernity that accompanied the rubber boom. With a preoccupation to align themselves with the new hegemony, *Mestizo* urban shamans, alternatively labelled S. *curanderos* ('curers') euphemistically, and S. *brujos* ('sorcerers') pejoratively, used tobacco in the form of cigars and cigarettes rather than pipes not only to mediate with the spirit-owners of their plant allies (S. *doctorcitos*, 'little doctors' – Luna 1986) but also to diagnose the cause of conditions presented by patients. This terminology replaced the native appropriation of Christian repression according to which spirit allies were S.Q. *llablonguna* ('devils'), and many shamanic plants were associated with the Devil. Two main contrasting categories, natural sickness (S. *enfermedad de Dios*), or sorcery (S. *mal de gente*) are still in use in the twenty-first century. Keshwa Lamas shamans still use the ancient art of pulsing together with tobacco smoking to diagnose and assess any illness that does not respond quickly to herbal home care or over-the-counter remedies. Pulsing enabled a dual diagnostic and divinatory use of tobacco smoke under the cover of European practices of taking the pulse. *Mestizo* shamans, independently, combined traditional uses of tobacco divination with European magical practices learnt in treatises of white and black magic imported into Amazonia since the nineteenth century.

The use of tobacco smoke to diagnose the cause of sickness, to render plant medicines effective beyond their mere empirical properties and to officiate with patients, distinguishes shamans from herbalists, who do not use tobacco either for preparing remedies or for curing. Seeing men (and some older women) relaxing while smoking tobacco in cigars or pipes, sitting on the thresholds of their houses in the evenings, it is not immediately obvious whether they are merely enjoying themselves or if, as shamans, they are at work, activating their connections with spirit entities, distant patients, ancestor souls, friends and enemies around them. Some shamans say that the art of partially absorbing smoke, the way of blowing the smoke and also the concentration in the activity are indications of truly shamanic tobacco smoking. These diacritical types of use however are blurred in practice and only clear in context.

The five categories of shamans recognized in the upper Amazon on the basis of their dominant plant media (*ayahuasca*, *toé*, tree barks, flower essences or tobacco) all use tobacco as a primary connecting substance in their relations to spirits, as a synergetic enhancer of the effects of the other mediating plants, and as the main tool of their therapeutic agency. In this way tobacco use is truly the hallmark of shamanism through history (cf. Hugh-Jones 1979a: 231; Fausto 2004: 158).

The central importance of tobacco use in shamanism, even in the more intensive path of tobacco shamans, remained muted without being hidden in *vegetalismo* as it peaked in the upper Amazon in the first half of the twentieth century. The continuum from recreational and ritual use, and from trade through debt peonage to indigenous exchange networks, both contributed to hide the function of tobacco as the upper Amazon indigenous peoples' substance of choice for connecting with the cosmos. I shall now go on to look in more detail at of the place of tobacco in regional upper Amazonian animist ontologies.

Local animist ontologies and shamanic agency

Among indigenous people of the upper Amazon, tobacco use is further differentiated along a continuum from secular to ritual by hunters and men opening new clearings in forest areas. Adherence to a set of dietary and behavioural restrictions (Q. *sasiku*) that is found throughout Amazonia with similar features, demarcates shamanic activity. Dieting and smoking are pre-conditions for shamanic agency in the cosmos. Hunters have a more limited agency but they use tobacco in ways that overlap with shamanic practice. They can use tobacco for its prophylactic or curative properties in a plain way but they can also associate themselves to the agency of shamans with a purposeful ascesis. In this section I highlight the close association between diet, tobacco and shamanic agency in relation to gender.

'*Plantas con madres*' ('Plants with mothers') are recognized both in the Amazon and the Andes, among main food crops, medicinal plants and plants with symbolic attributes. 'The Peruvians, we are told, believed that all useful plants are animated by a divine being, who causes their growth. These divine beings are called the Maize mother (*Saramama*) and Coca mother (*Cocamama*)' (Karsten 1926: 319). In the upper Amazon both domesticated and wild plants are classified according to whether they are animated by mother spirits or not. Those that do are regarded as 'powerful plants', whose subjectivities can be enlisted to prevail over those of less powerful beings which may encroach upon or attack humans in the cosmos, and even rob their souls, de-substantialising them. In animistic ontologies all entities in the cosmos are perceived as potential subjects, endowed with intentional agency and points of view (Halbmayer 2012). All shamanic plants, unlike commonly used medicinal plants, are 'plants with mother spirits' with a connotation of psychotropic attributes (Jauregui et al. 2011). The Keshwa Lamas, possibly due to the colonial development of their shamanism, are singular in the upper Amazon for the extent to which they attribute animals, elements and even some historical figures to a large number of plants as mother spirits in one of the most extensive medicinal floras of Amazonia. Shamans' control of cosmic beings as spirit allies is therefore determined by their dominion over plants during their training and the mediation enabled by plants is conditional upon tobacco use with them.

The importance of tobacco in the Amazonian gendering of the cosmos, reflected in the title of this book, is that it is categorized as a male plant, attributed with an overall synergetic male function as 'the father of all plants who have 'mothers'. Keshwa Lamas categorize cultivated Nicotianas as Q. *asnak panga* (strong aromatic leaves) that men handle. It is not gender per se but the reproductive agency of women that calls for their exclusion, except in rituals that are specifically focused on promoting fertility and reproduction, such as the historical marriage rituals of the Jivaroan peoples (Karsten 1926: 323–324).

In the cultural elaboration of the gendering of the cosmos as an animated forest (cf. Turner 1967), regardless of its many variations in Amazonia, men as hunters and shamans mediate with other beings beyond the sociality of localized networks of kin and affines (Q. *ayllu*). Besides the historical cultural differences between former Jivaroan peoples (Awajún, Wambis, Shuar, Achuar, and Shiwar) and the Forest Quechua in Ecuador and Peru (Canelos, Napo Quechua, Keshwa Lamas), all share animist cosmologies and ontologies (Descola 1996). These cosmologies, however, cannot be dissociated from a shared register of practical understandings and 'techniques of the body' (Mauss 1973), with a common sensory repertoire that receives slightly different emphases in particular groups. I draw on Brown (2007), Descola (1996) and Townsley (1993) in western Amazonia and Hugh Jones (1979b) and Hugh Jones (1979a) in northwest Amazonia among ethnographies that throw analytical light on shamanic practice. Actions in the sensory repertoire of shamans have often been described in travellers' accounts and in the anthropological literature but they have received relatively little attention due to either a focus on description (Luna 1986) or preoccupations with cosmology and ontology as cognitive domains (Croker 1985). Shepard (2004) offered a fresh focus on organoleptic aspects of ethnobotanical knowledge and plant use.

While men as hunters are procurers of game, and need to propitiate the non-human 'Masters of Game Animals' with culturally appropriate ritual behaviours, shamans oversee the reciprocity involved in not just hunting but all human activities related to the maintenance of personal human integrity and social reproduction. The balance of male and female forces in these different yet related activities requires attention that is imparted to babies from birth through tobacco smoke blown over their bodies and gendered amulets attached to their wrists, and assimilated by Keshwa Lamas group members during their entire life cycle. While men use tobacco, mostly in the form of smoke but also of chewing, as ways to protect their bodily integrity and maintain the separations between cosmic domains and between non-humans and humans in the forest, shamans take upon themselves the task of integrating male and female principles for the purpose of transcending these boundaries and acting on behalf of other humans.

Hunters use tobacco as a mimetic substance. They cover their own and their dogs' bodies with the scent of smoke or rubbed fresh leaves (of *N. tabacum* in preference to *N. rustica*), so that forest spirits can be delighted by its sweet scent and become benevolent, releasing game animals. Most spirits are fickle and can shift rapidly between friendly and hostile attitudes, requiring diverse tactics of self-humbling, seduction or defiance from hunters. Shamans on the other hand cultivate social relations with their spirit allies who first become 'like trade partners' or distant affines and are progressively drawn into the circle of close affinity and consanguinity through the birth of spirit children from spirit wives. The 'trade' of tobacco food with spirit helpers in exchange for their alliance in promoting well-being and an abundance of desired resources follows the same understanding as trading relations with 'other' indigenous groups or non-Indian outsiders.

Through their psychotropic effects, shamanic plants 'teach' novices about the interactions between people, plants and animals and 'show' them empirical and symbolic pathways to counteract the malevolent senders of sickness. The repeated ingestion of tobacco juice during long periods of strict fasting, in which the constant smoking of tobacco is also encouraged, is said to add an important dimension to the visionary effects of other powerful plants such as *ayahuasca* or *toé* since, in moderate doses, 'tobacco teaches in dreams'. Through the ingestion of tobacco, novices receive instructions about the plants that they need to work with and study in order to gain spirit allies in an individualized path of practice, within local and lineage patterns of knowledge transmission. 'We see different things with tobacco, which plants we need to follow, how to learn medicine, which spirits will come to us, animals'.

The best gift that a shaman can make when visiting his non-human kinsfolk, particularly the underwater spirits, is refined human tobacco. Spirits are said to be very fond of the fragrance of tobacco smoke or the aroma of tobacco juice. Some shamans say that spirits need to be fed tobacco smoke constantly in order to remain sweet allies as they experience cravings for tobacco (Wilbert 1987: 173) in the same way that humans are hungry for meat (cf. Fortis, this volume). No spirit can resist the attraction of tobacco and the interdependence that is created with humans in relation to tobacco. Traditionally, Keshwa Lamas shamans have had the role of guardians of the territories they inhabit, harmonizing perceived polarities between features of the landscape such as hilltops and lakes, river rapids and whirlpools, points of convergence of game animals (salt licks) and dangerous bogs or dry 'devil's gardens'. Even in a transformed and deforested landscape, Keshwa Lamas shamans continue to smoke and make tobacco offerings at certain points of contact between cosmic domains such as caves, cleavages in rocks (Q. *kaka siki*), roots and hollow trunks of ancient trees, around springs and on boulder stones thought to be the abodes of ancestors. Small bundles may also be hung or placed in selected sites with specific intentions.

The feeding of spirits with tobacco creates and augments the agential intent of shamans, supported by their allies' subjectivities that they hold inside them in embodied forms: the Q. *llausa* or Q. *yachay* ('knowledge phlegm') that shamans grow in their trachea and bronchiae, needs to be fed with tobacco smoke and in the case of strong shamans (Q. *sinchi sinchi yachak*) by tobacco juice. Inside the phlegm are not only small darts that are the expression of shamanic power but also 'live' small animals (Q. *karawa*) – scorpions, worms, spiders, centipedes, millipedes – that shamans acquire from others as gifts, by theft or by seizing them after they escape from the mouths of dying shamans. Without tobacco smoke and also tobacco juice as regular food, these entities become inactive and impotent, not responding to shamans' agentive intentions.

Very large pipes of strong tobacco are necessary to ensure the transfer of *karawa* to selected initiates, by regurgitating and re-swallowing their *yachay*. All shamans, however, also use regular, often daily tobacco smoking to maintain the visionary space that they enter under the effect of psychotropic plants, something they describe as contemplative study. For observers it may look no different from recreational pipe smoking for relaxing the mind, but for shamans this is a central connective activity that creates psychic bonds with spirits, patients, the whole cosmos and relational entities.

The feeding and nurturing (Q. *wiwa*) of plants tended by shamans with tobacco smoke is categorically opposed to the blood cravings of manioc among the Awajún (Brown 2007). Feeding spirits is antithetical to the social sharing of human food. The purpose of shamanic training diets is to withdraw from the activities of human sociality: the eating of game and strong fish involving fat, the flavouring of food with salt and chilli pepper, the drinking of manioc or maize beer and other forms of alcohol, sexual activity and social intercourse with women of reproductive age and, most importantly, with menstruating women. These are preconditions for shaman novices to become attractive to spirits in scent and demeanour, supplemented and supported by intensive tobacco smoking. This shamanic training diet however is not exclusive to novices. As first noted by Karsten (1926) and then by Métraux (1967), it is adhered to in all circumstances in which a group member's body boundaries are being changed or need restoring: around the growth and birth of babies and during the delicate process of their social integration during infancy (see Rahman, this volume); during rituals of initiation of boys and girls (that have now fallen into disuse in the upper Amazon), in cases of acute sickness (by the whole circle of adult close kin gathered around the sick person), and during shamanic training when men first acquire or reinforce their 'bodies of knowledge'.

The paraphernalia of tobacco use is quite succinct in the relatively object poor cultures of the upper Amazon. Symbolic associations of ritual objects used for the storage and consumption of tobacco with the gendering of the cosmos continue to be expressed in currently used Keshwa Lamas artefacts, in ways that are acknowledged by at least some group members. A shaman keeps his tobacco rolls with his possessions and only cuts or shaves off slices a little at a time, keeping them in a small satchel (Q. *shigra*) of cloth or anteater skin (Q. *shiwi*). Minced tobacco is kept in miniature ceramic pots that women make for husbands and close male relatives and decorate with the same motifs as those woven in men's belts.[10] Occasionally these designs are carved on the pipe cone. Tobacco can also be stored in forest snail shells (S.Q. *congompe*) that have symbolic associations linked with the hermaphrodite reproduction of these snails and the soft whitish pouches they develop when mating, which are compared to the *yachay* phlegm of shamans. The bag often also holds rolled cigars in corn paper or, now, industrial cigarette paper, together with personal charms such as black stones and quartz that are 'fed' by tobacco, a jaguar paw or a ring of alligator skin, pieces of wild camphor (*Laurus camphora*; S.Q. *alcamfor sacha*) for curing, and camalonga nuts (*Thevetia peruana*) and huayruru (*Erythrina americana*) for protection and treatment against sorcery.

Cone pipes have not changed much since Tessman collected and drew them in various parts of the upper Amazon in the 1920s. As ritual and symbolic objects, they now serve to differentiate shamans and aspirant shamans including foreign shaman apprentices from non-shamans who mostly use cigars or cigarettes. Pipes are carefully crafted in accordance with both the maker's and the user's connections with the cosmos as well as having regional cultural characteristics. As in the 1920s, their bowls are made of particular woods, either palm woods such as Aguaje (*Mauritia flexuosa*), or Shica Shica (*Geonoma interrupta*) both with feminine domain associations, or rosewood (jacaranda, *Dalbergia nigra*). The ducts are still made with the leg bones of Tanrilla (*Eurypyga helias*), birds that stand in shallow water and are associated with the water domain.

Boys start sharing local cigarettes with their fathers when they are ready to accompany their fathers or uncles to hunt, in the same progressive way as they are invited to take partake in *ayahuasca* or tobacco juice in men's circles. Young men only receive a pipe if they are interested in shamanic practice. Not all *Mestizo* urban shamans who have trained with indigenous shamans in the upper Amazon own and use pipes. *Ayahuasca* shamanism, which has led to the substitution of snuff tubes by pipes in eastern Peru (Gow, this volume), has also added to the rising demand for tobacco rolls. There is currently a proliferation not only of traditional upper Amazon cone pipe designs but also of wooden elbow pipes with mixed imported features (e.g. trolls, face designs of North American shamans, dragons) and variations on artistic motives related to Amazonian popular culture (e.g. mermaids).

Tobacco smoking and blowing in the ambivalent agency of shamans

Tobacco blowing practices are overt among cultural insiders but hidden from the view of Catholic agents who stigmatize them, Protestant agents who ban them and health authorities who attempt to eradicate them. There are glorified stories of shamans competing to kill birds at a distance with their blowing intent, and of shamans with wind (Q. *wayra*) as their spirit ally, who were able to dispel or attract clouds and change weather formations by tobacco blowing. Wherever tobacco is found in Amazonia, even in areas where snuffing is predominant over pipe use, shamans blow tobacco smoke as a main tool to cross over (via a metaphorical 'rainbow bridge'), dissolve and re-draw the boundaries of bodies and cosmic layers. The actions of blowing and sucking out, both mediated by tobacco smoke, are central to shamans' ambivalent agency through a specific sensory repertoire that links hunting and shamanism. While the 'sensual vitalities' of indigenous Amazonians (Santos-Granero 2006) have been noted in ethnographies since Seeger (1981), the sensory aspects of shamanic practice, particularly in relation to tobacco use, warrant more attention. upper Amazon people rate shamanship by the quality of the breath, voice and rhythm of performing shamans.

Both the actions of harming and curing using tobacco consist of 'blowing'. Shamans as sorcerers use a forceful blowing of tobacco smoke similar to blowing darts out with a blowgun for sending pathogens to their enemies, while shamans as healers use long and soft out breaths to blow over their patients' bodies after powerfully sucking out pathogens. While lesser shamans can only restore the integrity of bodies by removing pathogens sent by malevolent agents, fully fledged shamans with the controlled power to cure and harm have the ability to return pathogens to their senders in revenge and defeat them. Shamans suck out pathogens after blowing tobacco smoke on the area of the body where they have located intrusion. Sucking out, the opposite action to blowing on to a target, requires greater power/strength (*Q sinchi*) than blowing. There is a continuum of tobacco-assisted actions that is also a hierarchy of power ranging from blowing healing intent on a body, blowing a spell (positive or negative), blowing a pathogen, extracting a pathogen, blowing back pathogens to senders and sealing bodies (Q. *arka*) with powerful blowing.

Blowing tobacco smoke, preferably with the use of a dedicated shamanic pipe, is thus the required action for loosening, extracting and then re-sealing body boundaries, extracting pathogens or re-inserting souls to guarantee the integrity of bodies always at risk from external forces, human and non-human. The action of blowing is ambivalent according to the qualities of the blower and the conditions in which he (very rarely she) does so. The tobacco smoke is held in the mouth (some shamans describe this as a special skill that trainees need to master) and then projected softly and evenly. Blown tobacco smoke is believed to form an invisible covering that for a while protects the body not only from external infections but also from malevolent intentions or envy directed at persons. This is not esoteric knowledge or practice and spells and healing blowing are not the exclusive actions of shamans: fathers can blow tobacco smoke on their sick babies and small children;[11] hunters blow smoke on their dogs in preparation for going into the forest; older women protect young girls before festivals by blowing tobacco smoke all over their bodies with protective intent.

In contrast to the healing soft-blowing of tobacco smoke, the defensive blowing of tobacco water, made from either fresh tobacco leaves soaked in water overnight, or diluted tobacco juice from shaved pressed cured tobacco is only done by shamans. Forceful belching can be used to clear the throat and gargle before projecting the tobacco water or juice in patient's faces, eyes and noses (Q. *singadu*, liquid tobacco preparation for rhinal injection). The liquid can be mixed with camphor (either natural or synthetic), cologne (S. *agua florida* or *agua de Kananga*) and in extreme cases with diluted creosote (S. *creolina*) to counteract sorcery with a forceful implosive projection that involves the initial blocking of the thoracic diaphragm. This traditional blowing of smoke and tobacco water, reported since the nineteenth century in the upper Amazon and a standardized practice in *Mestizo* shamanism, has been recently altered in *ayahuasca* shamanism as blowing in people's faces is felt to be unpleasant and perhaps dangerous. Blowing is now done along patients' backs, as part of the revival of S. *baños de florecimiento*, flower baths.

Like the Achuar (Descola 1996: 232), Keshwa Lamas shamans believe that tobacco swallowed in the form of pellets 'operates as an internal magnet, making it possible to suck out and neutralize certain pains', particularly those caused by extreme fright. Sufferers may also be rubbed vigorously with tobacco leaves all over their bodies. Tobacco has a cooling and calming action while at the same time serving as a vehicle for substances or immaterial principles that are thereby transferred from the healer to the sufferer, or sorcerer to the victim.

The blowing of tobacco smoke is also agential for shamans in the context of the transformational ontologies of Amazonia. The body envelopes of particular categories of beings can be voluntarily or involuntarily acquired to modify the identity, appearance and behaviour of the bearer, shifting the 'perspective' of the bearer (Viveiros de Castro 1998). The Jaguar complex, widespread in Amazonian shamanism (Reichel-Dolmatoff 1975), has a negative twist among the Keshwa Lamas: shamans who shape shift as black jaguars (Q. *puma runa*) are feared as likely to turn against their own kin rather than attacking enemies. A strong and well-sealed body is impervious to intrusion or soul capture while young humans and debilitated persons are vulnerable: sorcery darts travel through the social body of the targeted individual to weaker relatives around him or her. Throughout Amazonia, personal growth is understood as a life trajectory from baby softness to the hardness of adult bodies that can hold souls securely. Shamans take upon themselves the task of maintaining the physical integrity of members of their social constituency that can be a household, hamlet or whole territory according to increasingly inclusive dominions.

These instrumental uses of the breath are not mechanical clinical actions. Their efficacy rests on the shaman's integrity as a therapeutic agent connected with allied forces in the cosmos. Before blowing tobacco smoke and sucking out pathogens, shamans need to engage their breath through silent rhythmical whistled exhalations (in rare cases inhalations) or as a soft voiced whistling that can vary with greater or lesser use of sibilants, fricatives or shh sounds. This whistling is a prelude to incantations, which are part of shamans' internal store of knowledge. Culturally standardized combinations of syllables and vowels (*nay-nay, rin-rin*) may be sung in transition from whistling to songs (Q. *ikaro*) attributed to particular powerful plants or to spirit allies. The whistling is associated with the use of shakapa leaf rattles (*Olyra latifolia*), that produce a rustling sound supposed to attract spirits. The wind-blowing-whistling-rhythm (in short repeated strokes produced by wrist shaking and followed now and again by an extended set of very rapid oscillations) while smoking a pipe or cigar produces a ritual space of shamanic agency in which intentions can be projected into effective actions mediated by cosmic allies called by the officiating shaman. Mediating efficacy rests on the combination of tobacco, breath and chant, each ensuring the potency of the other two.

In their chanting, upper Amazon shamans rely on a range of registers going from clear falsetto to guttural sounds. Since even tobacco shamans use both, their guttural sounds cannot be identified with the hoarse voices of intensive western smokers. When smoked after drinking *ayahuasca*, shamans extol the auditory effects of tobacco in sharpening receptivity to the voices of spirits or ancestors that come to take part in the ceremonies when called. Tobacco is said to elicit and activate advice and instructions from conjured up spirits in an extension of the counsel (S. *consejo*) ritually given by elders to young men and girls among the Keshwa Lamas. Tobacco makes us see and hear (S. *nos hace ver, nos hace oir*; Q. *rikurichi, uyarichi*).

Perhaps the most significant quality of shamanic tobacco smoke is its ability to elaborate on the vitality of breath and breathing. It is only through the production of tobacco smoke with one's breath and the singing of personal shamanic songs (*ikaro*) that the potential agency located in shamanic pipes and surrounding objects is released. Pipes and rattles then become journeying instruments rather than mere objects, assisting shamans to bring about altered states of consciousness either through the use of tobacco alone or with psychotropic plant brews. Unlike shamans of the northern Andes who make altars on which they arrange insignia and ritual objects of power, Keshwa shamans guide ceremonies using only their songs and the blowing of tobacco smoke on those present. All senses – smell, touch, eyesight, taste, to which must be added proprioceptic orientation and hallucinatory perception – are involved in shamanic healing rituals. They also include intense dreaming periods and enduring neurological alterations of perception in the following days or weeks. Proficient shamans are able to use the blowing of tobacco smoke to guide and control the visions of their patients, modulate effects as appropriate, either enhancing them or tapering them down according to patients' perceived needs. Tobacco blowing, powerful breath and clarity of intent are tools that upper Amazon shamans constantly cultivate.

The pharmacology of nicotine supports shamanic uses of tobacco

We saw above how the historical continuum between licit and counter-hegemonic ('diacritic') uses of tobacco in colonized parts of Amazonia may have supported, if not enabled, the continuity of shamanic uses. The sensory repertoire of shamanic agency, closely linked with Amazonian understandings of disease causation and healing, is pan-Amazonian and appears not to have changed much in time. As a third aspect of the 'tobacco ideology' that Wilbert alluded to, the collusion of the empirical and symbolic properties of tobacco cannot be ignored. In juxtaposing local understandings with scientific research findings from phytochemistry, pharmacognosy and pharmacology, Wilbert (1987) bridged an enduring gap between anthropology and ethno-sciences. Barbira Freedman (2002) has also referred to the properties of nicotinic receptors to throw light on Keshwa Lamas shamans' use of tobacco for opening and sealing their patients' bodies.

Descola's description of the Achuar's perceptions is applicable to the peoples of the upper Amazon more generally: 'Whatever the mode of its preparation, tobacco is believed by the Achuar to possess all kinds of extraordinary properties. Exhaled as smoke over afflicted parts, it cools and anaesthetizes them, at the same time serving as a vehicle for substances or immaterial principles that are thereby transferred from the healer to the sufferer. It plays exactly the same role when taken in an infusion, for the tobacco is believed to form an invisible covering that for a while protects the region of the body where it is applied from external infections .... In all its forms, it sharpens the senses and increases lucidity' (1996: 232).

Descola further comments that 'Treatments using herbal remedies are no more than palliatives in this kind of medicine, which is more at home with psychosomatic procedures than with herbalist prescriptions' (1996: 241). In saying this he reflects a view shared by many upper Amazon indigenous communities and, to a lesser extent, non-Indian urban shamans that all ailments are potentially caused by spells for which 'herbs' ('innocent' plants without mother spirits) are ineffective. Whether tobacco is used on its own or with other psychotropic plants, there is indeed a psychosomatic component to shamanic treatments. It is interesting however that the phytochemical compounds of selected and bred Nicotianas have made tobacco the mediator *par excellence* between humans and spirits in Amazonia. The widespread Amazonian practice of abstaining from salt, fat and sexual intercourse before and immediately after shamanic interventions may also be related to efficacy in facilitating the absorption of alkaloids contained in most plants-with-mother-spirits, with nicotinic neuronal receptors activating the chains of reactions related to neuro-endocrine responses to the plants' chemicals. Given the importance that forest people attribute to diets, there is still little research available on the interrelation between shamanic diets and Amazonian psychotropic plants.

In traditional Keshwa Lamas shamanic training, tobacco is administered in all forms (raw liquid, ingested buccally or rhinally, raw pellets, chewed or swallowed, boiled liquid, ingested rhinally or buccally, and concentrated paste). After initial training, neophytes may be drawn to use other plants than tobacco as their main medium of agency but they will continue to use tobacco (in smoke form) in all their shamanic activities. The ingestion of nicotine in different forms allows the sampling of different effects. Eaten or drunk tobacco induces a calming effect and enduring reduction of anxiety through its effects on the mucosa. In contrast, in snuffing, nicotine crosses the nasal membranes straight to the brain and the central nervous system, resulting in instant, fast but shorter effects. This complementary use of 'eating' and 'smoking' tobacco throws partial light on the distribution of preferred modes of tobacco use among Amazonian groups in different regions. The cultural absence of dry tobacco snuffing in the upper Amazon is surprising since it was a preferred mode of absorption among pre-Columbian Andeans and Renaissance European elites. Preference for absorption via either the lungs or the stomach and small intestine, or both in the case of rhinal ingestion, needs to be considered not only as a cultural choice but also in the local context of patterns of shamanic plant use and understandings.

The pharmacology of nicotine supports the role that tobacco plays in shamanic diets, complementing actions of cleansing and purging with emetic and laxative plants that Amazonian Amerindians in general and upper Amazon people in particular are keen on using regularly within a pan-Amazonian concern with cleansed and purged bodies as a foundation for health care and hygiene.[12] The ritual ingestion or ritual use of tobacco is generally dissociated from the consumption of normal food even when strict shamanic diets are not adhered to. All significant shamanic activities imply fasting. Tobacco is known to suppress appetite through the action of nicotine on the hypothalamus. The release of epinephrine triggered by nicotine also depresses hunger. Hunger contractions of the stomach are inhibited through the nicotine stimulation of sensory nerve endings in the buccal cavity, the stomach mucosa and the large mucosa surface of the small intestine due to parasympathetic stimulation in the gastrointestinal tract.

When hunters and trekkers must be on constant alert in the forest (as in the rest of the cosmos), nicotine hyperglycaemia, the elevation of blood sugar levels when the liver releases stored carbohydrates as an effect of ingesting tobacco by smoking or chewing on an empty stomach, is an advantage. Novice shamans resuming normal eating at the end of a fast are given a stringent progression of foods which master shamans blow tobacco smoke over to make them safe to eat without jeopardizing the delicate body-based assimilation of shamanic knowledge gained through the diet. If this is not done, this knowledge can be returned to its previous owner as if by a magnet, or turn aggressively against the new owner (S. *volteado*, S.Q. *cutipado*). The extreme care given to diet control supports J.E. Jackson's description of Amazonian shamans as mediators between ordinary food and 'soul food' (1983: 197).

Notwithstanding the availability of a wide range of over-the-counter drugs in most areas of the upper Amazon, tobacco is still the most valued therapeutic item that men take with them in the forest. No Keshwa Lamas man going into forest areas beyond community gardens boundaries (Q. *sacha ukupi*) leaves without tobacco in the form of either local cigarettes Q.S. *mapacho*) or loose cured tobacco in his small satchel. The empirical properties of Nicotianas, which may explain why the first Europeans to come across tobacco described it as a panacea, support its versatile uses in the forest as cosmos. The less 'humanised' the forest they walk through, the more at risk of spirit encroachment or attack hunters, or those who intend to act as founders of new settlements, are. Tobacco is offered as propitiating food to the mother-spirits of certain trees, particularly the Lupuna tree (Ceiba spp.), with a few pinches of tobacco placed in a hollow in the tree trunk or at the base of the tree. Tobacco is also scattered prophylactically along newly opened forest trails. Hunters who have succumbed to destructive encounters with forest spirits, revengeful actions from Masters of Game Animals or careless contact with dangerous (possibly poisonous) plants or sites that cause inadvertent humans to experience ceaseless vomiting or diarrhoea require the therapeutic use of tobacco blowing by expert shamans. Detailed research would need to be carried out to understand the alkaloids contained in the undergrowth of dangerous 'untamed' forest areas and the antagonistic effects of nicotine. The Lupuna sap is indeed known to be poisonous as well as psychoactive, as are the barks of the 'medicine trees' that the highest-ranking Keshwa Lamas shamans were specialists in using as S.Q. '*paleros*' or tree shamans of the upper Amazon. The traumas associated with extreme fright in rainforest thunderstorms or whirlwinds, as culturally constructed in folk illnesses specific to hunters, may well be helped by the nicotinic release of dopamine. Besides leaking his vitality through orifices, the hunter is said to become lethargic, idle, 'lazy' (Q. *afasiku*), the worst fate for an active Amazonian indigenous young man. In such cases further treatment may be prescribed, involving Insula ants (*Paraponera clavata*) that inflict painful stings. These possibly involve bioactive compounds that may have a synergetic effect with nicotine. The treatment of snake bites with tobacco juice, poultices and smoke is a specialized area of shamanic practice and it is now known that the venoms of some snakes are antagonistic to nicotinic acetylcholine receptors. Poison makers also use tobacco as a life-saving antidote to the toxic vapours of curare during its preparation.

In summary, we need to acknowledge the extent to which the Keshwa Lamas and other Amazonian Amerindians rely empirically on the pharmacological properties of nicotine. These properties cannot be separated from the anthropological analysis of Amazonian shamanism. Tobacco use supports both the heightened alertness of hunters as historical humans who have become ontologically separate from non-human subjects, and the connectivity of shamans in their approximation of the mythic time (Q. *ñaupa tempu*) with its undifferentiated communication between humans and non-humans in the forest as cosmos.

The shamanic handling of tobacco

Among cultivated Amazonian medicine plants, tobacco is the most needy of dedicated care over periods of at least four months. It requires rich black soils and, at least since the last century, is subject to diseases. Keshwa Lamas shamans are astute in their manipulation of growing conditions to achieve desired results, valuing aroma over the size of leaves in different varieties of Nicotiana species. They are constantly experimenting with plant mixtures while evaluating their effects on themselves and their patients. When they cure self-grown tobacco leaf material with wild honey, or mix it with wild plants, Keshwa Lamas shamans attribute the increased therapeutic potency of their tobacco to this influx of wildness. As in all Amazonian plant medicine, the symbolic effect of 'wild' (Q. *sacha*) components in relation to domesticated components is still little understood.

Upper Amazon peoples seem to have most particularly explored the modalities of smoking, buccal ingestion through eating, or drinking tobacco and rhinal ingestion of liquid tobacco rather than the snuffing of dry tobacco powder. Snuffing tobacco has not been documented in the upper Amazon, except for a possible overlap between pipes and snuff tubes in eastern Peru (see Gow, this volume). Keshwa Lamas shamans are familiar with the practice of snuffing that some of them have observed among other groups during their travels down the Amazon. In the same way that some Lamista hunters used imported bamboo tubes with lids to store their curare in the 1970s, some shamans enjoy keeping their cured tobacco in tubes obtained from distant trading partners who use snuffing tubes rather than in their traditional small gourds or forest snail shells. The use of dry tobacco snuffing using tubes is currently spreading through the expansion of *ayahuasca* shamanism in Amazonia and the rising use of *kambo*, frog poison (*Phyllomedusa bicolor*) in Iquitos and in Brazilian towns and in world capital cities. This increasingly popular practice is preceded with snuffing tobacco, derived from the possible traditional use of *Kambo* from the Matises who live near the Peru-Brazil border. This is one of several recent syncretic developments in *ayahuasca* shamanism; In the last decade, the experimental mixing of San Pedro cactus (*Echinopsis pachanoi*) (Q. *wachuma*); hallucinogenic mushrooms (psyllocybin) and Anadanthera peregrine with *ayahuasca* has become more common in shamanic centres catering for a *gringo* clientele (Barbira Freedman 2014).

In the upper Amazon, plant remedies made out of infusions or smoked plants are differentiated in both quality and strength from crude extracts obtained by expressing the fresh leaves or stems of plants, neat or in some water. Decoctions are the most concentrated preparations, only given to shaman trainees for drinking or rhinal ingestion under expert supervision. This continuum of use does not only apply to tobacco. Fresh Brugmansia plants are also used for inducing dreams, placed under pillows during sleep, with a milder effect than cooked preparations. Fumigations of plants under the platform beds or hammocks of patients are also used to deliver therapeutic plant smoke through inhalation and, shamans claim, transdermal effects.

It is plausible that tobacco water extracts prepared with fresh leaves crushed in water and tobacco drinking might predate tobacco smoking in the upper Amazon, with tobacco smoking becoming the post-Conquest preferred mode of consumption in the shamanism that co-evolved among pacified groups and local colonists. By the time Tessman undertook his comparative overview of cultures in the upper Amazon, all groups had cone pipes. At present, the drinking and eating of tobacco is still more widespread among Jivaroan peoples than among the Keshwa Lamas or Cocama except in the context of shamanic training, which may be attributed to the dominance of *Mestizo* shamanism. Different modes of preparation and consumption have continued to co-exist, with slightly differentiated attributions, in the same way as belt weaving and vertical looms, turtle-base spindles and spinning wheels are still used in parallel in the region.

Cultural revival movements now play an additional part in the selection of options regarding tobacco use, with renewed use of traditional pipes that were replaced by manufactured cigarettes during the second half of the twentieth century. Some *tabaqueros* (shamans who use tobacco as their main ally) who prefer green tobacco juice expressed from fresh leaves, rather than juice from soaked and grated rolls, dedicate themselves to the cultivation of their plants. Tobacco curing with honey has been resumed. Some *ayahuasqueros* use tobacco more than others and seek high quality tobacco for their pipes and for blowing over their brews; others use any tobacco that is available. The historical process of classification and categorization of shamanic plant use that *vegetalistas* engaged in has not resulted in the disappearance of ancient practices. On the contrary, it seems to have facilitated an overlap between colonial Amazonian popular culture and the underlying animistic ontologies anchored in understandings of health and sickness and in therapeutic practices. In the historical fluctuation of polarities of power between hinterland and riverine areas, forest and town, lowlands and highlands, downstream and upriver, the use of tobacco has been consistently revalued through the transformation of shamanism in the upper Amazon. Currently the international appeal of *ayahuasca* shamanism may be contributing to a secondary expansion of the tobacco path in Amazonia in spite of the global health campaigns directed against the consumption of tobacco.

Keshwa Lamas shamans also develop specialized plant use on the basis of their itinerant trainings with shamans in other ethnic groups (Barbira Freedman 2014).[13] They trade their knowledge songs (Q. *ikaro*) related to tree barks for songs that allow them to control other plants (some of which do not grow in their area of residence), associated spirits and cosmic domains and mostly, associated therapeutic/sorcery resources. The 'path of perfume' is sought more particularly from Shipibo shamans, who are seen as experts in seductive relations in the forest as a gendered cosmos and therefore whose medicine can be applied together with *ayahuasca* and tobacco to the valued area of men/women relationships and their related pathologies. When deepening their art of divination using tobacco, Keshwa Lamas turn to Cocama shamans (Q. *banco muraya, sumi runa*) whose mastery of the water domain as a space of transformational potentiality is highly valued. From people of the Marañón related to the Achuar and the Awajún, Keshwa Lamas shamans seek effective darts for protection against sorcery and revenge attacks. Many shamans from these Jivaroan groups (such as the Achuar – Descola 1996: 242–243) however think of Forest Quechua shamans as having superior knowledge and seek their songs. The dreaming ability of tobacco shamans (Wilbert 1987: 163) is said to allow them to better follow and guide the visions of their patients or of participants in *ayahuasca* group sessions, heightening their perception of collective and individual processes.

Discussion

In anthropological studies of Amazonian shamanism, understandings of the relation between soma and psyche have been fraught not only by Euro-American binarisms of body and soul, nature and culture that do not match those of Amerindians but also by a deeply instilled Judeo-Christian resistance to consider body-based practices as foundations for cognition and spiritual development. In spite of a considerable anthropological literature dedicated to the body in Amazonia (Taylor 1996; McCallum 2001; Vilaça 2005), remarkably little has been written on shared and differential physical and physiological aspects of shamanic training in relation to the development of 'bodies that know' in Amazonian shamanism.

Schultes's prediction (1967b: 293) that 'we shall see other narcotic stuffs assume greater roles and tobacco find a progressively less important role than it has been given in our ethnobotanical evaluation' does not appear to have come true. In this chapter I have used ethnographical material from the upper Amazon to draw attention to the actions and sensory repertoire related to tobacco use in relation to animistic cosmologies among hunters and shamans. In attempting to understand the bases for the historical resilience of shamanism in the upper Amazon, I have sought answers in the ethnography of both indigenous and non-Indian syncretic '*vegetalismo*' as intertwined through centuries of diacritical oppositions yet of dialectic integration. In the region of the Amazon most exposed to the hegemonic presence and the repressive powers of colonial secular and religious authorities and to the influx of Andean and mixed colonists, the practice of shamanism has served to preserve a distinctively Amazonian cosmology while continuing to thrive in the face of repression and to co-opt members of the dominant elites into the shamans' ranks. The particular sociality of upper Amazon peoples organized in small localized kindreds constituting loose territorial alliances[14] may explain continuity rather than ruptures such as those which S. Hugh-Jones reports for northwest Amazonia in the historical transformation of shamanism (1994). The internalization of condemned beliefs (plant spirits as devils) and the power of the oppressed (the Indian as potential powerful sorcerer) described by Taussig (1987) can be traced as part of the historical strategies of survival that allowed Keshwa Lamas shamans to sell their services to their oppressors. In spite of *Mestizo* urban shamans' self-portrayals as *vegetalistas*, the upper Amazonian shamanic system continues to remain explicitly ambivalent rather than relying on the diffuse sorcery accusations based on envy (S.Q. *envidia*) that Taussig presents as drawing Colombian colonists to local shamans. The current wave of extreme repression of all narcotic plant use including tobacco by Protestant Churches is causing a division among forest people – both members of indigenous communities and others – with a pressure on converts to exclusively use health post resources. It is too early to discern whether this new spread of Christianity in the upper Amazon will succeed in curbing shamanic practice. At the same time, younger shamans are becoming aware of the positive potential of a rejoinder with ecological discourse, the appeal of shamanism among *gringo* tourists and the place of plant knowledge in indigenous cultural revival movements.

The praxis of tobacco shamanism, closely linked with a pan-Amazonian set of understandings related to the body, the aetiology and treatment of sickness and the promotion of group fertility and wellbeing in a gendered cosmos, can be seen as providing a pragmatic counterpart to Amazonian mythology. Perhaps the most complex issue in Amazonian shamanism is that of agency in relation to intent. Psychosomatic effects, the use of metaphor, symbolic healing and mimesis are combined in the action of smoke blowing, while the physiological effects of tobacco smoke applied to skin, crown, hands and feet remain opaque to biomedical perceptions. The understanding of how Amazonian shamans transform their physiologies through the repeated use of psychotropic plants, without seeming to succumb to negative addictions in the process, is a challenge for physiologists and neuroscientists involved in nicotine research. Shamans' claims to use this acquired capability to cause psychosomatic alterations in others through tobacco smoke applied as an extension of their intentional out-breath are central to the study of Amazonian shamanism (see Rahman in this volume). An analysis of shamanic practice needs to address both local and scientific understandings of transformative actions within animistic ontologies. Many upper Amazon shamans would agree heartily, as they are not devoid of a good sense of humour, that symbolic efficacy is definitely an aspect of their practice. The Amazonian cosmos, in its regional variations, is replete with Jungian archetypes that delight the clients of new age *ayahuasca* shamans. In defence of the upper Amazon shamans, their powers of observation of natural phenomena and practical understandings of the effects, if not biochemical properties, of narcotic plants cannot be easily dismissed. In the context of their historical strategies, shamans across the ethnic categories of the upper Amazon have retained a practical logic that is never fully explicit but, even in the swelling suburbs of Amazonian towns, continues to nurture the lives of forest people. In the words of Richard Schultes (1973) 'Written records concerning the narcotics in the Americas… seem to indicate a deeper, more penetrating, more intimate part in native life.'

Notes

1. At the time of the Conquest, *N. undulata* was referred to as Tabacu Quechua (Benzoni 1565).
2. Wassén (1972).
3. Torres (1995, 1998) reviews archaeological evidence for the antiquity of psychoactive plant use in the Andes, among which *N. tabacum* and Anadenanthera seeds were most widely used as snuff in north Chile and in pipe smoking in northwest Argentina since the third millennium BC.
4. From the end of the sixteenth century, tobacco, praised for its many medicinal virtues in earlier publications (e.g. Monardes 1565), was condemned by the Inquisition in both Spain and England for fomenting commerce with the devil (Frampton's translation of Monardes (1577) 1925: 82).
5. Successive tobacco factories (S. *tabacaleras*) were in operation since the nineteenth century, leading to the current factory, Tabacalera del Oriente International, in Juanguerra, near Tarapoto, Peru. Now under Italian ownership, this factory relies on the mechanized production and processing of selected varieties of both *N. tabacum* and *N. rustic*a (bred for larger leaves) for export, rather than purchasing tobacco leaf material for processing from local producers. The bulk of *N. rustica* production was exported to France for the manufacture of Gitanes cigarettes until the late 1990s. Hybrids between *N. tabacum* and *N. rustica* have been developed since the beginning of the twentieth century in the American tobacco industry in the search for higher but palatable nicotine contents and varieties resistant to common pests and diseases.
6. Honey from Meliponia bees is preferred for use in all medicinal preparations including tobacco.
7. *Mapacho*, from the Quechua root word *mapa-*, 'dirty, soiled', became a generic Spanish term for *N. rustica* tobacco used in shamanism during the colonial period and continues to be used in this way.
8. The Amazon River and some of its tributaries was officially opened to the merchant-flags of all nations on the 7th of September 1867, with a Brazilian naval expedition which included the Peruvian steamers 'Morona', 'Napo', and 'Putumayo' (The American Annual Cyclopædia 1868: 94).
9. The Royal Council in Extraordinary, convened on the 29th January 1767 by Charles III, King of Spain, decreed the expulsion of Jesuits from all Spanish colonies in the Americas. The simultaneous suppression of the Jesuits in the Portuguese Empire, France, the Two Sicilies, Malta and Parma 1767 was the result of a series of political moves rather than a theological controversy. The suppression was an attempt by monarchs to gain control of revenues and trade that were previously dominated by the Society of Jesus (Moses 1919: 104–106).

10. Karsten (1964: 202) suggests the 'small ornamented clay pot which together with the ceremonial tobacco pipe forms his [the shaman's] most important equipment'.
11. 'By blowing tobacco juice on to a child, the father transmits some of his own vital energy to it on the very spot where it is most likely to impart strength, since the wrists are not only joints that are fragile – and therefore weak points in a body always in danger of fragmenting – but also the seat of the pulse, the very spot where separation between the inside and the outside of the organism is abolished and communication between the two becomes possible' (Descola 1996: 232).
12. Uses of *Ilex guayusa*, *Ilex vomitoria* and Q. *yawar panga* (*Aristolochia didyma*) are common in the upper Amazon within or without shamanic diets.
13. The displacements of people and most particularly men in extractive economies, presently logging and oil extraction, also promote encounters and exchanges between shamans from different ethnic groups in camps. Such exchanges supplement but do not replace the knowledge quests through which shamans gather their sources of power in their adult lives.
14. Lamas moieties may be a historical anomaly of this colonial *reducción*.

Part II
Shifting Perspectives

4

Singing White Smoke: Tobacco Songs from the Ucayali Valley

Bernd Brabec de Mori

en kano choronon / chorochorobainkin
pishayaketaananronki / nokon rome sheina
rome shei mediconin / medicina ayonxon
rome shei ininti / medicina aboxon…

I am going to release the world-in-the-song, and releasing, I am advancing;
after unfastening it, they say, I am going to convert my rolled-up tobacco,
the rolled-up-tobacco-physician into medicine.
The scent of my rolled-up tobacco I will entirely transform into medicine…
(Beginning of a song by Shipibo healer Gilberto Mahua,
performed on 22 January 2006)[1]

Ikara purutsu nanin katupitsara…

Let us sing this cigar…
From a Kukama magical song for fishing in Rivas (2004: 103).

Introduction: Tobacco is not important (any more)

Someone living in a so-called developed country, maybe in Europe, East Asia or North America, who wishes to acquire some data on how traditional medicine is conceptualized among the Western Amazonian indigenous group Shipibo-Konibo (mostly shortened to Shipibo) will probably grab his or her smartphone and type some keywords into a search engine. Results pop up as an incredibly long list. Surprisingly, most entries are in English rather than Spanish. They tell about medicine retreats in rainforest lodges, presenting healers called 'shamans' who know how to cure diabetes, cancer or even AIDS; the holistic experience of being part of a millennial chain of mystical knowledge can be purchased online, and all-inclusive trips to study jungle medicine with the most renowned shamans of true master-healer ancestry are fairly easy to book and may seduce the unwary (fees are mentioned later). Delving deeper into this database (maybe also feeding a video portal with the same keywords) one may discover that the Shipibo safeguard amazing techniques of how to sing songs encoded in embroidered geometric healing patterns (which can also be ordered online), patterns rendering what the shamans see in their visions induced by the 'entheogenic' or 'sacred' (or even 'divine') drink called *ayahuasca*. One who drinks *ayahuasca* – you will probably find out that within weeks an ambulant real shaman will also offer *ayahuasca* ceremonies very close to where you are – will be able to see incredible things, achieve illumination, and so on and so forth. Watching videos, one may also observe bone fide shamans blowing tobacco smoke, both over cauldrons full of boiling *ayahuasca* brew, as well as on the head and hands of an uneasy tourist suffering (and vomiting on) the effects of the brew. However, no tobacco-retreats are offered, no smoke-ins, and information about the traditional use of tobacco is rather hard to obtain. First comes *ayahuasca*. Next in the search engine ranking come the geometric designs and the songs called *ikaro* and far behind a few other 'master plants'. Somewhere far below – a few words on tobacco.

This chapter redresses the imbalance between the representation of *ayahuasca* and tobacco not only in contemporary search engines but in the literature. Much has been written about *ayahuasca* (especially among the Shipibo), for example, Luna and Amaringo (1991), Metzner (1999), Luna and White (2000), Labate and Jungaberle (2011), to mention only a few. Many of these publications are influenced by an ideology of 'psychedelics', mainly describing beneficial effects, or the 'white side' of *ayahuasca* use, including its applicability in biomedical contexts. Works offering a more critical scrutiny are rarer – but see Gow (1994) and Fotiou (2010a, b) among others, including some of my own and my wife's work (Brabec de Mori 2011, 2013 and 2014; Brabec de Mori and Mori Silvano de Brabec 2009a and 2009b). In contrast to the vast and still expanding research on *ayahuasca*, there is no publication I know of that is explicitly dedicated to tobacco use among the peoples of the Western Amazon. Titles may suggest it, such as Baer's essay 'The One Intoxicated by Tobacco. Matsigenka Shamanism' (1992), but even this then goes on to deal with *ayahuasca* rather than tobacco. Wilbert's seminal work, *Tobacco and Shamanism in South America* (1987) is somewhat superficial in its coverage of the Ucayali populations. It seems that writing about tobacco in this region is in some way impeded by the striking experience offered by *ayahuasca*, especially when approached in participant observation (and maybe by the allure of a much larger readership for authors who write about an exotic and spectacular hallucinogenic drug rather than one better known and less romanticized in the Western world). However, the present chapter may further explain *ayahuasca*'s steady ascent by analysing the decline of the use of tobacco.

The first section of this paper will summarize some historical data about the use of tobacco in former times. It appears that tobacco seems rather ancient (while *ayahuasca* does not). Thereafter, the role of tobacco in indigenous songs will be analysed with a series of examples from different indigenous groups of the region. An ethnomusicological approach to ethnopharmacology is seldom applied but can contribute to deepening knowledge about indigenous understandings of relations between magical action, substances such as tobacco, and the conceptualizations of cosmos and personhood. Song is the preferred mode of interaction and negotiation between human and non-human entities in the region. By combining results from the analysis of song texts with historical analysis and by taking into account the relative moral implications of tobacco and *ayahuasca* use, the chapter concludes with some thoughts about the influence of cosmopolitan attitudes to tobacco and *ayahuasca* on substance use in general and specifically tobacco in the context of drug tourism.

An almost historical review: Why tobacco is (still) important

Archaeological data in the Western Amazon is scarce, and evidence of substance use from the archaeological record is hard to obtain. The often-cited archaeological 'evidence' for *ayahuasca* use around 2,400 BC by Naranjo (1986) is invalid, as a careful reading of the source article reveals (cf. Brabec de Mori 2011: 24; Beyer 2012). The situation does not change when tracing prehistoric uses of tobacco. However, by analysing contemporary modalities of usage, reviewing the historical record and comparing linguistic and musicological data it appears that *ayahuasca* use in the Ucayali region is unlikely to be older than around 300 years (which is already a generous estimate, see Gow 1994; Bianchi 2005; Brabec de Mori 2011; Beyer 2012), while tobacco use among the same people is almost undoubtedly much longer.

One obvious line of enquiry is to look at the etymology of words for tobacco. Baer's (1992) essay 'The One Intoxicated by Tobacco' is based on a literal translation of *serip'igari*, the Matsigenka term for medical and ritual specialists, commonly called 'shamans'.[2] This term is closely related to *sheripiari*, the corresponding Ashaninka word, literally meaning 'tobacco drinker'. To complete the review of Arawakan languages spoken in the Ucayali valley, the Yine know such persons as either *kagonchi* or *monchi*. Though not obvious, Peter Gow suggests (personal communication) that *monchi* is likewise related to the 'drinking' of tobacco. In Panoan languages, the picture is less clear: the probably oldest Shipibo term for such specialists is *yobé* (i.e. 'power-charged seer'), along with *meráya*, a term probably derived from the Kukama clan name Murayari, and also present in Huni Kuin terminology as *mukroya*. However, it is interesting what these specialists were once reported as being able to do: they drank tobacco juice or licked tobacco paste and with that were able to change their shape (e.g. to transform into a jaguar), to enter the river and operate under water, or even to vanish and become 'spiritized' (*yoshina* in Shipibo terminology). This is similar to accounts from the abovementioned *sheripiari*, *monchi* and *serip'igari*.

Shepard (1998), for example, recounts an intriguing story about his own experience of 'eating' *opatsa seri*, a tobacco preparation, with a Matsigenka healer. In the following, I am going to review some accounts about techniques of *médicos* reported to me during my fieldwork by the specialists themselves. I will concentrate on the Shipibo, among whom I had most contacts, and I also draw on insights into their language. However, as outlined above, these concepts are shared among the whole Ucayali population including the river-dwelling mestizos (*ribereños*).

Indigenous people in the Ucayali valley prior to the European conquest probably did not smoke tobacco. The cigar (*rome shei*, see the initial quotation for this chapter) was probably introduced to them by Europeans, perhaps by those who had observed this practice among other indigenous groups. If this is true, the tobacco pipe (*shinitapon* in Shipibo, *kashimbo* in the regional Spanish dialect called Loretano) is not an ancient item among these people. About one hundred years ago, pipes were often carved in a way resembling elements from Western architecture (see some beautiful drawings on plate 26 in Tessmann 1928, reproduced in Figure 4.1)[3], maybe hinting at a connection to Europeans.

These 'architectural' elements are nowadays out of use. However, this does not mean that smoking could not evolve into a sophisticated practice, as will be shown in this chapter. The Shipibo term for pipe, *shinítapon*, for example, may carry a hint about some prior significance of tobacco use: it denotes the root (*tapon*) of a specific small palm tree (*shiní*), which was used for carving wooden splinters called *yobé* (synonymous with the ritual specialists). Such splinters, or darts, were used in sorcery, along with other palm tree darts such as those from the *wanin* palm (*Bactris gasipaes*, Palmaceae; *chonta* in Loretano, see an illustration of a dart in Tessmann 1928: 187). In order to use such splinters, a sorcerer (*yotomis*, i.e. 'power shooter') had to snap or blow them towards his victim, in a literal or symbolical sense – the splinter is the material manifestation of a magical energy that can travel much further distances than its material counterpart. Sorcerers carried such splinters in their chest; more precisely, the splinters were part of, or embedded in their *kenyon* (*mariri* in Loretano), a magical phlegm that was also regarded as a magical person dwelling in the specialist's chest. Having *kenyon* was the prerequisite for being a sorcerer or healer, because only by harnessing *kenyon* could magical darts be acquired, used, or removed from victims.

The healer Armando Sánchez (1937–2009) gave me a detailed account[4] on how to acquire *kenyon*, which I will present here in a shortened, somewhat streamlined, English translation:

> There is a tree that grows in the *tahuampa* [floodplains], its stem thick like this [shows c. half a metre] with yellowish fruits that the *gametana* fish loves to eat. In order to 'diet' the *mariri* [= *kenyon*] you have to carve a small hole into the stem on the side where the sun rises, before breakfast. Below the hole you fasten a small tin can with 'tobacco water', [that is, water in which tobacco has been seeped for several hours],

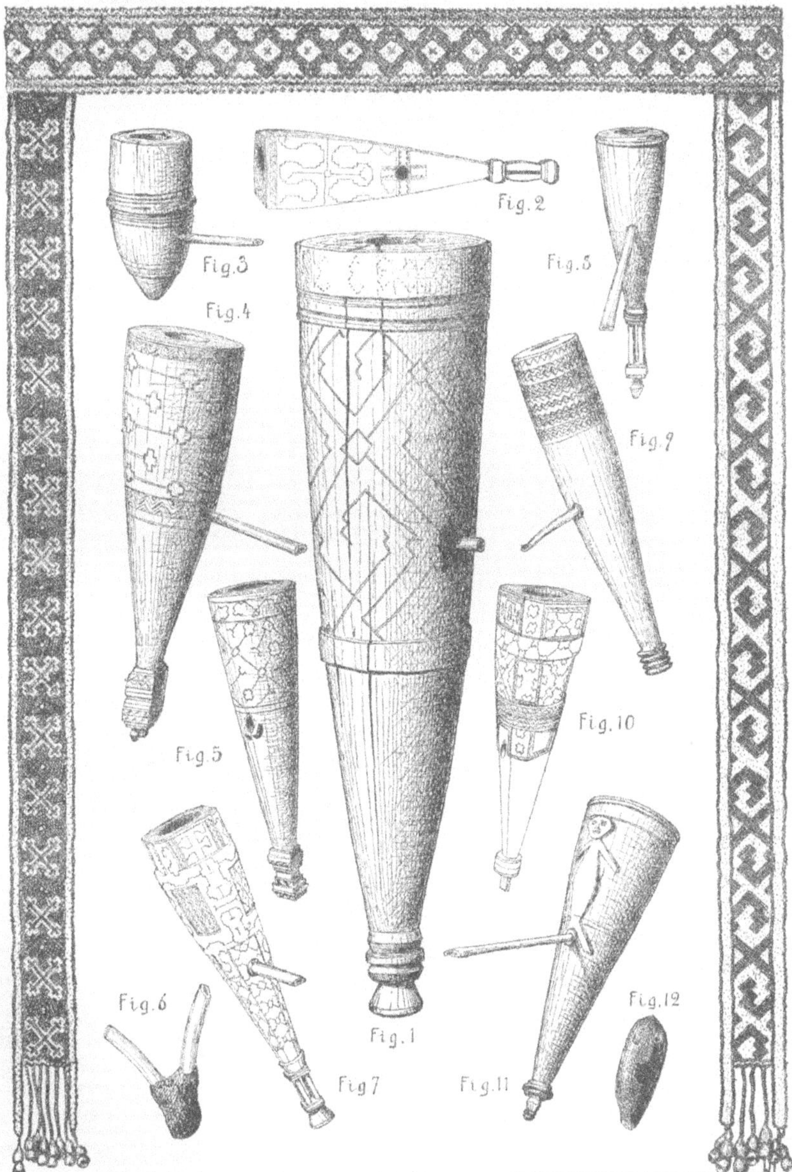

Figure 4.1 'Tobacco pipes, framed by [glass] pearl collars: Fig. 1–5, 7–11 Tobacco pipes. Fig. 6 Tool for insufflating tobacco dust into the nose. Fig. 12 Empty palm nut for storing tobacco dust. (Scale [of original print] 1:2.4)', translation by author, from Tessmann 1928: 100.

> and this must be carefully monitored. If a worm appears in the mixture, you can remove the can and take it home with you that same evening. Before that, however, you have to prepare another tobacco water. You take two females and two males of the white worms – don't take the black ones, they might kill us! – and put them into the new tobacco water. When you start your diet, you drink that with all the tobacco and the worms, and it will make you heavily drunk. The tree is called *inon atsa xeati* ['the jaguar's manioc beer'].
>
> After one week of strict dieting[5] you take your pipe and smoke tobacco. You have to swallow the tobacco smoke. With the smoke, the worm will come out, but you swallow it again. With more tobacco from your pipe, the other worm comes, already big – you have to do the 'diet' for six months, or maybe that's too much, three months – or better five. After that, when you want to bring forth your *mariri*, you swallow tobacco and it comes out. But it also can be nasty, when you smoke tobacco just like this [we were both smoking cigars], it eats the tobacco inside. And they ask you for more, they want their food.
>
> When you then treat a patient, and suck out the dart, you must not swallow it, it may still be alive, you have to burn or bury the darts. They live, like the *mariri* itself, it is alive! When it wants more food, it bites you inside your chest, so you have to drink some tobacco juice, and it will become docile, having gotten its food.

This account shows the direct link between sorcery darts and tobacco use. For the aforementioned treatment involving sucking a dart out of a patient's body, tobacco is likewise required. I observed several sucking treatments and was able to film[6] one conducted by Manuel Mahua (1930–2008), probably the last 'old-school' *yobé* among the Shipibo. Manuel did exactly what Armando told me: he first whistled a melody (*koxonti*) while holding his pipe close to his mouth. Then he lit it and swallowed the tobacco smoke. After a few drags, he produced the most astounding sound, like that of a growling jaguar, repeating this as the *kenyon* gradually came forth. When the slime was in his mouth, he sucked several times at the patient's affected part of the body. When he got the dart, he growled again and his son blew smoke over his whole body. Manuel then took the magic object out of his mouth and showed it to the audience before he buried it outside. At this occasion he produced a tooth and a worm-like little snake he called *kapókiri*.

Armando also instructed me in how tobacco is used as food for living stones called *inkanto*. Such stones can be obtained by various means and they circulate among sorcerers, but usually they conceal them and are wary not to show them to anyone. It is said that these stones can transform into jaguars or other predatory felines during night-time and attack their victims (in a physical as well as magical way). *Inkanto* stones should be kept in a bowl half filled with tobacco water, so they can 'drink' it when they want to – they are likewise fed with tobacco.

Although the above-mentioned techniques are – at least officially – out of use today, one more connection prevails, although it is somewhat cloudy in its consistency: the human voice (and sound in general, Brabec de Mori (forthcoming a)) is considered a substance in indigenous thought. A *médico*'s song may turn into matter in the world aspect ('perspective') of spirits. However, its substantiality is not obvious in 'our world'. In the whole Peruvian lowlands, magical songs are commonly termed *ikaro* (or *ikara*). As a verb for 'singing magical songs', the pseudo-Spanish *icarar* is very often used or likewise pseudo-Quechua *ikaray/ikarana*. Pieter Muysken (personal communication), a renowned linguist, told me that the word was not Quechua or northern Kichwa, although it is often mentioned as such, and figures in the Summer Institute of Linguistic's dictionary, together with a noun: 'ikara *s.* rito(s) *m.* mágicos(s) utilizando tabaco. [...] ikarana *v.t.* curar o hacer daño a una persona fumando y repitiendo fórmulas mágicas' (ILV 2002: 109).[7] Here, *ikara* is the name for any magical action ('rite') using tobacco, and the verb combines to expound the chanting of magical formulae. In line with Muysken, I doubt this etymology, and I prefer to derive the term from Kukama *ikara* which means 'song' (cf. Rivas 2004, eluded to in the opening quotation from Rivas; *ikara* is used for any songs, like drinking or courtship songs; on the central Ucayali, Kukama magical songs are most often referred to as *mariri*). Following this hypothesis, Kukama magical techniques using song spread through missions during the initial phase of conquest, proselytizing in the Peruvian lowlands during the seventeenth and eighteenth centuries. The Kukama, Kukamiria and Omahua (who all spoke a closely related language) were among the first groups to be 'reduced' into the missions of the Marañon and upper Amazon, which were some of the largest and most influential. These groups were then used as 'indios cristianos' in order to conquer, 'reduce' and baptize other surrounding indigenous populations. At the same time, missionaries tried to establish Quechua (the Inca's language) as a *lingua franca* among these groups who spoke many different languages (see Ardito Vega 1993: 69). Possibly at the same time, smoking was introduced or re-introduced to the region by Europeans (remember that indigenous people used to drink tobacco juice or paste). As was shown by Peter Gow (1994), magical techniques (and specifically 'ayahuasca shamanism') were spread among different indigenous groups via such missions and later in rubber tapper's camps. The possibly older association of tobacco use and magical chanting has probably taken on new forms in these places.

The analysis of indigenous songs shows that those indigenous groups who spent most time in or were in more or less stable contact with missions use very different musical styles today than those who were not (see also Brabec de Mori forthcoming b: 705). The melodic scales used by the Kukama, Shipibo and Yine, who since conquest dwelled on the main Ucayali River, are mostly pentaphonic, while the scales used by 'backwood' groups are triphonic or even amorphous. Another indicator is given by intonation: microtonal intervals, formalized speaking and excessive use of glissandi are very common among the interfluvial peoples, while the fluvial dwellers use a very 'clear' intonation in the sense of European tempered tuning. A strophic structure to almost any song is evident among them while virtually absent among interfluvial dwellers. This points towards a strong interaction between missionaries, the Catholic

Mass and the general singing style of the peoples in question. Remarkably, ritual songs among the Shipibo, Yine and Kukama are either closer to the interfluvial styles in almost all cases of songs performed outside of the *ayahuasca* context or even more complex in intervallic structure, using hexatonic or heptatonic scales, for example, and much longer sequences of phrases in the strophic structure, in the case of *ayahuasca* songs. Therefore, it appears that tobacco smoking, *ayahuasca* drinking and a synthesized singing style were 'co-invented' in this missionary context. Gow (1994: 107) also observes that the 'ayahuasca curing session', whose origin he places in exactly this social milieu of christened indigenous people in missions, 'implicitly parodies the Catholic Mass. This is most dramatically evident in the way in which the shaman blows tobacco smoke over each little cup of ayahuasca before it is given to the drinkers'.

Given that the Kukama were among the first to be 'reduced' in missions, followed later by the Shipibo and Yine, it can thus be explained how a Kukama technique (song – *ikara*) became adjunct, and even synonymous in ritual use, to tobacco smoking and consequently entered tradition as a (pseudo-) Quechua term in the whole region via the diffusion of *ayahuasca* use.

The 'Spanish' verb *icarar* is, however, most often applied to a magical technique obviously related to song but which is more specific. It is what Manuel Mahua did with his pipe before throwing up his *kenyon*: one holds a cigar or pipe close to one's mouth while whistling a melody. Some *médicos* insist that it is crucial to *think* the corresponding song's lyrics while whistling (cf. Olsen 1996: 259–260 for magical songs with 'imagined' lyrics or Piedade 2013 for spirits that are able to 'hear' human thoughts). When the cigar is then lit, the smoke is blown into the direction of the patient or victim in order to allow the song's efficacy to unfold. The cigar may be smoked by the same *médico*, but it can also be handed to another, taken away, kept for later and smoked by somebody else. The magically efficient song will still be 'in the smoke' which can be blown by anyone.

Today, *ikaro* or *ikara* are commonly understood as '*ayahuasca* songs' and are assumed to be age-old by the majority of authors. As indicated at the very beginning of the present text, most scholars dealing with *ayahuasca* and almost the entire popular and international *ayahuasca* community have appropriated the corresponding terminology without giving much credit to their tobacco-using predecessors and tobacco-related fundaments for the phenomena and techniques they are researching or (ab)using.

Spirits of the past: Tobacco songs

The most remote, in the sense of a Westerner mapping the upper Amazon, use of tobacco may occur among those few indigenous peoples who remain 'voluntarily isolated'. There is evidence (see Huertas Castillo 2002; Krokoszyński et al. 2007, among others) that many hundreds of individuals live along the Peruvian-Brazilian border, avoiding contact with towns and villages and, consequently, globalization. In 1958, a group of 27 individuals living in such circumstances and calling themselves the Iskobakebo was contacted and deported to the Callería River by US Protestant missionaries (see Brabec de Mori forthcoming b: 332 passim). I worked with the last few members of the Iskobakebo group, taking song recordings and translating these. The elder Winikera remembered magical songs that were performed before contact by the leader (healer/sorcerer) of this group and later by his deceased elder brother Meraketa. Winikera explained that the healer drank tobacco juice, sometimes together with an extract from *toé* (Brugmansia spp.). In this drunk state (*pae*) he started to communicate with non-human entities by singing. Winikera theatrically performed some of these songs. One of these is analysed in Brabec de Mori (forthcoming b: 350 passim), and shall just be briefly sketched here:[8] the singer repeatedly produces a sound mimicking the drinking of tobacco juice in between singing various passages in four distinctive musical forms: one form is marked by the syllables *jiji* and sung 'by the human', another two are sung 'by the macaw entity' and the fourth form is 'spoken' by the macaw. In the first part of the song, the human singer describes the macaw entity descending from a liana. The macaw then performs the healing, as perceived from its own perspective. After its successful intervention, it is given farewell. Returning to the perspective of the human singer, he mentions that they drink tobacco together to celebrate:

sakoboko ininon jiji	It ascends [again] along [my] liana,
nokon ibo shinira jiji	my master power.
chejebata irora jiji	The tobacco juice is good.
keshoroko rimaki jiji	We give us to drink each other,
taroko imai jiji	the [master power] gives me to drink [tobacco].
aunribikaista jiji	Thus [the master power] leaves again,
noko ishten menike jiji	I have already shared my happiness
nokon ointiroko jiji	from my very heart,
tayora menike jiji …	so the ill person is saved …

Tobacco here it is named *chejebata*, literally 'black-sweet'. It is unclear if this is a poetic metaphor or the 'original' Iskobakebo term for tobacco juice.[9] The macaw entity is not named but called 'my master power' (which is my free translation from *nokon ibo shini*). However, it is revealed in the parts sung 'by itself' (or by the transformed healer): it calls itself *jawan*, the common Iskobakebo term for the macaw. The following rendering of drinking tobacco juice is however clear and explicit. Here, tobacco juice, as Winikera explained, has the same function as maize beer in 'secular' Iskobakebo festivities: the healer and the macaw entity drink it together in order to celebrate. It is the spirit's maize beer – maize beer is also considered a basic nutritive among traditional Iskobakebo. Tobacco again is the food of the spirits.

However, the Iskobakebo do not perform healing or sorcery rituals anymore. They are so diminished in number that they are demographically swallowed up by the surrounding Shipibo and Spanish speaking population. Winikera's rendering is but a remembrance from a remote time and place.

The next example was performed by the aforementioned 'old-school' Shipibo *yobé* Manuel Mahua. When he performed the sucking of magical darts described above, he usually held his tobacco-filled pipe close to his mouth while whistling and *thinking* the appropriate lyrics before lighting the pipe and swallowing the smoke. When I asked him to do so, he agreed to openly sing the song so I could record the lyrics.[10] It is also a very long song so here again I only present the beginning and a short later excerpt:

ani ani míriko	This very big physician [*médico*]
nai xama meraya	this *meráya* [master healer] from the heaven's summit
koshi koshi míriko	this very powerful physician [*médico*],
bewa kenékeneya	I will bring, by the power of my well-patterned song,
shinítapon xamanbi	into the very centre of my tobacco pipe [*shinítapon*]
bewa xanichintaanan	and in there I will place the song accordingly.
jana rebon yasanai	Thereafter, I will set up the
maririka makina	*mariri*-machine at the tip of my tongue,
yasanakebainxon	And after I have set it up there,
makinanin yatanxon	the machine will grab
tsinkiáketanbanon	anything it attracts from all around…
…	
shinítapon tokantin	My tobacco pipe growls,
tonkari mariri	it growls forth the *mariri*,
ani ani mariri	the very big *mariri*,
toyoyoyo mariri	the *mariri* is elastic when I slurp it [onomat.]
cararara mariri	the *mariri* does *kararara* [onomat.]
piapia mariri	the *mariri* does *piapia* [onomat., or 'arrow-arrow'];
tinkotinin tsekarai	growling I bring it forth
yora meranoakan	from inside [my] body,
naman tsekaxonbanon	from the inside I will bring it forth.

The song describes in detail the process of summoning the *mariri* – the slimy entity dwelling in the singer's chest – by the means of his tobacco. Once brought forth into his mouth (the *médico* threw up several times producing a growling sound), the *médico* would suck at the patient's body and thus extract the object he thereafter showed to the people present.

In the first few lines, it becomes obvious that the '*miriko*' (S: *médico*) the singer mentions must be the tobacco he puts into his pipe. But it should be noted that it is also the song which is placed in the pipe, so here the song, the tobacco and the physician are synonymous. During the rest of the song, which is not transcribed here, Manuel mentioned many different kinds of splinters (*wexá*) that will be attracted and grabbed by his *mariri* machine, for example stone splinters (hinting at the *inkanto* stones), wooden splinters (hinting at *shiní* and *wanin* darts), rotten-wood splinters, among many others, most notably also snake and worm splinters (*kapókiri*).

Remarkably, the melodic-rhythmic structuring of this song is not entirely compatible with common Shipibo song style. It carries various references to downriver-dwelling Kukama singing style, including onomatopoetic syllables that are rare in Shipibo singing (including magical songs) but often excessively used by Kukama and Quechua *médicos* – another connection to the historical process mentioned above that connects singing, smoking and healing (or sorcery).

The third example song I recorded far upriver among the Yine on the upper Ucayali. It is a love magic song, which should likewise be performed (sung or whistled) while one holds a cigar or cigarette close to the mouth so it would be 'charged' with the song. This song is short and is printed here in full:[11]

jiweyogatyawaka	Into the whirlpool [in the river]
nutakanru nayirpowa	I put my tobacco [cigarette].
kapana gogompukote	Below the *kapana*-tree [species],
nutakanro mpotsiwate	I put the *alcalde*-bird [species].
kapana gonroteno	High up in the *kapana*-tree,
nutakanru katajiru	I put my brilliant,
katajiru nkoshichite	brilliant bird.

My Yine research associates explained that 'putting the tobacco into the whirlpool' would mean that the singer, charging his cigarette, would then blow the smoke on a spot in the river where the water is whirling – this whirlpool, which may also be considered a magical entity, then would 'take care of' the correct distribution of the song's power which is contained in the smoke. The persons who should be connected by love magic are mentioned as the two birds who are placed on the same tree.

The structure of this song is likewise remarkable, though in another sense. Among the Yine, there are two very different magical singing styles in use: First, the *ikara*, sung in *ayahuasca* sessions, always with foreign lyrics – mostly in Quechua-Spanish code-switching, but sometimes also in Ashaninka or Shipibo language – whose musical structure appears fairly similar to downriver Kukama or Quechua style singing. Second, songs like the one quoted above which come much closer to Yine *shikalchi* ('song', usually performed by women), although they are structurally distinct also from those. Most are sung in Yine language but unknown languages ('the spirits' language') also occur. These magical songs are not connected to *ayahuasca*; some of them are loosely linked to tobacco, as in the above example, or *toé*. These songs may be sung by anyone, they are not restricted to trained *médicos*. However, any singer has to perform 'correctly'. This means that the singer has to reproduce melodic and rhythmic structure along with the lyrics in a consistent way. This does not mean that only one structure exists which is sung by all people who know the song. On the contrary, each singer may use his own interpretation, but 'correctness' refers to internal coherency of these structures (cf. Brabec de Mori forthcoming b: 222–227). Another important factor for being effective, as my research associates pointed out, was 'to put faith' (*poner fé*) into the performance. Here, neither specific training nor any altered state is considered a prerequisite for efficiency, but a high degree of concentration and serious dedication by the singer. These songs are for curing, for love magic, for summoning or protection. It seems that this tradition of magical singing was already established when *ayahuasca* was introduced together with its' songs from the downriver Kukama and Shipibo.

Another example from the Ashaninka may complement this:[12]

sherisherityawako	Tobacco, tobacco, tobacco,
tziwankrokrokrorkro	*tsirootzi*-bird [onomat.],
tziwankrokrorokro	*tsirootzi*-bird [onomat.].
sherisherityawako	Tobacco, tobacco, tobacco,
tyawako tyawako	tobacco, tobacco,
tziwankrokrorokro	*tsirootzi*-bird [onomat.]

The song is a simple summons, and the singer explained that it was sung in order to communicate with the *tsirootzi*, a bird often referred to as an ambassador or omen and a favourite used by *médicos* for diagnosis and other means. Note that, along with the name of the bird merged with the onomatopoeia of its call, the lyrics mention tobacco in both its Ashaninka 'original' *sheri* and 'Ashaninkazized' Spanish *tyawako*. The singer further explained that the former *sheripiari* (*médicos*, 'tobacco-drinkers') sang such formulae when licking tobacco paste, but contemporary *médicos* could also sing similar formulae or songs during *ayahuasca* sessions.[13] Another research associate, César Caleb, explained to me that Ashaninka *médicos*, in former times, only used tobacco paste.

The final example stems from Shipibo singer and healer Rosa Valera and is taken from a night-time *ayahuasca* session. She sang for a young man living in urban context in order to 'open' him to receive good luck and commercial success in his working life. It is one of the rare occasions where she explicitly worked with her tobacco, and it is a very beautiful musical expression:[14]

nokon rome shei	My rolled-up tobacco
nete narakameya (2x)	lights it up from the inside.
min jakon kanobi (2x)	[It lights up] your beautiful world-in-the-song
kanoni rome shei	which is expanded by the rolled-up tobacco,
nokon rome sheikan	by my rolled-up tobacco.

min yora xaman	The interior essence of your body
mia soi axonon (2x)	I will make soft [like velvet],
ani *suerte* bitibo	so that it may receive the good luck.
en mia axonon	this I will do for you …
…	
ni tsonrabi	Not anyone
jaweatimakinkan	will be able to harm you.
earonki bewai	I, so it is said, am singing.
nete reshin tsoawa	The light-full and adorned *tsoawa*-bird
metsatira bewai	is singing beautifully.
ani kanoxamanbi	Inside of the immense world-in-the-song
panini rome shei	the rolled-up tobacco is hanging from the centre-top
nete narakameya	and it lights the world from its inside.
joi jakon tsitsoya	The beautiful words intertwine
rome sheitoninra	by the means of the cigar.
metsa rome sheikan	I am singing, so it is said,
earonki bewail	the beautiful rolled-up tobacco.
merayai bewail	I transform into a singing *meráya* [master healer],
inin *santo raina*	into the fragrant sacred queen,
rainara bewai	the queen is singing
min yora axoni	in order to cure your body.

In the first section of the song, Rosa describes how her glowing cigar lights up the sonic landscape she constructs by singing.[15] This landscape is expanded by her tobacco, that is by both its light and by its scent, which likewise extends this 'spiritual' landscape which is then identified within the patient's body. In the following part, not transcribed here, she mentions various instances from the patient's life and work which shall be improved as a result of her treatment. Then – like in the Iskobakebo example, it is again by the power of the song that transformation occurs. 'It is said' that Rosa was singing. With that she hints at the fact that this is being observed while she is already somewhere else, and somebody else. She describes herself as a singing *tsoawa* (a beautiful local bird species (zool. n. id.) which is often referred to by singing *médicos*). In the following passages, the cigar in her world-in-the-song intertwines with the sung words themselves; the tobacco *becomes* the song. Finally, the singer becomes a *meráya* (master healer) and joins this homunculus – the song, the scent, the cigar, the singing queen are all one entity who bestows its magical power on the patient's body.

In this series of tobacco songs, it may be noted that tobacco may be a person itself – as Gilberto Mahua in the opening quotation mentions a 'rolled-up-cigar-physician', his elder brother Manuel calls the tobacco in the beginning of his song 'a very big *médico*', which is also synonymous with the song itself. Rosa finally transforms into the tobacco, impersonating it. However, when transcending the worlds as in

Figure 4.2 'Jaguar transformation', painting by Milke Sinuiri (acrylics on canvas, 2007); reproduced with the kind permission of the Collection Ethnomedicine, Medical University of Vienna.

the Iskobakebo lyrics and the last example, tobacco is still a cigar, or a juice to be drunk (cf. Lima 1999: 102, where she describes that the Juruna shaman smokes a cigar together with the 'peccary shaman'). In the western Amazon, the perspectivist view of the world (Viveiros de Castro 1998; Lima 1999) is fairly consistent and plants are understood as persons as well as animals, spirits, and certain entities like lakes. However, tobacco is flexible. It transcends perspectives, still being a medium to smoke or drink for humans, peccaries, macaws, and spirits. At the same time it can be a person, usually a revered healer.

This last musical text further illustrates how tobacco and *ayahuasca* use may go together. However, the prior examples are now a reminiscence: both Armando, who instructed me how to acquire *kenyon*, and Manuel, who knew how to use it for sucking darts, are dead. They were among the last ones who actually held and practiced this kind of knowledge. The Iskobakebo Winikera only imitated his dead uncle and brother with his performance, and he taught nobody. Among Yine, I was told, there are still some people who know how to sing these magical songs but these persons are few and far between, and the remaining Ashaninka and Shipibo healers who still use tobacco are growing old. The younger ones generally turn to other things.

In the place of a conclusion: A painting

Instead of explaining in words how the transition happened from tobacco magic to *ayahuasca* commerce, I invite you to look at a work of art (Figure 4.2). It is a painting by Milke Sinuiri, a young Shipibo *ayahuasca* specialist who enjoys painting what he can see in his *ayahuasca* visions as well as themes from mythology and popular knowledge. He painted this picture in 2007 and it is now in possession of the ethnomedicine collection at the Medical University of Vienna. It was also reproduced and analysed in its artistic context in a prior publication (Brabec de Mori and Mori Silvano de Brabec 2009a).

The painter explained that this picture is about the good and the bad, about healing (*curanderismo*) and sorcery (*brujería*). Interestingly, the healer and the sorcerer are one and the same person, which is definitely evident in traditional indigenous medicine. However, the 'good' side on the left shows the person's human face, and at the lower left, an *ayahuasca* vine is naturalistically depicted. Above, a colourful 'mythical anaconda' crosses the dark blue sky (or outer space), a theme inspired by Pablo Amaringo, a well-known painter of *ayahuasca* visions (cf. Luna and Amaringo 1991). The left side, the 'good' side, is the *ayahuasca* side. On the right, the person shows a jaguar's face and smokes a tobacco pipe. On the top a big toucan looks down, a bird the Shipibo mostly associate with sorcery. Below it, two men face each other, the left one covered with white traditional Shipibo patterns. The one on the right appears covered by irregular red spots (measles?) – the healer and the sorcerer confronting each other in battle. Below them, a bunch of snakes emerges from the central person's chest, like the splinters mentioned by Manuel Mahua: snake splinters, living darts, the worms we swallowed during Armando's instructions. While the left side's background is the sky, the right side is bathed in red and yellow flames. This picture, better than a thousand words, demonstrates that nowadays healing is associated with *ayahuasca* while sorcery smells like tobacco.

I must turn to words again in order to further examine the moralities associated with each of these two remedies: *ayahuasca* and tobacco. Although in current *ayahuasca* tourism, there are cases of abuse reported (Peluso 2014), referring even to witchcraft (Fotiou 2010b), the general stance is to view the substance as a healing one, linked to romantic images of 'noble savages' and spiritual growth as reported at the very beginning of this chapter. It is the image on the right side in Milke's painting, the element that contemporary healers and *ayahuasca* entrepreneurs try to fend off, keep at bay, or at least ignore: sorcery.

In Amazonian reality, however, sorcery is always close at hand. This can be conceptualized if one considers that most Amerindian societies are based on a reciprocal understanding of the cosmos as described in many anthropological classics as well as more recent work (see for example Århem 1996; Fausto 2002; Halbmayer 2013, among others). In the case of 'medicine', one has to bear in mind that within what Descola (2005) calls an 'animic society' or a perspectivistic cosmos (Viveiros de Castro 1998), to heal means also to harm (see also Whitehead and Wright 2004). In the Ucayali region, a healer may cure a person who is ill – which implicitly means that the person was bewitched by a malign spirit, a powerful animal or plant, or by a human sorcerer. In any case, the healer has to overthrow the original cause of the illness in battle. In successful cases, the witchcraft is returned and will afflict its originator. Therefore the healer is simultaneously, from the other's perspective, a sorcerer. By the way, if the healer cannot overthrow the originator of the illness, he may return the witchcraft to one of the latter's relatives, in which case the episode can start again, reversed: the relative falls ill and consults a healer, who again …

This reciprocal view is incommensurable with the image nowadays pursued by western Amazonian specialists who frequently withdraw from work as *médicos* among their peers, to provide sensational experiences to drug tourists or to 'shaman apprentices' from so-called developed countries instead (see also Brabec de Mori 2014, among other essays in the same volume edited by Labate and Cavnar). This profound moral and cosmological dichotomy is further underlined by the Western view of tobacco as an addictive drug. I am reminded of a time when I assisted Gilberto Mahua in a daytime-consultation and curing session in 2007, one that did not involve *ayahuasca*. A young man consulted Gilberto because of his problems with addiction to other drugs. Gilberto took a perfume flask (*agua florida*), opened it and held it to his mouth while whistling (*icarar*, as described above), while I did the same thing with a cigarette. Gilberto finished his song, took some perfume into his mouth and blew it over the patient's body, while I lit my cigarette and blew smoke onto the patient's head and hands, something I had seen as regular practice in Shipibo tobacco healing rituals. We concluded the treatment, and then Gilberto took me aside and started earnestly to instruct me: 'you cannot use tobacco when treating somebody with an addiction problem, because tobacco by itself is an addictive drug!' This was a concept totally alien to traditional Shipibo uses of tobacco. It was a fragment of song lyrics by the same Gilberto, performed in January 2006, which opened this essay. Between performing this song and the aforementioned instruction, Gilberto had travelled outside Peru for the first time, conducting *ayahuasca* sessions among Westerners.

Notes

1. All song lyrics presented in this text are taken from the author's field recordings which are archived at the Phonogrammarchiv of the Austrian Academy of Sciences. The corresponding archive number for the recording from which this quotation is taken is D 5576.
2. I prefer not to use this introduced term because of its many popular connotations as well as its shrouded definition in anthropological discourse. In the Ucayali valley, Spanish-speakers usually call these people *curandero* (healer) or *brujo* (sorcerer). Indigenous people, besides using respective vernacular terms very often use the reinterpreted Spanish word *médico* (physician, doctor), even in first-language-discourse. I adopted the later term here and in other papers. I use male forms for *médicos* throughout, because what I describe here was and mostly still is considered exclusively the duty of men (although there appears a female *médica* later in the paper: she used to work together with her husband, which occurs sometimes).
3. On the same plate an object (marked as 'Fig. 6') can be seen, which was used for blowing tobacco powder into a peer's nose or even into one's own nose. This process is also shown in Harry Tschopik's film about the Shipibo, dating from 1953.
4. Recorded interview dating from September 19, 2003, archived at the Vienna Phonogrammarchiv under file D 4667.
5. The 'diet' mentioned by Armando refers to a general method of learning well known in the western Amazon: one applies some substance (e.g. drinks a decoction from a tree bark) and then retires into the wood or into a closed house observing strict alimentary and social (e.g. sexual) restrictions. During this period, the 'dieter' will get in contact with the spiritual aspect of the substance he used (e.g. the tree's 'owner') in order to learn diverse techniques, including songs, from this entities. After concluding the 'diet', the 'dieter' will thus be able to achieve things previously unavailable to him.
6. The film is archived under file V 1755 at the Phonogrammarchiv.

7. '*Ikara* is a magical rite that uses tobacco; *ikarana* means to heal or harm a person by way of smoking and repeating magical formulas'.
8. Performed by Pablo 'Winikera' Sangama in 2004, Phonogrammarchiv file D 5365.
9. To date, the Iskobakebo language is largely undocumented. The Iskobakebo I was working with spoke Shipibo almost fluently, and given that both are related Panoan languages, Shipibo deeply influenced their own way of speaking. The glossaries we recorded and translated appeared closely related to Shipibo, and that is where tobacco was translated as *rome*, which is also the Shipibo term. However, the language Winikera and his peers used in song appears different, and we suspect that it is closer to how they spoke before contact.
10. I observed the procedure several times, one of which I also filmed and for another I produced an audio recording: performed by Manuel 'Iskoniwe' Mahua in 2004, Phonogrammarchiv file D 5351.
11. It was performed by Marcelino Gonzales in 2004, Phonogrammarchiv file D 5366.
12. Performed by the *médico* Meyanto Vásquez in 2004 (D 5416).
13. There is a commercial CD recording available which was produced by an Ashaninka community on the upper Yuruá River in Brazil (Apiwtxa 2005). It contains, among other tracks, an extensive recording of an *ayahuasca* session, and the songs performed in this session either sound very similar to Meyanto's song quoted above or like the Kukama or mestizo style songs from downriver.
14. Excerpts from a performance by Rosa Valera in 2001, Phonogrammarchiv file D 4601.
15. The Shipibo term *kano* (which I translated as 'world-in-the-song') is too complex and its use in magical singing too sophisticated to be fully explained here; see instead Brabec de Mori (2012 and forthcoming b: 606 passim). It may be described here as the physical, material manifestation in the 'spirit world' of what is sung in 'our world'. That is, any magical song manifests as a 'landscape' in the spirit world, and this can be perceived by a *médico* under the influence of *ayahuasca*, but also in any altered state induced e.g. by fasting, or by drinking tobacco juice. Conversely, a song performed by a spirit in the 'spirit world' can manifest in 'our world' e.g. as a thunderstorm (cf. Brabec de Mori forthcoming a).

5

Cool Tobacco Breath: The Uses and Meaning of Tobacco among the People of the Centre

Juan Alvaro Echeverri

Introduction

When I lived in the Igaraparaná River with Kɨneraɨ, a tobacco healer, he advised me to stop smoking for a month. I looked too thin, my face had taken on a yellowish tinge and I was sweating too much, he said. He remarked that tobacco is strong and hot and that it might be heating up my body. I was a heavy smoker and reluctantly followed his advice; however, in the following weeks, I realized that my health was improving. When a full month had passed, I said to Kɨneraɨ that he had been right in advising me to stop smoking and that I was feeling much better. 'Well, yes', Kɨneraɨ replied, 'I told you that tobacco is strong'; and then, he added with utter conviction: 'But a man *must* smoke tobacco.'

Tobacco is a defence and a protection, he explained; the smell of tobacco makes your body appear fierce to animals and spirits. A man must smoke in the afternoon when he gathers with other men in the coca yard, in order to protect the space he sits in. He must also smoke when a thunderstorm threatens so as to avert it (because 'tobacco is electric'). A man should blow tobacco smoke on the legs and feet of women and children when they go to the gardens, so as to repel snakes and poisonous insects and animals, and it is paramount to travel with tobacco leaves or cigarettes to protect oneself, especially when undertaking risky tasks or meeting with strangers or powerful people.

His remarks on the proper manner of smoking struck me as a real novelty. He did not advise me to quit smoking altogether and to never again touch a cigarette – as is current in non-indigenous anti-tobacco campaigns – but rather, he advised me to learn about the uses of smoking. Smoking tobacco, besides fulfilling an everyday protective and healing function, is most importantly employed to induce a severe intoxication that enables a person to see the real causes of illnesses and misfortunes and to acquire a 'spirit of tobacco' to heal, as Kɨneraɨ did.

For the people I am describing in this chapter, smoking is a secondary, and largely inferior, use of the plant. Among them, today as in the past, tobacco is mainly consumed in the form of a thick decoction of tobacco juice mixed with vegetable salt, called *yera* (*ambil*, in local Spanish, from Quechua *ampi* 'poison'). They ingest this thick juice or paste by licking it, a practice that defines the cultural ensemble of groups of northwestern Amazonia who self-designate as the 'People of the Centre'. This expression encompasses seven ethnolinguistic groups of the Witotoan, Boran and Andoque linguistic stocks, which share a number of cultural traits and have a common social and ceremonial organization (Echeverri 1997; Griffiths 1998; Karadimas 2005; Gasché 2009; Londoño-Sulkin 2012; Pereira 2012). Their ancestral territory spans the area between the Caquetá and Putumayo Rivers in southeastern Colombia along the border with Peru, with a total population of about 10,000 people (DNP 2010). These people arguably constitute a single if fuzzily bounded society, in spite of their spatial dispersion and linguistic heterogeneity; besides much intermarriage among them, they share a rich ceremonial order that revolves around the consumption of coca and tobacco and in fact often hold rituals that bring together speakers of different languages. The People of the Centre understand themselves to be distinct from other neighbouring groups in that their men and women lick tobacco in daily life and on ritual occasions, while their neighbours merely smoke or powder their tobacco. Men lick the tobacco paste, generously admixed with ash salts, together with coca powder (Figure 5.1).[1]

Figure 5.1 Kinerai licking tobacco paste. (Photograph by O.L. Montenegro, Igaraparaná River, 1992.)

Tobacco licking has a limited distribution in South America. Johannes Wilbert (1987) reports tobacco licking by the now extinct Timote-Cuica in Mérida (Venezuela), the Chibchan-speaking Ijka and Kagabba in the Sierra Nevada de Santa Marta (Colombia), the Piro (with a question mark) and Ashaninka in the Peruvian foothills, and by the cultural ensemble of the People of the Centre in the Caquetá-Putumayo region (Colombia-Peru). Although the Timote-Cuica disappeared, the habit of licking tobacco remained in the Merida region and extended to the Gulf of Maracaibo and to the Venezuelan and Colombian *Llanos*, where it is called *chimó* (Kamen-Kaye 1971). The Ijka and Kagabba do not mix the tobacco paste with ashes or salt, although they do use an alkaline mixture (obtained from burning seashells) as an additive for the consumption of the leaves of coca (Reichel-Dolmatoff 1949). The use of tobacco paste among the Piro seems to be very marginal (see Gow, this volume); the Ashaninka do lick a tobacco concentrate called *sheri* (from which derives *sheripiari*, the term for shaman), but its preparation and components have not been fully documented (Elick 1969; Weiss 1975).

The tobacco paste is a moist substance and the product of a culinary process. As such, it contrasts with the more widespread use of tobacco smoking and tobacco snuff, which are dry substances and 'infra-culinary' – to use Lévi-Strauss's (1973: 68) expression. Lévi-Strauss proposed that the relationship between tobacco and honey could be defined as a series of oppositions: raw/cooked, burnt/moistened, supra-culinary/infra-culinary. Tobacco paste – a sort of tobacco honey – does not fit in these oppositions. Tobacco and honey appear to be on the same side of the opposition, as I will discuss below, and contrast with vegetable salt (burnt) and with coca powder (roasted). The meanings that these substances have for the People of the Centre and the uses they give to them in their discourse and practice can be fruitfully approached taking into consideration those oppositions that they themselves recognize. Although utilizing a structuralist language, my aim here is hermeneutic and ethnographic rather than seeking fundamental structures of the mind.

This paper discusses the uses and meaning of tobacco for the People of the Centre, relying mostly on insights from two elders: Kɨneraɨ (Hipólito Candre), an Ocaina-Witoto man who lived along the Igaraparaná River, introduced above, and Enokakuiodo (Oscar Román-Jitdutjaaño), who lives in the Middle Caquetá region, whom I will introduce in the next section.

Kɨneraɨ's advice on my smoking sprang from a fundamental view, which differs from contemporary non-indigenous beliefs concerning tobacco: a man *must* smoke and needs to know what smoking is for because tobacco *has a spirit*. In the pages that follow, I start with this central meaning in the first section, and follow with a discussion of the two closely associated substances that make up the tobacco paste: tobacco juice and vegetable salt. I then address the relationship between these and other substances in what I call the culinary space of the People of the Centre; by culinary space, I mean the set of technical processes and practices that ordain the two main spheres of production and consumption of substances: everyday meals (cassava bread, meat, starch drink and chilli sauce) and ritual substances (coca powder, tobacco paste and *manicuera* drink). On this basis I turn to the relation between tobacco, salt and honey to show a transformation from the opposition *dry* tobacco/*moist* honey, as posed by Lévi-Strauss, to the opposition *dry* salt/*moist* tobacco, in the case of the tobacco paste consumed by the People of the Centre. I conclude with a discussion of the technical processes of heating up and cooling down that define the basis of both tobacco's hazards (as articulated by Kɨneraɨ, above) and its healing power, encapsulated in the oration of the tobacco maker which ends the chapter.

Tobacco Woman

Enokakuiodo belongs to a Witoto Nɨpode clan. For most Witoto Nɨpode clans, tobacco belongs to women, and has its origins in the menstrual blood of the Tobacco Woman or the Woman of Abundance.[2] I have worked with Enokakuiodo and his family on the topic of vegetable salts for several years. Vegetable salts are extracted as the alkaline reagent for tobacco paste. When we first met in 1993, he told me the story of the Tobacco Woman, which I present here as it was narrated by his wife Alicia Sánchez, a Witoto woman (Figure 5.2).[3]

Figure 5.2 Alicia Sánchez. (Photograph by J.A. Echeverri, Yarí River, 1998.)

The myth begins with a hard-working woman, who appeared in dreams to a man who knew not of agriculture and eked a meagre existence in the forest eating only wild, uncultivated foods.[4] She appeared to the man during his dreams but would disappear again at dawn, returning to inside a little gourd, in which she was invisible. Then, Alicia said, the Tobacco Woman began to speak to the man: 'Man, receive me!

Man, it is for you that I came! Man, receive me well! You were also born for me; let us receive each other well.'

In order to capture her, he pretended to be asleep. When the woman passed in front of him, he grabbed her and did not let her go. She did not return to the little gourd and became like a person. That woman was tobacco. Alicia continued: 'This woman was indeed a hard worker; she planted many plants and fruit trees. She weeded under them; she cleaned under the manioc plants. That woman is a *kɨbaɨngo*, a hard-working woman.'

Then, envy reared its ugly face. The spirits of the mythological beings of the beginnings, whose visible manifestation in this world are game animals, were envious of humanity. The Tobacco Woman was 'raped' by those spirits and she no longer behaved as she used to. She could no longer live with the man and left his house. Alicia's husband, Enokakuiodo, explained this point, which Alicia glossed over: 'Formerly, the Mother was harmed. At this point [she said to the man]: "Man, this is none of your business, it is mine, it is I who was raped; but now I am searching; you are fine, you do not know".'

Before leaving, she told the man that she would return. For her to come back, he had to sweep the house and pile up the dirt by the foot of a peach palm. The man did as she demanded but she would not return. In dreams, she told him to look well into the dirt he had piled up. Watching carefully, he saw a little plant beginning to grow: it was a plant of tobacco. She taught him how to cook the tobacco leaves, how to add the vegetable slime to thicken it and how to process the vegetable salt to mix and produce tobacco paste. The Tobacco Woman told him that she would stay with him as tobacco paste. She had paramount power over all those who had attempted to debase her. She became a hunter, a devourer.

The strength Tobacco Woman had to look after and harvest cultivated plants was now turned into a hunting power against game animals.[5] The tobacco's power is her menstrual blood, represented in the tobacco paste.[6] Alicia explained: 'Then, tobacco means *blood*, it drains the filth in our body. A man must fast like that; he must fast for three days [his wife's menstrual period]: he works hard and does not sleep; in this way he fasts. It is a much forbidden thing.'[7] Enokakuiodo added: 'Then, [the evil spirits] fell into that menstrual flow; they were destroyed. As the story tells, the Mother accepted the seduction [of those evil spirits], but we, because we do not understand, we say that it is harmful for health.'

The last expression – harmful for health – was a deliberate reference to the caption that used to be written on the Colombian cigarette packages: *El tabaco es nocivo para la salud* ('Tobacco is harmful for health'). This caption disappeared in 2006, to be replaced with large photographs and captions explicitly portraying the purported dreadful consequences of tobacco smoking.

What is harmful is not tobacco, Enokakuiodo said, but the predatory capabilities of menstrual blood. This is what a man has to be careful of. Enokakuiodo further explained: 'At this point, now, it is the birth of tobacco. It is a woman. This is what a man cares about, this is what a man should avoid [women's menstrual blood], he guards that power.'[8] That female predatory capability targets all those evil beings that debased her. Enokakuiodo added: 'She devours everything, many bullet ants, many snakes, many illnesses; she devours them, yet no harm comes to her.' Bullet ants, snakes thorns, scorpions, spiders and illnesses are codified references to the plants from which vegetable salt is extracted (see Figure 5.3).

Figure 5.3 The Food of the Tobacco Woman: Salt. (Drawing by Oscar Román Muruy, Enokakuiodo's grandson, 2001.)

The tobacco decoction is mixed with those salts. We now turn to them.

Tobacco and salt: Blood and semen

That raped woman – tobacco – seeks revenge, Enokakuiodo explained; she is a devouring woman. This is menstruation: 'the poison that women have', he added. The process of preparing tobacco paste, where a vegetable slime and salts are added to the tobacco decoction, replicates the story of the Tobacco Woman.

Tobacco paste is prepared by boiling the fresh leaves of tobacco, prewashed with cold water. When the leaves have been thoroughly cooked – a process that may take more than a day – the whole decoction is strained to separate the pure juice of tobacco. This juice is brought to the boil again and simmered until it acquires a thick consistency and an intense purple colour. At this point the juice is mixed with a vegetal slime that serves as a thickening agent.[9] For the Witoto, this slime represents a pathogenic phlegm that, when found in the stomach, causes sleepiness; when in the throat, it impedes clear speaking. The very process of preparing the tobacco is understood to transubstantiate this phlegm into a component of the tobacco juice, rendering it harmless to people and 'defeating' it. Enokakuiodo explains: 'Then, inside our body, that phlegm is born. That is why it is mixed with the tobacco. One licks it [the tobacco paste], and it cleans the mouth and heals the throat.'[10]

After the slime is added, the cooking of the tobacco juice continues with much care, over a low flame, until the water evaporates and the paste becomes thick and elastic. The final product, a dark paste – a similar consistency to tar – is kept in a dry and warm place and can last for years (Figure 5.4). Each time it is consumed, a small gob of paste is mixed with a generous serving of vegetable salt.

The vegetable salts that are mixed with tobacco paste are made by burning plant material from a set of selected species, lixiviating the ashes by means of a filter, and dehydrating the resulting brine to obtain the dried salts (see Figure 5.5). Salt has a double meaning. On the one hand, it represents 'all the evils in this world', and in ritual discourse, it receives metaphorical names corresponding to harmful animals and elements of the forest. On the other, salt also represents the 'milk from the mother's breast', a substance purified by the process of burning and filtering (for a detailed explanation, see Echeverri et al. 2001; Echeverri and Román-Jitdutjaaño 2011; 2013).

Ash salts are mixed with tobacco paste (Figure 5.6); tobacco is the Mother, who defeated the evils of this world with her menstruation. Her menstrual blood swallows animals' spirits, a process of mixing that gives flavour and voice to the tobacco paste. This combination of substances is also explicitly compared to fecundation: ash salt is like semen and the tobacco paste is like menstrual blood.[11] Enokakuiodo explained: 'That salt [semen] seasons the tobacco [woman's blood]. "In the same way, when words are well seasoned, they are appealing", he [the Creator] said. On throwing it onto the woman, it was incorporated into her.'

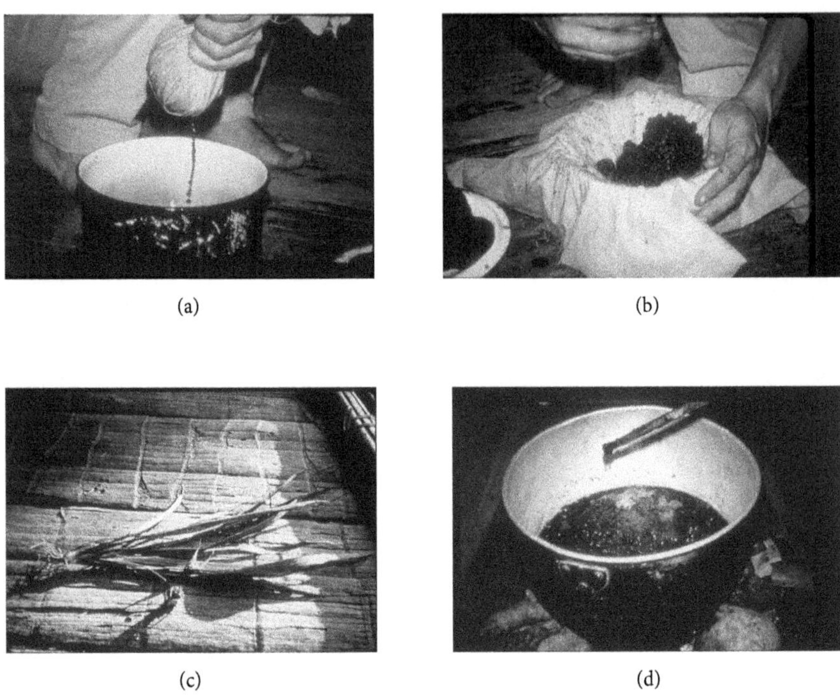

(a) (b) (c) (d)

Figure 5.4 Processing the tobacco paste: (a) filtering the tobacco juice; (b) squeezed tobacco leaves; (c) plant *Rapatea* sp. (*eraguai*) from which a slime is extracted to mix with the tobacco juice; (d) dehydrating tobacco juice mixed with the slime. (Photographs by O.L. Montenegro, Igaraparaná River, 1992.)

The vegetable salts fecundate the tobacco paste and make it speak, causing persons to speak well-seasoned speech. Salt-seasoned tobacco paste plays a central role in the ceremonial life of the People of the Centre. It is by means of a tobacco paste specifically enchanted for the purpose that a ritual master makes the formal invitations to his ceremonial allies. The host group of the ritual is in charge of the production of cultivated food, and the ceremonial duty of the allies is to bring forest game (representing illnesses that have been transubstantiated and rendered desirable) and perform the chants of the ritual. The tobacco paste has a significant exchange value: the ritual master uses it to 'pay' for both the work of the men and women of the host group and the ceremonial services (chants and game) of his ceremonial allies. Tobacco paste is also used in shamanry as a means of divination and as a weapon of attack and defence.

(a) (b) (c)

Figure 5.5 Processing the vegetable salt: (a) burning plant material; (b) filtering the ashes; (c) dehydrating the brine. (Photographs J.A. Echeverri, Yarí River, 1996.)

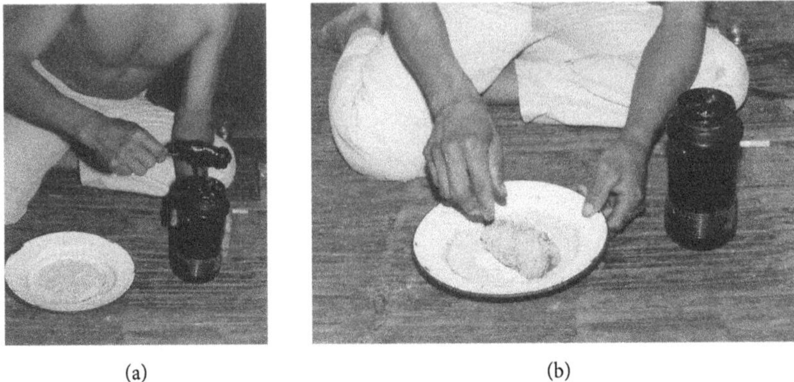

(a) (b)

Figure 5.6 Seasoning tobacco with vegetable salt (the salt is on the dish, and the pure tobacco paste is taken from the jar). (Photographs by J.A. Echeverri, Igaraparaná River, 1989.)

Tobacco paste is not only prepared by ritual specialists or shamans. Every adult man plants tobacco in his garden and prepares several kilos of tobacco paste for the year to come. He will extract vegetable salt and mix it with tobacco paste whenever he needs to treat an illness, go hunting, fell a new cultivated plot, take a trip or just to fill up his tobacco container, which is called *yerakɨ* in Witoto. This tobacco container is central in the dialogue between men. Men greet each other by offering and exchanging their tobacco paste and coca powder. The tobacco paste is an instrument for the formalization of agreements and transactions between men. The tobacco container is commonly referred as 'my wife' or 'my heart'.

Not only men possess and lick tobacco paste. Most women lick it and relish it mixed with a generous amount of vegetable salt. Women get their tobacco from their husbands, whom they usually actively help in the laborious process of harvesting and preparing the tobacco paste or from the tobacco 'payments' they receive for their work in the rituals. Children and youngsters also lick the tobacco paste that is given to them by adults. Youngsters who travel to the city to study carry specially blessed tobacco to protect them, help them in their studies and give them intelligence. Boys and girls who play sports also carry specially blessed tobacco paste to give them strength and defeat their opponents. Boys who like hunting or fishing likewise have their specially blessed tobacco paste to succeed in these activities.[12]

This form of tobacco use – tobacco paste mixed with ash salt – differs from other most widespread uses of tobacco in several crucial respects: it is a culinary product made by cooking and to that extent differs from inhaled or smoked tobacco, which Lévi-Strauss qualifies as supra-culinary; it is a moist substance consumed by licking, which contrasts with dry inhaled smoke and snuff; and, most importantly, its consumption requires a seasoning: vegetable salt. Tobacco paste thus fits squarely into the category of culinary products, to which we now turn.

The place of tobacco in the culinary space

By placing tobacco (paste) and coca (powder) in the culinary space of the People of the Centre, we want to stress that, in the natives' view, these substances are not conceived of as harmful and unhealthy 'drugs'. Rather, they are an integral part of the patterns of production and consumption of substances and of the production of bodies and persons.

Tobacco and coca are food, 'men's food', along with the everyday fare consumed by both women and men. Men produce tobacco and coca, women everyday food. The former substances are consumed mainly at night in a ritual setting, the latter are consumed mainly during the day in an everyday manner; each one has separate instruments and spaces for their processing, but both share the same technical processes and remarkably homologous notions about their adequate transformations and combinations.[13]

In People of the Centre's ordinary fare, there are four categories of foods: cassava bread, meat, chilli sauce, and manioc starch drink. These foodstuffs compose the core of everyday meals (Table 5.1). The two former are the main components, the two latter are complementary: the drink is drunk *after* the main meal (not simultaneously with it) and the chilli sauce is a seasoning of cassava bread and meat, and may take the place of meat if the latter is absent.

Cassava bread is made from toxic manioc which is cultivated by women, variously prepared by fermenting and pounding the tubers or grating them and extracting their starch, in both cases detoxifying the tubers; the resulting products are sifted and roasted. Meat is hunted or fished by men from wild sources, and prepared by women by boiling or grilling. The chilli sauce has a double seasoning process: a basic paste made from the poisonous juice of cultivated manioc (obtained during the preparation of cassava bread), flavoured first with (cultivated) chillies and afterwards with ants, insects and mushrooms, gathered by women from wild sources. The starch drink, prepared by women, combines starch, from cultivated manioc tubers, with a flavouring from fruits or honey, gathered by men from mainly wild sources. Table 5.1 synthesizes the sources of foodstuffs and the gender roles in their production.[14]

Table 5.1 Everyday foodstuffs.

Foodstuffs	Wild		Cultivated
	Male	Female	Female
Chilli sauce		Ants, mushrooms	Manioc juice (+ chillies)
Cassava bread			Manioc tubers
Meat	Game/fish		
Starch drink	Fruits/honey		Manioc starch

Ritual substances are of three sorts: coca powder, tobacco paste, and *manicuera* drink. Coca powder is prepared by roasting and pounding coca leaves, obtained from bushes cultivated by men, and mixing and straining them with the ashes from the leaves of a non-cultivated species. Tobacco is prepared by cooking tobacco leaves, cultivated by men, adding the gum from a wild species as a thickening agent, and seasoning it with salt obtained from wild plant species. The *manicuera* drink is elaborated by boiling down the poisonous juice of certain varieties of manioc (after the starch has been removed), cultivated and processed by women (see Table 5.2).

Table 5.2 Ritual substances.

Ritual substances	Cultivated		Wild
	Female	Male	Male
Tobacco paste		Tobacco syrup	Gum/ash salt
Coca powder		Coca leaves	Ashes
Manicuera drink	Manioc juice		

Both the *manicuera* drink and the meat are the result of the other gender's productive activity: male-obtained meat complements female foodstuffs, and female-cultivated and prepared *manicuera* drink complements male ritual substances. Also, there is a correspondence between the two main substances of each kind: chilli sauce and cassava bread, on the one hand, and tobacco paste and coca powder on the other. The technical and symbolic symmetries between coca powder and manioc bread have been pointed out by several researchers (Gasché 1971; Hugh-Jones 1979a; Karadimas 2005; Hugh-Jones 2007). Coca powder is 'men's cassava bread', writes Gasché (1971: 322–323), who points out that both are processed by pounding, straining and roasting, but in different order. The symmetries between tobacco paste and chilli sauce are also remarkable (cf. Hugh-Jones 1979a: 231–234). Tobacco and chilli are the only cultivated plants reproduced by seeds; the chilli sauce and the tobacco paste are produced by boiling and straining. Both are seasoned with wild substances, and both have the consistency of a thick, spicy syrup. 'Chilli sauce is women's tobacco paste', is a common expression.

This culinary space is structured by the two spheres that constitute society (and gender roles): the realm of women's labour on cultivated plots, where the bulk of non-meat food comes from, and the realm of male activity in the forest and the river – the main sources of 'meats'. In broad terms, these are the domains of reproductive consanguinity inside and affinity outside, and they are present at every level of the culinary space. I phrase this opposition as the divide between 'meat' and 'non-meat' foods. This distinction is indexed in indigenous discourse by two separate verbs: a person 'devours' *(rite)* meat and 'eats' *(guite)* non-meat. Meat and (non-meat) cassava bread are the components of the ordinary meals, just like tobacco and coca are the fundamental substances of ritual consumption.

Tobacco is associated with blood, as we saw above, and as such it belongs to the category of meat foods, and coca – 'men's cassava' – to non-meat. Coca and tobacco are the male equivalents of chilli sauce and cassava bread. The chilli sauce is licked, as is the tobacco paste, and is complemented with cassava bread in the same way in which tobacco paste is complemented with coca powder – the men's cassava.

Furthermore, both coca and tobacco are made up of meat and non-meat substances. The tobacco paste is composed of pure tobacco syrup processed by cooking the leaves of a cultivated plant, plus a vegetable salt obtained from the transformation of wild species. Coca is made by combining roasted and pounded leaves of the cultivated coca bush plus the ashes from the leaves of a non-cultivated species. The coca leaves and the tobacco syrup belong to the category of non-meat and the ashes and vegetable salt to the category of meat. This attribution is not only inferred from the cultivated and wild sources of each one, but it is also explicitly stated in discourse. The following excerpt clearly establishes the association between salt and meat:

meita ɨaibi	Then, that brine [meaning game]
fuui monifue urukɨ	will be, for the future generation,
taɨngojɨ fɨkaɨ *daaɨde afena*	the *complement* of their cassava bread.
nɨɨ nabedɨ ɨáibiza	This is the true brine;
baa fiia amena ibi nane daɨdɨkaɨ	that other [brine] is just the juice of a tree.
akie izoide ɨaibi kome abɨmo	In the same way, that brine is in our bodies,
ite kaɨmáre	as health.

This excerpt effectively details how brine (the base of vegetable salt) is game (meat), which is to be seasoned (and devoured) by tobacco (the Mother´s blood). Vegetable salt is obtained from the processing of wild plants, which come from the substances that the Creator cast out of his body in former times; those substances became, later on, vegetable and animal species. So, preparing salt is understood as killing an animal.

The quotation above introduces a fundamental concept of the culinary space: the adequate 'complementation' of meat-like substances with non-meat ones, expressed by the verb stem *fika-*. This verb has no straightforward translation into English or Spanish; it means to eat meat together with non-meat food.[15] In the following excerpt, Enokakuiodo explains how all the substances that the Creator cast out of his body into the world were to become the Mother's *fikariya* (the complement of her bread). Here again, salt = meat:

bebene nɨɨe mamena iidɨ bibi ɨaibi	Up here, this brine is against all those evil beings.
monifue jaabe daaɨiye monifue urukɨ	For the future generations it will be food,
fuuiadɨ fɨkáriye *mamériye daɨna*	later on they will *complement* their bread with it.

jáaeita badáaiitade	Formerly, it was evil,
bebénemo aiyi ñúe finoka	but up here it has been processed.
kue finoka daaide	'I processed it', [the Creator] says,
éiñoka fikari	'for the Mother to *complement* her bread'.

This complementation is attached to the proper construction of a person. To be well complemented is also to be well purified: *niiena fikaka, niiena ikofe* ('it is well *complemented*, it is like a strainer'). Straining separates and purifies; all processed substances (tobacco, coca, salt, cassava bread and chilli sauce) go through filtering (straining, sifting). The bottom of a strainer, charged with purified substance, is a conventional image for knowledge and experience; the pairing of combining with straining reinforces the idea that the axis of combination is made up of the most culturally elaborated and fully processed products – persons.

On the side of meat, we find the two foremost female and male substances: chilli sauce and tobacco paste; and on the side of non-meat, we find their complements: cassava bread and coca. Four verbs are employed to denote the consumption of these foods (see Figure 5.7).

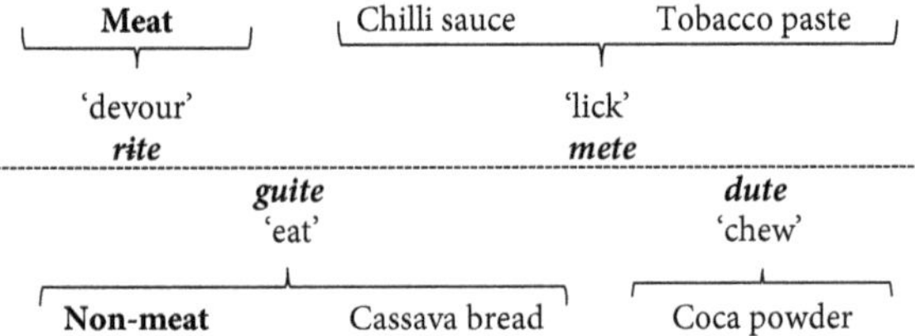

Figure 5.7 Verbs for consuming meat and non-meat foods.

On the meat side, the chilli sauce and the tobacco paste are both 'licked', whereas meat is 'devoured'; on the side of non-meat, the cassava bread is 'eaten' as are most non-meat foods – rice, plantains, corn, grains, excepting fruits – whereas only coca is 'chewed'.[16]

The verb 'to lick' *(mete)* is also used for the consumption of two key substances: salt and honey, to which we now turn.

Salt and honey

Honey and salt both come from vegetables. Lévi-Strauss (1973) already remarked that honey is considered a vegetable in many native taxonomies. Indeed, in the work we conducted on the species known to the Witoto to produce salt, we identified 57 plant species and one species of wild bee, which would seem to confirm it (Echeverri and Román-Jitdutjaaño 2011: 501, 2013: 8). The everyday and ceremonial position of honey in the lives of the People of the Centre seems to be inversely related to the everyday and ceremonial centrality of the tobacco paste (a tobacco 'honey'). To explore this relationship between honey and tobacco paste I will introduce two complementary myths narrated by Enokakuiodo, which I summarize next: the myths of the Salt Man and of the Honey Man (collected in March 1996, transcribed from Witoto and translated by S. Roman and J.A. Echeverri):

The Salt Man

After the spirit of Kudibini (an evil mythological character) was burnt, the Salt Man arrived to Maniyama's and lived with his daughter. He lived with her and did sorcery with the ash salt.

When he prepared ash salt, he burned himself in the fire. In this manner he would prepare salt and bring it home. His wife and relatives licked it and became ill.

His brother-in-law followed him. He saw how the Salt Man cleaned the place, piled up firewood, started the fire and when it was well lit, he jumped into it. When everything was reduced to ashes, the Salt Man would stand up again and would say, 'This salt is to pollute the mouth of Maniyama's daughter'.

The brother-in-law told it to his father. His father prepared a magical stick and gave it to him. The brother-in-law followed again the Salt Man, and after he jumped into the fire, the brother-in-law scattered the ashes with the magically prepared stick. In this manner, he destroyed the Salt Man.

The explosion of the Salt Man's entrails fell as the tree *jameda* (*Gustavia hexapetala*), and his image is a small toucan, who sings *oi, oi* (brother-in-law, brother-in-law).

The Honey Man

The Salt Man's brother, the Honey Man, arrived to Maniyama's, seeking revenge for the death of his brother. He lived with Maniyama's daughter and, like his brother, did sorcery with honey.

To collect honey he hit his forehead to make it bleed, and gave it to his family as honey. By licking it, they became ill.

They discovered what he had done, and his brother-in-law told his sister, 'This is no true honey; it is blood he gets by hitting his forehead. This is why we are ill'.

The Honey Man invited his brother-in-law to clear the underbrush. There, they saw a beehive that the Honey Man had magically prepared, and they both collected the honey. 'This is how I collect honey', the Honey Man said to his brother-in-law. Later on, the Honey Man invited his brother-in-law to fell the forest, and again he magically prepared a beehive in a tree. When the sun was in its highest, they perforated the hive. 'This is honey', the Honey Man said, 'where is the blood? Perhaps you were dreaming!' Maniyama's son began to lick honey. 'This is not the good honey', the Honey Man said, 'climb farther inside the tree'. When the brother-in-law got deeper into the hive, the Honey Man locked him up inside the tree.

Therein, that man became a little frog, who speaks *oi, oi* (brother-in-law, brother-in-law).

The two stories are remarkably complementary. Their sociological 'armature', to use Lévi-Strauss's (1973) expression, is identical – a conflict between affines. Their respective heroes are two brothers who marry, one after the other, the same woman and enter in conflict with the same brother-in-law. This identical armature is shown by those elements shared by both myths, which appear at the centre of Figure 5.8. The content of each myth is the systematic transformation of the other, with inverted outcomes: in one case, the hero is destroyed by the brother-in-law and in the other, the brother-in-law is punished by the hero; the Salt Man is scattered around in one myth, and the brother-in-law is locked up in the other; the former turns into a bird and the latter into a small frog. Figure 5.8 summarizes the comparison:

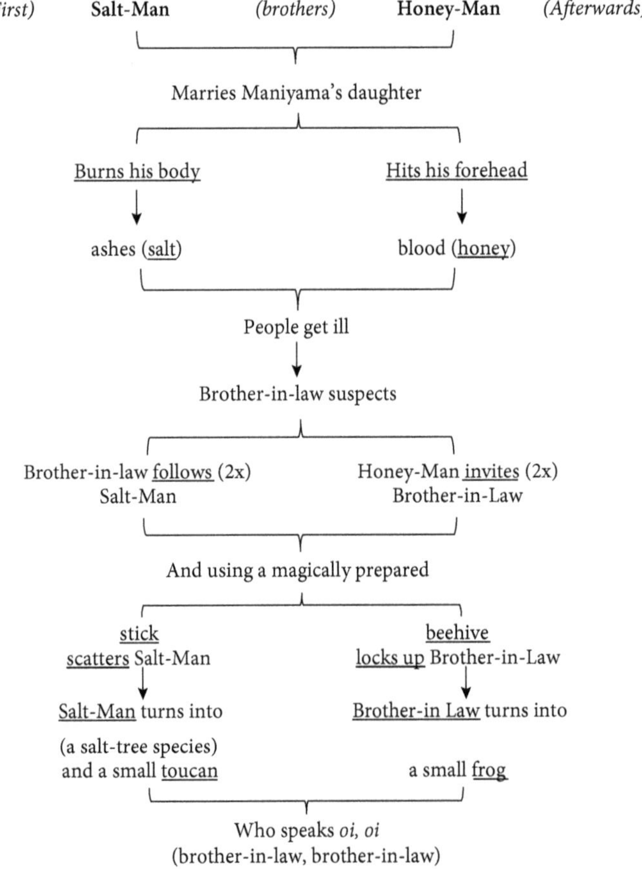

Figure 5.8 Comparison of the myths of Salt Man and Honey Man.

I will not attempt a complete interpretation of these two myths but will just pick up a few clues to try to understand the relation of moist (licked or drunk) and dry (smoked or inhaled) tobacco, through the mediation of honey and salt.

Both the Salt Man and the Honey Man prepared evil, poisonous versions of valued substances: salt and honey. The salt of the Salt Man came from his own body, was poisonous and had the objective of harming his in-laws; in contrast, the actual vegetable salt comes from the substances of the body of the Father Creator (source of the plant species in this world) and has the objective of capturing the mythological beings of the beginnings. The honey of the Honey Man came from his own blood, and was a poison against his in-laws, just like the actual tobacco is the blood (menstruation) of the Tobacco-Woman, aimed against the evil mythological beings of the beginnings. I summarize these clues in Table 5.3.

Table 5.3 Correspondences Salt-Salt and Honey-Tobacco.

	Myth's evil ***Salt***	**Proper** ***Salt***	**Myth's evil** ***Honey***	**Proper** ***Tobacco***
Source	Salt Man's body	Father creator's body	Honey Man's blood	Tobacco Woman's menstruation
Aimed against	In-laws	Mythological beings	In-laws	Mythological beings

What this simple comparison reveals is that the evil salt of the myth corresponds with the proper salt extracted nowadays and that the evil honey of the myth corresponds not with the actual honey consumed today but with the tobacco paste currently used. This is confirmed by the most remarkable opposition between the two myths: *dry* salt and *moist* honey, which is a transformation of the opposition *dry* tobacco (smoked or inhaled) and *moist* honey, in the myths studied by Lévi-Strauss, and *dry* salt and *moist* tobacco, in the culinary space.

This pair of myths serve as a transitional stage in the transformation of the place of tobacco from *dry* tobacco/*moist* honey to *dry* salt/*moist* tobacco. In other words, tobacco comes to occupy the position of honey, and salt the position of tobacco, as shown next:

Dry	**Moist**	
Tobacco	Honey	Myths of honey and smoked and inhaled tobacco (Lévi-Strauss)
Salt	**Honey**	**Myths of the Salt Man and the Honey Man**
Salt	Tobacco	Culinary space

It amounts to an inversion of the position of tobacco, mediated by honey and salt. This may shed light on the different ethnographic meaning of honey for the groups of the southern part of the continent, where honey is relished and the object of special festivals (cf. Lévi-Strauss 1973: 69 and passim), while for the People of the Centre honey is never consumed raw and has no comparable ritual importance. In contrast, a tobacco 'honey' is central in the ceremonial organization of the People of the Centre.

For the People of the Centre, only honey from two species of bees is deemed proper for consumption; the honey of other species of bees and wasps is not licked. Honey is never consumed raw but only boiled and mixed with other drinks/liquids. In some cases honey can be seasoned into the manioc starch drink. One of the main reasons that people do not drink raw honey is that it is considered to be blood. This association is clear in the interpretation of dreams; according to Kɨneraɨ: 'A dream of licking honey means you will suffer an injury' (Candre-Kɨneraɨ and Echeverri 1996: 59).

The aim of the consumption of tobacco and coca by a man is to care and heal his children, his wife and his cultivated plants. To heal is to cool down. Tobacco is a strong and hot substance, but also – through processing – a cool breath with healing power.

Conclusion: The oration of tobacco

All the substances in the culinary space are the result of three fundamental technical processes: heating, pounding and filtering. Of the three, heating is the main transformation. Tobacco is made by boiling the leaves of the plant; coca is processed through the roasting the leaves over a fire; all the products of manioc are made through fire processes: chilli sauce is boiled, just like tobacco; manioc bread is roasted over fire, just like the coca leaves; ash salt is made by burning vegetable material and the filtered brine is desiccated over fire. Finally, the *manicuera* drink is the result of boiling the juice of manioc, the starch drink is made by stirring manioc starch into boiling water; and honey – also – needs to be boiled to make it drinkable.

Fire has a transforming and humanizing power. In Enokakuiodo's discourse, fire is named as the Mother and, like tobacco, it is a devourer, a meat-eater. Fire is the founder of horticulture, the one that transforms the natural forest into cultivated plots, the one who decontaminates game meat, poisonous cassava and wild forest species, making them edible and healthy. Fire turns the natural into the humane and the harmful into the edible. This Fire-Mother is also the base of knowledge and wisdom – the wisdom of knowing nothing – as Enokakuiodo states: 'I know nothing, it is the Mother [fire] who prepares, it is the Mother who devours, the Mother does know about devouring. I know nothing, I only suckle from her breast, her breast is all I know. On the Mother's chest I am lying down.' What is crucial here is the coincidence of tobacco and fire. Both are female devourers of evil for the benefit of man, who only has to 'lie down' on her breast. She is a devouring fire against the evil beings and a resting place for man. She is hot and she is cool; it is a cool fire.

The description above brings us back to the start of this chapter. Kɨneraɨ's point about my tobacco smoking was that it was heating up my body; it was not about tobacco damaging my lungs or that it was a hazard that could cause me cancer. When, later on, Kɨneraɨ confided to me what he called 'the most fundamental oration of tobacco', I was left rather unimpressed. I imagined that such a fundamental incantation would refer to magical forces or give name to powerful spirits. Instead, the core of its images and wording were technical and culinary processes. He explained to me that the very basis of the healing power of tobacco was contained in the processes of making tobacco, salt and coca and particularly in the recurring process of heating up and cooling down. It took me years to begin to understand the meaning and power of this oration in all its concrete simplicity.

I will present this oration shortly, but let me first take from it a few leads about the use and meaning of tobacco for the People of the Centre. All the substances of the culinary space are meant to raise children and to construct true persons, but all of them are strong and hot and thus potentially harmful – particularly tobacco, salt and coca. It is the technical processes of heating, filtering and pounding that render them harmless to real people and furthermore beneficial or indeed necessary. Those technical processes are images of bodily processes and inducers of bodily conditions. Kɨneraɨ explained that preparing tobacco, coca and salt generates a healing capacity in the heart of the tobacco maker through the embodiment of those processes and particularly in the alternation of heating up and cooling down. I do not believe that Kɨneraɨ was worried because people smoke cigarettes – 'a man *must* smoke', he said – but rather, he was concerned with youngsters who do not know how to take care of (cool down) their wife (tobacco) and their children (coca and cassava).

Here is the incantation for making tobacco, the basis of the fundamental blessing for tobacco healing, narrated by Kɨneraɨ in April 1992. He pointedly noted that tobacco leaves are boiled for hours; they get very hot but finally they cool down. Ash salt is burned; it is on fire for hours, then gets reduced to ashes and cools down. Afterwards, the ashes are filtered with water and the resulting brine is put to boil; it gets very hot until it dries up and then it cools down. The coca leaves are toasted over the fire; they get very hot, until they dry up and cool down; the dry Cecropia leaves are made to burn; they flame up intensely and it looks frightening, but then it all cools down. Now, the pounded coca leaves are seasoned with the Cecropia ashes and strained together to obtain the coca powder; on the other hand, the vegetable salt is seasoned into the pure tobacco paste. Then, Kɨneraɨ continues (Candre-Kɨneraɨ and Echeverri 1996: 183, 185):

> Once it is mixed, he licks it [the tobacco paste]. After licking it, he puts a little coca powder in his mouth. In the mouth, the coca feels sweet and delicious, the heart bursts

> forth and gets healed. At this point – now truly – his breath is cool and sweet. Now, on the other hand, these words can be used as a healing spell. The breath of cooling down tobacco and cooling down coca is received in the heart as a healing spell – breath of tobacco, breath of coca. This is what the maker of tobacco heard in his heart, and it remained as a healing spell. A spell to cool down, a spell of our birth. In that manner this spell is received. Here, it concludes.

Acknowledgements

This chapter is based on a paper presented at the symposium 'The Changing Landscape of Tobacco Use in Lowland South America' (Durham University, 25–26 July 2013). Attendance to the symposium was made possible by a Santander Mobility grant and the support of Durham University, for which I am thankful. I thank Andrew Russell and Elizabeth Rahman, conveners of the symposium and editors of this book, for their careful editing, and Carlos David Londoño-Sulkin for his comments and criticism on a previous draft of this chapter.

Notes

1. The consumption of coca (*Erythroxylum coca* var. *ipadu*) in the form of a finely pound and strained powder mixed with ashes may have been adopted in post-Columbian times by the People of the Centre and is perhaps no older than the nineteenth Century, as suggested by linguistic, botanical and ethnohistorical evidence (Echeverri and Pereira 2005). Coca was incorporated into an already existing ritual complex where the use of tobacco was central.
2. In the 1990s, I witnessed a most peculiar series of debates among several elders of the People of the Centre about the 'gender' of tobacco; for some groups (two Muinane and some Witoto clans and the Andoque group) tobacco would be male, whereas for others (two other Muinane clans, and most Witoto Nɨpode clans) tobacco would be female. Carlos D. Londoño writes about the Muinane: '[T]here were differences between clans and language groups concerning the gender of tobacco itself: for some, the sweat-*cum*-seminal substance of the Grandfather of Tobacco was the origin of the Land of the Centre .... For others, the tobacco deity was the Mother upon whose shoulder the creator god created the land and placed it' (Londoño-Sulkin 2012: 97). This divergence remarkably appeared even between two sibling men of the same Muinane clan (cf. Londoño 2004). Fernando Urbina, a Colombian philosopher and collector of oral narratives from Muinane and Witoto, writes likewise: 'In my field journals there appear statements, taken from diverse knowledgeable men, of this kind: "In the Muinane tradition, coca is woman, while tobacco is man; among us, Witoto, it is the contrary"' (Urbina 2010: 145).

3. I transcribed and translated this version of the myth narrated by Alicia Sánchez from the sound track of the documentary *Ambíl y coca* ('Tobacco paste and coca'), recorded by her son Romualdo Román (available at http://www.youtube.com/watch?v=gZDuDvyBIyI). Thomas Griffiths recorded a similar story, in general outline, from a Witoto Nɨpode elder in Araracuara (Griffiths 1998: 298–300).
4. In this myth, tobacco is associated with the origins of horticulture. It is the Tobacco Woman who brings the knowledge not only to plant, but also to *process* cultivated plants (further below, I discuss the association of tobacco with fire, as a transforming and processing power, and its relation with culinary techniques). Wilbert argues that there are reasons to think that the cultivation of tobacco initiated at the same time that horticulture, and that tobacco may have been the oldest cultigen in the Americas (Wilbert 1994: 47).
5. Barbira Freedman (2010: 143), in an article about shamanic plants and gender, writes: 'The predatory imagery of shamanism is predominantly male, drawn from both hunting and warfare. Shamans heal by removing pathogenic "darts" from patients' bodies and they harm or kill by sending "darts" into their enemies' bodies. Hunting also involves the seduction of the game animals that are to become prey, with an imagery of sexual seduction.' This view contrasts with the hunting power of tobacco derived from women's menstruation, as narrated by Alicia and Enokakuiodo. Further on, she states (Barbira Freedman 2010: 151) 'Tobacco is considered to be the male catalyst that enhances the effects of all other shamanic plants. Lamista Quechua shamans frequently assert that tobacco is the "father of all plants", a male consort to the "mother spirits" of all shamanic plants'. Here, we have an interesting ideological divide between tobacco as a male hunting power and tobacco as female menstrual poison, which corresponds to a divide between the groups that use 'dart shamanism' and those who do not (as the People of the Centre). Female origins of tobacco are also narrated in other Amerindian traditions: in the mythology of the Pilagá Indians of the Chaco region, tobacco was originated from the ashes of the pubic hairs of a cannibal woman, killed by a cultural hero (Idoyaga Molina 2000: 210); and among the Yaqui, tobacco came into existence through the metamorphosis of an ugly woman (Kelley and Holden 1991: 95; Goodman 1993: 24).
6. Fausto writes about the relationship between tobacco and blood in an article about Parakanã shamanism, but in a different sense. He refers to the way a person becomes a shaman by eating like a jaguar (that is becoming a cannibal): 'Killing is conceived as a form of symbolic hematophagy because it is said that it "makes the killer's mouth smell of blood"' (2004: 161).
7. 'To fast' *(fɨmaide)* means following special dietary and other behavioural prescriptions. A man 'fasts' from his wife's menstrual period (and also the days after childbirth) by avoiding sexual contact with her, staying awake and busy working, consuming little food, and avoiding rage.
8. The expression 'nɨɨ ɨima rɨñénano', which I translate as 'this is what a man should avoid [women's menstruation]', literally means 'this is the meat a man should not eat'. It was a deliberate reference by Enokakuiodo to some Baptist preachers

who had been speaking of fasting from meat as a way to draw closer to God. For Enokakuiodo, those religious messages of 'not eating meat' – very much as those of 'not smoking tobacco' in public health policy – were misguided; the real 'sin' – and health hazard – is to indulge in sexual intercourse with a woman during her menstrual period.

9. Most commonly used species to obtain the slime are: *Rapatea* sp. (*eraguaɨ, baitokorɨ*); a vine of the Mapigiaceae family *(marakɨo)*; the pulp of the immature fruits of *Theobroma bicolor (mɨzeyɨ)*; the bark of *jɨko amena* (indet. tree: 'jaguar tree'); or manioc starch, when nothing else is available. Thomas Griffiths lists a few other species used as thickening agents by the Witoto Nɨpode (Griffiths 1998: 127). These species have no known phytopharmacological properties, with the exception of *jɨko amena*, which can cause intoxication and is 'used by ritual specialists and captains only' (Griffiths 1998: 127).
10. Irving Goldman, in a book on Cubeo religious thought, presents a spell for curing the pain in the throat, which also shows the relationship of tobacco with phlegm: 'There are two small grubs, one is red and one is white … He who is blowing turns the phlegm into two balls that are good and cool and sweet. The insect has tobacco and blows on the two little balls of phlegm and breaks them up and puts them aside … We are speaking of the little red fly, which sucks in the vine called *othyaime*. This vine has a raspy substance, which he is removing … He sucks away the phlegm. He takes away the pain from the throat and leaves it cool and sweet and renews us' (Goldman 2004: 343–344). It is by means of tobacco that the insect dries up the phlegm in the throat; the spell makes the analogy with the sucking of the raspy substance of the vine. It is remarkable that some of the slimes for tobacco used by the People of the Centre are obtained from vines, and that the combination of the tobacco with the slime is represented as the drying up of the phlegm in the throat.
11. Thomas Griffiths writes: 'Vegetable salt plants were the primeval hiding place of malevolent animals who plotted against the parental divinities and the Divine Son. Plants collected as a source of vegetable salt are identified in *rapue* [ceremonial discourse] as the "brain" of game animals to be eaten by the maternal divinity. In this context, people who set off to extract vegetable salt plant material sometimes remark that they are "going hunting"' (Griffiths 1998: 133).
12. The oration or blessing of the tobacco paste is performed by means of a chant, whistled (not sung aloud) over the tobacco by a specialist or a knowledgeable man or woman, right after the tobacco paste is mixed with the salt. These orations or blessing chants (*jɨɨra* in Witoto; *oración* or *conjura* in Spanish) are not public as are the chants performed in the rituals, they have a characteristic melodic pattern, and refer to properties and characteristics of animals, plants or natural phenomena that the person in charge of the oration wills to instil onto the tobacco paste – and by extension on the person who will lick it.
13. As discussed in the Introduction (this volume), Hugh-Jones (2007) distinguishes ordinary foodstuffs ('foods') and ritual substances ('non-foods') in Barasana society. The ordinary fare of the People of the Centre is much the same as that of the Barasana. Both groups share the use of coca, but they differ in that the former

use tobacco paste instead of cigars or snuff; nor do they drink *yagé* or alcoholic beverages. Hugh-Jones remarks that 'food' and 'non-food' 'are covert categories not verbally labelled in local languages' (2007: 64, n.16).

14. The most complete and insightful account of the technical processing of foods and its relation to cosmology and the production of persons is C. Hugh-Jones's Barasana ethnography (Hugh-Jones 1979a: 169 ff.). Her observations about Barasana processing of manioc equally apply to the People of the Centre.
15. Hugh-Jones mentions a similar concept among the Barasana people: 'Those who eat fish or game without manioc bread are severely reprimanded and told that they must combine meat and bread together' (2007: 57). He adds that the verb employed in this context is *ɨko-*, 'which has the connotation of mixing to produce some effect', and that in its nominal form, *ɨko*, 'refers to the leaf-ash added to coca and tobacco snuff to give it potency'. In the Muinane language, the prescription to children is *giraano midívehi* 'we mix big'; he verb *dívehi* refers to taking bites of manioc bread between bites of meat, fish, broth, or other meat food (C.D. Londoño-Sulkin, personal communication).
16. The coca powder is not actually 'chewed', but packed firmly inside the cheeks, where it slowly dissolves in the saliva.

6

Tobacco and Water: Everyday Blessings

Elizabeth Rahman

Introduction

For northwestern Amazonian Xié river dwellers of Brazil, tobacco is an ubiquitous plant. After dark, tobacco smoke pervades the communal house where men sit together and enjoy a smoke after supper. Visitors are also invited to roll a cigarette from the pouch of commercial tobacco (P. *Fumo Extra Forte Coringa*)[1] left on the table, together with the pages of a school exercise book that are used for rolling papers.[2]

Smoking tobacco is pervasive among men, after intra and inter-communal feasts and festivities, and older women may also share a cigarette in their company. Young children are sometimes asked to suck on and light cigarettes for their grandmothers to smoke, and I witnessed a four-year old, who had determinedly taken up the habit of his own accord, covertly smoking the butt-ends of discarded rolled cigarettes. Masticated tobacco leaves are also periodically applied to open and infected wounds to 'cool' them and thereby enhance the healing process. However, Xié river dwellers' primary interest is in smoking tobacco. This is true even among those lower-Xié river-dwelling evangelical communities whose doctrine prohibits smoking (Wright 2013: 176), but where male adolescents, I observed, continue covertly to smoke.

Roughly 850 persons live in manioc garden sites (P. *sitios*) and larger communities (P. *comunidades*)[3] dispersed along the stretch of the river Xié, a minor tributary which runs nearly parallel to the great Rio Negro, adjacent to the border with Colombia and Venezuela. I spent a year living on the mid-Xié river island-village community of Caranguejo,[4] together with my husband Carlos and my son, who turned five in the field. Our daughter, Sofia, was born in the field and subject to the same caring practices that I describe in this chapter. Xié river dwellers are composed of a range of ethnic heritages, but the Arawakan Warekena are considered the river's original inhabitants and most people identify themselves as Warekena. These people speak the lingua franca Géral,[5] Portuguese and a little

Warekena. Henceforth, words in Géral are prefixed with 'G.', words in Portuguese 'P.' and words in Warekena, 'W.'[6]

In the middle of the Xié river lie the enchanted waterfall rapids of Cumatí, and these form an important geopolitical divide between up-river Catholics and down-river evangelical communities. The affines of both tend to be from other Xié communities, but also include Arawakan groups from the Içana (Baníwa) and lower Rio Negro rivers (Baré), as well as other ethnicities. Elsewhere in Amazonia, tobacco lubricates relations between kin and more distant members of the same ethnicity (see Reig, this volume), but along the Xié it is mainly sourced from passing river merchants for which it is exchanged for manioc flour or forest derived products, such as the liana *cipó* (*Heteropsis flexuosa*) and the fibrous piassava palm (*Leopoldinia piassaba*), in the long-established system of debt-patronage (see Meira 1994). Why buy tobacco when they can cultivate it? The fault lay with their affines, I was told, who – once again – had neglected to share their tobacco and bring cuttings for them to plant.

Despite the dearth of tobacco proper along the Xié, *tauari* abounds. *Tauari* (*Couratari guianensis*) bark is used to produce home-made rolling papers. The *tauari* tree grows in seasonally water-logged lakes. Particular trees are designated as suitable according to their maturity, in regard to the quality of the bark and with sufficient time given for the bark to heal from previous extracts taken. The bark is sheared off the tree with a machete (see Figure 6.1, a) and then cut at a 45 degree angle so that a sharp point forms at the tip (b). The tip is then beaten with a stump, with the bark separating to form hundreds of wafer thin sheets of paper (c). These are then thoroughly washed in the river (d). As part of this process, the red pigmentation of the inner bark diminishes – as does its intense bitterness – and they are then left to dry in the sun. While commercialized rolling papers suffice for men's smoking, I was told that *tauari* papers are still and indeed 'should be' used for tobacco smoke blessings. Interestingly, in ritual contexts, it is *tauari*, rather than tobacco (G. *pitima*), that forms the linguistic basis for smoking: W. *umutauari*.[7] *Umutauari* is explained as 'blowing to cure', a process facilitated by the person conducting the 'blessing', the spell-blower or 'blesser' (P. *benzedor*).

Tobacco smoke blessings are performed by a blesser, an elder normally from a high-ranking sib (cf. Wright 2004: 104 on *mutawari*, 'chant-owner'). They involve the inhalation of smoke held in the mouth and then intentionally blown over the participant together with a muttered spell. Tobacco smoke blessings form an integral part of good care practices employed during pregnancy, childbirth, post-partum, during infancy and in early childhood, both for the perinatal family and for the infant itself. They are used as both a quotidian preventative health-care measure, throughout gestation, at the moment of birth, a week post-birth and throughout weaning; and as a curative, healing one, when infants suffer fright. The fact that infants are the special subjects of tobacco-blowing rituals has been noted by several other regional ethnographers (also this volume), and has been referred to as a form of 'involuntary

Figure 6.1 The processing of *tauari* (*Couratari guianensis*) to make rolling papers. (Artistically modified photograph taken by Elizabeth Rahman.)

smoking' with suggested narcotic effects (Wilbert 1987: 143). For Xié dwellers, however, tobacco alone is not understood to provoke an acute or ecstatic 'altered state' of consciousness (cf. Wilbert 1972; Gow 2013) or to have narcotic effects such as those experienced by a *pajé* (shaman), who in other contexts is described as 'drunk' when taking the psychoactive snuff *pariká* (*Virola calophylloidea*)[8] for divinatory diagnostic purposes.[9] But when it comes to curing, *pajés* still use tobacco spell-blowing as part of their healing repertoire for adults. This type of 'passive' or 'involuntary' smoking is seen to have a much more subtle effect.

This account of smoked tobacco takes perinatal smoke-blown blessings as its focus and attempts to consider tobacco in terms closest to Xié dwellers' – and other Amerindians' – own experiences and idioms of smoking. Tobacco is consistently cited as having the specific, highly valued, properties of repressing hunger, enhancing alertness, and lending qualities of lightness, levity and translucence to the consumer (e.g. Viveiros de Castro 1992: 131, 219; Wilbert 1987). This set of qualities is also recognized by pharmacological studies of the plant where they appear as an important manifestation of its psychoactive components; but they are also indigenous values actively cultivated outside the contexts of tobacco use (Santos-Granero 2012; Londoño-Sulkin 2012). Further, and specifically in northwestern Amazonia, tobacco is said to be cooling, drying, firming-hardening (Wright 1993) and 'closing' (Wright 2013: 87) and among Xié dwellers these properties, with the exception of drying, are also applied to water. These latter desirable characteristics are all specifically cited in the context of optimal neonatal growth and development and they appear more 'somatic' in that they relate more ostensibly to the cultivation of corporalities. From a Xié dwellers' perspective, tobacco and water blessings aid the drying out, firming up, closing off and cooling down of babies who are said to be leaky (they can't control their orifices), limp (they can't sit or stand up properly) and hot (suffer more from the heat than adults do). These qualities form part of the heated vitalities of infants. In order for them to grow and develop properly, they must be carefully regulated and controlled, and tobacco and water are key substances used to achieve this.

From all accounts tobacco blessings are an important, on-going component in the fabrication of body-persons and this is especially true in the development and growth of young infants. An existent literature examines the necessity of on-going hands-on care and the use of specific techniques, especially during infancy, as part of the fabrication of the 'mindful and relational bodies' of Amerindians (Vilaça 2005: 447; see for example Lagrou 2000: 160, on massage and moulding; Ewart 2000: 287–288, on tweaking; Belaunde 2001: 51, on surgical incisions). But tobacco and water, which are so salient to personal growth among Xié river dwellers, have remained absent from these discussions of perinatal person-making.

Tobacco smoke and water have remained elusive subjects perhaps because they are assumed to be 'just there', constant yet ephemeral, but also relatively intangible. As such these substances are assumed not to be subject to specific, bodily, techniques.

However, as I describe in this chapter, tobacco blessings and baby washing, when carefully executed, are precisely those nurturing acts that make babies grow and develop properly, maintaining them in good health. Taking this notion seriously, this chapter looks more closely at the specific techniques of use that render tobacco and water capable – as Xié dwellers contend – of having a positive, health-promoting effect.

Wakeful self-control, and self-domestication in the context of personal autonomy, consistently surface in the literature as near pan-Amerindian values (Overing 1989a,b). However, other than important insights into the idiom of sitting as a meditative, cool-minded capacity (Århem et al. 2004: 184, 200, 205, 215; S. Hugh-Jones 2009: 47–48) and the fact of hands-on 'mindful' care (Overing and Passes 2000), little research has been done on mindfulness as a cultivated state. Focusing not just on the everyday but on the minutiae of everyday performance, this chapter contends that tobacco blessings constitute mindful acts and that it is the minutiae of attention cultivated during these blessings that renders the substances of tobacco and water both health-promoting and body-making. This necessitates a more precise understanding of the term mindful as both a descriptor of the quality of a practice (as has already been employed in Amerindia) and as a concept (i.e. mindfulness).[10]

Mindfulness and techniques used to induce mindful states are not devoid of socio-ecological context, and for Xié dwellers, they unfold within the carefully negotiated dialectics of maintaining a mean-time equilibrium between the states of cool (but not too cool), dry (but not brittle) and hard (but not rigid) as socio-psychosomatic, personal qualities. This equilibrium, I contend, can be maintained if substances, plants, people and things are related to mindfully. This mindfulness, I argue, is cultivated in tobacco smoke blessings and describes how tobacco acts as a catalyst (Hugh-Jones 2007: 60–61; Barbira Freedman 2010: 115) that intersects substances, actively binding them together. In this way, tobacco lends body to human persons. I shall return to mindfulness as a useful heuristic device subsequently, but I wish first to focus on the ethnographic context that led me to this conclusion.

Tobacco, water and blood: Perinatal and early infant tobacco blessings

For Xié river dwellers, tobacco smoke blessings form part of a repertoire of techniques used to guide the emergence of hot (G. *saku*), limp (P. *molhe*) and humid neonates (G. *taina piranga*, lit. red child), to more (but not exclusively) cool, firm (G. *santo*, P. *duro*) and dry (G. *otipáua*, without fluids) social and personal states. Among neighbouring affines the Baníwa, with whom the Warekena share many similarities, newborns are completely 'open' and vulnerable to spirit attacks. The tobacco cigar and accompanying orations close, and sweeten, the body (Wright 2013: 87).[11] Thus tobacco smoke, among its other virtues which I go onto discuss, affords a coolness and dryness that mediates the volatile state of babies in extreme and leaky dampness. As the name of the baby's body suggests (G. *pira-miri*; *pira[á]* = body/fish; *miri* = little), this development from damp and limp to dry and firm is understood as an emergence from the river's water (lit. red water) to the land and is reflected in myth, both along the Xié and elsewhere (cf. S. Hugh-Jones 1979).

Rather than a radical shift from wet water to dry land however, the baby's emergence as a human being is brought about through a series of carefully executed – mindful – actions that mediate the transition. The execution of these actions facilitates the processual development of a strong, firm and purposeful (G. *kirimbawa*, P. *forte*) adult person, whose 'fish body' (G. *pira miri*) has become 'our body' (G. *pira yane*). However, even grown-up bodies, including those of 'hot' pregnant women who are full of blood (W. *tuya wemi*, lit. water women) must manage their personal states in reference to others and the wider environment.

Post-birth, the main concern is with the G. *maiwa* 'spirits'. Xié dwellers co-inhabit the river with the *maiwa*, the animal ancestors who populate the landscape and protect their animal 'children'. *Maiwa* live alongside Xié dwellers and appear as some of the most striking smooth stones, rocks and waterfall rapids which form the riverine landscape. In this petrified state, *maiwa* 'own' the animals that live around them and they mediate access to these for human subsistence. *Maiwa* may seduce or attack when humans behave inattentively (falling, slipping or otherwise injuring themselves) and when they fail to follow prescribed ways for living well (G. *kue katu*), including periodic fasting and bathing. This is especially the case during the perinatal period when these requirements are tightened. Other than following these prescriptions, people also avoid rousing the *maiwa* by performing protective perinatal rituals that 'close the *maiwa's* eyes'. Smoke blessings appear to be commonly used to disperse such 'spirits' and tobacco smoke repels them (also mentioned outside the perinatal context in Gow and Echeverri, both this volume). Parents who neglect to perform them however, make themselves and their children more generally susceptible to *maiwa*.[12] These persons also become more vulnerable to attacks by malignant *pajés* who can activate the *maiwa*, 'making them walk' and causing them to harm their intended victims. Aware of the *maiwa*, people follow a set of post-birth actions to ensure and restore good health during the perinatal period.

Post-birth blessings

Immediately after the umbilical cord is cut, the baby is bathed in a basin of river water fetched especially for that purpose. Before bathing begins, the water is blessed by a tobacco smoke blesser: sucking on a cigarette, taking and holding the smoke in his mouth without inhaling, the *benzedor* then pneumatically directs the smoke over the surface water of the baby's bath, muttering a barely audible blessing. This post-birth moment is one of silence and stillness, with the attention focused on the mist of smoke as it gently glides and disperses across the baby's bath water. Caranguejo village resident Aemilius explained to me about his own tobacco blessings, that he used them to ask the *maiwa* not to disturb the child. The focus then turns to bathing the baby.

To bathe the baby, a female relative, often the mother-in-law, supports the child one-handed, her right forearm and hand securing the baby across the chest in a forward-slumped seated position on her submerged foot. With the free (right) hand, water is cupped-up from the basin and dribbled down the baby's exposed back with increasing speed and frequency, changing from a delicately administered trickle-down-the-washer's fingertips to a vigorous, hand-fully cupped splash-washing. The water is splashed over the baby's head and dribbles down its face, chest and legs. This technique is invariably accompanied by a '*Brrrrin*' trumpeting noise as the washer forcefully expels air out between her vibrating lips. If the baby whimpers, it is consoled with back-patting and the washing continues. As the splash-washing increases in vigour, the '*Brrrrin*' sound becomes louder. The baby is then removed from the basin, dried with a cloth, breastfed and laid to sleep in his hammock. The first baby birth inaugurates an intensive routine of baby bathing (Rahman, forthcoming) – five times a day and up to 20 minutes a time.

Babies are bathed in this way because they 'feel hot' and so bathing 'feels good' to them. The more frequently they are bathed, the quicker they will grow and the stronger (*kirimba*) they will become. This is especially true if the weather is warm, when there is concern the baby will become 'dry' (P. *seco*)[13] or 'thin' (P. *magro*, that is, hard – G. *santa*, P. *duro*, – like bone, rather than firm and full). Fatness – being P. '*gordo*' – is a desirable characteristic of babies (cf. Ewart 2000: 288) and is part of what makes the developing *pira miri* a source of delight and wonder. Frequent bathing helps them 'grow lightly (P. *crescer ligeiro*, i.e. quickly)'[14] and babies that are regularly splash-washed are observed to be chubby, contented and of mild temperament. On teaching me this technique, one woman pointed to her four-year-old son and observed how 'firm' and 'strong' (G. *kirimbawa*) he was because he was bathed, and later bathed himself, with great frequency. Splash-washing stops when the baby has developed neck strength, can sit upright and has greater control of his orifices (no longer peeing and pooing indiscriminately). As such, splash-washing is seen as firming up both the form and the functioning of the anal and urethral orifices, which thereby gain control.

A week post-birth the baby then makes the transition from home basin-bathing to river bathing. This is marked by the *Iyumi* ritual, involving tobacco smoke and incense, which together form a sanctified concentration of the infant's early bathing-feeding-sleeping routine: Sitting perfectly still in the hammock, mother and child are immersed in the candied smoke of G. *chicantá* (P. *breu*), a plant resin placed on brazil wood (P. *pau brasil*) that is burned beneath the hammock for five to ten minutes producing a sweet wafting aroma. It is important that both the hammock and the baby are exposed to the fumes, as they form a single unit (cf. Walker

2009a). I was told that grass (P. *capim*), placed under the resin, is used 'to create more smoke' (P. *dar fumaça*), as G. *tátátinga*, literally 'white fire' (i.e. smoke), is an important part of ritual action. Simultaneously, a specially prepared cigarette will be lit. (This cigarette needs to have been blessed by a suitably qualified person, a *pajé* or blesser.) The father draws on this specially blessed tobacco cigarette, takes the smoke into his mouth and blows it over the mother and child, focusing on the crowns of their heads. He then blows smoke over the rest of the body, slowly moving down the torso, finally directing the least powerful breaths towards the legs and feet. The couple and child then rise and make their way down to the river, the father leading followed by the mother and child and (the paternal) grandmother. The father continues smoking the cigarette as they make their way to the river, holding the burning plant resin, until they reach the river bank. The father stubs out the cigarette while the plant resin, placed on the ground, burns for another ten to fifteen minutes.

The grandmother, babe-in-arms and mother wade into the water and the sweet-smelling fumes waft across the waters in their direction (see Figure 6.2). The fumes protect them from the potential 'shock' caused by the grandmother's splash-washing and 'make the ancestral spirit animals [*maiwa*] disperse'.[15] After washing, the mother swiftly returns home to breastfeed the baby. She then puts him to sleep in his hammock.

Water, fumes and smoke accompany the transition from hammock and home to river. They form part of the infant's guided discovery and subsequent frequent and active exposure to prolonged washing in cold water, where the water is picked up and splashed over a slumped and seated baby, actively engages the infant with its surroundings. What is more, riverine corporalities acquire bodily specificity and personal qualities consubstantial with the qualities of cool river water and cool tobacco smoke, as they move onto land. Xié dwellers appear to be referring to a certain firmness of form, muscles and sinews, which develops in tandem with socio-moral qualities and dispositions – the developing upright moral character of growing infants. Persistence, endurance and, perhaps most important, a flexible disposition in harmony with kin and environment, is part of this firming up of the body, where qualities of firmness are not only physical but are also associated with the cultivation of inner calmness. Based on the 'general principle that relations and processes outside of the body can be transferred to the body itself' (S. Hugh-Jones 1979: 119), water and tobacco cool down infants in their heated states, producing calm-minded and cool-bodied persons.

Hot emotions, including anger, are mitigated by bathing and infants who are conspicuously unruly become the particular focus of methodical cooling.[16] In the absence of bathing and tobacco smoke blessings, babies become infirm, suffer from leaking orifices (from which flow diarrhoea and mucus) and become limp and lifeless. Both water and tobacco play their role in the cultivation of cool, firm qualities. They are substances carefully mediated through specific techniques and mindful actions,

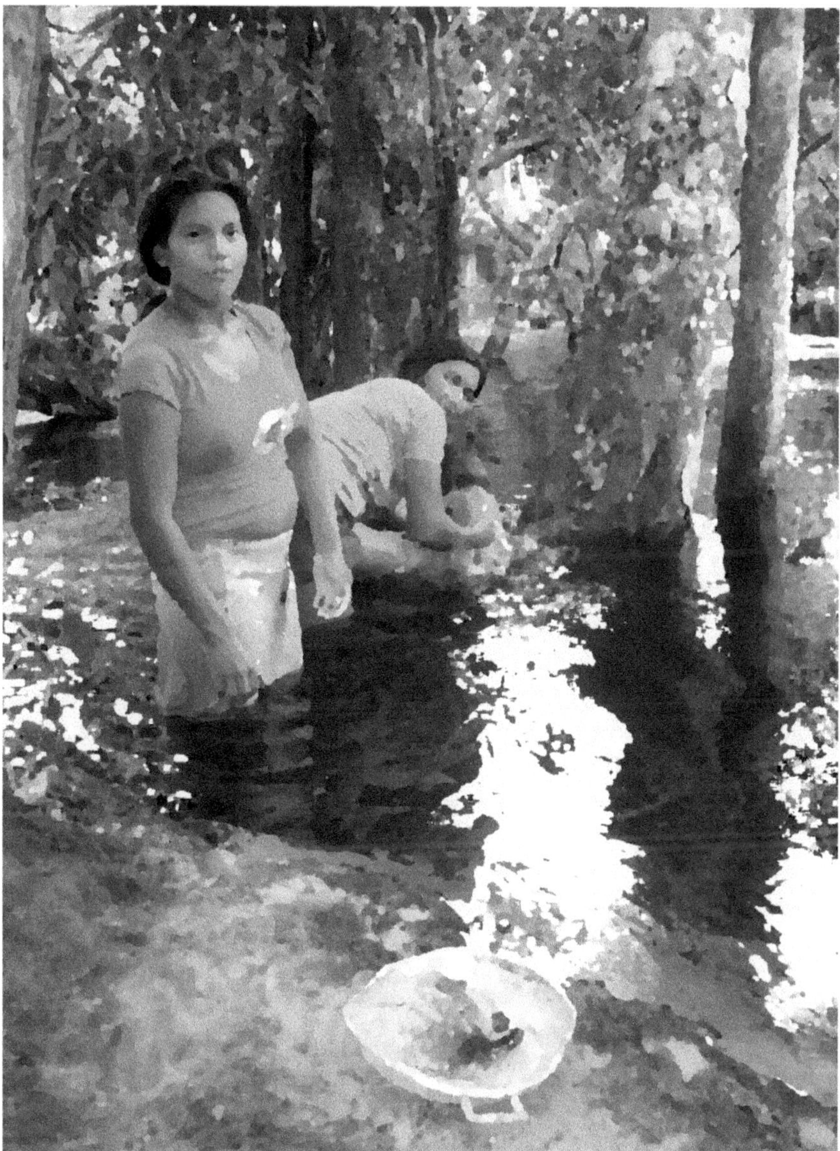

Figure 6.2 The *Iyumi* ritual: tobacco and smoke at the baby's first river bath. (Artistically modified photograph taken by Elizabeth Rahman.)

and the associated 'cooling' aspirated sounds (cf. Hill 2009b) the washer makes and the noise of splashed water itself, all work to achieve the effect of creating a properly embodied, 'cool' person.

The physiological and cognitive articulation of well-honed practices, such as tobacco blessings and splash-washing, encourage a full-bodied alertness, that is, bodily states and attitudes of mindful interaction and self-control, for baby and carer alike. Embodied experience is thus key to the active articulation and cultivation of people who are attentive to their environment and the beings (a range of human and non-human beings including kin, prey and predators) that inhabit it. What is more, these practices form part of a socio-physiological implicit pedagogy, whereby Xié residents seek to instil the morally upright qualities of tobacco and water on and into the neonate.

Weaning

The itinerary of tobacco smoke blessings continues when weaning begins, usually from around 4–6 months and invariably when the baby is observed to be 'looking' (G. '*o mayco*') and watching others eat. The first foods offered to an infant are highly prized cultigens, the fruit of the hard labour of family members. These are mild and bland, proximate, cultivated, heavily processed, 'cool' foods. Other foods are gradually incorporated into the infant's diet to include fish and 'hot' game, artfully caught and eaten by his kin. This increasing variety of foodstuffs moves along a continuum towards a diet of hot, piquant foods and the wilder, bloodier, forest-dwelling animals. These foods, while also subject to lengthy culinary preparation in order to remove all traces of blood, are also cooled by tobacco smoke blessings.

Food shamanism, by way of tobacco smoke blessings during weaning, is a moral responsibility of parents and rarely does anyone forgo what is perceived as a sensible precaution. For some families, a good *benzedor* can bless one category of fish and this is sufficient for the subsequent consumption of all other fish species. The same is true of small fish; small game; chilli pepper; large fish from the seasonally flooded forest (P. *igapó*) lakes and large game. If no powerful blesser is available, however, each type or species is blessed before the child consumes it. This occurs after bathing, in the baby's home and in the presence of the father and mother: In quiet seclusion, and after the family has bathed at dusk, the blesser speaks a few calm and quiet words, or mouths them, over a small offering of food, blowing also over the food, sometimes with, sometimes without the vehicle of tobacco smoke. The food is then safely eaten by the child. Bathing before taking foods – in this and in all other contexts – is an important way in which to cool down and close off the body, especially before eating the 'hot', heated and charged flesh of large predators.

If the body is perceived as an integrated vessel through which things flow in and out (C. Hugh-Jones 1979: 199), the way that it consumes foods is highly relevant.

The control of orifices is important since 'foods, excreta, smells, sounds, breath and visual images should all go in or out in a regular and controlled manner' (C. Hugh-Jones 1979: 199). They are organs which mediate flows into and out of the body, and like the body-enveloped-by-flesh, their functioning must also be firmed up and effectively controlled. These idioms are recurrent in myths which warn of the dangers of overly potent and piercing sounds, ravenous appetites and leaky vaginas and anuses, all of which can negatively affect health. For Xié dwellers, anal, urethral and oral orifices can be controlled by actively attending to their (firm, cool and quiet) regulation. Bathing and tobacco blessings during weaning orientate attention towards proper bodily functioning, allowing substances to be mindfully mediated before entering body.

Fright

Personal development is not just linked to the body-enveloped-by-flesh, rather a person is made whole by the integration of their developing fish-body, together with more intangible aspects: their image of themselves (G. *mira*, P. *imagem*, 'body-soul', shadow or reflection) and their soul (G. *anga*). Personal integrity reflects the distillation of these three elements in the self, which is also reflected in a firmly attentive bodily comportment and posture. In the case of infants, discussion of the soul, body and body-soul is normally limited to instances of sickness and fright (or S. *susto*), as it is known in the literature (Butt-Colson 1975: 300), is one common affliction for babies.

Any frightening or shockingly inappropriate interaction, including being caused to fall, being bathed inappropriately or being frightened by loud animal or bird noise-actions (*nerangaraxa*), all directly penetrate a child's soul (*anga*) which then becomes 'removed' (P. *afastado*). A child's *anga* is understood to be weak, vulnerable and easily and lethally detached from the physically tangible child itself: as one mother explained, fright, in distancing the baby's soul, causes the baby to cry 'because his soul is with the [P.] *majuba* [*maiwa*]'. Drastic or frequent shocks causing fright (G. *iyangasa*) will cause a child's soul aspect to have an overly loose connection to its body, which is evinced by crying and feverish states. The soul aspect is then drawn to the ancestral animal spirits (*maiwa*) and the child will begin an irreversible transformation manifested by death.

A mother with a frightened baby will seek a *benzedor*, or alternatively the blesser will hear the baby crying and approach the mother. Our youngest child, Sofia, was twice frightened in the field. This happened once when I was holding her and slipped on the muddy bank of the river when going to bathe; and before this, when we passed by the rapids at Cumatí when Sofia was a month old and she became affected by the potent, petrified remains of Cumatí's ancestral animal spirits (*maiwa*). On this occasion, the day after we returned to the village of Caranguejo Sofia was periodically crying, due to – as Caranguejo dwellers explained it – the fright she had had. Whilst my husband and I were arguing about how to quiet her, Caranguejo elder João, with whom we had travelled, arrived at our home. He asked if she had been crying more than usual and I confirmed that she had. He blew tobacco smoke on Sofia's head, then slowly directing it down her torso, and muttering an inaudible blessing, he cupped one hand, as if to scoop off the negative influence, and continued to blow on her crown. He then projected tobacco smoke over the baby and I, focusing on our crowns, and blew down our torsos several times while we sat in stillness in the hammock. He also repeatedly made the sign of the cross. This lasted no more than a few minutes, and it brought peace. My husband, both children and I then settled down to a restful sleep.

This remedy for fright always entails a short blessing, of five minutes or so, usually at either dusk or dawn and which may be repeated over several days. João, his son Soares and the indigenous health agent Aemilius all blew spells for Sofia with noticeable effect. I was told that blessings are frequently sought to draw the frightened soul back and that 'white' (i.e. biomedical) remedies were known to be useless in cases of fright.

During *umutauari* tobacco-blowing, I suggest that one's attention comes to settle on the intent-laden directionality of the smoke, propelled by the blesser: the blowing of tobacco smoke directs and establishes a clear, intended focus around which to orientate the attention. The aromatic smell of tobacco and its materiality offer powerful sensorial stimuli that awaken a person to the here and now. This creates a space in which time is suspended and attention is focused and directed to the full richness of the present moment. Aligning the attention is all the easier in the context of a rich sensory stimulus of which you are the subject. The tobacco-blower mediates with his own embodied presence. In the face of the apparently mundane, the perinatal family can attend all the more attentively to the minutiae of daily life, patiently resonating to the other's presence. Such focused attention is the baseline of the healthful person, or indeed, the very definition of a human person himself.[17]

Shamanic intervention

Tobacco is 'the hallmark of shamanic activity' (Fausto 2004: 158) and is used for both shamanic divination and for cure. For the Baníwa, Wright describes it as mythic performance, that involves Kuwai (the equivalent of the Amado for the Warekena) and the primordial shaman and deity Dzuliferi, also the 'owner of tobacco' (Wright 2013: 176). Noting how stanzas in myth parallel shifts in cure-healing séance, Wright states: 'Kuwai transforms into the shadow-soul of Dzuliferi. This transformation corresponds to the shift in the curing rite from localization of the soul of the sick and discovery of the sickness the soul has, to extraction by suction (jaguar mouth), water dowsing and smoke blowing to revive the soul of the sick. This occurs first in the Other World; if successful, the *pajé* is "authorized" to repeat the process on the patient in This World of the descendants' (Wright 2013: 83). Once sickness is located, the common techniques for cure include the aforementioned sucking out of the sickening agent (often a dart), the throwing of water, the blowing of tobacco smoke and the chanting of curing songs (e.g. Brabec de Mori, this volume). In these contexts, and beyond its scientifically evaluated medicinal properties, how else can tobacco work to cure?

When addressing the question of efficacy of ritual action, many studies highlight the psychosomatic effects of ritual practice. Ritual narrative has been understood as an important component that affects people's health, with semantics a way of making sickness intelligible to the sick person (e.g. Levi-Strauss 1963). Musical styles have aided in driving home their meaning (e.g. Hill 1985). These are compounded by the pneumatic power of shamanic breath, a power cogently made manifest by tobacco smoke (Butt-Colson 1956; Wilbert 1987; Cf. Hill 2009b; and by music, Hill and Chaumeil 2011).

Further studies focus on its important narcotic effects and the pharmacology of the tobacco plant. These have also been discussed in Wilbert's important study, where he suggests that tobacco blowing, often used with women and infants who do not normally smoke, may in fact induce some mild narcotic effect (through their 'involuntary smoking'). Through powerful symbolism (e.g. Hertz 1960 [1881–1915]; Douglas 1966, 1970) and psychosomatic efficacy (Moreno 1988, 1995; Wiseman 1999) and the intoxicating effects of nicotine, the shaman is seen as a therapist and the ritual use of tobacco has been understood as efficacious – and at least, highly persuasive.

Even minor blessings for the perinatal family and tiny infant, for fright for instance, appear to work. Possibly their efficacy further relates to the provision of a heightened sensorial experience, a 'quickening of the senses', which Desjarlais (1992, 1996) has convincingly suggested invokes 'presence'. In the context of Buddhist Sherpas, Desjarlais has argued that fright can be cured by a cacophony of actions, smells and sounds, which together comprise a repertoire designed to jump start a person's physiology. In Malaysia, Roseman (1988) has paid special attention to the 'pragmatic efficacy of aesthetic forms', and the artful manipulation of varied sensory stimuli by ritual specialists in order to induce vitality; while in Amazonia, Hill (1993) has pioneered the study of musical aesthetics. It appears then that a wide range of sounds, gestures, movements, powerful smells and substances are carefully composed in order to anchor a person back to the here and now. We get a sense of how sensory stimuli can be used to startle people into attentive life, by use of a more full-bodied magic (Abram 2010) – one of the more 'mystical' bodily techniques suggested initially by Mauss (1973[1950]: 386).

Furthermore, when we look closely at the *materia medica* and the specific techniques used during shamanic intervention (with adults), we find striking similarities to those that accompany infancy. Both tobacco and water are used, and the apparatus is also contiguous: the cylindrical cigarettes and water thrown from plant gourds (the latter are also used to feed infants). Even the trumpeting sound produced by the splash-washer mimics that of the maraca, often used for shamanic healing. The diet of 'cool' foods is the same for the sick person and the infant; as is recluse to their hammock, which is considered a 'cooling' place to be. This need not be construed as the metaphoric mimicry of infancy (cf. Goldman 2004: 147 in his discussion of ritual), but rather, I suggest, affords an induction and informal education that exposes infants early on to tobacco and water and suggests how they might appropriately respond to these stimuli. As such, rituals during infancy maximize 'the information available in the total environment' (Jackson 1983b: 335) and launch an infant's initiation into a world of potent smells and sensations. Later in life – in taking people back – in a condensed form, these self-same stimuli may be used effectively to induce cure. Within such a hypothesis, shamanry becomes potentially much more effective for an indigenously raised patient – attuned to these stimuli and made in Amerindia – than for an outsider.

Unlike infancy however, with curative interventions for adults, shamanic language also becomes salient, working as a type of what Uzendoski and Calapucha-Tapuy (2012) call 'somatic poetry'. They suggest (Uzendoski and Calapucha-Tapuy (2012): 29, 25) that 'language works together with imagery, sound, smell, and taste to produce a holistic communicative experience', unfolding in an 'animated universe of flowing energies' (also see Hill (1985) and the seminal piece based outside Amazonia by Bahr and Haefer (1978)). These perspectives are foregrounded in ethnomusicological research which, since Blacking (1977), has pointed towards 'transcendental somatic states' and experiences of 'resonance'.

Other-than-auditory sensorial stimuli, including tactile, olfactory and the visual senses evoke 'presence' (De Martino 1972; Desjarlais 1992, 1996) 'sensory attentiveness', 'hereness' (Desjarlais' 1996), 'resonance' or 'co-respondence' (Ingold 2000). It has been suggested they induce what might be described as a distinct 'mode of attention' (Csordas 1994), that I have expounded as mindfulness. At this level, shamanic intervention functions at both symbolic and somatic levels, the two of which are difficult to separate in the practice of an alchemic art. Alchemy also has its specific *apparati*.

Smoking mindfully

Since Rivière's notion that tubular devices for Amerindians are 'not simply technical or aesthetic objects but also some sort of energy transformers' (1969: 157), we find recurrent examples of the significance of tubes in relation to Amerindian socio-cosmologies: hair tubes, flutes and blowpipes are revealed as technical choices intimately intertwined with societal and personal virtues (on spears and blowpipes, Rival 1996; on blowguns, palm trees and ancestor spirits,

Erikson 2001). In Arawakan northwestern Amazonia, the focus has been on the metaphorical umbilical cord that, among other things, links agnatic ancestors to newborns (Wright 1998; Hill 2009a). Discussing the similitudes between a range of tubular devices controlled by men (the flute, the blowpipe, the shaman's body), Chaumeil (2001: 90) explains:

> ... the act of blowing mobilizes the entire body of the shaman. The shaman gets his supplies of magical darts from forest spirits after negotiation, and ingests them through the mouth. Once swallowed, the darts slide down the digestive tube (lubricated with phlegm) into the stomach (equivalent to the quiver), where they are kept and fed with tobacco smoke (regularly swallowed by the shaman), and where the 'digestive' process is stopped, given that the efficacy of the darts depends on their being expelled upward by going back along the digestive tube lining, and not downwards (as excrement). The darts, which are deviated towards the shaman's arms, are not equivalent to undigested, vomited food. The shaman's stretched-out arms become a kind of launching pad, or blowpipe.... This killing arm, a kind of magical pipe connected to the stomach by the digestive tract, is not unlike the ancient war flute made with the humerus of an enemy. In both cases we find a similar process activated by blowing through an organ. This tubular model of shamanic aggression prevails throughout Amazonia and does not presuppose the actual use of blowpipes in hunting. What matters here is the principle, that is, breath contained within a tube.

Breath contained in a tube is exactly what smoke manifests and the cylindrical cigarette reveals itself as an excellent technical device through which to transform energy[18] – when accompanied by the appropriate technique. There is an art to smoking, and tobacco-blown blessings use the bodily techniques of taking tobacco smoke into the mouth and pneumatically projecting it. In cure-healing and protective contexts, cigarettes are smoked with applied concentration, focusing on either the directed expulsion of breath and intent-full smoke-blowing; or, in the context of divination and initiation, they involve deep inhalation, the holding of breath and the closing of the glottis to retain it, and its measured expulsion. Many Amerindian languages convey this latter smoking technique using the verbs 'to eat' and 'to ingest' or 'digest' (rather than 'to smoke'). See for example, among the Araweté (Viveiros de Castro 1992: 131) and the Yanomami (Reig, this volume); while the Shipibo see tobacco as 'food' (Brabec de Mori, endnote 14 of the introduction to this volume). In both contexts, smokers are aware of and also modify their breathing to adjust the amount of smoke produced. And in both, the cylindrical cigar mediates the oral orifice – the mouth – and the intake of air into and out of the organism and facilitates this shift in attention.[19]

It is curious that mindfulness has recently been used as a way to give up smoking, but only by first making the person smoke actively, with awareness (Carim-Todd et al. 2013; Elwafi et al. 2013). In fact, the way that shamans take deep lungfuls of 'digested' smoke, makes shamanic smoking akin to yogic *pranayama* breathing, even if the *prana* – the vital breath – is poisonous smoke. This type of (albeit smokeless) mindful breathing has been shown to have a number of positive neurophysiological effects on the body, on mood and on depression (Burg and Michalak 2011). From the Xié dwellers' perspective, when combined with tobacco smoke, they actively promote a focused, attentive and relaxed state. It should come as no surprise then that smoking is done sitting on stool, the northwestern idiom most commonly used to portray mindful, meditative modes (Århem et al. 2004: 184, 200, 205, 215; S. Hugh-Jones 2009: 47–48).[20] As Wilbert (1987: 93) summarizes, 'Besides offering comfort and rest, the stool provides the smoking man who occupies it a self – and world – centred space for meditative communication with the metaphysical powers.' Further research may reveal that smoking mindfully is better for health than the 'fast food' smoking that characterizes workers' breaks and the heavily stressed. I have suggested that such breathing techniques are used to master the effect of tobacco rather than vice versa.

Mastering the intoxicating effects of tobacco in these contexts means that shamans become 'diaphanous', 'smooth and lightweight' (Viveiros de Castro 1992: 131; Fausto 2004: 166), all positively valued qualities that render the connection between body and soul more pliable (Viveiros de Castro 1992: 195), thereby allowing the soul to detach and undertake the necessary journeying. Thus, mediating and controlling the effect of tobacco by mindful breathing – and sometimes through tobacco-induced 'controlled hyperventilation' (Wilbert 1987: 91) – allows the shaman to become 'disembodied actively, not passively' (Viveiros de Castro 1992: 195). This is important for such lightness can be negative if it is a state provoked by malignant sorcery or is otherwise uncontrolled or done 'passively': the involuntary (or uncontrolled, e.g. Rival 2005) detachment of soul substance, such as in cases of fright, can lead all too easily to death (e.g. Vilaça 2005).

Tobacco and others

Ritually smoked cigars are most prevalent during ceremonial exchange, with (potentially predatory) human affines; and (equally predatory) animate others (see Fortis, this volume) and we may then conclude that, first and foremost, cigars are used to mediate ambivalent relations with a number of beings, both human and otherwise, in the Amerindian cosmos.[21] While cigars may be used to mediate energy flows in and out of the body-covered-by-flesh, cylindrical devices also 'transform untamed, dangerous energy into controlled, socialised energy' (Chaumeil 2001: 81). In this final section of the chapter, I consider how cylindrical cigars offer a means through which to cool and calm a special type of relation – that with the potentially fiery affine.

During the Christmas festivities the entire Tartaruga community came to visit Caranguejo village, where many of their affinal relations live. Manuel, their leader (P. *capitão*), *pajé* and the prolific father of 12, lit a huge cigar in the crowded community centre and, sitting next to my husband, he divulged some of his knowledge to him. Manuel remained sociably well-composed through the evening's drinking and smoking.[22]

Manuel's grand cigar expounds his power as a leader, a shaman and a father, able to mindfully mediate this, and other, substance (-persons). The cigar also affords a visual recollection of his virility and we see that cigars and penises on the one hand;[23] and gourds (used in pipes and tobacco preparation) and vaginas on the other, are often juxtaposed in the literature (e.g. S. Hugh-Jones 1979, 2009). By penetrating them, men 'open up' women, and in some ethnographic contexts, this is understood to provoke a girl's menarche and the flow of blood (e.g. among the Cashinahua, McCallum 2001: 17). Accordingly then, both blood (likened to the murky-burnt amber of the 'black' river waters of the Xié) and tobacco are two potent 'outward substances' or substance-mediums, which 'cause the necessary bodily and psychic dispositions to meet others' (Fausto 2004: 166).

Smoking tobacco is linked to the river and the mythic and ritual process of world-opening, described in some detail for Xié dwellers' neighbouring Arawakan affines, the Baníwa (Wright 1998) and Wakuénai (Hill 1993). While wafting tobacco smoke gives rise to the twisted course of the Içana river (Garnelo 2003), the flow of menstrual blood – the river's murky waters in myth (Wright 2013: 191) – indicates fertility and the potential to reproduce society (Rahman 2014). World-opening has been identified as a mytho-historical ritual practice that facilitated the occupation of new lands and the incorporation of diverse peoples (Hill and Wright 1988) as part of the Arawakan expansion (Hornborg and Hill 2011).

Driven by a logic of the incorporation of others, rather than the forced submission or expulsion of local groups (e.g. Makú),[24] the Arawakan complex (Santos-Granero 2002) is thought to have been widely dispersed throughout South America. But establishing and maintaining such, potentially fiery, affinal relations with newly encountered resident groups, requires cool-minded composure and perchance also, cool tobacco breath. While tobacco blows open the cool paths to conviviality, perhaps too, the up-take of smoking can be linked to an increase in affinal encounters – with tobacco as an attractive trade item- and potentially an important part of the Arawakan complex. This would not only explain the uptake of smoking in the context of colonialism but also smoking as the process of de-affinizing the other (as with shamanic séances with non-human beings, see Fortis this volume), a process that also occurs for the heated sub-human neonatal guest (who must be de-affinized and made into kin, Gow 1989; Rival 1998; Vilaça 2002). With reference to the introduction to this chapter, it also illuminates why children, now in their submissive position, are expected to light the cigarettes of their grandmother 'owners', and why many of the Makú ethnicity, acting as servants (see Silverwood

Cope 1972: 104; Santos-Granero 2009c: 210–232), are known as 'the people who light cigars' (Hugh-Jones 2007: 52).

Tubular forms penetrate others, at both literal and metaphorical levels, and where 'indigenous socio-logics is based on physiologics' (Seeger et al. 1979: 13) they serve to reproduce both persons and the societies they live in. Smoked tobacco then mediates domains of existence and facilitates relations with others, traversing borders and acting as a broker, in the same way in which the shaman does (see introduction to this volume).

Conclusion

Through its ethnographic focus, this chapter has redressed the neglect of the question of perinatal tobacco use and in doing so, argues for a move away from the detailed fact of hands-on care, to more closely examine the minutiae and mode of mindfully attentive caring acts. Thus, while sensuous engagement with the world – including its plants – constitutes part of living well with others (both people and plants) and helps mould the body; what determines the capacity of others to make self is precisely the mode or quality of their interactions. This may be described as cool-mindedness, a personal quality and at once a somatic, psychological and social state that co-opts substances to its end. From this perspective, it becomes clear that tobacco is not just a substance used, but rather, that it is an alchemical agent able to constitute and make bodies.[25] Mindful engagement affects the effects of this ubiquitous plant and the artful use of tobacco, to orientate the attention, makes people well by making them aware.

Tobacco blessings are important for personal development not least because they have the potential to materialize a potent mode of interacting: tobacco blessings both cultivate and manifest the more generalized personal virtue of maintaining a controlled open, closely attentive, alert and wakeful disposition.

The indeterminacy and ambiguity afforded by bodily praxis, as opposed to the more hard core data derived from linguistic analysis for example, has meant that the analysis and efficacy of full person, mind-body interactions has remained elusive. Casting this in a new light, recent research into mindfulness, which is also increasingly seen to be beneficial for perinatal well-being (Hughes et al. 2009), offers the possibility of making ethnographically based, healthful practices intelligible to a wider audience. However, mindfulness initiatives during the perinatal period (CALM; MBCP) tend to focus on breathing and other generic recommendations, irrespective of environmentally and culturally specific techniques (cf. Panter-Brick et al. 2006). For this reason, I have further situated mindful practice with regard to prevailing and specific, morally evaluated (cf. Santos-Granero 2011) substances (of tobacco and water) and their associated techniques as they manifest along the Xié river.

Tobacco blowing and water-splashing firms or reintegrates aspects of emergent persons, making them potent and strong (*kirimbawa*) rather than flaccid, weak and infirm (*pitua*). In other contexts, tobacco blessings (*umutauari*) draw together the aspects of self that make a person whole, reintegrating soul (*anga*), the developing body-image (*mira*) and the tangible body-enveloped by skin itself (*pira yane* or in the case of children, *pira miri*). Health and sickness are defined by the proper integration of these aspects which are the baseline for productive and joyous and healthful interdependence. Tobacco, used mindfully, makes emergent and grown persons potent, strong and healthy – and even '*extra forte*' as the Coringa (commercial rolling tobacco) branding suggests.

I have argued that when tobacco is squarely located in this wider, somatic, 'body ecologic' (Hsu 2007), we can see it as instrumental in the project of drying, cooling and gathering a person into one 'seated' place. Ecological rubrics at work in the body, reverberate beyond the body proper, demonstrating a complex somatic symbiosis that extends out in both time and space. And thus, I have suggested that a methodological and analytical shift that collapses substance-based and equally psychologically based analyses may shed further light on both.

Acknowledgements

In developing this chapter for publication, I thank Robin Wright and Jonathan Hill for their comments. I also thank my co-editor, Andrew Russell, for his edits as well as the comments and corrections from co-authors in this volume. I am also grateful to have received funding for my doctoral fieldwork and for writing up. For various awards and grants, I thank The Institute of Social and Cultural Anthropology, The School of Anthropology and Museum Ethnography, Linacre College and the University of Oxford. The British Federation of Women Graduates, I thank for their generous scholarship. Thanks also go to The Royal Anthropological Institute for the Olivia Harris Award.

Notes

1. 'Extra Strong Coringa Smoke' is a popular brand in the municipality of São Gabriel da Cachoeira. The packet bears the catchphrase 'let's smoke' (P. '*vamos a pitar*').
2. Today most individuals use the pages of exercise books as rolling papers and get these from the local school teacher.
3. P. '*Comunidade*' is the common appellation for riverine dwellings since the end of the 1960s when Salesian missionaries instigated the *Comunidades Eclesiais de Base* (Oliveira 1981: 31; 1995: 150 cited in Lasmar 2005).

4. To protect their identity, pseudonyms are given for both village and personal names appearing in this chapter and images are artistically modified.
5. Nheengatu, Ñengatú, Géral, or Yeral in Colombia and Venezuela, is a simplified form of the ancient Tupi, a trading language, and the official language of the municipality.
6. There is fair degree of linguistic mixing; hence these categories should be taken as no more than a general guide.
7. The latter part of the word '*tauari*' appears to be of Arawakan stock and relates directly to the tree bark. However, the etymology of this term is further clouded by lingua Géral, in which '*ari*' denotes intended growth and transformation, while '*umutu*' alludes to taking or ingesting. What is striking however is that neither appears to relate to the tobacco plant.
8. On its preparation, see http://www.isuma.tv/es/hohodene/searching-for-parika-amazonian-shamans-revitalization-project
9. While the two forms of smoking cannot be – and indeed should not be – categorically distinguished, their intended aims and methods nonetheless diverge (in the case of the former, to protect, prevent and cure; and in the case of the latter, to find and negotiate the release of the pathogenic agent, or in other contexts, simply to have a good and sociable time).
10. Mindfulness is the 'process of regulating attention in order to bring a quality of… awareness to current experience… within an orientation of curiosity, experiential openness and acceptance' (Bishop et al. 2004: 234). It effectively describes, 'the condition of being alive to the world, characterised by a heightened sensitivity and responsiveness in perception and action, to an environment that is always in flux' (Ingold 2006: 10).
11. Conversely, the process of body hardening among the Cashinahua involves heating up or 'cooking' the child post-birth, so that the infant will be 'washed in warm water and then placed in a hammock over a basin containing hot coals' (McCallum 1996: 354). Thus it would appear that these concepts are not universal and possibly the result of a complex interface between distinct eco-niches.
12. Also see the shamanic diagnosis for Wright's (2013: 57) fractured right femur – and a degenerative disease of the joints called Morquio's disease – as the consequence of parental neglect, due to them not having performed the correct oration to avert the gaze of water spirits. The idiom – of 'pushing away the gaze' – is also similar.
13. In contrast, Twigg (2000: 27) states how, in early modern England and France, bathing became seen as dangerous to the body. She specifies 'skin was regarded as porous; and water, especially hot water, was believed to penetrate the body and weaken its vital fluids. Young children were no longer bathed in water since its action would prolong the softness of a system that was already too moist; the process of growing up was seen as a process of drying out'. Accordingly, she notes a preference for 'dry washing', 'rubbing down' or 'wiping down' with the fortifying and strengthening properties of perfumes and spirits.
14. On lightness as a quality of vitality, see Santos-Granero (2012: 192).

15. For the Baníwa, the *maiwi* or *umawalinai* (aquatic water-spirits) are further pacified by throwing chilli pepper into the river (Wright, personal communication).
16. According to Hill (2009b, 1985) the musical process of cooling metaphors (cf. Levi-Strauss' 'cooling out' 1963) occurs simultaneously on emotional and intellectual levels, and transforms harmful emotions (anger, envy) into healing, health-promoting ones (calmness and generosity).
17. Consistently, in daily life, persons are evaluated according to their dexterity, and above all their lack of clumsiness. Recently, Xié dwellers have taken to asking the rhetorical question, 'Were you born yesterday?' when co-community members are lackadaisical in their execution of tasks. Mindful performance is constantly compelled, exigent and expected, and those who 'lack mind' are likely to be sub-human sorcerers.
18. Among the People of the Centre, when the *Couratari* tree is felled and burned to make ash salts (to be mixed with tobacco paste), it takes on the appearance of a giant self-smoking cigar (Echeverri, personal communication). Perhaps as an indexical suggestion, this is why the tree, rather than tobacco itself, forms the linguistic basis for smoking (see introduction to this chapter and Note 7).
19. In the myths of the closely related Wakuénai, tobacco acts to switch people's consciousness; it can wake them up or put them to sleep (Hill 2009c). A mythic example of mindfulness? (Hill, personal communication).
20. '... an activity described as cooling, relaxing, and peaceful – [that it] is synonymous with learning, contemplation, and meditation and has connotations of stability, rootedness, and fixity. A wise person has a "cool seat", an irritable person a "hot seat", and a thoughtless or flighty person "does not know how to sit". A person's stool is thus an aspect of his or her character' (Hugh-Jones 2009: 48).
21. On virtual and real affinity, see Viveiros de Castro (2001).
22. As with the consumption of alcohol, one's controlled consumption is dependent not on the quantity consumed, which can be enormous, but on the quality of its consumption. Measured consumption is an aspect of a person's centred personality, for people are frequently judged by their ability to withstand the affects pain, hunger and the influence of 'drugs'.
23. The *couratari*'s fruits – the bark of which is used for rolling papers – has the form of a penis (Echeverri and Román-Jitdutjaaño 2013).
24. Makú is a linguistic group that incorporates the ethnicities of Hupda, Yuhupde, Dow, Nadöb (Brazil) and Kakwa and Nukak (Colombia). It is an Arawak word meaning non-speaker (as opposed to Wakúenai, 'speakers of our language', and for the Baníwa Hohodene, refers to their non-quite-human unfinished people and their 'grandfathers' (Cornelio and Wright 1999). In these contexts, Jackson (1983a: 149), based on her research with Tukano-Bará, succinctly clarifies the issue: 'The term Makú is generic ... and like several other terms ... can at times designate nothing more precise than the "wild" Indians of a given region – those least contacted, least clothed, and who are alleged to practice no farming, have no houses, and lead a totally nomadic existence.' This internally generated disparity between 'wild' not-entirely-people on the one hand; and 'civilized'

'true people' (Jackson 1983a: 159) on the other, would appear to be an important feature of indigenous classification throughout Lowland South America (Gow 1993; in central Brazil, also see Ewart, 2013).

25. This is a reversed logic to studies highlighting the pharmacological importance of Nicotiana species – and hence tobacco as a drug – as determinant of the uptake of smoking (see for example, Oyuela-Caycedo and Kawa, this volume). Rather, the perceived effects of tobacco find their place within a system of virtues that upholds the effects that the plant induces. Wilbert (1987) makes a similar point in his discussion of 'natural modelling' in tobacco shamanism, in which he claims the action of nicotine provided empirical support for the pre-existing beliefs of Amerindian shamans – see Barbira Freedman (this volume).

Part III
Changing Landscapes

7

Commercial Cigarettes and *Tamï Ale* among the Wayana in Northern Amazonia

Renzo S. Duin

Figure 7.1 Wayana *pïjai* ('shaman') blowing smoke onto a patient. Engraving by Edouard Riou for Jules Crevaux (1883: 301). 'The *pïjai* inhales the smoke of a cigarette [...] and projects it with force while blowing like a whale onto the place where the ailment is located' (Jules Crevaux 1883: 299).[1]

> *There is yet another profitable commodity to be reaped in Guiana, and that is by Tobacco, which albeit some dislike, yet the generality of men in this kingdome doth with great affection entertaine it. It is not only in request in this our Country of England but also in Ireland, the Netherlands, in all the Easterly Countries, and Germany; and most of all amongst the Turks, and in Barbary [i.e., northern Africa] [...] The Tobacco that was brought into this kingdome in the yeare of our Lord 1610 was at the least worth 60 thousand pounds.*
>
> Robert Harcourt (1928: 36 [1613])

Introduction

Tobacco in the form of non-commercial cigarettes is widely used throughout Amazonia, and particularly in Guiana,[2] during healing practices by the *pïjai* ('shaman'), as vividly described by Jules Crevaux (1883: 299) and illustrated by Edouard Riou in Figure 7.1. While tobacco in the Western world is considered harmful and deadly, in Amazonia it is used in healing practices. From the latter perspective, one can argue that tobacco kills the evil spirit that causes ailments. Robert Harcourt, in the other opening quote above, mentioned that in the early seventeenth century most men 'in this kingdome doth with great affection entertaine [tobacco]', and he pointed out that tobacco as a commodity is very profitable and in high demand in Europe and beyond. What happened around this time, to draw on Arjun Appadurai, is that tobacco changed its 'regime of value' (1986: 15). In other words, this indigenous Amazonian product underwent a cultural redefinition as a trade item that became incorporated into the western regime of value. In this essay, I focus on the role of tobacco, in both the form of commercial cigarettes and traditional long cigarettes (*tamï*) made with locally grown tobacco (*tamï ale*) among the Wayana of the upper Maroni River (border between French Guiana and Suriname). Two questions that are at the foundation of this essay are (1) have commercial cigarettes affected the role of the local shaman (*pïjai*)? and (2) has the role of *tamï ale* in the *pïjai's* work been replaced or rearticulated by commercial cigarettes? Harcourt's description points to the long entwinement of tobacco in the lifeways of indigenous Amazonian people and their interaction with traders from Europe.

A deep-historical perspective (see Oyuela-Caycedo and Kawa, this volume) may shed light on the role of both commercial cigarettes and *tamï* (the traditional long cigarette) in the *pïjai*'s work. I am in the fortunate position that a few rare items in varying formats, such as a television broadcast (Leuk 1959a, b), photo books (Darbois 1956, Mazière and Darbois 1959), a published explorer journal (Crevaux 1883) and objects in a museum collection [Pitt Rivers Museum inventory number 1964: 2: 73], all relate to the very same region where I have conducted my field research since 1996, namely the upper Maroni River, border between Suriname and French Guiana. Moreover, I am working together with individuals – as well as with their children and grandchildren – who feature in Leuk's 1959 broadcast and Darbois' 1950s photo books or who manufactured objects currently held in the Pitt Rivers museum collection. Furthermore, genealogies of these individuals relate directly to the people mentioned in Crevaux's journal more than a century ago. This set of data spans over 125 years and allows me to analyse whether or not commercial cigarettes have affected the role of the local shaman (*pïjai*) and if *tamï* (the traditional long cigarette) has been replaced or rearticulated by commercial cigarettes.

Before discussing *tamï* and commercial cigarettes, let me dwell for a moment on the terms *pïjai* and shaman. I prefer the local Wayana term *pïjai* over the more generally used 'shaman' and have used it throughout this chapter. The Amazonian term '*pajé* or *piaii*' (Whitehead and Wright 2004: 2), '*pagé*' (Thévet 1558), '*piayé*' (Biet 1664) and other semantic variations, became known to the European audience *before* the term 'shaman' was introduced in 1672 by Avvkum Petrovich. Not only did the term shaman originate from *Siberia*, but Petrovich presented it as a verb '*to do the shaman*' (Narby and Huxley 2004: 18, emphasis added). The verb 'to do the shaman' can be translated in Wayana as *tïjumkai* (root *jum* = 'father'). For these reasons, I am reluctant to use the term 'shaman' for Amazonia and advocate for the use of *pïjai*, *piaii* (Carib) or *pajé* (*língua geral*). Furthermore, healing is not only performed by the *pïjai*; there are several Wayana (both male and female) who know *ëlemi* chants that are performed in curing ceremonies.[3] These *ëlemi* chants support curing of wounds inflicted upon the corporeal body. As will be elaborated upon in a moment, *ëlemi* chanters may use commercial cigarettes during these healing ceremonies whereas the Wayana *pïjai* prefers the traditional *tamï ale*.

First, I will describe and discuss the broadcasts of *Voyage sans Passeport* (Leuk 1959a, b) where commercial cigarettes are being handed out. This occasion, unique in the sense that the exchange of commercial cigarettes is recorded on film, was certainly not the first time that the Wayana of the upper Maroni River came in to contact with commercial cigarettes.[4] This broadcast and voice-over demonstrates that the Wayana of the upper Maroni River in the 1950s were already situated within an ever-expanding global network. Next, I will discuss *tamï ale* based on my personal experience in the field, comparing this to the account by Jules Crevaux some 123 years earlier. This will enable me to demonstrate either the continuity or the discontinuity of the role of tobacco in the practice of the *pïjai*. I will conclude with a consideration of the social aspects of tobacco smoking and the different uses of *tamï ale* on the one hand, and of commercially produced cigarettes on the other. As I am not a smoker, I cannot relate to the practice of smoking and the different tastes. However, I have been treated by a *pïjai* with *tamï ale*, and have assisted in other *pïjai* sessions; so I can draw on these personal experiences. Although tobacco has not been a primary focus of my research (Duin 2009, 2012), I draw on information gathered throughout the years to conceptualize the role of tobacco and to gain insight into the different use of *tamï ale* and commercial cigarettes.

Commercial cigarettes handed out to the Wayana in 1959

24 January 1959. Kawemhakan, Lawa, upper Maroni River, Surinamese bank. A one-legged *bagnard* (i.e. a French political convict)[5] in the characteristic striped prison outfit undertook an expedition to the upper Maroni River. The *bagnard* arrives by canoe at the indigenous Wayana village known as Kawemhakan. His aim is to find local guides to help him find the much sought after blue *morpho* butterfly. Supported by two crutches, the one-legged *bagnard* climbs the steps cut in the clay riverbank to arrive in the public place of the village named 'High Place' (Kawemhakan in Wayana).

Upon arrival in the village, the *bagnard* establishes himself on a small bench in a circle of seven men and several children. Three women are standing in the background. The men are well dressed with numerous bead strings, mirror necklaces, loin-cloths, some have a shining armband and rings, and three men wear the feather crown known as *pumali*.[6] One man has stuck a macaw tail feather between the bead-strings of his upper arm. Having recruited five native guides, the *bagnard* departs by canoe in search of the butterflies. While the canoe of the film crew had an outboard motor, the search for the butterflies is done *à la rame* (by means of paddles).

This staged visit of the *bagnard* to the Wayana or *Roucouyennes* was broadcasted in two episodes in the series *Voyage sans Passeport*, namely *Guyane: les Indiens* (Leuk 1959a) and *Guyane: sur le Maroni* (Leuk 1959b). When the *bagnard* first begins to climb the steps towards the village, he has a cigarette in his mouth, and when he explains how to catch the butterflies with his net, a young Wayana boy is standing in the middle of this circle smoking. It is only the following week that the gift of commercial cigarettes is broadcast. It becomes clear that these broadcasts are staged reenactments, partly drama, partly documentary, situated between fiction and fact, but which demonstrate the attitudes and bodily dispositions of the Wayana in the 1950s as regards to commercial cigarettes.

The second broadcast by Gilbert Leuk (1959b) among the Wayana of the upper Maroni River begins with a demonstration of traditional fishing by bow and arrow. Next, we return to last week's scene where the Wayana men are sitting on their wooden benches in a circle in the village square. The *bagnard* is handing out commercial cigarettes. He draws out cigarettes from the packet one by one and hands them to each man in turn. The first Wayana man sitting next to the *bagnard* keeps his eyes on the cigarette as it is brought out. The second man does not show much interest in receiving a cigarette. Then two cigarettes are handed to the next man who has a small boy of about three years old on his lap. One of these two cigarettes he hands to the man next to him because he is out of reach of the *bagnard*. Another man, who is standing, reaches out to obtain a cigarette. Next, the *bagnard* walks behind the men, who remain seated on their benches and one by one, he lights the cigarettes with his lighter. The men are inhaling the cigarettes. Some hold the cigarette in their right hand, between thumb and index finger, yet most hold the cigarette in their left hand, between index and middle finger. The adolescents in particular smile broadly while they smoke the commercial cigarettes. And then the small boy takes centre stage, having got off his father's lap. He stands firm with a toy bow and arrow in his left hand, and a cigarette in his right, between his index and middle finger. He is happily smoking the cigarette that was given to his father. Inhaling deep into his lungs, blowing out big plumes of smoke, he demonstrates this is not the first time he has smoked a cigarette. The scene ends with a close-up of the face of the young boy proudly smoking.

The voice-over of the all-knowing cinematographer and the female interviewer of the programme are rather derogatory: when Leuk first states that they are handing out cigarettes, the interviewer asks if the Wayana have had cigarettes before, to which Leuk replies 'No, never before.' Rather than providing more information about the cigarettes, Leuk talks about the payments for filming. 'We stayed about two days among the Indians to shoot this footage. In the beginning, I could take pictures and they [the Wayana] did not ask for anything. When we left, it cost us 100 to 150 French francs to take one photograph.' 'Which you had to give?' 'Yes, you had to give it. They did not accept otherwise. If we had stayed eight days, it maybe would have cost us 500 francs per image. There is no set tariff… ' Then Leuk is interrupted by the interviewer who asks 'But what do they do with that money?' After all, *Voyage sans Passeport* emphasizes how far we are from 'civilization'. 'Their money', Leuk replies, 'they [i.e., the Wayana] travel to Saint-Laurent; they conduct "expeditions"; they go to the city where they buy lots of things, which are normally sold to them in exchange for gold. For example, they buy things for their kitchen.' Meanwhile, the footage of the Wayana smoking commercial cigarettes continues, and when the little boy appears the interviewer comments 'But they really smoke at a young age there… !' 'Indeed. As you see… like a chimney!' the film-maker replies. 'Certainly… and he continues… ' 'Indeed'. 'Indeed, surprisingly' the interviewer and the film-maker concur.

In the past, the Wayana tried to make money out of every transaction in order to purchase Western goods. This continues today, and most purchases are made for the kitchen, above all aluminium and enameled pots, pans and plates. Apparently, no commercial cigarettes are purchased by the Wayana, at least not until recently, the only exception being Paranam, son of the village leader of Kawemhakan where the *bagnard* handed out his commercial cigarettes as discussed above. Paranam told me in 2000 that he had been employed as a Dutch government official to monitor the activities on the upper Maroni River since 9 June 1969, that is, only a decade after Leuk's broadcast, and as such he had easy access to commercial cigarettes. Paranam embodied the ongoing globalization of the Wayana. His extended personhood, through the photographs of Dominique Darbois (1956; and particularly Mazière and Darbois 1959), reaches far beyond the Guianas. Meanwhile, the globalizing world encroached upon him. Paranam was a man living in limbo; while being Wayana, he had a hard time belonging to the local indigenous Wayana community, but neither would he ever really fit into the western Dutch/Surinamese society. Paranam was from a long lineage of shamans and his father provided him with *tamï ale* from a young age, as it is common practice for would-be *pïjai*'s to be taught to smoke. Paranam's sons continue to be entwined with this ongoing globalization of the Wayana, and they continue to attempt to make money out of every transaction to purchase Western goods such as TVs and computers.

Wayana today identify the boy smoking in the 1959 broadcast as a son of a Wayana man, also from the earlier mentioned village of Kawemhakan, named Sintaman. Sintaman himself features in the broadcast while having his son on his lap and, later, watches over his son who smokes a commercial cigarette. In 1963, a few years after the broadcast of *Voyage sans Passeport*, British anthropologist Audrey Butt-Colson collected several unused specimens of long cigarettes (*tamu*) from Kawemhakan as well as some used cigarettes with charms from a proximate village (Figure 7.2). Traditional long cigarettes (*tamu* or *tamï*)[7] consisting of tobacco leaves (*tamï ale*; *Nicotiana* spp.; in Wayana, *ale* is 'leaf') rolled (*timisike*) in thin sheets of inner tree bark (*okalat*; *Couratari guianensis*; in the Maroon trade language of Suriname this tree is also referred to as *ingi pipa* 'Indian pipe'), are used by the *pïjai*.

Figure 7.2 Samples of new and used *Tamï ale*, the traditional long cigarettes with locally grown tobacco (*tamï ale*), along with okalat inner tree bark wrapper (*Couratari guianensis*), collected by Audrey Butt-Colson in 1963 in the Wayana villages of Kawemhakan, Suriname (new) and Twenke, French Guiana (used cigarettes), both located at the Lawa, upper Maroni River (Pitt Rivers Museum inv.nr. 1964: 2:73). (Photograph by Renzo Duin 2012.)

A tradition of *tamï ale* among the Wayana

Some fifteen years ago, during one of my first visits among the Wayana of the upper Maroni Basin, I suffered from sunstroke, or so I thought. I had a severe headache. My head was spinning as I stood up, so I decided to stay in my hammock. I stayed with Ronnie, a nephew of Paranam, and neighbour of the *pïjai* who had made the long cigarettes for Audrey Butt-Colson in 1963. Ronnie decided to invite a *pïjai*. I told him it was not necessary, assuming that if I had sunstroke, my headache would be gone by the next day. 'Do not die!' Ronnie's family told me. Ronnie asked if I had a packet of cigarettes. I had brought a packet of cigarettes with me, although this was the first time that a Wayana had asked me for any. I thought his request ill-timed, yet my headache was too severe to even begin arguing about it. 'In my backpack' I said.

Ronnie went through my backpack and left with the whole packet. 'Do not die!' Ronnie's wife and daughter said again. 'Great' I thought, 'and why must he now leave with an entire packet of [commercial] cigarettes?'

That evening, just after sunset, Ronnie's daughter came to my hammock and told me to come to the place in front of the house of her grandmother. A table and chair were carefully positioned in front of it. 'Where does it hurt?' the *pïjai* asked. I indicated my temples, where I could feel the blood was pulsating through my veins. Then he took his long cigarette and began inhaling. He blew a cloud of smoke onto my left temple, in the self-same fashion as is depicted in the engraving by Edouard Riou for Jules Crevaux some 123 years earlier (Figure 7.1). Here, the *pïjai* in that picture is wearing a feather cape and feather headdress whereas the *pïjai* who treated me was wearing a short, T-shirt and a baseball cap. Then the *pïjai* began to suck on my left temple. He spat and took another puff of his long cigarette. He sucked and spat again. Another puff. Then, the same procedure on the right temple. Another puff from his *tamï ale*, and blew the smoke over my head. He then massaged my head, from the front to above the ears. Then he clapped his hands in the air and said it was done. If the pain was gone next day, I would have to pay him, he said. According to this *pïjai* my headache had been caused by the dangerous evil spirit of *sisi-je*, Mother Sun. The next day, the headache was indeed gone. It turned out that Ronnie had taken my commercial cigarettes as an incentive for the *pïjai* to come and treat me that evening.

On 24 November 1878, in the Wayana village of Pouimro, upper Paru de l'Este. Jules Crevaux (1883: 299), during his explorations of the upper Paru and Citaré, requested information from the *pïjai* Apipa, who was known to be well-travelled, as any well-respected *pïjai* should be. Crevaux, who is a medical doctor himself, addressed Apipa as 'colleague'. At sunset, Apipa prepared himself for a consultation. The patient was sitting outside on a bench, amidst the spectators, just like I had done some 123 years later.

> The *pïjai* inhales the smoke of a cigarette that is passed to him already lit, and blowing like a whale, he forcefully projects [the smoke] on the sick part. Then he sucks with his mouth [on the sick part] and blew with violence to chase away the evil he just sucked out. This diabolical scene lasts more than two hours; it ends with a prescription that can be summed up in a word: diet, diet. The patient will not eat peccary, curassow, or big fish, not drink manioc beer, etc. My colleague will receive a hammock as payment, but only after the patient recovers completely. (Crevaux 1883: 299; Figure 7.1)[8]

Unlike my treatment, a small enclosure with leaves of '*ouapou*' [= *wapu*] was constructed in a corner of the house (Crevaux 1883: 299). Based on similar structures built today, it can be concluded that this was a *mïmnë* or *tokay*, an enclosure about two to three metres in diameter, and some two metres high, made out of dense layers of vertically arranged fronds of the *kumu* palm (*Oenocarpus bacaba*) or *wapu* palm

(*Euterpe oleracea*). No chinks of light are permitted through the palm frond walls. This kind of enclosure is only constructed after dusk and stripped down before dawn. It is at this ephemeral place that the *pïjai* invokes the spirits, in the past as is today.

On 16 August 2000, at sunset, in the same village where I was treated a year earlier, a young Wayana husband brought *kumu* palm fronds into the village. He said that his grandfather would arrive in a moment to treat his wife who was very ill. At 8.30 p.m., the young husband, together with the husband of his wife's sister-in-law, began making make an enclosure in a corner of the house of their mother-in-law. Half an hour later, the *pïjai* entered the enclosure. First some chanting was heard. All spectators who were sitting on long benches around the enclosure of palm fronds ask, one after another, '*Ëh?!*' I had also been invited to sit and ask in search of the evil spirit who caused this malady. Some two hours later, around 10.45 p.m., a second sound emanated from the enclosure. It was the high-pitched voice of *ipo*, the water monster, my neighbour told me. Then there was rustling and swooshing in the palm-fronds, around and around. '*Kaikui*', (the monstrous jaguar), my neighbour informed me again, in a soft-spoken voice. Then it was quiet. It was cold. The full moon rose in a cloudless sky. Cassava beer was distributed to those present. A small fire was lit for the attendants to warm themselves. This fire was shielded, so as not to attract the evil spirit *jolok*. Then the next of kin, one by one, continued to ask for the evil spirit, '*Ëh?, ëhhh?!*' After midnight, at 12.20 a.m., the *pïjai* briefly left the enclosure to reenter with the patient to begin the session of smoking, sucking, chanting and thumping the ground. Palm fronds were rustling. Kinsmen, one by one, continued to ask '*Ëh?, Ëhhh?!, Ëh.*' At 6.00 a.m., just before sunrise, the palm fronds had been removed. Some small *tamï ale* butts remained on the ground. The *pïjai* had taken the larger pieces with him. The patient was sitting by the fire, warming herself. The *pïjai* had returned to Kawemhakan. This *pïjai* session very much resonated with what Jules Crevaux (1883: 299) witnessed some 123 years previously.

Another occasion for smoking *tamï ale* was by the village leader at dawn as was photographed by Dominique Darbois in 1953 (Darbois 1956; Mazière and Darbois 1959). Some Wayana elders remember how, before sunrise, the village leader ordered a fire to be started in the village plaza. All men and children gathered around the fire in the centre of the village. While the cigarette was burning, the village leader told stories – stories of times long ago (*uhpak aptau eitoponpë*); legends, myths and stories of wars. While the cigarette was burning, Wayana oral tradition was kept alive. History was in the making. Along with the use of *tamï ale* at dawn facilitating early morning storytelling, this unique Wayana social memory is perishing.

Commercial cigarettes and *tamï ale* in the twenty-first century

It appears that the distribution of commercial cigarettes in the late 1950s by the *bagnard* filmed by Leuk had little to no impact on the role of *tamï ale*. As we saw above, a few years later, Audrey Butt-Colson collected some new cigarettes from Kawemhakan where the *pïjai* invited on 16 August 2000, lived. This is not to say there was no influence from the Dutch or the American evangelical missionaries.[9] Quite the contrary, the son of the *pïjai* (and father of the young husband whose wife was seriously ill) was trained by the missionaries and leads the Sunday mass in the local church of Kawemhakan that was inaugurated in 1999. Wayana have found a way of living where Sunday church, the *pïjai*, and Western medication exists side-by-side. So too *tamï ale* and commercial cigarettes can exist side-by-side. Perhaps a *pïjai* can use 'modern' commercial cigarettes for 'modern' illness, but for traditional illness, such as the attack by *sisi-je*, relief was found in *tamï ale*.

The general literature classifies both *tïjumkai* ('to do the *pïjai*') and the chanting of *ëlemi* under the generic 'shamanism'. There is however a clear distinction between the *pïjai*, who materializes internal complaints, and the *ëlemi*-chanter who treats wounds inflicted upon the corporeal body. Commercial cigarettes can be used during *ëlemi*-chants. Commercial cigarettes are not considered as powerful as *tamï ale*, although they are recognized to have some characteristics that make them useful for treating certain corporeal problems. For example in 2004, during an expedition in the Tumuc-Humac Mountains, Pajakwale, a grandson of the *pïjai* who had made the long cigarettes collected by Butt-Colson some forty years earlier, requested a commercial cigarette from one of the other expedition members. This was the first time during the expedition that he had asked for a cigarette. Rather than taking his time and enjoying a cigarette at this amazing panorama over the Amazon rainforest, he smoked the cigarette with short but firm puffs. His short but firm inhalations allowed him to extract the tar paste from the commercial cigarette and spit it onto his hand. The extracted tar paste was smeared over the air hole of what appeared to be a bot fly larva (Fr. *ver macaque*, *Dermatobia hominis*). After about half an hour, Pajakwale placed both thumbs on each side of the air hole, and with force, pushed the larva out of the body – the cure for the 'itchy feeling' that one of the expedition members was experiencing on the side of his body, under his arm. This rather specific use of commercial cigarettes for a particular healing practice is unlikely to replace the *tamï ale* as used by the *pïjai*.

There is only one Wayana who was known for smoking large quantities of commercial cigarettes, namely Paranam, son of Janamale, the village leader, founder of Kawemhakan, and an important interlocutor. Apart from him, one rarely sees a Wayana smoking a commercial cigarette. To refresh my memory, I viewed earlier video recordings. One occasion, which was so distinctive that I had remembered it, was during the presentation of basketry items in 2003. A brother of the young wife that underwent the *pïjai* treatment in 2000, as described and discussed earlier, was present during the presentation of basketry items. He was about fifteen years old. Although he had not produced any basketry, he had arrived to see the commotion. He stood aside, leaning against a tree. He was wearing blue jeans, Adidas sneakers, a red T-shirt, and a red bandana. In his right hand, between index and middle finger, he had a commercial cigarette. Rather than engaging in the local practice of presenting the basketry, and related ceremony, he tried to get the attention of the girls passing by. As he explained later, he was unaware of local traditions. He later moved to Cayenne, the capital of French Guiana, and works today as a heavy construction excavator driver. He only returns to the upper Maroni River during the December holidays between Christmas and New Year's Eve, to see his family. Both Paranam and this adolescent Wayana were raised within Wayana society but were attracted to the European lifestyle, whether it be Dutch or French. Smoking commercial cigarettes within Amazonian societies reflects a desire for Western modernity (cf. Barletti, this volume). Kopytoff (1986: 89) wrote on the drama of personal biographies that 'a person's social identities are not only numerous but often conflicting, and there is no clear hierarchy of loyalties that makes one identity dominant over the others'. Regarding the case of the Wayana, the impossibility of choosing between clashing identities, that is, Amerindian versus a European lifestyle, is materialized through the use of *tamï ale* and commercial cigarettes. Although both items are tobacco based, the former embodies an Amerindianization of conviviality whereas the latter materializes a longing for Western oriented modernity. This drama of the social fields of *tamï ale* and commercial cigarettes embodies the friction between conflicting valuation and uncertainties of identity that is increasingly taking place in Wayana indigenous communities.

Conclusion

When Wayana smoke *tamï ale*, it is always in a context of sociality, if not conviviality, whether it be at dusk during a *pïjai* session where all next-of-kin are present to help search for the evil spirit responsible for an internal ailment, or at dawn when the village leader used to tell his traditional stories. We have seen commercial cigarettes used to invite a *pïjai*, during healing sessions in combination with *ëlemi* chants and as an individual practice indicating a desire for Western modernity. I therefore argue that the traditional role of *tamï ale* is not rearticulated or replaced by commercial cigarettes, neither has the latter affected the role of the 'shaman' (*pïjai*). The power and qualities of commercial cigarettes are always trumped by the traditional *tamï ale*.

In this chapter, I have attempted to provide a picture of a global trend, the spread of tobacco and tobacco products, in one area of tobacco's historical 'source' region. Further research on the topic is needed. Of particular interest is the question of why it is that commercial alcohol (rum, whisky and beer) has spread so quickly among the Wayana, whereas commercial tobacco has hardly gained ground even after its introduction into the area more than a century ago – in contrast to some of the other Amazonian communities discussed in this book. Commercial cigarettes among the

Wayana in French Guiana and Suriname have not, in more than a century, replaced or rearticulated the role of *tamï ale*. Among the Wayana of Guiana, *tamï ale* and commercial cigarettes each play a role in different social fields that are situated in a dramatic friction: *tamï ale* is directly related to the Guiana tradition of conviviality, whereas commercial cigarettes are mostly used by young individuals who have an insecure identity.

Acknowledgements

First and foremost, I thank the conveners, Andrew Russell (Durham) and Elizabeth Rahman (Oxford), for inviting me to the workshop and editing the English text. The research project *Beauty and the Feast* (2010–2014), of which I am the Principal Investigator, is funded by the Dutch National Science Foundation (NWO-VENI # 275-62-005). The 2012–2013 fieldwork allowed for research on the most recent situation regarding the use of commercial cigarettes and traditional indigenous cigarettes among the Wayana of the upper Maroni Basin. Interpretations made are the responsibility of the author.

Notes

1. '*Le piay hume la fume d'une cigarette [...] et la projette avec force en soufflant comme un cachalot sur la partie malade*' (Crevaux 1883: 299).
2. Guiana, or the 'Island of Guiana', encompasses Venezuela east of the Orinoco, Guyana, Suriname, French Guiana and Brazil east of the Rio Negro and north of the Amazon.
3. Many Wayana man and women know *ëlemi* chants and know recipes for herbal cures, yet these men and women are not considered *pïjai*. Many *ëlemi* chants are sung in Apalai, including the ones published as 'Wayana' (de Goeje 1941). Just as different *pïjai* master different methods, different *ëlemi* chanters know different chants. *Ëlemi* chanters are not hierarchically ranked, other than they simply know different chants. When people have flesh wounds, they go to an *ëlemi* chanter (male or female) proven to be effective in healing this kind of wound. Internal illness is treated and materialized by the *pïjai*.
4. During the 1903 Gonini expedition, tobacco was rationed at one hundred gram per person per week (Franssen-Herderschee 1905: 6), and during the 1937 border expedition tobacco was rationed at one package (with paper and matches) per person per week (van Lynden 1939: 90).
5. Saint-Laurent is located at the mouth of the Maroni River, and it is there that a prison camp ('*bagne*') was located, made famous in the beginning of Henri Charrière's 1969 book *Papillon*. The prison officially closed in 1946, the same year the colonial penal system was abolished, though many former prisoners remained in French Guiana.

6. Unfortunately this broadcast in the grey tones of black-and-white film does not authenticate the richness of red, yellow, and metallic blue against a background of green and blue hues.
7. *Tamï* resonates with both *tamo* (1. grandfather, 2. ancestor) and *tametei* (twilight, between about 6.30 p.m. and 7.00 p.m.) referring to the time a *pïjai* arrives at his patient.
8. '*Le piay hume la fume d'une cigarette qu'on lui passé tout allumée et la projette avec force en soufflant comme un cachalot sur la partie malade. Puis, il fait ventouse et soufflé avec violence pour chaser le mal qu'il vient d'aspirer. Cette scène diabolique duree plus de deux heures; elle se termine par une prescription que l'on peut résumer en un mot: diète, diète. La malade ne mangera pas de pakiri, de hoco, de gros poisson, ne boira pas de cachiri, etc. Mon collègue recevra en payement un hamac, mais à une condition, c'est que le malade se rétablira complètement*' (Crevaux 1883: 299).
9. The American evangelical missionaries have run a Sunday school in Kawemhakan. Since the independence of Suriname in 1975, and with the establishment of the first school in French Guiana, many Wayana from Kawemhakan have crossed the Maroni River during the past decades. French Guiana is a French overseas department. Wayana residing on the French bank have been provided with French identity cards since 2000 and obligatorily follow the French educational system.

8

Landscapes of Desire and Tobacco Circulation in the Yanomami Ethos

Alejandro Reig

> *A newly arrived guest stretches silently in the hammock appointed to him. Conversation will not be started until after having received from his host some food lying beside him in a basket, and a chewing of tobacco. Any festival begins with the ceremonial offering of meat and boiled plantain. Through cooked food and tobacco, a full entrance is done into culture, which is to say into exchange.*
>
> Lizot (1984: 157)

This chapter explores the significance of tobacco among the Yanomami in daily life and in relations between distant villages, suggesting that its consumption and circulation conveys the always unfinished condition of a sociality based on circulation and exchange. I look at these issues by examining the connection between people, consumption and place; the Yanomami subsistence pattern as an incomplete gestalt with different components; and the role of want and need in everyday life. The examination of the practice of tobacco consumption and circulation within these contexts is suggested by Yanomami myths that account for the different food staples given to the people by ancestors, tobacco among them, in which the latter appears expressing a powerful and mobilizing desire.

Yanomami tobacco, *pẽẽ nahe*, is everywhere in daily life. We can see the wad bulging under the lower lips of men (and, to a lesser extent, of women and children); placed upon the beams of the house or on top of pieces of wood on the ground while people converse or eat; and passing between the hands and mouths of friends or kin. Its wide leaves can be seen drying over the fire and wrapped in bundles on the backs of visitors to distant allied villages as a token of exchange. In the gardens, always composed of a number of basic food and useful staples (plantain and bananas, manioc, yam, cocoyam, sugar cane, maize, arrow-cane and cotton among them) tobacco plants always festoon sections of the clearing. A wad can be placed in the mouth of a corpse before its cremation at a funeral (Lizot 1988: 867), but tobacco is not used ritually in this sociocultural context, unlike other Amerindian societies.

Rather, the secular, everyday micro-rituals it materializes pertain to the register of pleasurable consumption and exchange, and in that tobacco plays a central role in the Yanomami good life. In villages close to a mission, health post and school, where many adults are engaged in paid jobs as nurses, teachers or representatives of diverse national institutions, some people have replaced the traditional practice of sucking the tobacco wad with the smoking of cigarettes. However, the aspects of tobacco use and circulation I will highlight are not traversed by an opposition between change and tradition. Rather, I will suggest that these practices of consumption and sociality display complementary aspects that get emphasized or downplayed differentially in contrasting socio-geographical contexts.

The technical process of Yanomami tobacco making is probably not unlike that of other peoples: after being harvested, the leaves are put to dry over the fire and then wrapped in bundles. In order to make a wad, a leaf is extracted and processed individually each time. It is first soaked in water in a gourd or bowl, then put over the ashes of the hearth, which adhere to the wet surface. The leaf is then amassed between the hands and folded into a small and elongated lump. It can then be tucked under the lower lip, the upper lip or behind the cheek. These placements are respectively called *karepou*, *hɨɨpou* and *hopou* (Lizot 2004: 309–310). A good piece may last several days, slowly losing its strength and transforming from strong and efficacious (*wayu*) to tasteless or neutral (*nosi* or *okewe*).

Tobacco is conceptualized as food (Lizot 2004: 255), in part because it serves to diminish hunger (Cocco 1987: 306), and it comes together with cooked food in the cycle of reciprocal gifts both with visitors from another village and within the village (Lizot 1984: 157). Its circulation, however, not only differs from that of game meat but also from that of vegetables harvested in the garden. While every man who tends a garden usually has his share of tobacco in it, tobacco tends to circulate more freely between neighbours in the same village than does manioc and other tubers or plantains, items which are usually consumed within the nuclear or extended family.

Tobacco is easily shared between people in an amiable relationship. As expressed in the opening quotation by Lizot, handing a wad of tobacco to a visitor from another village is one of the gestures of good etiquette which open the micro-cycles of sharing that form the backbone of Yanomami sociality. This is, however, a more formalized exchange than those occurring between close friends or kin. On a casual meeting in a path in the forest or in the village, a friend or kinsperson will say that his wad has become tasteless or that he doesn't have one: the other person will extract the piece from his mouth and divide it in two, giving away half, which the requestor will quickly insert under his lip, and conversation will be resumed.[1] As a mobile staple, tobacco is not, however, just given away. Only discrete quantities circulate in the casual manner just described, and it enters into trade on the occasion of visits to other villages. Within a village, the differences in tobacco produced by different gardeners may be subject to a more intense coveting that the rest of agricultural produce. A laborious farmer may be asked for some of his tobacco by those with less of it. Eventually, if failing to redistribute, the hardworking gardener will suffer the theft of some of his leaves by the lazier gardener, leading sometimes to serious conflicts (see Chagnon 1968: 37; Lizot 1980: 37). Dried tobacco leaves may also be taken out of the bundle at the productive gardener's home by covetous individuals when the owner is not there.

Tobacco has possibly become an essential staple because it helps to create both an atmosphere of sociable exchange and an alert disposition to any individual task. The extended timeframe of the pleasure it affords, coupled with the mixture of awakening and relaxation it produces, facilitates its circulation in a somewhat looser manner than other staples, creating a platform for diverse relations of exchange. Tobacco configures a central social need and when it is lacking it is substituted by other plant leaves, such as cotton (Lizot 1984: 14–15), *yaraka henaki* plant (*Phyllanthus piscatorum*), a fish poison (Gertsch et al. 2004) and *yapi mahekoki* plant (Trichilia sp. *Meliaceae*) (Cocco 1987), some of which are also likely to have psycho- and physio-active effects. As a practice of consumption and conviviality tobacco can be placed together with other foodstuffs and stimulants, such as the *epena* hallucinogenic drug made from wild plants,[2] and *yupu una*, a beverage made of a mix of crushed crab shells, ashes from the bark of the *korori kefi* tree (*Couratari multiflora*, Lecythidaceae), water and pepper (Capsicum sp.). Alertness, satisfaction and stimulation of the senses are common to these three experiences, in very different degrees: *epena* is a powerful vision-inducing hallucinogenic, while tobacco is a mild alertness-inducing drug; *yupu una* provides oral satisfaction and feelings of satiation together with the stimulant effect of the saline mix and the peppers. But a defining feature of all the experiences with these substances is the centrality of sharing and exchange within them: they provide a basis for specific situations of social interaction.

The collective consumption of *epena*, both in its ritual uses (the funerary ceremony, healing shamanism, initiations) and its everyday uses (sharing of news and loose conversation between men in the public plaza), is a fundamental practice of Yanomami sociality. Tobacco consumption, as we have said, is a prevalent and ubiquitous practice done both individually and in the company of others, with less psychotropic effects than *epena* and done in a non-performative way, contrary to the ritual uses of the latter. I have seen the delicious *yupu una* sauce, sipped on its own or together with roasted shrimp, taken in what seems to be a binding moment between a few commensals, two young men or a mature couple, its intensity emphasized by the silent consumption of the hot peppers. Putting together these three practices of shared substance ingestion and their different degrees of physical and psychoactive effects, we can understand something of the varying intensities and degrees of consciousness necessary to maintain the convivial atmosphere of Yanomami society. This society cannot be fully appreciated if such activities are overlooked, as they play a central role among the practices by which the social *ethos* is supported and maintained.

The exchange and consumption of Yanomami tobacco has been well described (Chagnon 1968, Lizot 1984, Cocco 1987), but a deeper investigation that considers the wider societal relations it enables is still due. Here, I will suggest some relations of tobacco with people, places and desires, and some possible pathways for its research.

The affordances of places

Tobacco, food and hallucinogens mediate ties between people, but the three also express the links between people and the surroundings in which they procure food: they define places of environmental offerings and consumption which provide 'affordances' (Gibson 1977) that serve to qualify people or villages from certain areas. Lizot has stated that most basic forest and agricultural staples are generally widespread in the Yanomami region, with a dearth of some products (such as the curare arrow tip poison) in only a few areas. But products from faraway places can also be preferred, and exchange is pushed by the drive to socialize rather than by scarcity (Lizot 1988: 554). However, Fuentes (1980: 64–65) has reported a differential abundance of *fisiomi* (*Anadenanthera peregrina*), the basic tree for the production of *epena*, in the upper Ocamo region (which encompasses my research area), compared to areas closer to the Orinoco. During my fieldwork, between 2007 and 2011, the relative availability of tobacco and *epena* was a subject of comment between lowland riverine villages and upriver mountain villages and stimulated visits and exchanges. While I have not seen any record of *yupu una* (or its *korori kefi* bark ingredient) appearing as a token of exchange, its consumption, less generalized today, is also tied to the socio-natural environment, as it tends to disappear in villages which rely on circuits of exchange with national society. As a traditional practice with an important role in providing sodium to a saltless diet (Cocco 1987: 305), it is still crucial in distant villages not in contact with sources of industrial salt (on the processing of salt, see Echeverri, this volume).

Together with food, tobacco and *epena* stand out as resources that connect friendly villages in times of relative need. In this manner, they constitute material staples that enable webs of ecological and socio-political exchanges which underpin the reproduction of the symbolic order of society. During the wet season, for example, people from less gifted areas of the forest may come to visit and stay for long periods at the villages of their kin in more plentiful areas. This is not necessarily expressed in terms of their need for food, but together with the need to be close to their people living far away. The village of *Shakripiwei*, in the *Shitari* area of the upper Ocamo River in which I did my fieldwork, had a population of around 50 people. It received several long-term visits from a group of more than a dozen relatives of the leader of one of the village factions between the rainy seasons of 2008 and 2009. These were people from the villages of *Horeape* and *Kanoshewe* in the Parima B area, known for its scarcity of game and poor harvest yield. The visitors went on daily foraging trips to obtain game and forest fruits as did the locals, but they also ate the garden produce of their hosts. Food was particularly scarce in Parima B that season, while *Shitari* still had quite abundant forest resources. The reason for visiting was explained to me by the leader of the group in terms of coming to live with 'our people' (*ipa kepe*), but an adolescent girl also said to me: 'it is much better to be here, there is lots of food and I had been longing to see mother's sister (*amiye*)'. Her statement clearly links the affordance of sociability with food availability, sharing and eating, with physiological and social needs expressed as one.

With regard to tobacco, individual people from downriver may move to visit upriver villages, or upriver interfluvial people may visit other friendly villages when their harvest is finished, driven simply by relative tobacco scarcity. They will bring specific items of exchange to secure the needed bundle. My guide from a lowland village, a middle-aged mission-educated and river-settled Yanomami man, would take me upriver and suffer the entire walk up to the *Shitari* mountains to be able to get some of the local tobacco in exchange for some fish hooks. This was quite an effort for him, as he is now used to motorized river travel and short, level walks to his nearby garden. But he had stopped sucking tobacco and was more interested in the cigarettes that he asked me to bring him from the city each time I entered the field. The *Shitari* tobacco that he traded was due to end up with his son-in-law or another of his fellow villagers. Another man, a friend and shaman from this downriver area, asked me to bring a forest plant hallucinogen for him from the upriver villages to which I was headed. Forest and agricultural produce are thus interwoven with webs of socio-political interrelations on a wider regional scale, allowing a complementation between ecologically differentiated areas.

In my wider ethnography of Yanomami place-making, I have revised the various ways in which the relation with places constitutes a marker of identity. From the wide to the narrow, these include the distribution of foraging areas for different villages of a population group; the statement of differences from others by means of how specific activities are carried out in certain forest areas; the inscribing and imbuing of places with meaning through naming and discursive practices, and physical intervention and transformation of the forest. Specific meshes of place-meaning play upon a set of categorically differentiated spaces: garden, village, paths and 'closed', lush '*paimi*' forest with no visibility, devoid of trails (Reig 2013). The places in which groups of people are located and the resources they manage to mobilize become part of the things that characterize them vis-à-vis other groups, within a socio-political ethos in which the village is the centre of the world and alterity increases radially outside of it (Albert 1985: Ch. VII). Given that the Yanomami ritual and socio-cosmological regime precludes any permanent attachment to place and to dead relatives or ancestors (Clastres and Lizot 1978: 130–131; Lizot 2007: 320–321), these situated identifications constitute important markers of difference. Particular practices and forms of resource use are attributed to people from different areas. For example, in my field site, I was told about how the people of *Wanat^ha*, a village to the northwest, still nestled in the mountains but lower in the altitude gradient and much closer to the Ocamo River, cooked big fish they got from the river in their funerary rituals, instead of meat. Similarly people from Ocamo, a village at the mouth of the Ocamo upon the Orinoco, performed the consumption phase of the funeral in a different way than them, and so on. These differentiations serve to constitute useful regional identifications, which always depend on the perspective of the speaker.

The occurrence and consumption of forest and garden produce, including tobacco and other stimulants, and their identification with people and places, takes place against a background of movement. Apart from seasonal trekking outings by factions or hunting expeditions, mobility in a Yanomami village may appear as a continuous helter-skelter scattering. Seen from the outside, it is surprising to see how individual people or families are always prone to disappear from the village without seemingly any prior notice. Looked at within the context of daily coexistence and respective socio-political weight of male leaders, their prestige or wealth of relationships or the state of affairs between a man and his wife, these sudden departures appear less arbitrary. Visits to distant places not only allow an escape from and amelioration of social tensions, disarm the build-up of gossip-related malaise and make it possible to get trade objects. As Feather says of the Nahua (2009), this 'restlessness' also affords the possibility of incorporating the perspective of others, doing what they do, eating what they eat. On a certain occasion in the early 1990s, I was serving a meal to a couple of adults that had brought me back on a canoe journey to the Mavaca mission post on the banks of the Orinoco, after I had visited their village in the Manaviche River, where Jacques Lizot was then working. A local, mission-educated and fully clothed bilingual man that I had been interviewing the week before entered the house and sneered at the two crouching men in loincloths gulping rice with sardines. These were '*waikasi*', wild Yanomami, from his point of view. He addressed me, shrugging:

> Mind you, when I visited Caracas, we had Coca-Cola with ice… stewed beef with potatoes… we smoked…

This feast had taken place at the home of a well-known explorer, a field partner of the anthropologist Napoleon Chagnon who was in the middle of a dispute in those days with the local missionaries and the anthropologist who hosted me. Beyond the evident conjuring of jealousy and the affirmation of his socio-political alliances, my bilingual interlocutor expressed a scale of places and their differentially valued affordances: the city where he engaged with local whites, ate proper white men's food and smoked like them; the 'interface' Yanomami village (Kelly 2011) where he engaged with transient whites such as me, who had little more than canned fish and rice to offer to someone like him, who knew better; and the upriver villages of wild Yanomami (usually sneered at by school-educated Yanomami because 'they still eat mice and snakes'). Distant places afford specific experiences with substances and food, as well as the experience of other environmental qualities. And they provide this because places constitute sensorial and material loci of incorporation.

The examples listed above help us to understand that the social value given to places, which are always *places of people*, may emerge through both the performance of certain behaviours and incorporation of substances. We will see later that these two aspects are also present in tobacco consumption. In a register of oral performance, for example, the two types of ceremonial dialogues, the 'language of the inside' *patamou* and the 'language for the outside' *wayamou* (Carrera 2005: 316–336) serve to forge local identifications, and to strengthen and repair intra-village relations and those with more or less distant neighbours, respectively. These practices of word exchange create and re-create certain configurations of sociality. But beyond these discursive performances and, in a complementary note, when places are looked at from the perspective of food and stimulants consumed and shared, we can find a consubstantiation between people and their places phrased on a register of embodiment. During inter-village visits people seem to loosely embody the specificities of their places. When visiting each other people carry these place-characteristics with them, and these can be strategically foregrounded in certain situations. For example, the relative scarcity of their lands can be stressed by visitors when visiting kin in a more plentiful area of the forest, thus providing the basis for exchange, for both an ecological and affective complementation. Like Western gastronomic or gourmet tourists, Yanomami people characterize places in terms of differential food and pleasure affordances.[3] When the young adults from *Shakripiwei* came back from the regional capital of La Esmeralda where they had been taken as patients or as companions of those in hospital, their stories abounded with how they drank lots of soft drinks and 'ate mixed' all the time – rice with canned tuna, pasta with sauce – like the *napë* (non-Yanomami people). It is within this horizon that traditional tobacco consumption and sharing seems to display its capacities for social linkages and mobilization.

Lack, want and completion in everyday life and myth

I have said that tobacco may serve to enact a different hue of exchange relations than those which other food staples serve to materialize. And I have also said that the degree of formality of its exchanges differs depending on whether it circulates between co-residents (*yahit^{h}erimi*) or between locals and visitors from another village. When a host hands a wad to a visitor from a neighbouring village, tobacco always serves to perform a welcoming procedure, facilitating immediate exchange with a gesture of quick incorporation, a sort of instant 'making kin out of the other' (Vilaça 2002). The visitor may sit down on the ground close to his host's hammock and say '*kamiye keya*' – 'it is me', or 'I have arrived'. This sole gesture is an invitation to reciprocate the gift of the visitor's presence: after being given the piece of tobacco, sooner or later he will receive some portion of food that is then eaten or hung over the fire. The visitor and the host will eat together and catch up on recent news: who has gone to the forest, who else has gone to visit another village or has come from another village to visit; where there is a conflict in a distant community, who brought the news about it and how. And at some point the visitor will express a need: his hammock has been burnt or torn apart because it was old, he has no machete, he is lacking a bowl like the one belonging to the host, obtained from a chain of trade that goes beyond this group of mountain villages to the river's edge, where somebody received it initially from a doctor. Frequently, after saying what he wants, the visitor will exclaim: '*ya fõri*', 'I need it intensely, I am craving for it' or '*ya proke*', 'I am empty', 'I am without anything', 'I am lacking (something)'. For those who are being asked, the ones who demand are exhibiting their dearth (of something). They put themselves in a pitiful or shameful position, *nö preaaɨ* (Lizot 2004: 269), showing themselves as 'poor me'. This expression is always related to somebody witnessing this state. *Nö preaaɨ* thus demonstrates a vacuum, one's emptiness or *manque*, to borrow a term from psychoanalytical discourse.[4] The expression for not having tobacco underlines the emptiness of the mouth (Lizot 1984: 14), stressing the importance of oral satiation (cf. Gow 1989).

The Yanomami moral code puts certain values in a central place, which may be seen in their highest, idealized form in an intensely emotional situation, such as a funerary ceremony. Then the virtues of the deceased are praised in lamentation: generosity, bravery, beauty, efficiency in hunting, fishing and farming (Lizot 2007: 305). Taking these as a point of departure to ascertain the wider logics of the *ethos* may help us understand why certain behaviours perform such a central role. Generosity, and to a certain extent magnificence or prodigality (in providing food, words or appropriate retaliation when due), seems to be the constant that traverses this moral regime. On a more affective level, Alès has underscored the central place of acting to impede the suffering of your loved ones within the Yanomami moral economy: it is through this that solidarity and conviviality are achieved (Alès 2000: 137). These two complementary drives may serve to illuminate why the exhibition of oneself as *being in need* is such a repeated attitude: it probes the interlocutor's generosity, challenges him to respond within the framework of the moral code and serves to maintain the affective atmosphere of life in common.

As I have shown, the consumption and sharing of tobacco occurs within this moral field: it mediates the circulation of gifts, food and services between people. But the physical, emotional and symbolic satisfaction it provides seems to be charged with further connotations related to the perception of the social ecology as a totality. This becomes evident when we make an interconnected reading of the myth of the origin of agriculture and that of the origin of tobacco. I will begin with the first of them, 'The Master of Banana Trees', which has been extensively analysed by Lizot (1989, 1994) and Carrera (2005). They emphasize how this myth establishes the role of reciprocity and exchange as a foundation of the Yanomami moral regime and sociality. I summarize it here, following Lizot's original recording of the myth:

> The ancestors did not know about plantains and they ate earth with the animals they hunted. *Hõrõnami* was in the middle of the forest when rain announced itself. He made a shelter and spoke out in ceremonial *wayamou* phrases his intentions to cut down a tree and fetch a honey-comb attached to it, against the backdrop of a mountain. Then Ghost – *Poreriwë* – appeared, carrying a load of plantains in a basket, with ripe bananas on top. Even if flabbergasted by the encounter, *Hõrõnami* managed to ask who the revenant was, and what the fruits were. Ghost, who hid himself from sight and had a very bad stutter when speaking, denied initially knowing what the plantains were. Then he changed his attitude and spoke of all the varieties of plantain and bananas he had harvested, and invited *Hõrõnami* to eat them. The latter tasted the ripe fruits and got dizzy, making Ghost laugh: he said people always lost their mind when eating them for the first time. Ghost lived in a house by a plain at the base of a mountain, where he had a garden, but was now camping in the forest. *Hõrõnami* said that after tasting the bananas, people in his village would surely want to have more of them. The other one replied that his name was Ghost – *Poreriwë* – that he used to take shortcuts in the forest instead of paths, and that if they came to his house to ask for plantains they would find it empty and he would not give them any. They both departed. Ghost went through the bush and eventually ended up in a path, and *Hõrõnami* left taking the bananas with him and reached his village. Everybody asked him about those new fruits he hung over his hearth, but he remained silent, warming himself up and ignoring the insistent questions. Finally he told them how he got them out of his encounter with Ghost, and subsequently distributed them. The people in the village ate the bananas and got dizzy (from Lizot in Wilbert and Simoneau. 1990: 153–155).[5]

Lizot emphasizes the central place of generosity and reciprocity in this myth, expressed through the proper exchange of words and goods. Ghost is an ambiguous being between the dead and the living and his stinginess is evident in his refusing to share food and give out words properly (he has a stutter). He thus falls outside the proper grounds of sociality (Lizot 1994: 224). By means of a deconstruction of the discursive plot, Carrera further illuminates Ghost's asociality (2005: Chs. 5–6) as it appears in the different voices that make up the narration. It becomes evident in the words of *Poreriwë* giving his location only in a physical geographical space; while the voices of the Yanomami (*Hõrõnami* and the myth-teller) emphasize that Ghost lives alone, outside a social space. A person is only understood as human if living in a local group, a community of relations (Lizot 1994: 110–118).

I would like to underline some complementary aspects of this story that illuminate our subject: these are the way in which this key issue of exchange is staged in contrasting productive and spatial contexts, and how these appear to be enacted in a sort of ecological transition. In terms of the productive contexts, the narration highlights the importance of food coming from the garden for a proper living. Its incorporation – through Yanomami agency – serves to overcome a time of incompletion and suffering, that of exclusive foraging, when people 'ate earth'. The story thus displays the two components of Yanomami ecology, which are to remain an incomplete gestalt as long as they are not integrated by an act of giving – by exchange. But the narration also seems to stage, with some hints on proper emplacement and behaviours, an unfinished sociality connected to these non-agricultural times. The *wayamou*, the central Yanomami ceremonial discursive exchange between speakers, which allows peace-keeping and is performed between men from allied communities, is shown to be practiced in the forest, outside its proper village space, and without an interlocutor.[6] This theme of asociality seems further stressed in *Hõrõnami's* refusal to speak with the people in the village, maybe under Ghost's contagion. The reading of these two aspects as underscoring asociality is strengthened by the loss of consciousness of those eating cultivated food for the first time. It is as if in a liminal transition (of society) between not-having and having garden food, all the perils of life at the limits of humanity emerge. These are expressed in silences and stutters, soliloquies, *out of placeness*, and a transitional dizziness or loss of self-awareness. The incorporation, both of the knowledge of farmed plantains and of those eaten in the village, would signal the closure of the crisis of the liminal phase.

The story also displays a classification of landscapes. As Carrera has pointed out, Ghost speaks of his emplacement by just giving geographical references, and by revealing his asociality (his house, where he lives alone, will be found threateningly empty). Ghost also refuses to walk a proper path. And a path (*pei yoka*), is an eminently social space, produced by the act of walking (Lizot 2007: 290). He instead traverses the closed forest, and then ends up in a path, as if stressing the ambiguity of a coming and going between wild and domesticated spaces. But he also says that he has his garden (and his house) on a plain at the base of a mountain. Looked at on an ecological register, foothills as this one appear to be empirically recognized as a type of space good for planting, even if not part of an explicit classification (see Alès 2003: 400–401, 407–408; Lizot 1980: 51–52). The mountain *Shitari* people of my field site, for example, were planning to move their gardens towards the foothills closer to the Ocamo River peneplain. Subtly, the key cultural knowledge transferred by *Hõrõnami's* agency from Ghost to people is not only that of agriculture, but also that of a landscape awareness tied to it.

Recapitulating the elements so far displayed, I propose that this foundational narrative establishes some of the cornerstone elements of Yanomami economy and society, that it stages a transition from wild to domesticated consumption by means of some emplaced behaviours and changes of consciousness, and that it displays an awareness of landscape related to the incorporation of agriculture.

The myth of the origin of tobacco offers further clues to illuminate these issues. I summarize it here:

> *Nosiriwë* walks through the forest weeping, because he is in need. He cries '*peshiyë, peshiyë, peshiyë!*' as he walks. He finds some blue-headed parrots eating *pahi* and *moshima* fruits and asks them for a bunch. They ask him why he is crying; he says he is in need of something. They give him the fruits and he continues wandering and weeping, finding some more parrots eating *reshe* fruits. They also interrogate him and give him the fruits he asks for, which he eats without satisfying himself. 'I am crying because there's something I don't have', he says. Once again he finds parrots eating, eats a little and goes on lamenting.
>
> Finally he finds Kinkajou, who is eating fruits sitting on the branch of a tree. He has left his axe in the ground with a cut of tobacco in the handle. *Nosiriwë* again voices his craving, and asks Kinkajou for some fruit. They are tasteless, says Kinkajou, who has guessed *Nosiriwë's* need, and tells him to take his tobacco cut instead. *Nosiriwë* inserts the tobacco under his lip and shouts his satisfaction: '*Aye, ayë, ayë*'. He then goes away, and all over the places where he spits on the way back, tobacco plants grow (from Lizot in Wilbert Simoneau 1990: 168–169).

In another version of the myth the unsatisfied wanderer – this time called *Kuripowë* – reaches a village carrying his lamentation, and the people stay in fear in their hammocks because of his strange behaviour. They show him a path and urge him to go after a group of women that have gone that way, so he can have sex with them and calm his desire. He says he does not want to take the women, and resumes his lamentation in the forest path: 'I need something, I need something.' He then finds the one who finally gives him tobacco and after getting satisfied goes on a ridge path, spitting and causing the tobacco to grow, attracting hummingbirds that feed on the sweet flowers (Wilbert and Simoneau 1990: 169–170).

Lizot underlines how the myth exploits the ambiguity of the wanderer's cry of *peshiyë*, derived from *pëshi*, a verb usually expressing sexual desire, but also used for tobacco craving (Lizot 1975: 19). I find the most powerful image in this narration to be that of the man wandering in the forest driven by a desire so strong that it makes him weep but that he cannot express. The different forest beings that he finds in his journey try unsuccessfully to calm his anxiety with wild fruits, and the stages of his path are riddled with frustration. Tobacco serves here as a vehicle to stage an unfulfilled, inexpressible and mobilizing want. This staging of a desire, unable to speak its name but insistently voicing its non-fulfilment as a mobilizing *lack*, seems to display metonymically the need for the social, to reveal that 'desire is always desire of the Other' (Lacan 1966: 814, 1989: 238). What is expressed here is a craving for commensality and exchange, a need for society, finally (and provisionally) satisfied with the donation of a cultivated plant, which has since become a central staple in Yanomami gardens. Juxtaposed with the previous story and read on a socio-ecological register, we could suggest that here, again, the life of fruit-eating forest beings is experienced by the forager in want as a *crisis of completion*. But this crisis is taken to resolution in the gift that allows the fulfilment of the nameless desire, after which *Nosiriwë* traverses the landscape in a fecundating manner, taking both the role of a seed-dispersing forest animal and that of a farming man. So, while the myth of the origin of plantains inaugurates agricultural times, the story of the discovery of tobacco rounds off this inauguration by stressing the satisfaction achieved with it. It builds its plot upon a similar crisis of an incomplete ecology, emphasizes the anxiety of times of only wild food and resolves it by incorporating a farmed plant. Plenitude is obtained through social interaction which enables productive life.

However provisional this interpretation might be, it must be stressed that the mythical landscapes summoned here to illuminate a current social practice and its significance are not for the Yanomami a faded past occurrence. On the contrary, they are empirically, conceptually and actively realized today. Lizot has recorded the myth being used by gardeners when planting the crop, uttering a propitiatory spell recalling the events of the discovery of tobacco by *Nosiriwë* and how *Hashoriwe* (the mythical Kinkajou) gave it to him (1980: 36). As Overing (2004) has observed, mythical and current landscapes are inextricably connected in the production of everyday life. This connection surfaces in vivid contexts of actions recalling productive social values and practices while also staging, without discontinuity, a certain foundational folly of existence.

Discussion

I have highlighted some aspects of tobacco in its customary practices of exchange and consumption as well as the complementary relation between this consumption and the configuration of social landscapes and places. I have proposed that to understand tobacco among the Yanomami we should explore its conceptualization in an interface register between stimulants such as the hallucinogenic drug *epena* and food. This I believe to be an open path for research, in order to discern tobacco's significance and place among other practices with a finer lens and to explore further the different social engagements in which it appears, associated with or separated from other staples of Yanomami commensality.

In dealing with tobacco, as with other drugs which are regulated, prosecuted and medicalized in Western society, research should not overlook the central aspect of the enjoyment they provide, and how this pleasure connects with wider identifying dimensions of social experience (Bunton and Coveney 2011). This precaution takes a special meaning in cases such as this one, in which indigenous tobacco is neither of ritual use nor provides a strong intoxicating resource for other social engagements but is instead woven into the central warp of everyday wellbeing (cf. Sarmiento Barletti, this volume). The functions of intoxication and ritual transportation served by the *epena* drug in Yanomami society provide an experiential intensity for discerning the different organizational levels of the cosmic landscape. Tobacco, less psychoactively intense and providing other forms of physical satisfaction, permits self-possessed social activities (e.g. work, hunt, play, love, trade) and has a role in all the fundamental webs of exchange that connect social groups and places. But both these substances are so central because they are delicious to the consumer. And in Yanomami society the delight of tobacco is added to the diverse practices that constitute a social ethos which emphasizes commensality and a joyous and celebratory (but also antagonistic) affirmation of existence.

The way in which changes in tobacco consumption affect the convivial engagements of which it forms a part is an open question in this context. When I did my fieldwork, I used to bring leaves donated by a tobacco company to give to my collaborators, which were very much appreciated because of their size and strength.[7] I learnt that I was no pioneer in this, as missionaries had been doing it for a long time for the villages in the contact axis of the Orinoco River. In their long-term residence with the Yanomami, some priests incorporated tobacco leaves from industrial plantations into the things they transported to the Yanomami cooperatives or as gifts to the people. The tobacco I brought to the mountain villages where I worked, however, was not much coveted in the downriver villagers where I always spent a few days before travelling upriver. Even if they received tobacco leaves, the downriver village people I knew much preferred me to bring them cigarettes as gifts.

Many adults in these downriver villages have substituted traditional tobacco sucking with smoking. Putting aside the actual physical effect of the drug, I find it difficult to make equivalence between tobacco smoking and sucking a tobacco wad, given the 'eat, talk and exchange' ambience the latter makes possible. Yanomami are proverbially eloquent in trade or political matters. In these villages, for example, frenzied discussions about a new local councillor or another representative of the many political posts created by the state occur, with everyone talking at once. Such an ambience appears less well served by cigarettes compared to a flavoursome wad of tobacco under the lip. Smoking, apart from its individual lonesome consumption, when done in public seems to be more likely to be an aspect of the performance of a 'civilized' individual. To dress as a *napë* (a *criollo*), speak Spanish, read and write, engage in politics or in healthcare and also to smoke are part of the many practices that configure the universe of 'becoming white', *napeprou* (Kelly 2011). Instead of replacing traditional usage wholesale, smoking seems to be incorporated among the plural registers of the relational ethos. Thus, if what characterizes the regime of traditional tobacco practices is convivial consumption, in the social landscape of change in interface villages this new practice, smoking, seems to have installed itself as one of the components of the perspectival *habitus* of the foreigner. If we follow Londoño Sulkin´s proposition concerning the existence of an 'Amazonian package' (2012) with a plural configuration of incorporation of otherness, fabrication of bodies and perspectival ontology, we could say that instead of 'sharing of substances to make bodies', it is the 'incorporation of otherness' component which seems to be intensified in these contexts.

Conclusion

To conclude, I would like to suggest that what gives traditional tobacco practice its central place in Yanomami existence is that it serves as a 'libidinal machine', an enabling mechanism of sociality charged with desire, to expand the webs of exchange at different scales: among friends and kin, between villages, between distant villages and landscapes. It serves to stage a need for something undetermined, and satisfies it in determined material exchanges and encounters. Once consumed it goes tasteless, so triggering the need for further encounters and exchanges. A geography of desire is apparent when people mobilize themselves to travel from one region to another to visit kin and make the best of their resources, news and people. And it is then that the full potentiality of tobacco as a social phenomenon appears: it is a vehicle for the statement of difference and its reduction, and for experiencing the always imbalanced nature of the regime of exchange and its temporary solution. But it is a pleasurable solution and one that traverses the realms of the social, the ecological and the psychological.

Acknowledgements

I wish to thank Elizabeth Rahman and Andrew Russell for their invitation to the symposium 'The Changing Landscape of Tobacco Use in Lowland South America', and their careful editing of this chapter, as well as all the symposium participants for a rich discussion. I thank Javier Carrera and Johanna Gonçalves for their discussion and comments on the manuscript; Laia Soto for her guidance on reading Lacan on the subject of desire and Roger Norum for his proofreading of this text.

My fieldwork between 2007 and 2011 was supported by CAICET, Centro Amazónico de Investigación y Control de Enfermedades Tropicales and Fundación La Salle de Ciencias Naturales. The processing of my material and writing of my thesis was supported by a grant from the Porticus Foundation via the Wataniba socio-environmental affairs work group.

Notes

1. Neighbours in a tense or pre-conflict situation may, however, reject an offer of tobacco, fearing it might contain harmful – poisonous or magical – substances (Carrera, pers. comm).

2. According to Fuentes (1980: 64–67), *epena* maybe a semi-domesticate.
3. This resonates with the approach of Cunill Grau (2007), who has spoken of a geography of the senses to account for the different regions of Venezuela.
4. The French *manque*, lack or deficiency of something, is understood as the cause of desire in psychoanalysis (one desires because one is lacking in something). To show oneself as 'desiring' subjects is to expose oneself as lacking, as being in need. 'But let us articulate that which structures desire. Desire is that which is manifested in the interval that demand hollows within itself, in as much as the subject, in articulating the signifying chain, brings to light the want-to-be, together with the appeal to receive the complement from the Other, if the Other, the locus of speech, is also the locus of this want, or lack' (Lacan 1989: 200, see original in 1966: 627).
5. See also Lizot (1989: 83–86).
6. It must be said that a solo performance of a *wayamou* to stop the rain from coming is also a cultural possibility. But this does not deny the asocial resonances of the fact that *Hõrõnami* performs a dialogical ritual while in solitude in the bush.
7. Marshall writes extensively about similar uses of tobacco as 'currency' and 'a token of friendship, conviviality and sociality' among anthropologists in Oceania (2013: 89–100).

9

Of Tobacco and Well-being in Indigenous Amazonia

Juan Pablo Sarmiento Barletti

[Tobacco] shows me the reality of things. I can see things as they are. And it gets rid of all the pains.

Ashaninka shaman to Narby (1998: 30)

Smoking [tobacco] killed at least 100 million people worldwide last century, and ten times that will meet the same fate in the 21st century if present smoking rates persist.

Kohrman (2008: 10)

Introduction: The everyday use of tobacco in indigenous Amazonia

I will never forget the first time I saw an Ashaninka[1] man blow tobacco smoke on his young child. I was drinking manioc beer with a group of Ashaninka men when I suddenly noticed Sebastian, our host, blow tobacco smoke on the top of his son's head, followed by his hands and then his feet – long puffs of smoke that the child seemed to find soothing. I knew what Sebastian was doing to his young son (getting rid of the *susto*[2] that affected him), and I knew that he knew what he was doing (even if untrained, every Ashaninka man carries some shamanic knowledge, many times just mimetic). I had felt a similar soothing feeling a few days earlier when a *sheripiari* (an Ashaninka shaman) had blown tobacco on my crown. Still, I could not help but flinch: tobacco smoke on a child? In the United Kingdom, I instinctually move my cigarette away when I walk past small children and am now used to smoking outside pubs in the winter or to being banished to people's gardens or doorsteps. To be fair, my Ashaninka informants have not been exposed to constant warnings on second-hand smoking, although they are told that smoking kills every three months during visits by the brigades of the Peruvian Ministry of Health. Packs of cigarettes now also have health warnings printed on them.

How, if tobacco is 'the world's greatest cause of preventable death' (Kohrman and Benson 2011: 329), do we start to understand and explain its important place within different indigenous Amazonian ethos of wellbeing? This is a very complicated issue, as evident in the contrasting statements about tobacco use given by Narby and Kohrman at the beginning of this chapter. This issue is especially complex when we take into account that a large number of studies on wellbeing in Euro-American societies have health as one of its key aspects, or even as synonymous with it (see, for example, Mathews and Izquierdo's 2009 model of wellbeing involving health, happiness and prosperity). Most studies on wellbeing come from the domain of psychosocial health, based on an understanding of wellbeing in terms of mental health (e.g. Deci and Ryan 2008). Some studies focus on the detrimental influence of tobacco, bundled with other 'harder' drugs, on human wellbeing. Yet Izquierdo has shown that even if Matsigenka people (an indigenous Amazonian group closely related to Ashaninka people) are getting healthier according to objective measures, 'they feel that their wellbeing is in drastic decline' (2009: 67) due to the impact of extractive industries working in their territory. The important role tobacco plays in indigenous Amazonian ideas of wellbeing is obvious in ritual practice, ranging from its use in healing (e.g. Narby 1998: 119) to its use in practices aimed at the fabrication of human beings (e.g. Londoño-Sulkin 2000: 171). These findings are unsurprising as most studies of tobacco use in the region centre on the ritual use of the plant. By contrast, I am interested in tobacco's non-ritual uses in the Ashaninka pursuit of *kametsa asaiki*.

Kametsa asaiki ('living well') is aimed at the creation of the *Ashaninkasanori* ('real Ashaninka person') through the teaching of three interconnected knowledge sets. The first is the control of antisocial emotions (e.g. anger, jealousy, stinginess and sadness) and the everyday practice of the socially constructive ones (e.g. love and happiness). The second is adopting and displaying an ethos of hard work and being generous with the product of such work. The third is related to the second and is associated with relationships of care (e.g. feeding, bathing and protecting) between people who relate to each other as *Ashaninkasanori*. An important aspect of these relations is the emphasis on commensality and the enjoyment of socially productive substances (e.g. 'real' food, medicinal plants) while avoiding the negative ones. These three sets of knowledge are evidence of the hard work that goes into the creation of Ashaninka 'strong bodies' and 'happy faces' (*cuerpos fuertes* and *caras felices*). Ashaninka people are no strangers to the use of tobacco (*pocharo*) in these processes. Wilbert (1987: 126) notes that Ashaninka people enjoy four out of the six uses he found for tobacco in Amazonia: drinking, licking, taking as snuff[3] and smoking but not chewing it or using it in enemas.[4] Historically, tobacco was commonly used as *sheri* (tobacco paste), made from boiled down tobacco leaves. This form of tobacco lends its name to the Ashaninka shaman, the *sheripiari*. Weiss (1975: 62) translates *sheripiari* as 'he who uses tobacco' and 'he who is transfigured by tobacco', while Elick (1969: 203–204) suggests the word combines *sheri* and *piai* ('a rather common designation for the shaman in northern South America'). Baer (1992), translates the Matsigenka term *seripigari* as 'he who is intoxicated by tobacco'.

One of the many things I looked forward to as I prepared for fieldwork among the Ashaninka people was the chance to smoke their tobacco or taste their tobacco paste, which I had read was mostly used for shamanic purposes. I was not only curious of its taste but also of its renowned potency. Texts based on fieldwork in the 1960s (Elick 1969; Weiss 1975; Varese 2002) describe tobacco paste, commonly used at the time, as a bittersweet and very strong substance that could induce hallucinations. This is not surprising as Narby, working with Pichis Valley Ashaninka groups, highlights that their tobacco 'contains up to eighteen times more nicotine [than] Virginia-type cigarettes'. (1998: 120) My informants say that *sheri* was so strong because some Ashaninka men combined *kamarampi* (*ayahuasca, Banisteriopsis caapi*) and tobacco for a potent paste.

This chapter steps away from the analysis of the use of tobacco in ritual practice, important though that is, to concentrate on the everyday use of the plant.[5] I am not claiming that the everyday use of tobacco utterly contradicts the meanings and symbolism it carries in ritual practice or shamanic discourse. Rather, I want to show the important links that exist between tobacco and wellbeing outside ritualistic activity. For this, I will look at the everyday uses of tobacco among people living by the Ene and Bajo Urubamba rivers of Peruvian Amazonia. These two areas have very different historical experiences, an important element when considering tobacco use.

The first part of this chapter will discuss how the planting of tobacco by Ashaninka groups in the Ene River is part of a larger reconciliatory effort in the wake of the Peruvian internal war (officially 1980–2000). This conflict was caused by *Sendero Luminoso*'s attempt to topple the Peruvian state and led to the deaths of between 6,000 and 8,000 Ashaninka people, out of almost 70,000 deaths in the whole country.[6] Ashaninka villages include people who were active on different sides during the war and people who lost family or friends due to the violence. The current Ashaninka project of reconciliation not only seeks to create convivial relations among people but also to rearticulate their social relations with *aipatsite* ('our earth/territory/soil') and the powerful spiritual agents living within it. Ene Ashaninka people posit that the perceived lack of soil productivity and game they are currently experiencing is due to the anger of *aipatsite* and the different *ashitarori* (*dueños*, 'owners'/'masters') at what happened during the war. The violence also led to the fleeing of *maninkari* spirits ('those who are hidden', 'good forest spirits') who aid *sheripiari* in their healing practices and guide the souls of the dead to the afterlife. Any possibility of renewing their pursuit of *kametsa asaiki* is impossible without an attempt to enjoy positive social relations with *aipatsite*. Ashaninka people not only need the 'real' food they plant and hunt in the forests but also need to reclaim their living spaces from the wandering souls of the dead who have become demons.

The second part of this chapter explores the everyday use of cigarettes by Bajo Urubamba Ashaninka people. These groups seldom plant tobacco, instead buying it as cigarettes or in leaf bundles (*mapacho*) from *mestizo* traders. I will argue that, in this case, the use of cigarettes cannot be understood separately from the consumption of other manufactured goods such as clothing, radios and *trago* (cane alcohol). For this, I will look at the meaning attributed to these goods by those who purchase and consume them. From this I will propose that cigarettes are one of the objects that my informants use to define being 'Peruvian' and 'civilized'. Their enthusiastic consumption of these goods allow them to access the world of Peruvians, 'become Peruvian' and through this interact as *Ashaninkasanori* in a context of state oppression, colonization and extractive industries that make it harder for them to live in their desired way. So, rather than being a tool of colonial or capitalist control, cigarettes are part of a set of tools that enables them to be who they want to be.

Of tobacco and reconciliation in the Ene River

Although I have only made short visits to the Ashaninka villages by the Ene River, I have met many people that were born in that area but left it during the worst years of the war to find refuge in villages of the Bajo Urubamba, Tambo and Ucayali rivers. I have also enjoyed long conversations with Ene Ashaninka people in Satipo, the largest town in that area.

Evelina, one of my *comadres* in the Bajo Urubamba, left the Ene in the early 1990s. She went first to a *nucleo poblacional* (camp for internally displaced people) set up by the army and the indigenous self-militia (Sp. *ronda*, Ash. *ovayeriite*, 'the warriors') in the Tambo River, after which she moved to the Ucayali and finally to the Bajo Urubamba. Evelina longed for the Ene and kept in touch with her family via radio but was very cautious about going back. She tried to convince me not to go and warned me:

> *Compadre* you have to be very careful, things over there are not *conforme* ['agreeable' but really denotes normality]. The land has been made to taste too much blood from all the violence, people have tasted too much blood, they have killed and so they are not like us .... People can't go back to where their houses used to be, their kin have been killed and left [in the forest] unburied. Many of my kinsmen died there, it was very sad .... They say that the *maninkari* have left to the higher areas,[7] disgusted with all that happened and now there are only *kamaari* ['demons'], making people sick.

Similarly, one of Caruso's (2012: 126) Ashaninka informants in the Ene River told her that 'the bloodshed was huge in these forests, and that also had a big impact on the *maninkari* .... The *maninkari* are good people, good spirits, who don't like being around evil .... They don't like death and blood, and all of this was a great shock to them .... They went far away, into the highlands'. I have recorded more narratives stating serious worries about the departure of *maninkari* spirits and about the wandering souls of the dead in the Ene as well as the Tambo River, which also saw a lot of fighting.

Weiss notes that Ashaninka people fear the souls of their dead because 'the souls of the dead can, and usually do, become demons' (1975: 302). I was told that these souls, carried by sadness and solitude, roam their former homes to visit their kin and attempt to take them to the afterlife for company. During Weiss' fieldwork (late 1960s) the houses and all the possessions of the dead were burnt to prevent these houses from becoming 'a focal point of ghostly or demonic visitation' (1975: 433). This is more complex if we take into account that my informants also consider that *Sendero* cadres were demons, and that 'the soul of someone who has been attacked by a demon, and only such a soul, will itself become a demon after death unless destroyed by fire' (1975: 435). This complicates any return to their former villages as people were not buried properly and their houses were not burnt. Hence, there is a possibility that the ghosts of the deceased might return as demons, would not recognize their former kin and would attack them. Weiss writes:

> Demons consider human beings ... their legitimate prey. [The] hordes of evil spirits in the universe are driven by an insatiable urge ... to attack and inflict maximum damage upon any human being they encounter ... they inhabit, not the ends of the earth as do the good spirits, but actual [Ashaninka] territory ... and thus constitute an ever-present danger. (1975: 165)

The role of *maninkari* spirits is key in assuring rest for the souls of the dead as they are called upon to guide these souls to the afterlife. For example, Weiss describes a burial practice in the Perene River that:

> includes notifying the *maninkari* of the death by whistling over a cupped hand at the gravesite .... The *maninkari* then come and ... [the deceased] accompanies them body and soul back to their place of residence ... up on the mountain ridges or up in the sky, becoming *maninkari* themselves .... They look down from their vantage points at the living, and ... they descend to visit. (1975: 438)

War pushed *maninkari* spirits to reclusivity. Thus, the souls of the Ashaninka killed in the war are trapped and are possibly becoming demonic. This would make them unable to recognize their kin and attack them. Souls that do not depart with *maninkari* spirits also risk becoming *peari*, 'the soul of a dead person, or any demon for that matter, taking the form of a game animal' (1975: 290).[8] A *peari* is recognized as 'emaciated, [with] pustules, tumors, or patchy fur, is infested with worms, or has unhealthy-looking organs' (1975) and is never eaten.

I later asked Evelina about life in the Ene before the war. She said:

> Oh *compadre*, it was beautiful! So much game, so much fish.... My father would always find something [in the forest], bring it back to our house and my mother would cook it and we would eat it happily. We had feasts, people would come and visit to drink manioc beer and dance, people would play their drums, their flutes.... It was beautiful! We lived peacefully.... But life there is very different today, there is not as much game or fish.... Some people have not been able to throw their sadness away [after the war]...they fight when they get drunk, they don't know how to live well.

Evelina makes a definite connection between people not knowing how to live following *kametsa asaiki* precepts and her perceived lack of game and fish. Another Ene Ashaninka woman told me that the reason for the lack of game in the area was that the owners/masters were angry for the abuses committed against their animals during the war. I enquired if this was due to overzealous hunting but she replied it was because soldiers and *Sendero* cadres had raped those animals.

Many Ashaninka people worry about the perceived lack of *aipatsite's* productivity since the war. Emilio told me that *aipatsite* had not only reduced its usual yield due to the bloodshed but also because of extractive industries and cocaine production:

> It's different now. When I was young plants grew huge! It was easy, people knew the *ivenki* [magical plants] for many plants, and they grew beautifully! But now I hear people can't grow their plants so easily, the land is not the same...it's like it doesn't want to produce [*producir*] any longer...it's angry with people for all the deaths...it's tasted so much blood.... And all those chemicals being used when they make cocaine upriver makes it worse.... There are those plans to build the dam at *Pakitzapango* that we hear about on the radio that will flood [the area]...and all the *empresas* ['companies' but refers to extractive industries]. It makes me so sad.

Similarly, Julio told Caruso (2012: 126) that:

> [T]he soil changed after the violence. Until 1991, there were many good places to plant crops.... But many places, after the war, began to dry up, like a punishment. Or perhaps because so many people were killed, or maybe we shouldn't have buried the people where they died – maybe they were buried in sacred places. It seems that we've bothered the land [*la hemos molestado a la tierra*], which is a part of ourselves. Also our produce was always good before the war, but no longer.

The imagery of *aipatsite* soaked with blood fits with *Sendero*'s plan in which violence was 'the Redeemer...the Mother of History' (Degregori 2011: 67). Indeed, Abimael Guzman, *Sendero*'s leader and ideologue, insisted each village would be required to pay its quota of blood as part of the one million lives it would take to topple the Peruvian state. Ashaninka narratives of war tell of murder and torture, and of how people in *Sendero* camps were fed human remains, including foetuses, breasts and penises (Sarmiento Barletti 2011). These actions transformed former Ashaninka kinsmen into demons, preventing them from recognizing their former friends and family.

Aipatsite was exposed to human and demonic cruelty during war and now the state and other outsiders continue disturbing it with plans for a hydroelectric dam, exploratory tests for gas and oil extraction and the production of cocaine. The resulting lack of productivity threatens *kametsa asaiki* as it is impossible to create *Ashaninkasanori* without the food they plant and the game they hunt. Thus, the project of reconciliation in the wake of war is not only aimed at former combatants and victims but also includes the refashioning of human relationships with *aipatsite*, which is key for any renewal of the pursuit of *kametsa asaiki*.[9] Space prevents me from expanding on these reconciliatory efforts but I want to focus on the important role of tobacco in rearticulating social relations in this area.

Ethnographies dealing with Ashaninka people highlight the close relationship between tobacco and *maninkari* spirits. According to Weiss (1975: 260), even if the *maninkari* by definition 'cannot be seen', humans can nonetheless see them 'by the continual ingestion of psychotropic drugs, especially tobacco and *ayahuasca*'. Similarly, Narby (1998: 118) points out that '[*maninkari*] spirits had an almost insatiable hunger for tobacco'. This link is common elsewhere in the region. Wilbert (1987: 173–174) lists fifteen different Amazonian societies who consider tobacco as a food for the spirits. Likewise, Sullivan (1988: 653) writes that 'tobacco smoke is a prime object of the craving of helper spirits'. Similarly, Yagua people consider tobacco 'a food for the spirits in general' (Chaumeil 1983: 110), the people of the Vaupes 'considered [tobacco] to be ... the food of spirits' (S. Hugh-Jones 1979: 210), Bororo people pay tobacco to *bope* spirits 'for their activities on behalf of men' (Crocker 1985: 202), and the Matsigenka shaman feeds his crystals 'tobacco daily. (...) [If not] his auxiliary spirits, which materialize in the crystals, will leave him' (Baer 1992: 87).[10]

Tobacco shamanism is an important part in how Ashaninka people deal with the sadness they say takes control of some of them in the wake of war, leading many to committing suicide (Caruso 2012: 109). Yet, the everyday use of tobacco is also important in their reconciliatory projects as they cultivate tobacco in their gardens as the plant, and not just its smoke, attracts *maninkari* spirits back from exile and repels demons who abhor tobacco.[11] Gray (1996: 136) makes a similar point by stating that '[tobacco] is cultivated by Arakmbut men to keep away harmful spirits', and C. Hugh-Jones (1979: 110) writes that tobacco is used by people in the Vaupes to cleanse a house after a death. One of my informants noted the power in tobacco, as the plants are frequented by the *tsonquiri* (hummingbird), considered as an important shamanic aide.[12]

Yet, it is also in the actual work involved in cultivation that people show *aipatsite* their resolution to live moral lives together and leave the violence of war behind. By cultivation I am not only referring to tobacco but also to the foodstuffs (e.g. manioc, rice) and cash crops (e.g. coffee, cocoa) that are now key to the Ashaninka economy. Families organize *minga* work parties and invite their kin and close friends to help them open new gardens or harvest their crops. These are instances of group work that are described as happy or beautiful moments as people joke and drink manioc beer throughout the workday. *Mingas* end with a meal prepared by the family organizing the *minga* for all attendees. These instances of group work are counterpoised to how non-indigenous Amazonians in the area are said to avoid working in large groups, understood as them showing a lack of care for their kin. The war made *mingas* impossible as men were constantly patrolling and there was no easy access to manioc beer. Today Ashaninka people can *trabajar tranquilo* ('work peacefully') with whomever they want to invite to their gardens, actively showing themselves as socially productive beings displaying an ethos of hard work that is an important part of *kametsa asaiki* and of relating to *aipatsite* in a positive manner.

Thus, Ashaninka people are creating positive social relationships with *maninkari* spirits and *aipatsite* as part of their communal process of reconciliation. The cultivation of tobacco allows them to attract spirits back to their territory and also show *aipatsite* that people are working hard at the moral relationships put forth in *kametsa asaiki*. We can see that Ashaninka post-war processes are not just about going back to a romanticized past, but they seek to re-articulate the ties between Ashaninka people, *aipatsite*, and *maninkari* spirits to face the new challenges presented by their current social and political context.

The planting and use of tobacco in the Ene River does not mean that Ashaninka groups do not buy cigarettes. They do, but I will argue that we must consider the purchase and consumption of cigarettes from a different analytical angle. Let's move to the Bajo Urubamba to show what I mean.

Tobacco and Peruvianness in the Bajo Urubamba

Miqueas asked, as I took another drag of the cigarette we were *pichangueando*,[13] 'Juanito, what are those cigarettes called? Are they Peruvian?' I handed him the pack of Golden Beach cigarettes, which Miqueas inspected while I explained that the brand name was English. 'Ah, so they are *gringo* cigarettes?' Miqueas asked as he handed the pack back to me, seemingly confused. I said I was not sure and looked on the side of the pack to find out they were made in Peru. Miqueas seemed happier: 'So they *are* Peruvian cigarettes! No wonder they are so good and strong!'

Golden Beach cigarettes are not the nicest I have ever smoked but they were very cheap in Lima and readily available in bars and shops in Atalaya, the district capital. Currently, a pack of cheap cigarettes cost four *Nuevos Soles* (£1), or four cigarettes could be purchased for £0.25. For comparative purposes, my Ashaninka informants are paid £3 for a day of work, £6 for a large live chicken and around £0.25 for a kilo of husked rice. In Atalaya, £1.25 bought two kilos of good rice, a gallon of *trago* (cane alcohol), half a gallon of the cheapest petrol, a night in one of the most inexpensive hostels in town, a used t-shirt, two shotgun shells or a plate of food in the town's market.

I asked Miqueas about the strength of the tobacco we were smoking: surely it was not stronger than the tobacco used in *sheripiari* practices. I told him I had smoked tobacco in the Ene River and it had made me feel sick as I had inhaled it when I should not have. Miqueas agreed, 'You don't know how to smoke that tobacco ... it's strong!' But he also said things are different in the Bajo Urubamba: '[Ene Ashaninka people] still know how to plant tobacco or know how to use *sheri* .... There are no good shamans left [in the Bajo Urubamba], that's why you hear so much about witches.[14] Our ancestors knew how to work that tobacco but now we don't.' It was generally agreed that the best shamans were in Atalaya and that they were not Ashaninka. But even so, the very few *sheripiari* I know in the area have replaced the diagnostic and healing use of tobacco paste with *mapacho* tobacco purchased in Atalaya. This tobacco is smoked in rolled-up cigarettes or pipes.[15] I was assured that the use of *mapacho* did not negatively affect the healing processes.[16] While factory-made cigarettes are avoided in *ayahuasca* ceremonies, I have seen men blow cigarette smoke on their children, and Elick recorded cases of *sheripiari* using cigarettes in the 1950s (Elick 1969), again on children.[17]

At the time I wondered why they went from using a substance they produced or gathered (there are some species of wild tobacco) to one they had to purchase with the very little money they made. My informants are not reluctant to plant cash crops as they grow, among many others, rice, coffee, cocoa and different kinds of beans. These they sell in Atalaya, or keep for their family's consumption or to sell to other villagers. Most Ashaninka men I met smoke, albeit at very different degrees, and it was not rare to see women smoking either, although never in the same *pichangas* as men.[18] In fact, one of the first Ashaninka phrases I learned was *pipoaka*, roughly translated as 'do you smoke?' So, why spend money on tobacco when you could grow it? I soon realized I was posing the wrong question, influenced by my desire for my informants' self-sufficiency at a time when the colonist/capitalist frontier further complicated their lives. My doctoral fieldwork coincided with renewed attempts by the Peruvian state to limit indigenous land tenure, an expansion of permits for gas exploration and extraction in the area, plans for a series of hydroelectric dams, the continuous presence of cocaine producers and traders in the area and open state repression against indigenous Amazonian protesters that lead to the tragic events at the *Baguazo* (5 June 2009), labelled by the international press as the 'Amazonian Tiananmen'.

Upon my arrival, I had been heartbroken by the general lack of 'traditional' material culture, with every household owning a series of industrially produced goods. My host Joel apologized as his electric fan had stopped working the previous week (although I still do not know if he was joking). The very few people that owned a *cushma*, the long traditional tunic, only ever wore them for political meetings and even then still preferred to wear trousers and shirts. I soon learned that the wages men earned from working timber and the meagre profits families made from selling cash crops were used to buy goods like televisions and DVD players. These would rarely be used as their owners could seldom afford to run the village's electricity generator. Families in the area had received corrugated metal sheets for their houses as compensation payments from a petrol company but even if everyone exalted how beautiful the houses looked, very few slept in them as the roofs made them unbearably hot in the dry season.

Today, the organization of 'beautiful' villages resembles the organization of Peruvian towns. Villages are made up of houses built in very close physical proximity to each other, as opposed to the dispersed settlements in which their ancestors lived in the past. Houses are organized in grids, usually around a centre that includes the football pitch as a sort of plaza. This area is surrounded by public buildings (e.g. the school, medical post, communal house) and a place for a mast and Peruvian flag. Most Ashaninka people in the area are completely bilingual in Ashaninka and Spanish. Most of them use the latter in their daily interactions, to the point that most young people can understand Ashaninka language but do not speak it fluently. As opposed to other areas, it is not common for people to have Ashaninka surnames and those young parents who do prefer to give their children surnames in Spanish. From afar, this might look like acculturation and I initially associated their attitude as forced change driven by the intense and cruel process of debt-slavery and colonization that indigenous groups in the area faced until a few decades ago (see Gow 1991, 2001; Garcia Hierro et al.1998). I could not help feeling that they had finally succumbed to decades of governmental pressure to become Peruvian 'multicultural' citizens and individual consumers. I quickly realized how wrong I was.

Stephen Hugh-Jones, reflecting on the issue of material goods in indigenous Amazonia states '[T]here is something deceptively straightforward about the oft-repeated story of forest Indians, seduced by worthless trinkets, pressured to accept unwanted and unnecessary goods, turned into undiscriminating consumers forced to sell their labour and produce on a ruthless market, who begin by losing their heads, and end up losing their autonomy and their culture as well.' (1992: 51) In a similar vein, Fischer (2000) shows that the goods owned and desired by Xikrin Kayapo people, which an outsider might consider unnecessary luxuries, are actually an essential part of their social reproduction. I want to follow these analyses that highlight the importance of examining manufactured goods beyond their obvious utilitarian value to understand the everyday consumption of cigarettes among my Ashaninka informants in the Bajo Urubamba. I propose that this consumption is only one aspect of the way they understand their current identity as *civilizados* ('civilized') and *peruanos* ('Peruvians'), which reinforce their pursuit of becoming an *Ashaninkasanori*.

Ashaninka people posit that all beings are made from both material and immaterial substances from very different origins and acquired through different relationships.

Thus, 'Peruvianness' is defined by the consumption of material goods such as those listed above, including cigarettes. Here, I follow Santos-Granero's statement that 'scholars... have overlooked the material dimension of people-making processes by focusing mainly on the social relations that go into the making of a person' (2012: 183). Yet, the 'thing' is not separated from social relations. As I have showed elsewhere (Sarmiento Barletti *forthcoming*), the acquisition of material goods from without Ashaninka society has become key to their pursuit of *kametsa asaiki* and the fabrication of people as *Ashaninkasanori*.

I must clarify something before moving on. My Ashaninka informants understand being Peruvian as separate from citizenship. They distinguish Peru as a nation, which they imagine themselves a part of, from *el estado*, the Peruvian state. The state is an exogenous oppressive force, associated with extractive industries, unfair laws aimed at limiting their territory and even *Sendero*. Contrastingly, my informants are proud of being Peruvian. This is obvious from the countless hours they spend practicing the national anthem in front of the Peruvian flag in the run-up to Peru's independence day, their pride at having DNIs (the Peruvian identity card), at having a title for their land and, for some, at having 'served the fatherland' (*servir a la patria*) by enlisting for military service.[19] Peruvianness is also implied in the use of industrially made clothing and other Peruvian products. This consumption is explained as part of a process of 'becoming Peruvian' in which they tap into the 'civilized' knowledge of Peruvians.

My Bajo Urubamba informants identify themselves as 'civilized' and contrast themselves to the Ene Ashaninka people who they imagine as 'not having civilized/woken up yet' (*todavia no han civilizado/despertado*), reflected in their use of traditional clothes and face designs and eating a diet closer to that of their ancestors. The related notions of 'being civilized' and 'being Peruvian' are now an important part in the everyday fabrication of *Ashaninkasanori*. Veber (1998: 384) notes that 'the notion of civilization is borrowed from settlers but carries somewhat different connotations and meanings... "becoming civilized"... refers primarily to the acquisition... of non-native knowledge that may allow a wider range of maneuver vis-à-vis, and control over, relations with settlers'. So, if Ashaninka people include a series of manufactured goods in their everyday practices, they do so because they allow them to enjoy a different perspective: the 'Peruvian' perspective. Vilaça argues (2010) that Wari' people's desire for these goods cannot be reduced to their use value, but should be understood as responding to their desire to explore the perspectives of 'whites'. Basing her argument on Viveiros de Castro's (1998) discussion of Amazonian perspectivism, Vilaça argues that Wari' people want these goods in order to acquire the knowledge associated with 'being white' and thus to 'be Wari' being white'. Thus, while it used to be that only shamans had the possibility of engaging with two different perspectives simultaneously, Wari' people in general are able to do so when they consume manufactured goods associated with 'whites'. Like Wari' people, my Ashaninka informants are Ashaninka while being Peruvian.

They consume cigarettes, one of the many signs of 'Peruvianness', as a creative engagement that strengthens their everyday pursuit of *kametsa asaiki*.

Cigarettes are definitely understood as being non-Ashaninka products.[20] Some of my Bajo Urubamba informants who studied at the Catholic missionary schools in the Tambo River in the 1970s and 1980s associated smoking cigarettes with the Peruvian and Spanish priests in these missions. The missions were places where they had changed their traditional clothes for shirts and trousers and had learned how to eat chicken and sweets. The otherness of cigarettes is also present in the stories of how people learned how to smoke as this was usually done in non-Ashaninka settings, most commonly in timber camps and during military service in which Ashaninka men interact with *mestizos* for months at a time. Both of these instances were also cited as moments that allowed men to learn or improve their Spanish. As such, being or not being able to smoke cigarettes conveys a person's ability to interact with outsiders in a 'civilized' manner.[21]

Even if my informants may smoke cigarettes as a way of being Peruvian, this does not mean that they do it in the same way that other people living within Peru do. I suggest that this is related to how 'as far as Ashéninka are concerned, they themselves are the centre of their world; other people may have their own centres, but these are not important to the Ashéninka' (Veber 1998: 384). This lets them place everything around them in an order based on their own categories and so they define and control definitions of 'Peruvianness'. For example, an irate Ashaninka man in a communal meeting I attended, after being told that the Peruvian government would build a hydroelectric dam in the area, asked, 'Is this government Peruvian?' Similarly, I was repeatedly told that *Sendero* cadres and petrol companies were not Peruvian. As I mentioned earlier, cigarettes are commonly smoked in groups, at least in pairs. Some of my informants pointed this out as an Ashaninka way of consumption as it reflects the way in which manioc beer and food are ideally consumed. My informants point out that, as opposed to *mestizos* in Atalaya, they share in the consumption of these substances to show that they care for each other.[22]

Even when smoking in bars in Atalaya we all smoked from the same cigarette, passed from man to man. The filters of the cigarettes shared in these rounds would come back to me soaked in the saliva of every other man in the round, which is why my informants did not share cigarettes with just anyone. I have never seen Ashaninka people get into *pichangas* with *mestizos* or Andeans, but then, the people that my informants identify as such would probably not partake in the rounds due to their prejudice of indigenous Amazonians as unhygienic. I understood the idea of consubstantitality in smoking better when I noticed my *compadre* Chato picking up all of the cigarette butts we left behind after smoking in his house, carefully disposing of them in the area where his family also threw away leftover food. At first I thought he was just tidying up or trying to hide how much we had been smoking. But I was wrong, again, as Chato explained: 'You can't just leave these lying around *compadre*, there are lots of witches [in these villages].' Cigarettes and left over food, like fingernails and hair clippings, carry with them parts of their users and can be used against them by a *matsi* ('witch'). I thanked Chato, and he advised me, 'it is not like it used to be, there are no powerful *sheripiari* to deal with witches'.

In a sense, sharing cigarettes, and also *trago*, allows men to associate without needing female labour to provide them with the means for sociality.[23] Manioc beer parties, or even a leisurely drink at sundown, are not possible without the participation of women as they are the ones that prepare it. The circles of smokers of cigarettes and drinkers of *trago* allow people to reach the highly desirable state of *shinkitaka* (S. '*mareacion*'; in this context, referring to drunkness)[24] faster than by drinking manioc beer. This turns cigarettes and *trago* into an important part of contemporary Ashaninka sociality at a time when there are not enough of the desirable resources (e.g. game) to redistribute to other households. In today's *pichangas*, cigarettes stop being a thing to become invested with the properties of social relations that are important for *kametsa asaiki*.

Conclusion: Learning from the everyday use of tobacco in indigenous Amazonia

It seems as if the power that indigenous Amazonians attribute to tobacco in shamanic or other kinds of ritualistic practice is so strong that anthropological analyses have ignored the less explicitly 'mystical' everyday functions of the plant. There are many studies outside anthropology of everyday uses of tobacco in different 'cultures' (although these are usually equated to nationalities) aimed at finding ways to get people to smoke less, guided by Euro-American models that equate wellbeing with health.

Based on how Ashaninka people add tobacco to the factors that contribute to their wellbeing, I want to propose a question to a wider scholarly debate that I have posed elsewhere (Sarmiento Barletti *forthcoming*): to what extent do discourses and ideas of wellbeing reflect ways of thinking about the world? Briefly, with the rise of personal wellbeing as both a popular concept and a notion of 'virtue' that is in high demand, most wellbeing research tends to focus on self-knowledge, individual agency and self-responsibility. These studies are characterized by a lack of attention to cultural variations in understanding and usage of the term. Ashaninka people's uses of tobacco as part of their pursuit of wellbeing may clash with Euro-American conceptions of the 'good life', but it also shows that different conceptions of humanity beget different approaches and discourses of wellbeing (see Sarmiento Barletti and Ferraro n.d.).

Even if smoking kills, the different uses of tobacco among Ashaninka people are all related to *kametsa asaiki*. In the Bajo Urubamba River, what looked like a tool of the colonial/capitalist frontier for the transformation of indigenous people into individual consumers turns into an instrument aimed at becoming and being

Peruvian. This is an identity that reinforces *kametsa asaiki* and thus being an *Ashaninkasanori* at a time when colonial/capitalist pressures make it harder to do so. In the Ene River, tobacco becomes one of the different ways through which people create positive social relations with *aipatsite* and *maninkari* spirits after the violence they all experienced during the Peruvian internal war. This discussion highlights how there can be different approaches to tobacco not just between but within an Amazonian society and shows how different uses and conceptualizations of tobacco are shaped by the historical context in which particular groups live.

Reviews of the anthropological literature on tobacco call for more critical studies on the power relations involved in the tobacco industry, in advertising and between smokers, especially when it comes to indigenous societies (Kohrman and Benson 2011). I agree with how necessary these studies are. For example, Brady (2008) has shown how colonists calculatingly exploited Australian Aboriginal people's addiction to nicotine, and by that imperilled them both economically and biosocially. Yet, Ashaninka people present a different case, not only because tobacco is a native plant but also because they conceive of themselves as 'masters of the Universe' (Veber 2000: 18), rather than the 'victims of progress' whom Bodley (1972) prophesied would soon be exterminated in an ethnocidal catastrophe. Oppressive powers such as the state, extractive industries and *Sendero Luminoso*, in attempting to control Ashaninka social practices, may have transformed their society but have not changed their conception. The resilience of Ashaninka social practice is illustrated in their desire to pursue *kametsa asaiki* in spite of the obstacles set by these and other outsiders.

Rather than one of control, the Ashaninka experience of tobacco is one of a creative rearticulation of relationships and models of identity that grants new symbolic and practical uses to different forms of this plant as part of communal projects through which people seek their desired mode of wellbeing. Tobacco empowers more than just Ashaninka *sheripiari*, who create relationships with spirits in order to heal, protect and provide for their people. The everyday use of tobacco allows my informants to become *Ashaninkasanori* by becoming more Peruvian, in a process of Peruvianness that is defined by markers they have set themselves. But it also allows them to become *Ashaninkasanori* by inviting spiritual outsiders into everyday social interaction and actively mending the relationships that were broken during the cruelty of war.

Notes

1. Known as *Campa* until the 1980s, Ashaninka people are speakers of an Arawakan language. Estimates put their population at around 100,000 people, with most of them living in Peruvian Amazonia. Around 2,000 of them live in the Brazilian state of Acre.

2. 'Fright', a category of behaviour disturbance caused by contact with different kinds of neutral or evil spirits. See Rubel et al. (1985) and Logan (1993).
3. Weiss includes the name for snuff tubes in his list of Ashaninka words but makes no reference to snuff in his text, based on fieldwork in the 1960s. Elick makes no mention of snuff in his thesis, based on fieldwork in the 1950s and 1960s.
4. I have been told that some Ene River *sheripiari* do chew tobacco (Sandro Saettone, pers. comm.).
5. See Overing and Passes (2000) for an argument in favour of an analysis of indigenous societies based on their everyday life.
6. See Degregori (2011) for a general but insightful account of *Sendero* and the war in the Peruvian Andes and Caruso (2012) and Sarmiento Barletti (2011) for accounts of the conflict in Ashaninka territory.
7. '*Kanuja*'. These areas are imagined as pristine, rich in game and other resources and inhabited by Ashaninka people living like their ancestors used to.
8. Ideas of the wandering dead are common elsewhere in Amazonia (e.g. Lagrou 2000: 152).
9. Bovensiepen (2009) makes a similar point in her study of post-conflict landscape rehabilitation in East Timor. By living, growing and reproducing on the lands of their ancestors, her informants renew their group's relationships with the earth.
10. Elick found the same practice among Pichis River *sheripiari* (1969: 208–209).
11. It is worth noting that in parts of the Ene River people plant tobacco close to their houses rather than in their gardens which are usually away from villages (Sandro Saettone pers. comm.).
12. A similar point was made by Weiss' informants, who consider *tsonkiri* as the owner of tobacco (1975: 259). The neighbouring Yanesha people also make this link (Santos-Granero 1991: 111).
13. Denotes 'sharing' but I am not sure of its origin; my informants only use it in reference to cigarettes. Ashaninka people rarely smoke alone, unless there is a specific reason for doing so like avoiding the ruthless *manta blanca* fly or repelling demonic spirits when walking in the forest at night. *Pichanga* is a word commonly used in the Peruvian coast for informal football matches but I have been told that it can also be used as a euphemism for group rape in *mestizo* Amazonia.
14. People in the Ene River said the same thing: the good *sheripiari* had died during the war and many people showed dissatisfaction with the *sheripiari* who survived, as they had not used their supposed power to counter the *Sendero* (Antonio Sancho, pers. comm.).
15. Although the form of the material has changed, the techniques employed are still very similar. Tobacco paste requires *sheripiari* to hold the paste in their mouths and then to spit it on to the afflicted area. Smoking from pipes/rolled-up cigarettes requires them to hold the smoke in their mouths and then to blow it on the affected area. In both cases, they then suck the afflicted area to extract the cause of the affliction.
16. Some informants proposed that *mapacho*, as it comes from outside Ashaninka villages, is 'more powerful' than the tobacco cultivated by *sheripiari*. As Laenerts

points out for another Ashaninka group, 'the most interesting ethnomedicinal plants are deemed to be those from people living closer to the urban society (...) [T]hose plants must be powerful, because Western or mixed-blood people are obviously powerful... Real health depends on your place in the world, i.e. your interconnection with other living beings, rather than on a local chemical reaction in some particular part of your body' (2006: 143). Gow (1994) has made a similar point concerning *ayahuasca* in Western Amazonia.

17. This suggests a different stance to cigarettes than that of Matsigenka people (see Rosengren 2006: 809) who make sharp distinctions between cigarettes and shamanic tobacco. Perhaps the huge influx of money and material goods into Matsigenka villages as compensation payments by petrol companies has affected this distinction as cigarettes are so readily available. It is noteworthy that I only saw cigarettes used by Ashaninka people during healing practices involving children. This may have to do with the different relationships that shamans and non-shamans have with tobacco in its different forms and with children's 'weaker' bodies.
18. Smoking rounds, like manioc beer rounds, are gender-based.
19. This creates a complex Peruvianness that may pose obstacles to conviviality in villages as young men leave the armed forces with ideas of masculinity and leadership that clash with Ashaninka ones.
20. There is a possibility, which I have not discussed with my informants, that the use of manufactured goods does not challenge their Ashaninkaness because these goods were originally Ashaninka. A myth proposes that whites only have the knowledge to produce industrial goods because they kidnapped Inka, a *sheripiari* who knew how to produce these goods. In a sense, all Peruvian goods *are* Ashaninka or transformations of Ashaninka products. See Weiss (1975: 419–425) for an account of the myth.
21. As opposed to Nahua or Amahuaca people who until recently raided timber camps for manufactured goods.
22. An Ashaninka person has only ever offered me a cigarette to smoke on my own during anniversary feasts. These were usually offered by young friends of mine, advertising that they could afford them!
23. Of course, smoking as a form of socializing is not uncommon elsewhere. See Kohrman's (2008) work in Chinese hospitals, Nichter's et al. (2004) work on how North American women smoke in groups to lessen negative perceptions or Reed's (2007) work in a Papua New Guinean prison. The latter is closer to the Ashaninka case as groups of inmates share cigarettes, and men are strategic, for different reasons, about who they share a smoke with.
24. I can only agree with Weiss' (1975: 243) statement that '[t]he ideal psychic state of the [Ashaninka] is one of inebriation'.

10

Smoking Tobacco and Swinging the *Chicha*: On Different Modes of Sociality among Guna ('Kuna') People

Paolo Fortis

Smoking tobacco was a pervasive feature of the everyday life in the Guna village of Ogobsuggun[1] located on an island in the middle-eastern section of the San Blas archipelago, off the Atlantic coast of Panama, as I observed while conducting fieldwork in 2003 and 2004. Drinking *chicha*[2] was similarly common – a drink made with ground toasted maize, or alternatively with sugar cane juice, and consumed either fermented ('bitter') or unfermented ('sweet'), depending on the occasion. Both tobacco and *chicha* are key components of Guna sociality and in what follows, I aim to look at the relationship between these two substances and how they correspond to different modes of sociality in a Guna lived world.

My partner and fellow anthropologist Margherita Margiotti and I were both heavy smokers during fieldwork and, despite the tropical heat and humidity, kept smoking tirelessly throughout our stay in the village. We used to bring back a good number of cartons of Marlboro Light from our trips to Panama City and lived in fear of finishing them before our next visit to the metropolis. These we both smoked ourselves and distributed to our Guna friends and hosts. Whenever we were in company, which was most of the time, and decided to smoke a cigarette, it was unthinkable not to offer one to all the adult men and elder women in our company. If there was one thing we quickly learned to do, it was sharing our tobacco provisions with our hosts, friends, informants and people we would occasionally meet. Often, visitors coming to the house of our hosts asked us for a cigarette with the usual expression *ubie*, 'I want to smoke.' I remember a middle-aged unmarried woman, nicknamed Warakkwa, 'thin one', who used to come to Raquel's and Nicanor's house and sit down, waiting to be offered a cup of drink or a bowl of *dule masi* – coconut soup with plantain and fish. When either Margherita or I were present, she would always ask us for a cigarette, which she would smoke eagerly sitting inside the house.

During the night gatherings in the communal house of the village, which were attended by all adult men, as opposed to the morning gatherings attended by women, I had the unspoken obligation to distribute cigarettes to the men sitting on the same bench as me and sometimes even to some of those sitting in front of and behind. Moreover, every time I interviewed an adult member of the village, especially in the case of elder specialists, the conversation was punctuated by our respective lighting of numerous cigarettes, which were of course provided by me. In brief, I always had to make sure to carry a sufficient provision of cigarettes with me before leaving the house in order to satisfy all my companions' requests. Luckily, cigarettes in Panama then were a great deal cheaper than in Italy.

Guna ways of smoking

People in Ogobsuggun used to smoke exclusively menthol cigarettes, which consequently were almost the only type available on the island. They bought single cigarettes in the local shops, mostly of Colombian make and sold by traders who had their base in Cartagena and stopped their boats regularly on each island selling different kinds of goods. In some ways, our Marlboro Light might have provided an exotic counterpart to the menthol cigarettes they consumed on an everyday basis and which we were forced to smoke after our provisions finished, which regularly occurred sooner than we had expected. When asked why they smoked menthol cigarettes, people normally answered that they liked their fresh taste and on a recent fieldwork trip, I heard calling other types of cigarettes *cigarillos calientes*, 'hot cigarettes'.

In my experience, most Guna adult men and elder women enjoyed smoking and never refused a cigarette upon being offered one. Younger women, on the other hand, very rarely did so. The latter often commented that they found smoking unpleasant and that the taste of cigarettes was too bitter for them. Sometimes jokingly they puffed from a cigarette, only to cough and laugh out loudly afterwards. I also noticed that boys, especially if unmarried, did not usually smoke, while adult and elder men engaged more frequently in such activity. There seemed therefore to be both a gender and an age division in the way people consumed tobacco, young women being at the lowest point of consumption and elder men at its highest. Also, while adult and elder men smoked publicly, like in the gathering house or standing outside their houses on the village pathways, elder women never did so, except when they attended healing rituals. For such occasions a few elder women, alongside a number of adult men, were invited, upon payment, to attend the ceremony as 'tobacco smokers', *waar uedi* or *biba uedi*, 'pipe smokers'. During such occasions, they smoked pipes to assist the chanter in the performance of the healing session.

People in Ogobsuggun used to smoke in a number of different occasions, and I would caution against describing any of these as purely recreational (cf. Gow this volume). Differently from the way I conceived of smoking, as chiefly an individual activity – which retrospectively I see as a sort of defence against the almost too intense sociality of daily life during fieldwork – Guna people seemed to conceive of smoking chiefly as a relational pursuit. I can hardly recall anybody who had the habit of smoking alone and certainly I cannot remember anybody who was as dependent on smoking as I was at the time. The only case that comes to my mind is that of Wagala, an old widow, who lived with her daughter's family, and used to ask us for two cigarettes at dusk – one to smoke in company and the other for when she lay in her hammock because, she said, it would keep her warm before sleeping.

Although cigarettes were consumed in a variety of different occasions, smoking appeared crucial during healing and puberty rituals, where tobacco smoke functioned as a means of metaphysical communication enhancing the agency of those involved in the performance of specific ritual tasks. I observed three different forms of tobacco consumption: as industrial cigarettes, in store-bought pipes and as locally produced cigars.[3]

During trips to the mainland forest with Guna men going to work in their gardens, or collecting firewood or coconut, I used to take a packet of cigarettes with me, but people found it weird that I smoked while walking. Guna men used to smoke only when resting after intense work activities like felling trees, clearing new gardens or gathering maize. Once, when I was accompanying Rotalio Pérez, a Guna man in his forties, to his garden, we encountered a group of women, who, after exchanging the usual greetings – 'where are you going?' and 'what are you doing?' – commented to him that they got scared before meeting us because they had smelled the smoke of my cigarette from a distance. That, Rotalio later explained to me, is usually the sign that a *wagsabbur*, a 'forest stranger', is in the vicinity. *Wagsabbur* are strangers that could be found wandering in the forest. They might be *guerrilla* escapees who cross the border with Colombia, drug smugglers or both.

Encounters with foreigners in the forest were highly feared by women who travelled alone, since, I was told, there had been cases of rape in the past. For this reason, Rotalio told me, it is extremely unusual that Guna men smoke when walking in the forest. However, I also suspect that men working alone in the forest rarely smoke because tobacco has the quality of establishing communication with the non-human world. Since the forest for Guna people is home of the most powerful and predatory spirits, like those of trees, animals and demons, it would not appear too surprising that Guna men consider smoking as not an entirely safe activity to be carried out in a forest (cf. Fortis 2012a: 23–39). *Wagsabbur* are therefore those non-Guna people who travel in the forest careless of its inhabitants and showing a remarkable ignorance of its potential threats. In this sense, their misuse of tobacco could be interpreted as an index of their other-than-human nature, a characteristic that I most likely shared, especially at the beginning of my fieldwork.

In contrast, smoking on the island was considered a safer activity and men smoked regularly during night meetings in the gathering house, where the air was heavy with smoke and where the chiefs sung long chants from the mythical tradition and political matters were also discussed collectively (see Howe 1986). On a small table, the village secretary (*el secretario del pueblo*) sold single menthol cigarettes, which were stocked in the village hall and provided a form of income to be spent on public affairs. When finishing singing, and while the village spokesman gave a speech interpreting their chants, the chiefs often lit cigarettes or pipes and rested their throats by emitting puffs of tobacco smoke.

Another moment when men and elder women smoked collectively was during puberty ceremonies held in occasion of the menarche of a girl or few years after it. These ceremonies lasted between one and three days, and people collectively drunk fermented *chicha*. When intoxicated by this strong brew, men and women smoked cigarettes and pipes that, they explained, were meant to satisfy the animal spirits that also attended the ceremony. Animal spirits (*bonigana*) are among the guests invited to participate in puberty rituals, alongside all adult members of the village and distant kinspeople from other villages. After asking further about the role of tobacco during puberty rituals, I learned that smoking cigarettes and pipes provided animal entities with their own fermented *chicha*. Tobacco smoke is the *chicha* of animals, Guna people told me on several occasions. They drink it – so human participants smoke a plenty – and the animal spirits enjoy getting drunk with it, as human beings do with *chicha*.

'Smoking tobacco', *waar ued* in Guna language, is a key component of all healing rituals, shamanic initiations and puberty rituals. During these occasions, besides commercial cigarettes and pipes, long cigars, made with locally produced tobacco are smoked by ritual assistants. *Waar suid*, 'long tobacco', refers to the long cigar made by rolling dried tobacco leaves and closed at one end by tying it with a string. This was the only way in which locally produced tobacco was smoked by Guna people during my fieldwork. However, people in Ogobsuggun made it clear to me that they did not cultivate tobacco any more. It was their distant kinspeople living in the interior region of Bayano, in the Darién forest beyond the San Blas range, who still cultivated it and made such cigars. When people from Bayano visited Ogobsuggun, they brought cigars – either to sell them or to offer them as a gift to their hosts and friends. Otherwise, when a large quantity of cigars was needed in preparation for a village wide healing ritual, people went to Bayano to buy them. Let us now take a closer look at the association between tobacco and the two forms of *chicha*, fermented ('bitter') and unfermented ('sweet'), which constitutes the central concern of my paper.

Bitter *chicha*

During the preparatory stages of puberty rituals the most important task is that of preparing *inna gaibid*, 'bitter *chicha*', by mixing ground toasted maize and powdered cacao with the boiling juice squeezed from large amounts of sugar cane. When the liquid has cooled down, it is then transferred into large clay jars lined against the wall inside the *inna nega*, '*chicha* house', their open tops closed with large *bijao* leaves (*Calathea lutea*). Furthermore, small Spanish pepper pods are placed on top of the leafy lids in order to ward off animal spirits that might come and taste the *chicha* and thus ruin it (Prestan Simón 1975: 145). The *chicha* is left fermenting in the jars for a period of a week to ten days.

When this time has passed it is the task of the master *chicha* maker to taste the fermented beverage. This person was called in Spanish *el quimico de la chicha*, which was the translation of the Guna *inna sobedi*, 'he who makes/transforms the *chicha*'. At the time of my research, only one man was recognized as being a fully fledged master *chicha* maker and was called by both villagers in Ogobsuggun and in the neighbouring village of Ustupu to 'taste the *chicha*' in preparation for their ceremonies. His name was Aurelio Smith. Aurelio had a group of pupils, some of whom had been following him on *chicha* tasting sessions for years, waiting to 'graduate' as *inna sopeti*, while he had previously learned from his father. Aurelio invited me twice to join the group, and during these occasions, I had the chance to participate in the tasting of the fermented *chicha*. This was done in a ritualized way where we sat on a row of wooden stools: Aurelio, the most experienced *sopeti* at one end, and I, the least experienced one at the opposite end. Two men were in charge of opening one jar at a time and each one of us tasted its contents. After tasting the *chicha* from each jar, a man (*waar saedi*, 'tobacco blower/maker') holding a long cigar started a sort of hopping dance from one foot to the other, stopping in front of each one of us to put the lit end of the cigar in his mouth and blow the smoke on our face. This operation was repeated as many times as the number of jars to be tasted, with the obvious consequence that at the end of the tasting sessions, we were all happily inebriated.

During these sessions Aurelio, contemporaneously tasting and giving lessons of taste, judged the state of fermentation and the taste of the content of each jar. If the *chicha* from a jar was considered too alcoholic it would be mixed with warm water or unfermented maize *chicha*. If, on the contrary, it was too low in alcohol, it was given more time to ferment. Also, if the taste of some jars was considered too 'bitter', *gaibid*, or else tasted like 'copper', or 'shellfish', some crushed dried tobacco from the long cigars was sprinkled in it. This would cause the *chicha* from the bad tasting jars to acquire the taste from the good tasting ones.

Smoking, drinking and sociality

Two ways of smoking are therefore practiced during puberty rituals. One is the 'passive' smoking of *chicha* makers during tasting sessions; the other is the 'active' smoking of *chicha* drinkers during the ceremony itself. If the former way entails the smoking of long cigars locally produced by the one assistant, the latter entails the intensive smoking of commercial cigarettes and store-bought pipes by all the attendants. Also, on the one hand, during tasting sessions smoke is 'exhaled', or 'blown' (*saet*), so that *chicha* makers can receive it on their faces. The same treatment, as I shall describe below, is reserved for the ritual chanter during healing sessions and to the small wooden figurines acting as auxiliary spirits. On the other hand, when drinking collectively people 'inhale' (*ued*) the smoke of their own cigarettes and pipes. This is reminiscent of the way in which elder women and men 'actively' smoke through inhalation when they assist at healing sessions, as briefly mentioned above. They smoke both cigarettes and pipes and collect the ashes in small calabashes. The rationale behind this operation is that tobacco ashes are the fermented *chicha* of animal spirits, which need to be appeased to retrieve the sick person's soul (cf. Howe 1976). Both forms of smoking, by exhalation and inhalation, are therefore practiced in puberty ceremonies and healing rituals, but they are used for diverse ends.

Both in puberty ceremonies and healing sessions tobacco ashes assume, through a perspectival logic (Viveiros de Castro 1998), the position of fermented *chicha*. What human beings see as ashes, animals see, and indeed taste, as beer. Therefore, the tobacco smoked on the occasion of puberty rituals *is* the fermented *chicha* of animals. Normally kept at distance from the village, lest people fall prey to their malevolent intentions and get sick or die (Chapin 1983; Fortis 2012a: 40–66), animal entities are instead invited to participate in puberty ceremonies and to share in the festive and cheerful atmosphere created by human beings. They listen to the songs that people sing, hear their feet stomping on the ground during their dances and indeed desire to drink alcoholic *chicha* and get drunk with it, as human beings do. The drunkenness of animal entities is to be considered one of the key factors for the good accomplishment of puberty rituals. The ritual entails a number of sung performances conducted by the main specialist, the *gamdur*, the 'flute man', who invites animal spirits to participate in the ritual. Through his life-long ability and experience in mastering these incredibly long and powerful chants, the *gamdur* has to make sure that the animal entities feel happy and satisfied, but at the same time he needs to make sure that their proximity does not turn into danger for human beings. For this reason, a number of taboos, sexual and alimentary, have to be followed by those involved in hosting and preparing the ceremony. If these taboos are not respected, the *gamdur* and the *inna sobedi* might become ill and even die as a consequence of the attack of animal spirits.[4]

Animals are not the only 'others' invited during puberty rituals. The whole village gathers during such ceremonies. Affines, or completely unrelated persons from the same village, share the same festive mood, and otherwise potentially hostile relations are eased by the collective inebriation. Moreover, visitors from other Guna villages often come and stay for the duration of the festival. These visitors are called *girmar*, a term used to indicate the mother's brother (MB) and father's brother (FB) but also meaning 'ghosts' and 'forefathers'. This multiplicity of meanings seems to me to point, on the one hand, to the 'spatial' distance that separates ego from the MB, who moves out of the house when he marries and from the FB who always happens to live in another household, Guna people being a matri-local society. On the other hand, ghosts and forefathers are people 'temporally' distant. They do not share the time of human beings. They are no more among the living and can only be encountered in the forest as ghostly figures, in dreams or in mytho-historical narratives.

In anthropological terms, during puberty ceremonies the village is prototypically open to alterity in its different forms: unrelated people from within the village, distant kinspeople from other villages and animals all participate in the drinking party.[5] Despite the generally positive mood during drinking ceremonies, the atmosphere can get heated and sometimes quarrels abruptly transform into violent fights, which nonetheless are quickly forgotten when people become sober again. When people get 'drunk'(*mummud*), after drinking great quantities of *chicha*, they easily lose their temper and act without 'thinking'(*binsaed*), thus unable to acknowledge the relations that link them to other people. Guna people used to ask me, half-jokingly, whether I was scared of participating in drinking ceremonies, since I might get involved in a fight and get punched, although this never happened. Also, when men become drunk, they engage in singing competitions. Sitting near one another, ritual singers start performing healing chants, singing loudly and showing off both their specialist knowledge of long chants and their strong, hoarse, low-pitched voices. Competition and violence seem therefore to be among the characteristic aspects of puberty ceremonies, and although the actual occurrence of the latter might be less often than people admit, its potentiality was quite clear both at the physical and metaphysical levels.

Puberty ceremonies were also among the aspects of Guna life that encountered the earnest opposition of missionaries and policemen. Between the 1900s and 1920s, Catholic and Protestant missionaries tried, with limited success, to establish missions in some Guna villages and one of their very first objectives was that of preventing young Guna men from getting drunk during puberty ceremonies. As the Catholic priest Leonardo Gassó was disconcerted to note in the summer of 1907, two puberty rituals were celebrated a week apart in the village of Nargana (Howe 1998: 45–46). Likewise, Panamanian police put much effort into opposing the celebration of puberty rituals in Guna villages, trying to substitute them with rural traditional dancing events which Guna people were forced to attend. In the effort to acculturate Guna people and to impose a sense of order on what national authorities perceived as chaos, a ban was issued against puberty rituals in 1919 (Howe 1998: 180). In particular, what Panamanian policemen located in the San Blas outposts seemed to fear most was the uncontrolled and riotous behaviour of drunken Guna men. The element of animosity that was normally expressed in Guna puberty ceremonies, alongside other more convivial elements, seems therefore to have received particular attention from non-Guna outsiders concerned with trying to convert, control and 'pacify'.

But animosity was, and is not, the only element to characterize *chicha* ceremonies. Marriages can also be agreed during puberty rituals. On these occasions the families of the bride and the groom speak and find an agreement. After that, the groom is mockingly 'abducted' and carried by three or more men of the bride's family to her house where he will start living and contributing to the daily workload (cf. Prestan Simón 1975: 92–93). The often jovial tipsiness caused by drinking fermented *chicha* makes people better disposed to each other and breaks the barriers of communication normally existing between families that do not consider themselves as related.

The theme of drunkenness as conducive to smoother relations with affines but as also potentially dangerous, is present in a series of myths that I have analysed elsewhere (Fortis 2012a). In these narrations, the culture hero Dad Ibe and his siblings organize two drinking ceremonies to celebrate the marriages of Dad Ibe and his sister Olowaili, respectively to the daughter of Biler, the trickster and Urgunaliler, the thunderstorm master. Both marriages were diplomatically conceived by the culture heroes not only as a way of establishing alliances with but also of defeating their enemies, the ancestors of the contemporary animal species. During these ceremonies, they invited the grandchildren of Biler to participate. They were different animals who still had a human form. The latter got drunk and started fighting between themselves so Dad Ibe, through the help of a shamanic stone, kicked them out of the *chicha* house and transformed them into the different animal species that Guna people know nowadays. Moreover, in one version of this myth, narrated to me by Nicanor Pérez in Okoposukkun in 2004, the *chicha* that Dad Ibe prepared for the animals-*cum*-affines-*cum*-enemies, instead of being made with sugar cane and maize, like the one he and his siblings drunk, was made with *ina nusu* (*Spieghelia anthelmia*), a medicinal plant used to kill intestinal worms, but which if taken in high doses can be lethal to human beings. In this last mythic narrative then, the difference between humans and animals in ancient times is stressed not so much by appealing to their different bodily appearance, since they all had human appearance, but instead to their perceptual differences. *Chicha* for human beings is a drink made with maize and sugar cane, while for animals, we are told, it is made with a poisonous plant.

A further perspectival trope emerges when we focus on Guna people's statement that the ashes of tobacco smoked by drunk people during drinking ceremonies are the fermented *chicha* drunk by animal entities, which, as Nicanor told me, in mythic times was actually a poison, hence a quintessential 'anti-food'. This should not appear surprising as, in the second volume of the *Mythologiques*, 'From Honey to Ashes', Lévi-Strauss opens with a demonstration of how among Amerindians honey – and similarly beer – share with tobacco the quality of oscillating between the category of food and that of poison.[6] Although the fermented *chicha* drunk during Guna puberty rituals is not a poison, its bitter taste and its alcoholic composition place it outside of the Guna category of 'food'.[7] Guna people consume fermented *chicha* only on the occasion of puberty rituals, its bitter taste standing in opposition to their predilection for sweet drinks in daily life, which I shall discuss in the next section.

Sweet *chicha*

Sweet drinks included sweetened coffee, chocolate drink, *madun*, a drink prepared with ripe plantain, and *inna ossid*, 'sweet *chicha*', made with unfermented maize. All these beverages were sweetened, rather excessively to my taste, with white sugar, which was consumed in huge quantities by each Guna household during my fieldwork. Among these drinks the one considered quintessentially nutritious (and therefore included in the category of 'people's food', *dule masi*), was *inna ossid*, 'sweet *chicha*'. This drink was also the one available virtually every day in Guna households. Each household always had a good provision of maize cobs, which were kept toasting in a wooden structure supported by four poles overhanging the cooking fire. To prepare sweet *chicha* dry toasted maize grains were ground and boiled in a big iron pot and left to cool. Although its taste was originally sour, it was served with added sugar.

Sweet unfermented *chicha* was drunk during the day to quench thirst and, if available, offered to kinspeople and friends visiting the house. It was kept in small metal pots in the cooking house and when a woman took a cup of it she made sure to scoop up some of the ground maize that had deposited on the bottom of the pot. Guests were usually given a glass of fresh water after drinking sweet *chicha* to rinse their mouth and get rid of the maize grains; then they spat out the water to one side on the ground with remarkable precision. People often stressed the good property of *inna ossid* in contributing to make the bodies of their kin strong and healthy. They compared it to *dule masi*, the coconut and plantain soup eaten with fish, which constituted the main and by far the most desired meal. Other drinks like *madun* were also praised, as opposed to coffee and cocoa drinks that, although often drunk and easily available, were not considered 'real food'. Most adult men used to take a bottle of *inna ossid* to the forest, or just some ground maize and sugar, which they diluted with fresh river water. This was considered the best way of coping with the intense heat and hard work in the forest gardens. Men did not spit the residual ground maize when drinking *inna ossid* in the forest but instead ate it. Thanks to its not purely liquid but more substantial composition, *inna ossid* was considered a food.

Women made *inna ossid* in their own kitchen. Prepared and offered exclusively by women, it was the outcome of the combined, although temporally disjointed, work of both sexes, since maize was sown and harvested by men. Similar to the rest of the daily food, which if in abundance could be offered to visiting kinspeople, sweet *chicha* was mainly consumed by co-residents. On the contrary, 'bitter *chicha*' (*inna gaibid*), as noted above was not considered food. Its consumption was unrestrained and led to vomiting; its composition was liquid and was always drunk cold. It was prepared outside people's houses, in the communal *chicha* house. The collection of sugar cane in the forest, the squeezing of its juice in the community mill (*trapiche*), and the subsequent stages of preparation were carried out collectively, sometimes involving children. Men and women worked together during the preparation of the *chicha*, stirring and filtering the boiling liquid. Its final maker, overlooking its fermentation, was a man, the maker of *chicha*. If *inna ossid* was the quintessential convivial food, shared by co-residents and making their bodies similar, *inna gaibid* was the vehicle to bring together unrelated people for a limited amount of festive time. If the former was conducive of an ethos of peacefulness, the latter, despite its mood enhancing quality, had an element of animosity and entailed a more or less latent degree of violence. We can also point out that those who drink bitter *chicha* together might eventually end up offering each other sweet *chicha* if they become related through a marriage. Interestingly enough, those who usually share sweet *chicha* tend not to drink bitter *chicha* together, since women tend to stay sober in order to help their husbands when they are too drunk to get back home by themselves.

Let us now focus on a further instance of the association between *chicha* and tobacco in the Guna lived world. In the next case, both substances respectively oscillate between sweetness and smoke and bitterness and ashes, retaining the capacity to create peaceful and convivial relations on the one hand and mediate inimical and predatory ones on the other.

Healing

There are striking similarities between the *chicha* and tobacco nexus in puberty rituals, shamanic initiations and healing rituals. The last two cases show almost the same internal organization and due to space constraints, I only deal with the latter here.[8] Both puberty ceremonies and healing rituals are witness to elaborate forms of exchange with alterity, both human and non-human. In the case of the former, as we have seen, animal spirits are invited to participate and are offered fermented *chicha* in the form of tobacco ashes in exchange for their peaceful return to their underworld villages once the ceremony finishes. This is reminiscent of the myth in which Dad Ibe, in occasion of his marriage with the daughter of the trickster Biler, transformed the ancestors of animals into their present day forms. Furthermore, as mentioned above, during puberty ceremonies the bride's kinsmen may 'abduct' the groom, taking him by force into the girl's house in order for the couple to start living together. In the case of healing rituals, animal spirits are offered fermented *chicha* as a way of persuading them to relinquish the soul or, rather, one of the immaterial doubles of the sick person. In most cases, I was told, the 'abduction' of a person's soul/double was carried out by an animal spirit's chief, who wanted to acquire a spouse for one of his/her children (cf. Vilaça 2002). If the abducted soul was not retrieved, it would remain to live with its animal companion and its earthly body would die.

During one healing ritual in which I was invited to participate in October 2004, the chanter, Aparicio del Vasto, worked with the help of three female 'pipe smokers' (*biba umala*), a male 'cigar smoker' (*waar saedi*) and a person in charge of burning cacao beans, *sianar daggedi*, literally 'he/she who looks after the cacao burner'. During the curing session, which was held after sunset, Aparicio sang for more than four hours directing his chant to his auxiliary spirits, who travelled in the metaphysical realm to find the abducted soul of the sick person kept hidden in a village of animals invisible to normal human beings. Auxiliary spirits are lodged in small wooden carved anthropomorphic figures and are colloquially called *nudsugana*, or *suargana* (Figure 10.1).

Figure 10.1 Guna wooden figures (*nudsugana*). (Photograph by Paolo Fortis.)

Aparicio had taken his wooden figures a few days before the curing session and set them in a box below the hammock of the ill woman who was separated from the rest of us by a curtain. During the performance of the ritual, he stopped singing twice, during which time the cigar smoker stood up and, with the lit end of the long cigar in his mouth, puffed the smoke on Aparicio's face and on all the other assistants four times. His way of smoking was the same as that of the *waar saedi* during Aurelio's tasting sessions. Meanwhile, during the whole duration of the ritual the three elder women kept smoking their pipes and collected the ashes in small calabashes.

In healing rituals like this, tobacco is used both as strengthening sweet *chicha* and inebriating bitter *chicha*. I suggest that during the session the chanter, his assistants and the wooden auxiliary figures become similar in that they establish a form of communication, whereby the chanter and the wooden figures are the closest. I was told that the chanter masters the special language spoken by *nudsugana* and by animal entities. This is the language in which healing chants are sung. In brief, chants use the vocabulary of daily life to construct highly imagistic speech patterns the meaning of which, although possible for a non-specialist to guess, is highly esoteric (see Sherzer 1983). By chanting, that is speaking the 'language of spirits', Aparicio became of a kind with them for the duration of the ritual, as did the pipe smokers. The only difference between them was that Aparicio was able to control his interactions with the spirit world and to master the whole ritual. By virtue of having stopped menstruating, the elder women pipe smokers were able to withstand close relationships with the spirits and were essential to the accomplishment of the healing process.[9] For this reason, the chanter and his assistants are treated similarly to auxiliary spirits and fed the food of the latter, tobacco smoke.[10] Human participants in the healing ritual thus *become* 'spirits'. In this way, tobacco smoke is used as a vehicle of conviviality between humans and non-humans, making them temporarily of the same kind for the purpose of establishing close positive relationships with a view to curing sick human persons. In this sense, chanter and assistants perceive tobacco smoke in the same way as *nudsugana*, as sweet *chicha*.

Tobacco ashes are understood to be the same substance both in healing rituals and in puberty ceremonies: the fermented *chicha* drunk by animal spirits. The chanter summons female *nudsugana*, the auxiliary spirits, to bring the ashes/*chicha* to the animal spirits. They in turn, seduced by the beauty of the *nudsugana*, cannot refuse to drink it and quickly get drunk. Similar to puberty rituals female auxiliary spirits are 'those who swing the *chicha*', *inna obanedi*, referring to the swaying movement of female dancers who carry half gourds full of fermented beer and offer them to dancing drinkers who meet them at the centre of the *chicha* house. Swinging the *chicha* is therefore the typical way of offering the fermented drink during festivals and involves an element of cheerfulness and exchange between the sexes, who attend to each other by singing and dancing. By the same token, male *nudsugana* play the diplomatic side of the battle and convince the drunken animals to reveal where they hide the soul/double of the sick person. Once this is discovered, they can sneakily retrieve it and restore it to its original owner. A remarkable difference thus appears between tobacco smoke and ashes in the context of healing rituals; while smoke is equally perceived as sweet *chicha* by human beings and *nudsugana* – that is, there is concordance – ashes are perceived differently by human and animal beings – there is discordance. Thus, while sweet *chicha* has the property of traversing specific perceptual boundaries, bitter *chicha* stresses the limits of those very boundaries.

At this point, I need only introduce one last element: the food of *nudsugana*. As anticipated above, these auxiliary spirits receive the same treatment as the ritual chanter and the *chicha* maker, that is, the smoke of long cigars is blown on their faces. Tobacco smoke is the sweet *chicha* of *nudsugana*; it is their food, which gives them the force to 'work hard' and fight the animal spirits. The smoke/*chicha* is consumed by these powerful beings through their nose. As can be clearly seen by the way these figures are carved, *nudsugana* have no mouth. Instead they have a long pointed nose, which is a key indicator of their other-than-human nature (cf. Fortis 2012a: 87–92, b). Guna people stress the fact that, in contrast to both *nudsugana* and white people, they themselves have short flat noses.

Guna people are aware of the alterity of these powerful beings and through daily acts of conviviality aim at familiarizing them. As I discuss elsewhere (Fortis 2012a: 178–180), people look after these protective figurines in their daily life in order to incorporate them in the house as a particular type of co-resident by washing and feeding them. In this way they ensure that the protector spirits 'remember' their hosts when the latter are in need.

Nudsugana are normally kept in plastic or wooden boxes inside the dormitory house of almost all Guna households to protect people against the predatory attacks of malicious spirits. Once I observed Wagala lighting a pipe filled with tobacco and, covering the bowl with one corner of her fabric skirt, blowing on it so that she could direct the smoke coming out of the mouthpiece towards the *nudsugana* gathered in a wooden box inside the house. Rotalio, her son-in-law, told me that Wagala was giving them 'sweet *chicha*' so they would be strong and alert during the night, watching over the sleep of the family.

Conclusions

Different ways of smoking tobacco – 'inhaling' (*ued*) and 'blowing' (*saed*) – correspond to different types of *chicha* – 'bitter' 'fermented' (*gaibid*) and 'sweet' 'unfermented' (*ossid*) – and consequently to these convivial and predatory social relations. At the same time this suggests a reading of the different moral behaviours associated respectively to humans on the one hand and animals and foreigners on the other hand. The former are capable of establishing consubstantial relations based on the production and circulation of 'real food', which they should consume moderately and without greed according to the appropriate moral attitude towards sharing that distinguishes 'real people' from 'strangers' and 'others'. The latter are considered more prone to, besides the excessive smoking of cigarettes, the excessive consumption of inebriating drink (anti-food) that, in Guna terms, besides being produced by non-kin and not being circulated through the usual paths of relatedness, leads to the boisterous behaviour that stands in stark opposition to the tranquil everyday life that co-villagers strive to pursue. We could even suggest that tobacco smoke and sweet *chicha* stand in relation to the 'cooked' in the same position as tobacco ashes and bitter *chicha* stand in relation to the 'rotten'. But instead of appealing to a division between 'human culture' and 'non-human nature', following Stolze Lima (2000), I wish to point to a division between a 'human quality', characterized by a certain degree of morality, including Guna people and the familiarized *nudsugana* spirits, and an 'animal quality' that, from a human perspective, is characterized by a distinctive lack of morality and an excess of predation. Neither 'qualities' nor moral attitudes are essential and unchangeable traits of any single living being, human or otherwise.

Commercial cigarettes and pipes are mainly smoked to produce the ashes that are served as bitter *chicha* to animals. This active form of smoking corresponds to the anti-food character of tobacco. Drinkers of bitter *chicha* smoke when they are not engaged in eating food and are instead prone to vomiting. Pipe smokers inhale the smoke during healing rituals, occasions when they have to follow a number of taboos, including restraining from sex and from eating certain types of food. Men resting during work in the forest inhale the smoke of their cigarettes to placate their hunger; the same thing that they do in the gathering house, a place where everyday food is never consumed.[11] By contrast, the passive form of smoking corresponds to the food character of tobacco. Smoke from long cigars is blown on *chicha* makers during tasting sessions. It is explicitly meant to prevent them from getting drunk while they taste the *chicha* from the several jars from which the entire village will drink. The smoking of *nudsugana* as noted above is a form of feeding too and is carried out inside the house, the quintessential place of conviviality.

If different ways of smoking correspond to different forms of sociality, it is interesting to note how the greater access to commercial tobacco, in the form of cigarettes, was happily embraced by Guna people in the past century when Guna population in the recently created island villages grew dramatically. The consequence of this has been that Guna people have had to work hard to maintain a safe and peaceful everyday life. Since the possibility of splitting and creating new villages is less of an option now than it was in the past, social life has had to elaborate new mechanisms to deal with internal conflicts.

Puberty rituals maintained an important role in Guna village life and have survived repeated attempts by missionaries, policemen and schoolteachers to eradicate them during the past century. By the same token, healing rituals have played a crucial role in dealing with the multiplication of predatory attacks from extra-human forces. The intensification of productive activities carried out on the mainland to provide food for the highly populated island villages has often had the consequence of upsetting the invisible dwellers of the forest causing the spread of epidemics. Guna people have thus found new allies in their wooden auxiliary figures, which are arguably endowed the spatio-temporally transformed powers that Guna specialists once themselves possessed before moving to the islands (Fortis 2011). Thus, far from revealing a growing addiction to commercial tobacco at the expenses of a supposedly 'traditional' use, the consumption of cigarettes has come to occupy a crucial place at the intersection of the differential modes of sociality in the transforming lived world of Guna people.

In this chapter I have argued that, for the Guna, tobacco smoke is the sweet *chicha* of *nudsugana* – auxiliary spirits – and tobacco ashes are the bitter *chicha* of *bonigana* – animal spirits. In line with Lévi-Strauss' argument in 'From Honey to Ashes' (1973), this double association seems to point to a system whereby both tobacco and *chicha* oscillate between the position of food and that of anti-food. Given the 'convivial' character of sweet *chicha* and the 'spirited' one of bitter *chicha* described above, tobacco seems to be the metaphysical counterpart of the maize drink, mediating the relation between human beings and auxiliary spirits on the one hand and human beings, animal spirits and unrelated people on the other. In brief, tobacco does at the metaphysical level what *chicha* does at the physical one; they both index consubstantiality with beings to be made similar and mediate predatory relations with 'others'.

Acknowledgements

Fieldwork among Guna people in 2003 and 2004 was funded by a Doctoral Scholarship granted by the University of Siena and by a Short Term Fellowship from the Smithsonian Tropical Research Institute. A trip in 2014 was funded by the Seedcorn Fund of Durham University. I am grateful to Guna people in Ogobsuggun for their hospitality and helpfulness through my research. I also wish to thank Elizabeth Rahman and Andrew Russell for inviting me to contribute to the present volume and the participants at the workshop 'The Changing Landscape of Tobacco Use in Lowland South America' for their helpful comments and highly interesting discussion.

Notes

1. I use here the new orthography for transcribing the Guna (previously spelled 'Kuna') language devised by a group of Guna linguists and officially adopted by the Guna General Congress (Orán and Wagua 2011). The main difference with previous forms of transcription, including the one I so far adopted, is the use of the voiced stop consonants g, b, d instead of the previously used k, p, t.
2. *Chicha* is the term used throughout Spanish-speaking Central and South America to indicate different types of fermented and unfermented drinks, which can be made with maize, manioc or different types of fruit.
3. However, it should be noted that chewing tobacco was reported among the Colombian Guna from the Urabá Gulf in the 1950s by the missionary Severino de Santa Teresa (1924: 218). See also Wilbert (1987: 127).
4. With great sadness Margherita and I learned in 2005, after we had returned back home, that Aurelio Pèrez had died. Aurelio was already ill during our stay in Ogobsuggun and said that despite the fact that he was given different plant medicines they all seemed to be ineffective in curing his illness. People in the village commented that this was because the illness had been caused by the revengeful attack of animal entities angered by the fact that the father of a pubescent girl, who the previous year had hosted a puberty ceremony for which

Aurelio was the *inna sobedi*, had broken the taboo and had had sex with his wife during the fermentation period of the *chicha*.

5. Guna people call those people who are not their kinspeople '*an ibmar suli*', literally 'not my thing'. As Margiotti (2010) argues, it is difficult to identify a category of affines among the Guna and there are not preferential categories of marriageable peoples.
6. See Londoño-Sulkin (2012: 97–103) for a study of the convivial and predatory qualities of tobacco among the People of the Centre (cf. Echeverri this volume).
7. See Margiotti (2010) for an insightful analysis of the differences between the daily preparation and distribution of food carried out predominantly by grandmothers in Guna households and the latter's inebriation during puberty rituals, when the preparation of food becomes thus responsibility of younger women who do not usually drink alcoholic *chicha*. This would suggest an interesting parallel between young women's avoidance of tobacco and of fermented *chicha*. Both substances share the quality of enhancing relations with the non-human world.
8. For more information on the use of tobacco during Guna shamanic initiations, see Fortis (2012a: 152–174).
9. This by no means entails that Guna women have lesser ritual capacities than men. See Fortis (2012a: 110–132 and 2014) for a discussion of female specialist skills.
10. See Baer (1992) for a discussion of the use of tobacco among Matsigenka shamans who feed their auxiliary spirits tobacco daily.
11. On a few occasions, crackers and squash drinks were distributed among attendants in the gathering house. However, Guna people did not consider that 'real food'.

Bibliography

Abram, D. (2010), *Becoming Animal*, New York, NY: Vintage Books.

Abruña-Rodríguez, F., Vicente-Chandler, J., Pearson, R.W. and Silva, S. (1970), 'Crop Response to Soil Acidity Factors in Ultisols and Oxisols: I. Tobacco', *Soil Science Society of America Journal*, 34(4): 629–35.

Albert, B. (1985), *Temps du Sang, Temps Des Cendres: représentation de la maladie, système rituel et espace politique chez les Yanomami du sud-est (Amazonie brésilienne)*, Doctoral thesis, Paris X – Nanterre University.

Alderete, E., Erickson, P.I., Kaplan, C.P. and Prez-Stable, E.J. (2010), 'Ceremonial Tobacco Use in the Andes: Implications for Smoking Prevention among Indigenous Youth', *Anthropology and Medicine*, 17(1): 27–39.

Alès, C. (2000), 'Anger as a Marker of Love. The Ethic of Conviviality among the Yanomami', in J. Overing and A. Passes (eds), *The Anthropology of Love and Anger: The Aesthetics of Conviviality in Native Amazonia*, London: Routledge, 133–51.

Alès, C. (2003), 'La horticultura yanomami yla problemática de los medios de sabanas en la Amazonia venezolana', in C. Alès and J. Chiappino (eds), *Caminos Cruzados: Ensayos en Anthropologia social, Etnoecologia y Etnoeducacion*, Mérida: IRD Editions/ULA-GRIAL, 389–422.

American Annual Cyclopædia, The (1868), *The American Annual Cyclopædia and Register of Important Events of 1867*, New York, NY: D. Appleton and Co.

Antonil, A.J. (2012), *Brazil at the Dawn of the Eighteenth Century*, translated and edited by T.J. Coates, Dartmouth, MA: Tagus Press.

Apiwtxa (2005 [2000]), *Homapani Ashaninka, Français*. CD audio, Cruzeiro do Sul: Asociacao Ashaninka do rio Amonea e Taboca Anapyiri.

Appadurai, A. (1986), *The Social Life of Things: Commodities in Cultural Perspective*, Cambridge: Cambridge University Press.

Ardito Vega, W. (1993), *Las Reducciones Jesuitas de Maynas. Una Experiencia Misional en la Amazonía Peruana*, Lima: CAAAP.

Århem, K. (1996), 'The Cosmic Food Web: Human-Nature Relatedness in the Northwest Amazon', in P. Descola and G. Pálsson (eds), *Nature and Society: Anthropological Perspectives*, London: Routledge, 185–204.

Århem, K., Cañón, L., Angulo, G. and García, M. (2004), *Ethnografia Makuna*. Gothenburg and Bototá: Acta Universitatis Gotoburgensis/Instituto Nacional de Anthropología y Historia.

ASH [Action on Smoking and Health] (2008), *Beyond Smoking Kills: Protecting Children, Reducing Inequalities*, London: ASH.

Baer, G. (1992), 'The One Intoxicated by Tobacco. Matsigenka Shamanism', in E.J.M. Langdon and G. Baer (eds), *Portals of Power: Shamanism in South America*, Albuquerque: University of New Mexico Press, 79–100.

Bahr, D. and Haefer, J. (1978), 'Song in Piman Curing', *Ethnomusicology*, 22(1): 89–122.

Bakewell, P. (2010), *A History of Latin America to 1825*, Malden, MA: Wiley-Blackwell.

Ballaré, C. (2009), 'Illuminated Behaviour: Phytochrome as a Key Regulator of Light Foraging and Plant Anti-herbivore Defence', *Plant, Cell and Environment*, 32(6): 713–25.

Barbira Freedman, F. (2002), 'Tobacco and Curing Agency in Western Amazonian Shamanism', in P.A. Baker and G. Carr (eds), *Practitioners, Practices and Patients: New Approaches to Medical Archaeology and Anthropology*, Oxford: Oxbow Books, 136–60.

———. (2010), 'Shamanic Plants and Gender in the Healing Forest', in E. Hsu and S. Harris (eds), *Plants, Health and Healing: On the Interface of Ethnobotany and Medical Anthropology*, Oxford: Berghahn, 135–78.

———. (2014), 'Shamans' Networks in Western Amazonia: the Iquitos Nauta Road', in B.C. Labate and N. Clavnar (eds), *Ayahuasca Shamanism in the Amazon and Beyond*, Oxford: Oxford University Press, 130–58.

———. (n.d.) 'Shamans' Networks and Indigeneity in Western Amazonia, Past and Present', Seminar paper, Centre of Latin American Studies, University of Cambridge.

Bates, H.W. (1873), *The Naturalist on the River Amazons*, 3rd edition, London: Bradbury and Evans.

Belaunde, L. (2001), *Viviendo Bien: Género y Fertilidad Entre los Airo-Pai de la Amazonía peruana*, Lima: Centro Amazónico de Antropología y Aplicación Práctica.

Bennett, B.C. (1992), 'Hallucinogenic Plants of the Shuar and Related Indigenous Groups in Amazonian Ecuador and Peru', *Brittonia*, 44(4): 483–93.

Benson, P. and Kirsch, S. (2010), 'Capitalism and the Politics of Resignation', *Current Anthropology*, 51(4): 459–86.

Benzoni, G. (1565), *Historia del Mondo Nuovo*, Venice: F. Rampazetto. [English Translation (1857) *History of the New World*, London: Hakluyt Society].

Beresford-Jones, D.G., Whaley, O., Ledesma, C.A. and Cadwallader, L. (2011), 'Two Millennia of Changes in Human Ecology: Archaeobotanical and

Invertebrate Records from the Lower Ica Valley, South Coast Peru', *Vegetation History and Archaeobotany*, 20(4): 273–92.

Berounský, D. (2013), 'Demonic Tobacco in Tibet', *Mongolo-Tibetica Pragensis*, 13(2): 7–34.

Beyer, S. (2009), *Singing to the Plants: A Guide to Mestizo Shamanism in the Upper Amazon*, Albuquerque: University of New Mexico Press.

———. (2012), 'On the Origins of Ayahuasca', Online blog entry, 25 April 2012. Retrievable from http://www.singingtotheplants.com/2012/04/on-origins-of-ayahuasca/

Bianchi, A. (2005), 'Ayahuasca e xamanismo indígena na selva peruana: O lento caminho da conquista', in B.C. Labate and S.L. Goulart (eds), *O uso ritual das plantas de poder*, Campinas: Mercado de Letras, 319–29.

Biet, A. (1664), *Voyage de la France Equinoxiale en l'Isle de Cayenne, entrepris par des françois en l'année 1652*. Paris: Chez François Clozier.

Bishop, S.R., Lau, M., Shapiro, S., Carlson, L., Andersen, N.D. and Carmody, J. (2004), 'Mindfulness: A Proposed Operational Definition', *Clinical Psychology: Science and Practice*, 11: 230–41.

Blacking, J. (1977), *The Anthropology of the Body*. London: Academic Press.

Bodley, J. (1972), *Victims of Progress*. California: Mayfield Publishing Company.

Bovensiepen, J. (2009), 'Landscapes of Life and Death in the Central Highlands of East Timor', *Anthropological Forum*, 19(3): 323–38.

Boxer, C. (1962), *The Golden Age of Brazil, 1695–1750: Growing Pains of a Colonial Society*, Berkeley, CA: University of California Press.

Brabec de Mori, B. (2011), 'Tracing Hallucinations: Contributing to a Critical Ethnohistory of Ayahuasca Usage in the Peruvian Amazon', in B.C. Labate and H. Jungaberle (eds), *The Internationalization of Ayahuasca*, Zurich: Lit-Verlag, 23–48.

———. (2012), 'About Magical Singing, Sonic Perspectives, Ambient Multinatures, and the Conscious Experience', *Indiana*, 29: 73–101.

———. (2013), 'La transformación de la medicina Shipibo-Konibo. Conceptos etno-médicos en la representación de un pueblo indígena', in E. Sigl, Y. Schaffler and R. Ávila (eds), *Etnografías de América Latina. Ocho ensayos* (Colección Estudios del Hombre 30), Guadalajara: Universidad de Guadalajara, 203–44.

———. (2014), 'From the Native's Point of View: How Shipibo-Konibo Experience and Interpret Ayahuasca Drinking with "Gringos"', in B.C. Labate and C. Cavnar (eds), *Ayahuasca Shamanism in the Amazon and Beyond*, New York, NY: Oxford University Press, 206–30.

———. (forthcoming a), 'El oído no-humano: Los agentes en las canciones indígenas, un "eslabón perdido" ontológico?', in B. Brabec de Mori, M. Lewy and M. García (eds), *Mundos audibles de América. Cosmologías y prácticas sonoras de los pueblos indígenas*, Berlin: Gebr. Mann.

———. (forthcoming b), *Die Lieder der Richtigen Menschen. Musikalische Kulturanthropologie der indigenen Bevölkerung im Ucayali-Tal, Westamazonien*, Innsbruck: Helbling.

Brabec de Mori, B. and L. Mori Silvano de Brabec (2009a), 'Shipibo-Konibo Art and Healing Concepts. A Critical View on the "Aesthetic Therapy" ', *Viennese Ethnomedicine Newsletter*, 11(2–3): 18–26.

———. (2009b), 'La corona de la inspiración. Los diseños geométricos de los Shipibo-Konibo y sus relaciones con cosmovisión y música', *Indiana*, 26: 105–34.

Brady M. (2008), 'Health Inequalities: Historical and Cultural Roots of Tobacco Use among Aboriginal and Torres Strait Islander People', *Australian and New Zealand Journal of Public Health*, 26: 120–4.

Brandt, A.M. (2007), *The Cigarette Century: The Rise, Fall, and Deadly Persistence of the Product that Defined America*, New York, NY: Basic Books.

Brewer, J.A., Mallik, S., Babuscio, T.A., Nich, C., Johnson, H.E., Deleone, C.M., Minnix-Cotton, C.A., Byrne, S.A., Kober, H., Weinstein, A.J., Carroll, K.M. and Rounsaville, B.J. (2011), 'Mindfulness Training for Smoking Cessation: Results from a Randomized Controlled Trial', *Drug and Alcohol Dependence*, 119 (1–2): 72–80.

Brown, M.F. (2007), *Tsewa's Gift: Magic and Meaning in an Amazonian Society*, Tuscaloosa, AL: University of Alabama Press.

Bruhn, J.G., Holmstedt, B., Lindgren, J.E., and Wassén, S.H. (1976), 'The Tobacco from Niño Korin: Identification of Nicotine in a Bolivian Archaeological Collection', *Ethnographical Museum of Gothenburg Annual Report*, 45–8.

Bruno, M.C. (2014), 'Beyond Raised Fields: Exploring Farming Practices and Processes of Agricultural Change in the Ancient Lake Titicaca Basin of the Andes', *American Anthropologist*, 116(1): 130–45.

Bunton, R. and Coveney, J. (2011), 'Drugs' Pleasures', *Critical Public Health*, 21(1): 9–23.

Burg, J. and Michalak, J. (2011), 'The Healthy Quality of Mindful Breathing: Associations with Rumination and Depression', *Cognitive Therapy and Research*, 35(2): 179–85.

Butt-Colson, A. (1956), 'Ritual blowing: Taling – A Causation and Cure of Illness among the Akawaio', *Man*, 56: 49–55.

———. (1975), 'Birth Customs of the Akawaio', in J.H.M. Beattie and R.G. Lienhardt (eds), *Studies in Social Anthropology: Essays in Memory of E.E Evans- Pritchard by His Former Oxford Colleagues*, Oxford: Clarendon, 285–309.

———. (1977), 'The Akawaio Shaman', in E.B. Basso (ed.), *Carib-Speaking Indians: Culture, Society and Language*, Tucson, AZ: University of Arizona Press, 43–65.

Candre-Kɨneraɨ, H. and Echeverri, J.A. (1996), *Cool Tobacco Sweet Coca: Teachings of an Indian Sage from the Colombian Amazon*, London: Themis Books.

Carrera Rubio, J. (2004), *The Fertility of Words: Aspects of Language and Sociality among Yanomami People of Venezuela, DPhil thesis*, University of St Andrews.

Carim-Todd, L., Mitchell, S. and Oken, B. (2013), 'Mind-Body Practices: An Alternative, Drug-Free Treatment for Smoking Cessation? A Systematic Review of the Literature', *Drug and Alcohol Dependence* 132(3): 399–410.

Carneiro da Cunha, M. (1998), 'Pontos de Vista sobre a Floresta Amazônica: Xamanismo e Tradução', *MANA*, 4(1): 7–22.

———. (2009), 'Um difusionismo estrutural existe?', *Cultura com aspas e outros ensaios*, São Paulo: COSAC NAIFY, 115–22.

Caruso, E. (2012), *Being at the Centre: Self and Empire among Ene Ashaninka People in Peruvian Amazonia*, PhD thesis, University of Kent.

Chagnon, N.A. (1968), *Yanomamö: The Fierce People*, New York, London: Holt Rinehart and Winston.

Chamberlayne, J. (1682), *The Natural History of Coffee, Thee, Chocolate, Tobacco*, London: Printed for Chistopher Wilkinson.

Chandless, W. (1866), 'Ascent of the River Purus', *Journal of the Royal Geographical Society*, 35: 86–118.

Chantre y Herrera, J. (1901), *Historia de las misiones de la Compañía de Jesús en el Marañón español, Provincia de Maynas*, Madrid: Imprenta J. Ayrial.

Chapin, M. (1983), *Curing among the San Blas Kuna of Panama*, PhD dissertation, University of Arizona.

Chaumeil, J-P. (1983), *Voir, savoir, pouvoir. Le chamanisme chez les Yagua du Nord-Est péruvien*, Paris: CNRS.

———. (2001), 'The Blowpipe Indians: Variations on the Theme of Blowpipe and Tube among the Yagua Indians of the Peruvian Amazon', in L. Rival and N. Whitehead (eds), *Beyond the Visible and the Material: The Amerindianization of Society in the Work of Peter Rivière*, Oxford: University Press, 81–99.

Chevallier, A. (2013), 'From Ecological Constraints to Cultural Identities: Pre-Columbian Attitudes Toward Food', in M.I.J. Davis and F.N. M'Mbogori (eds), *Humans and the Environment, New Archaeological Perspectives for the Twenty-First Century*, Oxford: Oxford University Press, 97–116.

Clastres, H. and Lizot, J. (1978), 'La part du feu. Rites et discours de la mort chez les Yanomami', *Libre*, 3: 103–33.

Cocco, L. (1987), *Iyewei-teri: quince años entre los yanomamos*, Caracas: Libreria Editorial Salesiana, Escuela Técnica Popular Don Bosco.

Cooper, J.M. (1949), 'Stimulants and Narcotics', in J.H. Steward (ed.), *Handbook of South American Indians*, Volume 5, Smithsonian Institution: Bureau of American Ethnology, Bulletin 143, 525–58.

Cornelio, J. and Wright, R. (1999) *Waferinaipe Ianheke: a Sabedoria Dos Nossos Antepassados*, Rio Aiari, São Gabriel da Cachoeira, Amazonas: ACIRA/FOIRN.

Crevaux, J. (1883), *Voyages dans l'Amérique du Sud*. Paris: Hachette.

Crocker, J.C. (1985), *Vital Souls: Bororo Cosmology, Natural Symbolism, and Shamanism*, Tucson, AZ: University of Arizona Press.

Csordas, T. (1994), *The Sacred Self: A Cultural Phenomenology of Charismatic Healing*. Berkeley, CA, London: University of California Press.

Cunill Grau, P. (2007), *Geohistoria de la sensibilidad en Venezuela*, Caracas: Fundación Empresas Polar.

Daley, C.M., James, A.S., Barnoskie, R.S., Segraves, M., Schupbach R. and Choi, W.S. (2006), ' "Tobacco Has a Purpose, Not Just a Past": Feasibility of Developing a Culturally Appropriate Smoking Cessation Program for a Pan-Tribal Native Population', *Medical Anthropology Quarterly*, 20(4): 421–40.

Darbois, D. (1956), *Yanamale, Village of the Amazon*. London: Collins.

Deci, E. and Ryan, R. (2008), 'Hedonia, Eudamonia, and Well-Being: An Introduction', *Journal of Happiness Studies*, 9: 1–11.

de Goeje, C. (1941), 'De Oayana-Indianen', *Bijdragen tot de Taal-, Land- en Volkenkunde van Nederlandsch-Indië*, 100: 70–125. Leiden: Brill.

Degregori, C.I. (2011), *Qué difícil es ser Dios. El Partido Comunista del Perú-Sendero Luminoso y el conflicto armado*, Lima: Instituto de Estudios Peruanos.

de Martino, E. (1972 [1988]). *Primitive Magic: The Psychic Powers of Shamans and Sorcerers*, Bridport: Prism Press.

Denevan, W.M. (2001), *Cultivated Landscapes of Native Amazonia and the Andes*, Oxford: Oxford University Press.

———. (1996 [1993]), *The Spears of Twilight: Life and Death in the Amazon Jungle*, London: Harper Collins Publishers.

———. (2005), *Par-delà nature et culture*, Paris: Editions Gallimard.

Desjarlais, R. (1992), *Body and Emotion: The Aesthetics of Illness and Healing in the Nepal Himalayas*, Philadelphia, PA: University of Pennsylavania Press.

Desjarlais, C. (1996), 'Presence', in C. Laderman and M. Roseman (eds), *The Performance of Healing*, London: Routledge, 143–64.

Dickau, R., Bruno, M.C., Iriarte, J., Prümers, H., Betancourt, C.J., Holst, I. and Mayle, F.E. (2012), 'Diversity of Cultivars and Other Plant Resources

Used at Habitation Sites in the Llanos de Mojos, Beni, Bolivia: Evidence from Macrobotanical Remains, Starch Grains, and Phytoliths', *Journal of Archaeological Science*, 39(2): 357–70.

Dickson, S. and O'Neil, P. (1958–1969), *Tobacco: A Catalogue of the Books, Manuscripts and Engravings Acquired since 1942 in the Arents Tobacco Collection at the New York Public Library from 1507 to the Present*, New York, NY: New York Public Library.

DNP [Departamento Nacional de Planeación, Colombia] (2010), *Aspectos básicos grupo étnico indígenas*, Bogotá: DNP, Dirección de Desarrollo Territorial Sostenible, Subdirección de Ordenamiento y Desarrollo Territorial.

Douglas, M. (1966), *Purity and Danger: An Analysis of Concepts of Pollution and Taboo*, London: Routledge.

———. (1970), *Natural Symbols: Explorations in Cosmology*, Barrie and Rockliff: Cresset Press.

Duin, R. (2009), *Wayana Socio-Political Landscapes: Multi-Scalar Regionality and Temporality in Guiana*, PhD dissertation, University of Florida.

———. (2012), 'Ritual Economy: Dynamic Multi-Scalar Processes of Socio-Political Landscapes in the Eastern Guiana Highlands', *Antropológica*, 117: 5–53.

Earle, T.K. (1987), *Archaeological Field Research in the Upper Mantaro, Peru, 1982–1983: Investigations of Inka Expansion and Exchange*, Los Angeles, CA: Institute of Archaeology, University of California, Los Angeles.

Echeverri, J.A. (1996), 'The Tobacco Spirit's Game: From Oral to Written Expression in the Amazon Basin', in M. Preuss (ed.), *Beyond Indigenous Voices*, Lancaster, CA: Labyrinthos, 115–22.

———. (1997), *The People of the Center of the World. A Study in Culture, History and Orality in the Colombian Amazon*, PhD dissertation, New York, NY: New School for Social Research, Faculty of Political and Social Science.

Echeverri, J.A. and Pereira, E. (2005), '"Mambear coca não é pintar a boca de verde": Notas sobre a origem e o uso ritual da coca amazônica', in B.C. Labate and S.L. Goulart (eds), *O Uso ritual das plantas de poder*. Campinas: Mercado de Letras 117–85.

Echeverri, J.A. and Román-Jitdutjaaño, O. (2011) 'Witoto Ash Salts from the Amazon', *Journal of Ethnopharmacology*, 138(2): 492–502.

———. (2013), 'Ash Salts and Bodily Affects: Witoto Traditional Environmental Knowledge as Sexual Education', *Environmental Research Letters*, 8(1): 015034–46.

Echeverri, J.A., Román, Ó.J. and Jitdujaaño y Román, S. (2001), 'La Sal de Monte: Un Ensayo de Halofitogenografía Huitoto', in C. Franky and C. Zárate (eds), *Imani Mundo. Estudios en la Amazonia Colombiana*, Bogotá: Universidad Nacional de Colombia, 397–477.

Echeverría, J. and Niemeyer, H.M. (2012), 'Nicotine in the Hair of Mummies from San Pedro de Atacama (Northern Chile)', *Journal of Archaeological Science*, 39(7): 1951–9.

Echeverría, J., Planella, M.T. and Niemeyer, H.M. (2014), 'Nicotine in Residues of Smoking Pipes and Other Artifacts of the Smoking Complex from an Early Ceramic Period Archaeological Site in Central Chile', *Journal of Archaeological Science*, 44: 55–60.

Ehrenreich, P. (1948), 'Contribuição para a Etnologia do Brazil', *Revista do Museu Paulista*, 14: 279–312.

Elferink, J.G.R. (1983), 'The Narcotic and Hallucinogenic Use of Tobacco in Pre-Columbian Central America', *Journal of Ethnopharmacology*, 7: 111–22.

Elick, J. (1969), *An Ethnography of the Pichis Valley Campa of Eastern Peru*, PhD thesis, University of California Los Angeles.

Elwafia, H., Witkiewitzb, K., Mallika, S., Thornhil, T., Judson, V. and Brewera, A. (2013), 'Mindfulness Training for Smoking Cessation: Moderation of the Relationship between Craving and Cigarette Use', *Drug and Alcohol Dependence*, 130: 222–9.

Erikson, P. (2001), 'Myth and Material Culture: Matis Blowguns, Palm Trees, and Ancestor Spirits', in L. Rival and N. Whitehead (eds), *Beyond the Visible and the Material: The Amerindianization of Society in the Work of Peter Rivière*, Oxford: Oxford University Press, 101–21.

Ewart, E. (2000), *Living with Each Other: Selves and Alters amongst the Panará of Central Brazil*, PhD thesis, University of London.

———. (2005), 'Fazendo Pessoas e Fazendo Roças Entre os Panará do Brasil Central', *Revista de Antropologia*, 48(1): 9–35.

———. (2013), *Space and Society in Central Brazil: A Panará Ethnography*, London: Bloomsbury.

Facundes, S. da Silva (2000), *The Language of the Apurinã People of Brazil (Maipure/Arawak)*, PhD thesis: The University of New York at Buffalo.

Farabee, W. C. (1922), *Indian Tribes of Eastern Peru*, Papers of the Peabody Museum of Archaeology and Ethnology, Harvard University, Volume 10, Cambridge, MA: Harvard University Press.

Fausto, C. (2002), 'Banquete de gente: comensalidade e canibalismo na Amazônia', *Mana - Estudos de Antropologia Social*, 8(2): 7–44.

———. (2004), 'A Blend of Blood and Tobacco: Shamans and Jaguars among the Parakanã of Eastern Amazonia', in N.L. Whitehead and R. Wright (eds), *In Darkness and Secrecy: The Anthropology of Assault Sorcery and Witchcraft in Amazonia*, Durham, NC: Duke University Press, 155–78.

———. (2007), 'Feasting on People: Eating Animals and Humans in Amazonia', *Current Anthropology*, 48(4): 497–530.

———. (2008), 'Donos demais: maestria e domínio na Amazônia', *Mana*, 14(2): 329–66.

Feather, C. (2009), 'The Restless Life of the Nahua: Shaping People and Places in the Peruvian Amazon', in M. Alexiades (ed.), *Mobility and Migration in Indigenous Amazonia: Contemporary Ethnoecological Perspectives*, Oxford: Berghahn, 69–85.

Feinhandler, S.J., Fleming, H.C. and Monahon, J.M. (1979), 'Pre-Columbian Tobaccos in the Pacific', *Economic Botany*, 33(2): 213–26.

Fischer, W. (2000), *Rain Forest Exchanges: Industry and Community on an Amazonian Frontier*, Washington, DC: Smithsonian Institute.

Fortis, P. (2011), '*Nuchu* and *Kwarìp*: Images of the Past in Central and South America', in P. Fortis and I. Praet (eds), *The Archaeological Encounter: Anthropological Perspectives*, University of St Andrews, Centre for Amerindian, Latin American and Caribbean Studies Occasional Publication, 204–33.

———. (2012a), *Kuna Art and Shamanism: An Ethnographic Approach*, Austin, TX: University of Texas Press.

———. (2012b), 'Images of Person in an Amerindian Society: An Ethnographic Account of Kuna Woodcarving', *Journal de la Société des Americanistes*, 98(1): 7–38.

———. (2014), 'Artefacts and Bodies among Kuna People from Panama', in E. Hallam and T. Ingold (eds), *Making and Growing: Anthropological Studies of Organisms and Artefacts*, Farnham: Ashgate, 89–106.

Fotiou, E. (2010a), *From Medicine Men to Day Trippers: Shamanic Tourism in Iquitos, Peru*, PhD thesis in Anthropology, University of Wisconsin-Madison.

———. (2010b), 'Encounters with Sorcery: An Ethnographer's Account', *Anthropology and Humanism*, 35(2): 192–203.

Frampton, J. (1925) *Joyfull Newes Out of the Newe Founde Worlde (Cover Title: Frampton's Monardes)*, with an Introduction by S. Gaselee, combining material from the 1577 and 1580 volumes, London: Constable and Co.

Franssen-Herderschee, A. (1905), 'Verslag van de Gonini-expeditie', *Tijdschrift van het Koninklijk Nederlands Aardrijkskundig Genootschap*, 22: 1–159.

Fry, C. (1889), *La gran region de los bosques; o, ríos peruanos navegables: Urubamba, Ucayali, Amazonas, Pachitea y Palcazú. Diario de viajes y exploraciones… 1886, 1887 y 1880*, 2 Vols, Lima: Imprenta de B. Gil.

Fuentes, E. (1980), 'Los Yanomami y las plantas silvestres', *Antropológica*, 54: 3–138.

Garcia Hierro, P., Hvalkof, S. and Gray, A. (1998), *Liberation Through Land Rights in the Peruvian Amazon*, Copenhagen: IWGIA.

Garnelo, L. (2003), *Poder, Hierarquia e Reciprocidade: Saúde e Harmonia Entre os Baniwa do Alto Rio Negro*, Rio de Janeiro: Fiocruz.

———. (2007), 'Cosmology, Environment, and Health: Baniwa Food Myths and Rituals', *História, Ciências, Saúde –Manguinhos*, 14: 191–211.

Gasché, J. (1971), 'Quelques prolongements sociaux des pratiques horticoles et culinaires chez les indiens Witoto', *Journal de la Societé des Americanistes*, 60: 317–27.

———. (2009), 'La sociedad de la "Gente del centro" ', in F. Seifart, D. Fagua, J. Gasché and J.-A. Echeverri (eds), *A Multimedia Documentation of the Languages of the People of the Center. Online Publication of Transcribed and Translated Bora, Ocaina, Nonuya, Resígaro, and Witoto Audio and Video Recordings with Linguistic and Ethnographic Annotations and Descriptions*, Nijmegen: DOBES-MPI. http://corpus1.mpi.nl/media-archive/dobes_data/Center/Info/1.3_Sociedad.pdf (accessed 10 April 2014).

Gately, I. (2001), *La Diva Nicotiana: The Story of How Tobacco Seduced the World*, London: Simon and Schuster.

Gertsch, J., Gertsch-Roost, K. and Sticher, O. (2004). 'Phyllanthus piscatorum, ethnopharmacological studies on a women's medicinal plant of the Yanomamï Amerindians', *Journal of Ethnopharmacology*, 91(2): 181–188.

Gibson, J. (1977), 'The Theory of Affordances', in R.E. Shaw and J. Bransford (eds), *Perceiving, Acting, and Knowing: Toward an Ecological Psychology*, Hillsdale, NJ: Erlbaum, 67–82.

———. (1979), *The Ecological Approach to Visual Perception*, Boston, MA: Houghton Mifflin.

Glaser, B., Guggenberger, G., Zech, W. and de Lourdes Ruivo, M. (2003) 'Soil Organic Matter Stability in Amazonian Dark Earths', in J. Lehmann, D.C. Kern, B. Glaser, and W.I. Woods (eds), *Amazonian Dark Earths: Origin, Properties, Management*, Dordrecht, Netherlands: Kluwer, 141–58.

Goldman, I. (2004), *Cubeo Hehénewa Religious Thought: Metaphysics of a Northwestern Amazonian People*, New York, NY: Columbia University Press.

Gomes, F.S. (2002), 'A "Safe Haven": Runaway Slaves, *Mocambos*, and Borders in Colonial Amazonia, Brazil', *Hispanic American Historical Review*, 82(3): 469–98.

Goodman, J. (1993), *Tobacco in History: The Cultures of Dependence*, London: Routledge.

Goodspeed, T.H. (1954), *The Genus Nicotiana: Origins, Relationships and Evolution of Its Species in the Light of Their Distribution, Morphology and Cytology*, Waltham, MA: Chronica Botanica.

———. (1961), *Plant Hunters in the Andes*, Berkeley, CA: University of California Press.

Gow, P. (1989), 'The Perverse Child: Desire in a Native Amazonian Subsistence Economy', *Man*, 24(4): 567–82.

———. (1991), *Of Mixed Blood: Kinship and History in Peruvian Amazonia*, Oxford: Clarendon Press.

———. (1993), 'Gringos and Wild Indians: Images of History in Western Amazonian Cultures', *L'Homme*, 126–8: 327–47.

———. (1994), 'River People: Shamanism and History in Western Amazonia', in N. Thomas and C. Humphrey (eds), *Shamanism, History and the State*, Michigan: University of Michigan, 90–113.

———. (2001), *An Amazonian Myth and Its History*, Oxford: Oxford University Press.

———. (2002), 'Piro, Apurinã and Campa: Social Dissimilation and Assimilation in Southwestern Amazonia', in J.D. Hill and F. Santos-Granero (eds), *Comparative Arawakan Histories: Rethinking Language Family and Culture Area in Amazonia*, Urbana and Chicago, IL: University of Illinois Press, 147–70.

———. (2013), 'Dormido, Borracho, Alucinando: Estados Corporales Alterado a Través de la Ayahuasca en la Amazonía Peruana', in B. Caiuby and J. Bouso (eds), *Ayahuasca y Salud*, Barelona: los Libros de la Liebre de Marzo, 66–87.

Gray, A. (1996), *The Arakmbut: Mythology, Spirituality, and History*, Oxford: Berghahn.

Griffiths, T. (1998), *Ethnoeconomics and Native Amazonian Livelihood: Culture and economy among the Nɨpóde-Uitoto of the Middle Caquetá Basin in Colombia*, D Phil thesis, Faculty of Anthropology and Geography, St. Antony's College, University of Oxford.

Haberman, T. (1984), 'Evidence for Aboriginal Tobaccos in Eastern North America', *American Antiquity*, 49(2): 269–87.

Halbmayer, E. (2012), 'Debating Animism, Perspectivism and the Construction of Ontologies', *Indiana*, 29: 9–23.

———. (2013), 'Securing a Life for the Dead among the Yukpa. The Exhumation Ritual as a Temporary Synchronisation of Worlds', *Journal de la Société des Américanistes*, 99(1): 105–40.

Harcourt, R. (1928), *A Relation of a Voyage to Guiana by Robert Harcourt 1613*. Edited with introduction and notes by Sir C. A. Harris. London: Hakluyt Society, second series, no. LX.

Harter, E.C. (1985), *The Lost Colony of the Confederacy*, Jackson: University Press of Mississippi.

Hastings, G., de Andrade, M. and Moodie, C. (2012), 'Tobacco Harm Reduction: The Devil is in the Deployment', *British Medical Journal*, 345: e8412.

Hernandez, F. (1942), *Historia de las Plantas de Nueva España. Medico e Historiador de su Majestad don Felipe II Rey de Espana y de las Indias, y Protomedico de todo el Nuevo Mundo*, Mexico: Imprenta Universitaria.

Herndon, W.L. and Gibbon, L. (1854), *Exploration of the Valley of the Amazon*, Washington, DC: A.O.P Nicholson, Public Printer.

Hertz, R. (1960 [1881–1915]), *Death and the Right Hand*, Aberdeen: Cohen and West.

Hill, J. (1985), 'Myth, Spirit Naming, and the Art of Microtonal Rising: Childbirth Rituals of the Arawakan Wakúwenai', *Revista de Musica Latinoamericana*, 6(1): 1–30.

———. (1993), *Keepers of the Sacred Chants: The Poetics of Ritual Power in an Amazonian Society*, Tucson, AZ: University of Arizona Press.

———. (2009a), *Made-from-Bone: Trickster Myths, Music, and History from the Amazon*, Urbana, IL: University of Illinois Press.

———. (2009b), 'Materializing the Occult: An Approach to Understanding the Nature of Materiality in Wakúwenai Ontology', in F. Santos-Granero (ed.), *The Occult Life of Things: Native Amazonian Theories of Materiality and Personhood*, Tucson, AZ: University of Arizona Press.

———. (2009c), 'Hearing is Believing', *Journal of Consciousness Studies*, 16(6–8): 218–39.

Hill, J. and Chaumeil, J.-P. (eds) (2011), *Burst of Breath: Indigenous Ritual Wind Instruments in Lowland South America*, Lincoln, NE: University of Nebraska Press.

Hill, J. and Santos-Granero, F. (eds) (2002), *Comparative Arawakan Histories: Rethinking Language Family and Culture Area in Amazonia*, Urbana, IL: University of Illinois Press.

Hill, J. and Wright, R. (1988), 'Time, Narrative and Ritual: Historical Interpretations from an Amazonian Society', in J.D. Hill (ed.), *Rethinking History and Myth: Indigenous South American Perspectives on the Past*, Urbana, IL: University of Illinois Press, 78–105.

Hornborg, A. and Hill, J. (eds) (2011), *Ethnicity in Ancient Amazonia: Reconstructing Past Identities from Archaeology, Linguistics, and Ethnohistory*, Boulder, CO: University Press of Colorado.

Howe, J. (1976), 'Smoking Out the Spirits: A Cuna Exorcism', in P. Young and J. Howe (eds), *Ritual and Symbol in Native Central America*, University of Oregon Anthropological Papers, 9.

———. (1998), *A People Who Would not Kneel: Panama, The United States and the San Blas Kuna*, Washington, DC: Smithsonian Institution Press.

———. (2002 [1986]), *The Kuna Gathering: Contemporary Village Politics in Panama*, Tucson, AZ: Fenestra Books.

Hsu, E. (2007), 'The Biological in the Cultural: The Five Agents and the Body Ecologic in Chinese Medicine', in D. Parkin and S. Ulijaszek (eds), *Holistic Anthropology: Emergence and Convergence*, Oxford: Berghahn, 91–126.

Huertas Castillo, B. (2002), *Los pueblos indígenas en aislamiento. Su lucha por la sobrevivencia y la libertad*, Lima and Copenhague: IWGIA.

Hughes, A., Williams, M., Bardacke, N., Duncan, L.G. and Goodman, S.H. (2009), 'Mindfulness Approaches to Childbirth and Parenting', *British Journal of Midwifery*, 17(10): 630–5.

Hugh-Jones, C. (1979), *From the Milk River: Spatial and Temporal Processes in Northwest Amazonia*, Cambridge: Cambridge University Press.

Hugh-Jones, S. (1979), *The Palm and the Pleiades: Initiation and Cosmology in Northwest Amazonia*, Cambridge: Cambridge University Press.

———. (1992), 'Yesterday's Luxuries, Tomorrow's Necessities: Business and Barter in Northwest Amazonia', in C. Humphrey and S. Hugh-Jones (eds), *Barter Exchange and Value*, Cambridge: Cambridge University Press, 42–74.

———. (1994), 'Shamans, Prophets, Priests and Pastors', in N. Thomas and C. Humphrey (eds), *Shamanism, History and the State*, Ann Arbor: Michigan University Press, 32–75.

———. (2007), 'Coca, Beer, Cigars and *Yagé*: Meals and Anti-Meals in an Amerindian community', in J. Goodman, P.E. Lovejoy and A. Sherratt (eds), *Consuming Habits: Global and Historical Perspectives on How Cultures Define Drugs*, 2nd edition, London: Routledge, 46–64.

———. (2009), 'The Fabricated Body: Objects and Ancestors in Northwest Amazonia', in F. Santos-Granero (ed.), *The Occult Life of Things: Native Amazonian Theories of Materiality and Personhood*, Tucson, AZ: University of Arizona Press, 33–59.

Idoyaga Molina, A. (2000), *Shamanismo, brujería y poder en América Latina*, Buenos Aires: CAEA-CONICET.

ILV [Instituto Lingüístico del Verano] (2002), *Shimikunata asirtachik killka. Inka Kastellanu. Diccionario Inga-Castellano (Serie lingüística peruana 52)*, Lima: ILV.

Ingold, T. (2000), *The Perception of the Environment: Essays on Livelihood, Dwelling and Skill*, London: Routledge.

———. (2006),'Rethinking the Animate, Re-animating Thought', *Ethnos*, 71(1): 9–20.

Izquierdo, C. (2009), 'Well-Being among the Matsigenka of the Peruvian Amazonia: Health, Missions, Oil, and "Progress" ', in G. Mathews and C. Izquierdo (eds), *Pursuits of Happiness: Well-Being in Anthropological Perspective*, Oxford: Berghahn, 67–87.

Jackson, J.E. (1983a), *The Fish People: Linguistic Exogamy and Tukanoan Identity in Northwest Amazonia*, Cambridge: Cambridge University Press.

Jackson, M. (1983b), 'Knowledge of the Body', *Man*, 18(2): 327–45.

Jauregui, X., Clavo, Z.M., Jovel, E.M. and Pardo-de-Santayana, M. (2011), '"Plantas con madre": Plants that Teach and Guide in the Shamanic Initiation Process in the East-Central Peruvian Amazon', *Journal of Ethnopharmacology*, 134: 739–52.

Kamen-Kaye, D. (1971), 'Chimó: An Unusual Form of Tobacco in Venezuela', *Botanical Museum Leaflets, Harvard University*, 23(1): 1–59.

Karadimas, D. (2005), *La Raison du Corps: Idéologie du Corps et Représentations de l'Environment chez les Miraña d'Amazonie Colombienne*, Paris: Éditions Peeters.

Karban, R., Baldwin, I.T., Baxter, K.J., Laue, G. and Felton, G.W. (2000), 'Communication between Plants: Induced Resistance in Wild Tobacco Plant Following Clipping of Neighboring Sagebrush', *Oecologia*, 125: 66–71.

Karsten, R. (1926), *The Civilization of the South American Indians, with Special Reference to Magic and Religion*, London: Kegan Paul, Trench, Trubner and Co.

Karsten, R. (1964), 'Studies in the Religion of the South American Indians East of the Andes', in A. Runeberg and M. Webster (eds), *Commentationes Humanarum Litterarum XXIX.1*, Helsinki: Societas Scientiarum Fennica.

Kawa, N.C. (2016), *Amazonia in the Anthropocene: Soils, Forests, Plants, People*, Austin, TX: University of Texas Press.

Kawa, N.C. and Oyuela-Caycedo, A. (2008), 'Amazonian Dark Earth: A Model of Sustainable Agriculture of the Past and Future?', *The International Journal of Environmental, Cultural, Economic, and Social Sustainability*, 4(3): 9–16.

Kawa, N.C., Rodrigues, D. and Clement, C.R. (2011), 'Useful Species Richness, Proportion of Exotic Species, and Market Orientation on Amazonian Dark Earths and Oxisols', *Economic Botany*, 65(2): 169–77.

Keller, F. (1875), *The Amazon and Madeira Rivers: Sketches and Descriptions from the Note-book of an Explorer*, London: Chapman and Hall.

Kelley, J.H. and Holden, W.C. (1991), *A Yaqui Life: The Personal Chronicle of a Yaqui Indian*, Omaha: University of Nebraska Press.

Kelly, J.A. (2011), *State Healthcare and Yanomami Transformations: A Symmetrical Ethnography*, Tucson, AZ: University of Arizona Press.

King James 1st (1604), *A Counterblaste to Tobacco*, London: Imprinted by Robert Barker.

Knapp, S., Chase, M.W. and Clarkson, J.J. (2004), 'Nomenclatural Changes and a New Sectional Classification in Nicotiana (Solanaceae)', *Taxon*, 53(1): 73–82.

Kohrman, M. (2008), 'Smoking among Doctors: Governmentality, Embodiment, and the Diversion of Blame in Contemporary China', *Medical Anthropology*, 27: 9–42.

Kohrman, M. and Benson, P. (2011), 'Tobacco', *Annual Review of Anthropology*, 40: 329–44.

Kopenawa, D. (2013), *The Falling Sky Words of a Yanomami Shaman*, Cambridge MA: Harvard University Press.

Kopytoff, I. (1986), 'The Cultural Biography of Things: Commoditization as Process', in A. Appadurai (ed.), *The Social Life of Things: Commodities in Cultural Perspective*, Cambridge: Cambridge University Press, 64–91.

Kovarik, A., Dadejova, M., Lim, K.Y., Chase, M.W., Clarkson, J.J., Knapp, S. and Leitch, A.R. (2008), 'Evolution of rDNA in Nicotiana Allopolyploids: A Potential Link between rDNA Homogenization and Epigenetics', *Annals of Botany*, 101: 815–23.

Krokoszyński, Ł., Stoińska-Kairska, I. and Martyniak, A. (2007), *Indígenas aislados en la Sierra del Divisor (Zona fronteriza Perú-Brazil)*, Iquitos, Lima and Poznań: AIDESEP and UAM.

Kruse, A. (1951), 'Karusakaybë: der Vater der Mundurukú', *Anthropos*, 46: 915–32.

Kurasawa, F. (2004), *The Ethnological Imagination: A Cross-Cultural Critique of Modernity*, Minneapolis, MN: University of Minnesota Press.

Labate, B. C. and Cavnar, C. (eds) (2014), *Ayahuasca Shamanism in the Amazon and Beyond (Oxford Ritual Studies)*, New York, NY: Oxford University Press.

Labate, B.C. and Jungaberle, H. (eds) (2011), *The Internationalization of Ayahuasca*, Zürich: LIT.

Lacan, J. (1966), *Écrits*, Paris, Editions du Seuil.

———. (1989), *Écrits: A Selection*, Translated by Alan Sheridan with a foreword by Malcolm Bowie, London and New York, NY: Tavistock/Routledge.

Laenerts, M. (2006), 'Substances, Relationships and the Omnipresence of the Body: An Overview of Ashéninka Ethnomedicine (Western Amazonia)', *Journal of Ethnobiology and Ethnomedicine*, 2: 49–67.

Lagrou, E. (2000), 'Homesickness and the Cashinahua Self: A Reflection on the Embodied Condition of Relatedness', in J. Overing and A. Passes (eds), *The Anthropology of Love and Anger: The Aesthetics of Conviviality in Native Amazonia*, London: Routledge, 152–69.

Lambeck, M. (2010), *Ordinary Ethics: Anthropology, Language and Action*, New York, NY: Fordham University Press.

Land, T., Keithly, L., Kane, K., Chen, L., Paskowsky, M., Cullen, D., Hayes, R.B. and Li, W. (2014), 'Recent Increases in Efficiency in Cigarette Nicotine Delivery: Implications for Tobacco Control', *Nicotine and Tobacco Research*, Advance Access doi: 10.1093/ntr/ntt219

Lasmar, C. (2005), *De Volta ao Lago de Leite: Gênero e Transformação no Alto Rio Negro*, São Paulo: Editora UNESP.

Leuk, G. (1959a), 'Guyane: les Indiens' (broadcast: 17 January 1959, 12 min.37s.), *Voyage sans Passeport* http://www.ina.fr (accessed 7 February 2012).

———. (1959b), 'Guyane: sur le Maroni' (broadcast: 24 January 1959, 11 min.20s.), *Voyage sans Passeport* http://www.ina.fr (accessed 7 February 2012).

Lévi-Strauss, C. (ed.) (1963), 'The Sorcerer and His Magic', in *Structural Anthropology*, Volume 1, New York, NY: Basic Books, 167–205.

———. (1973 [1966]), *From Honey to Ashes: Introduction to a Science of Mythology 2*, London: Jonathan Cape.

———. (1992 [1964]), *The Raw and the Cooked: Introduction to a Science of Mythology 1*, London: Penguin Books.

Lewis, R.S. (2011), 'Nicotiana', in C. Kole (ed.), *Wild Crop Relatives: Genomic and Breeding Resources, Plantation and Ornamental Crops*, Berlin: Springer-Verlag, 185–208.

Lewis, S. and Russell, A. (2011), 'Being Embedded: A Way Forward for Ethnographic Research', *Ethnography*, 12(3): 398–416.

Lima, T.S. (1999), 'The Two and Its Many: Reflections on Perspectivism in a Tupi Cosmology', *Ethnos*, 64(1): 107–31.

Lizot, J. (1975), *El hombre de la pantorrilla preñada*, Caracas: Fundación La Salle.

———. (1977), 'Population, Resources and Warfare among the Yanomami', *Man*, 12(34): 497–517.

———. (1980), 'La Agricultura Yanomami', *Antropológica Caracas* (53): 3–93.

———. 1984. *Les Yanomami Centraux*. Paris: Ecole des Hautes Etudes en Sciences Sociales.

———. (1988), 'Los Yanomami', in J. Lizot (ed.), *Los Aborígenes de Venezuela, Vol. 3, EtnologíaContemporánea*, Caracas: Fundación La Salle-Monte Avila Editores, 479–583.

———. (1989), *No patapɨ tëhë. En tiempos de los antepasados. Texto de lectura 2*, Caracas: Vicariato Apostólico de Puerto Ayacucho.

———. (1994), 'Words in the Night: The Ceremonial Dialogue – One Expression of Peaceful Relationships among the Yanomami', in L. Sponsel and T. Gregor (eds), *The Anthropology of Peace and Nonviolence*, London: Lynne Reiner Publishers, 213–40.

———. (2004), *Diccionario enciclopédico de la lengua yãnomami*, Caracas: Vicariato Apostólico de Puerto Ayacucho.

———. (2007), 'El mundo intelectual de los Yanomami: cosmovisión, enfermedad y muerte con una teoría sobre el canibalismo', in G. Freire and A. Tillet (eds), *Salud Indígena en Venezuela, 1*, Caracas, Venezuela: Ministerio del Poder Popular para la Salud, 263–322.

Logan, M.H. (1993), 'New Lines of Enquiry on the Illness of Susto', *Medical Anthropology*, 15: 189–200.

Londoño, C.D. (2004), *Muinane: Un proyecto moral a perpetuidad*, Medellín: Editorial Universidad de Antioquia.

Londoño-Sulkin, C. (2000), '"Though It Comes as Evil, I Embrace It as Good": Social Sensibilities and the Transformation of Malignant Agency among the Muinane', in J. Overing and A. Passes (eds), *The Anthropology of Love and Anger: The Aesthetics of Conviviality in Native Amazonia*, London: Routledge, 170–86.

———. (2005), 'Inhuman Beings: Morality and Perspectivism among Muinane People (Colombian Amazon)', *Ethnos*, 10(1): 7–30.

———. (2010), 'People of No Substance: Imposture and the Contingency of Morality in the Colombian Amazon', in M. Lambek (ed.), *Ordinary Ethics: Anthropology, Language and Action*, New York, NY: Fordham University Press, 273–91.

———. (2012), *People of Substance: An Ethnography of Morality in the Colombian Amazon*, Toronto: University of Toronto Press.

Luedke, T. and West, H. (2006), *Borders and Healers: Brokering Therapeutic Resources in Southeast Africa*, Indiana: Indiana University Press.

Luna, L.E. (1984), 'The Concept of Plants as Teacher among Four Mestizo Shamans of Iquitos, Northeast Peru', *Journal of Ethnopharmacology*, 11: 135–56.

———. (1986), *Shamanism among the Mestizo Population of the Peruvian Amazon*, Stockholm: Almqvist and Wiksell.

Luna, L.E. and Amaringo, P. (1991), *Ayahuasca Visions: The Religious Iconography of a Peruvian Shaman*, Berkeley, CA: North Atlantic Books.

Luna, L.E. and White, S.F. (eds) (2000), *Ayahuasca Reader. Encounters with the Amazon's Sacred Vine*, Santa Fe, NM: Synergetic Press.

Lynden, A.J.H. van (1939), 'Op Zoek naar Suriname's Zuidgrens. De Grensbepaling tusschen Suriname en Brazilië. 1935–1938'. *Tijdschrift van het Koninklijk Nederlands Aardrijkskundig Genootschap. Tweede Reeks*, 56: 793–881.

Lyon, W.S. (1998), *Encyclopedia of Native American Shamanism. Sacred Ceremonies of North America*, Santa Barbara, CA: ABC-CLIO.

Mann, C.C. (2011), *1493: Uncovering the New World Columbus Created*, New York, NY: Vintage.

Marcoy, P. (1875), *Travels in South America from the Pacific Ocean to the Atlantic Ocean*, 2 Vols, London: Blackie.

Margiotti, M. (2010), *Kinship and the Saturation of Life among the Kuna of Panama*, PhD dissertation, University of St Andrews.

Marshall, M. (2013), *Drinking Smoke: The Tobacco Syndemic in Oceania*, Honolulu: University of Hawai'i Press.

Mathews, G. and Izquierdo, C. (2009), 'Introduction: Anthropology, Happiness and Well-Being', in G. Mathews and C. Izquierdo (eds), *Pursuits of Happiness: Well-being in Anthropological Perspective*, Oxford: Berghahn, 1–19.

Matteson, E. (1954), 'The Piro of the Urubamba', *Kroeber Anthropological Society Papers*, 10: 25–99.
———. (1965), *The Piro (Arawakan) Language*, Berkeley and Los Angeles: University of California Press.
Mauss, M. (1973 [1950]), 'Techniques of the Body', *Economy and Society*, 2(1): 70–88.
Mazière, F. [text] and Dominique, D. [photos] (1959), *Parana, Boy of the Amazon*, Chicago, IL: Follet Publishing Company.
McCallum, C. (1996), 'The Body That Knows: From Cashinahua Epistemology to a Medical Anthropology of Lowland South America', *Medical Anthropology Quarterly*, 10(3): 347–72.
———. (2001), *Gender and Sociality in Amazonia: How Real People are Made*, Oxford: Berg.
McDaneil, P.A. Malone, R.E. (2007), '"I Always Thought They Were All Pure Tobacco": American Smokers' Perceptions of "Natural" Cigarettes and Tobacco Industry Advertising Strategies', *Tobacco Control*, 16: e7.
McGonigle, I. (2013), 'Khat: Chewing on a Bitter Controversy', *Anthropology Today*, 29(4): 4–7.
McNeill, A. and Munafò, M.R. (2013), 'Reducing Harm from Tobacco Use', *Journal of Psychopharmacology*, 27(1): 13–18.
Meira, M. (1994), 'O Tempo dos Patrões: Extrativismo, Comerciantes e História Indígena no Noroeste da Amazônia', in *Cadernos Ciências Humanas*, Belém: MCT/CNPq/MPEG, 2.
Métraux, A. (1967), *Religions et Magies Indiennes d'Amérique du Sud*, Paris: Gallimard.
Metzner, R. (ed.) (1999), *Ayahuasca: Human Consciousness and the Spirits of Nature*, New York, NY: Thunder's Mouth Press.
Miller, D. (2005), 'Introduction', in D. Miller (ed.) *Materiality: an Introduction*, Durham, NC: Duke University Press, pp. 1–50.
Monardes, N. (1565–1569), *Historia Medicinal de las Cosas que se Traen de Nuestras Indias Occidentales*, Sevilla: Hernando Diaz.
Moore, K., Bruno, M.C., Capriles, J.M. and Hastorf, C. (2010), 'Integrated Contextual Approaches to Understanding Past Activities Using Plant and Animal Remains from Kala Uyuni, Lake Titicaca, Bolivia', in A.M. VanDerwarker and T.M. Peres (eds), *Integrating Zooarchaeology and Paleoethnobotany: A Consideration of Issues, Methods, and Cases*, New York, NY: Springer, 173–203.
Moreno, J. (1988), 'The Music Therapist: Creative Arts Therapist and Contemporary Shaman', *The Arts in Psychotherapy*, 15(4): 271–80.
———. (1995), 'Ethnomusic Therapy: An Interdisciplinary Approach to Music and Healing', *The Arts in Psychotherapy*, 22(4): 329–38.

Moses, B. (1919), *Spain's Declining Power in South America, 1730–1806*, Berkeley, CA: University of California Press.

Naranjo, P. (1986), 'El *ayahuasca* en la arqueología ecuatoriana', *América Indígena*, 46(1): 117–27.

Narby, J. (1998), *The Cosmic Serpent: DNA and the Origins of Knowledge*, New York, NY: Penguin.

Narby, J. and Huxley, F. (eds) (2004), *Shamans through Time*, New York, NY: Tarcher: Penguin.

Nater, L. (2006), 'Colonial Tobacco: Key Commodity of the Spanish Empire, 1500–1800', in S. Topik, C. Marichal and Z. Frank (eds), *From Silver to Cocaine: Latin American Commodity Chains and the Building of the World Economy, 1500–2000*, Durham, NC: Duke University Press, 93–117.

Nichter, M. Nichter, M., Vuckovic, N., Tesler, L., Adrian, S. and Ritenbaugh, C. (2004), 'Smoking as a Weight-Control Strategy among Adolescent Girls and Young Women: A Reconsideration', *Medical Anthropology Quarterly*, 18: 305–24.

Nordenskiöld, E., Fuhrken, G.E., Leijer, G.M.E., Leijer, M., Kantule, R.P. and Wassén, H. (1919), *Comparative Ethnological Studies*, Volume 1, Göteborg: Elanders Boktryckeri Aktiebolag.

Norton, M. (2008), *Sacred Gifts, Profane Pleasures: A History of Tobacco and Chocolate in the Atlantic World*, Ithaca, NY: Cornell University Press.

Okamuro, J.K. and Goldberg, R.B. (1985), 'Tobacco Single-Copy DNA Is Highly Homologous to Sequences Present in the Genomes of its Diploid Progenitors', *Molecular and General Genetics*, 98: 290–8.

Olmstead, R.G., Bohs, L., Migid, H.A., Santiago-Valentin, E., Garcia, V.F. and Collier, S.M. (2008), 'A Molecular Phylogeny of the Solanaceae', *Taxon*, 57(4): 1159–81.

Olsen, D.A. (1996), *Music of the Warao of Venezuela. Song People of the Rain Forest*, Gainesville etc.: University Press of Florida.

Orán, R. and Wagua, A. (2011), *Gaymar Sabga. Diccionario Escolar Gunagaya-Español*, Panama: Equipo EBI Guna.

Overing, J. (1989a), 'Personal Autonomy and the Domestication of Self in Piaroa Society', in G. Jahoda and I.M. Lewis (eds), *Acquiring Culture: Cross Cultural Studies in Child Development*, London: Croom Helm, 169–92.

———. (1989b), 'The Aesthetics of Production: The Sense of Community among the Cubeo and Piaroa', *Dialectical Anthropology*, 14(3): 159–75.

———. (1990), 'The Shaman as a Maker of Worlds: Nelson Goodman in the Amazon', *Man*, 25(4): 602–19.

———. (2004), 'The Grotesque Landscape of Mythic "Before Time": The Folly of Sociality in "Today Time". An Egalitarian Aesthetics of Human Existence',

Kultur, Raum, Landschaft. Zur Bedeutung des Raumes in Zeiten der Globalität Jahrbuch des Österreichischen Lateinamerika-Instituts, 6: 71–92.

Overing, J. and Passes, A. (2000), 'Introduction: Conviviality and the Opening up of Amazonian Anthropology', in J. Overing and A. Passes (eds), *The Anthropology of Love and Anger: The Aesthetics of Conviviality in Native Amazonia*, London: Routledge, 1–30.

Oyuela-Caycedo, A. (2004), 'The Ecology of a Masked Dance: Negotiating at the Frontier of Identity in the Northwest Amazonia', *Baessler-Archiv*, 52: 54–74.

Panlõn Kumu, U. and Kenhiri, T. (1980), *Antes o Mundo não Existia: a Mitología dos Indios Desana*, São Paulo: Livraria Cultura.

Panter-Brick, C., Clarke, S.E., Lomas, H., Pinder, M. and Lindsay, S.W. (2006), 'Culturally Compelling Strategies for Behaviour Change: A Social Ecology Model and Case Study in Malaria Prevention', *Social Science and Medicine*, 62(11): 2810–25.

Peluso, D. (2014), 'Ayahuasca's Attractions and Distractions: Examining Sexual Seduction in Shaman-Participant Interactions', in B.C. Labate and C. Cavnar (eds), *Ayahuasca Shamanism in the Amazon and Beyond (Oxford Ritual Studies)*, New York, NY: Oxford University Press, 231–55.

Pendell, D. (2010), *Pharmako/Gnosis: Plant Teachers and the Poison Path*, Berkeley, CA: North Atlantic Books.

Pereira, E. (2012), *Un povo sábio, um povo aconselhado: Ritual e política entre os Uitoto-murui*, Brasilia: Paralelo 15.

Petrovich, A. (2004), 'The Shaman: "A Villain of a Magician Who Calls Demons" [1672]', in J. Narby and F. Huxley (eds), *Shamans Through Time*, New York, NY: Tarcher: Penguin, 18–20.

Pickergill, B. (2007), 'Domestication of Plants in the Americas: Insights from Mendelian and Molecular Genetics', *Annals of Botany*, 100: 925–40.

Planella, M.T., Collao-Alvarado, K., Niemeyer, H.M. and Belmar, C. (2012), 'Morfometría Comparada de semillas de Nicotiana (solanaceae) e Identificación de Semillas Carbonizadas Provenientes de un Sitio Arqueológico en Chile Central', *Darwiniana*, 50(2): 207–17.

Prance, G.T. (1972), 'Ethnobotanical Notes from Amazonian Brazil', *Economic Botany*, 26(3): 221–37.

Prestan Simón, A. (1975), *El Uso de la Chicha y la Sociedad Kuna*, Mexico, DF: Instituto Indigenista Interamericano.

Proctor, R.N. (2011), *Golden Holocaust: Origins of the Cigarette Catastrophe and the Case for Abolition*, Berkeley, CA: University of California Press.

Rahman, E. (2014), *Made by Artful Practice: Health, Reproduction and the Perinatal Period among Xié River Dwellers of Northwestern Amazonia*, DPhil thesis: University of Oxford.

———. (forthcoming), 'Intergenerational mythscapes and infant care in northwestern Amazonia, in K. Quereshi and S. Pooley (eds), *Reproductive Cultures: Kinship, Social Practice and Inter-Generational Transmission*, Oxford: Berghahn.

Rahman, E. and Echeverri, J.A. (eds) (forthcoming), 'The Alchemical Person', *Tipití: Journal of the Society for the Anthropology of Lowland South America* (Special Issue).

Ramos, A.R. (2012), 'The Politics of Perspectivism', *Annual Review of Anthropology*, 41: 481–94.

Ramos, D. (2013), *Círculos de coca e fumaça: Encontros noturnos e caminhos vividos pelos Hupd'äh (Maku)*, DPhil thesis, Universidade de São Paulo Faculdade de Filosofia, Letras e Ciências Humanas Departamento de Antropologia.

Ramsey, S.L. (2011), 'Nicotiana', in C. Kole (ed.), *Wild Crop Relatives: Genomic and Breeding Resources, Plantation and Ornamental Crops*, Heidelberg: Springer-Verlag, 185–208.

Reed, A. (2007), '"Smuk Is King": The Action of Cigarettes in a Papua New Guinea Prison', in A. Henare, M. Holbraad and S. Wastell (eds), *Thinking Through Things: Theorising Artefacts in Ethnographic Perspective*, London: Routledge, 32–46.

Reichel-Dolmatoff, G. (1949), 'Los Kogi: Una tribu de la Sierra Nevada de Santa Marta, Colombia', Tomo I, *Revista del Instituto Etnológico Nacional*, 4: 9–298.

———. (1975), *The Shaman and the Jaguar*, Philadelphia, PA: Temple University Press.

———. (1976), 'Cosmology as Ecological Analysis: A View from the Rainforest', *Man*, 11(3): 307–18.

Reig, A. (2013), '*"When the Forest World Is not Wide Enough We Open up Many Clearings". The Making of Landscape, Place and People among the Shitari Yanomami of the Upper Ocamo Basin, Venezuela*', DPhil thesis, University of Oxford.

Rival, L. (1996), 'Blowpipes and Spears: the Social Significance of Huaorani Technological Choices', in P. Descola and G. Pálsson (eds), *Nature and Society: Anthropological Perspectives*, London: Routledge, 145–64.

Rival, L. (1998), 'Androgynous Parents and Guest Children: The Huaorani Couvade', *Journal of the Royal Anthropological Institute*, 4(4): 619–42.

———. (2005), 'The Attachment of the Soul to the Body among the Huaorani of Amazonian Ecuador', *Ethnos*, 70(3): 285–310.

Rivas Ruiz, R. (2004), *Ipurakari. Los Cocama-Cocamilla en la várzea de la Amazonía peruana*, M.A. thesis, Lima: Pontífica Universidad Católica del Peru.

Rivière, P. (1969), 'Myth and Material Culture: Some Symbolic Interrelations', in R. F. Spencer (ed.) *Forms of Symbolic Action*, Seattle, WA: University of Washington Press, 151–66.

———. (1999), 'Shamanism and the Unconfined Soul', in M.J.C. Crabbe (ed.), *From Soul to Self*, London: Routledge, 70–88.

Robicsek, F., Coe, M.D. and Goodnight, B.A. (1978), *The Smoking Gods: Tobacco in Maya Art, History, and Religion*, Norman, OK: University of Oklahoma Press.

Roller, H.F. (2010), 'Colonial Collecting Expeditions and the Pursuit of Opportunities in the Amazonian Sertão, c. 1750–1800', *The Americas*, 66(4): 435–67.

Romesh, D. (2000), 'Relational Wealth and the Quality of Life', *Journal of Socio-Economics*, 29(4): 305–40.

Roseman, M. (1988), 'The Pragmatics of Aesthetics: The Performance of Healing among Senoi temiar', *Social Science and Medicine*, 27(8): 811–8.

———. (2006), 'Transdimensional Relations: On Human-Spirit Interaction in the Amazon', *Journal of the Royal Anthropological Institute*, 12: 803–16.

Rubel, A.J., O'Nell, C.W. and Collado, R. (1985), 'The Folk Illness Called Susto', in R.C. Simons and C.C. Hughes (eds), *The Culture-Bound Syndromes: Folk Illnesses of Psychiatric and Anthropological Interest*, Dordrecht: D. Reidel, 330–50.

Russell, A., Wainwright, M. and Mamudu, H. (2014), 'A Chilling Example? Uruguay, Philip Morris International, and the WHO's Framework Convention on Tobacco Control', *Medical Anthropology Quarterly*. DOI: 10.1111/maq.12141.

Russell-Wood, A.J.R. (1998), *The Portuguese Empire, 1415–1808: A World on the Move*, Baltimore, MD: Johns Hopkins University Press.

Sabaté, L. (1925), 'Viaje de los misioneros del Convento del Cuzco a las tribues selvajes de los Campas, Piros, Cunibos y Shipibos por el P. Fr. Luis Sabaté en el año de 1874', in P.F. Bernardino Izaguirre (ed.), *Historia de las misiones Franciscanas y narración de los progresos de la geografía en el oriente del Perú; relatos originales y producciones en lenguas indígenas de varios misioneros, 1691–1921*, Volume 10, Lima: Talleres tipográficos de la Penitenciaría, 7–317.

Santa Teresa, S. de (1924), *Creencias, ritos, usos y costumbres de los indios catíos-indios cunas de la prefectura apostólica de Urabá, Colombia*, [s.n.], Bogotá.

Santos-Granero, F. (1991), *The Power of Love: The Moral Use of Knowledge amongst the Amuesha of Central Peru*, London: Athlone Press.

———. (1998), 'Writing History into the Landscape: Space, Myth and Ritual in Contemporary Amazonia', *American Ethnologist*, 2: 128–48.

———. (2002), 'The Arawakan Matrix: Ethos, Language, and History in Native South America', in J. Hill and F. Santos-Granero (eds), *Comparative*

Arawakan Histories: Rethinking Language Family and Culture Area in Amazonia, Urbana, IL: University of Illinois Press, 25–50.

———. (2006), 'Sensual Vitalities: Non-Corporeal Modes of Sensing and Knowing in Native Amazonia', *Tipití: Journal of the Society for the Anthropology of Lowland South America*, 4(1): 57–80.

———. (2009a), 'Introduction: Amerindian Constructional Views of the World', in F. Santos-Granero (ed.), *The Occult Life of Things: Native Amazonian Theories of Materiality and Personhood*, Tucson, AZ: University of Arizona Press, 1–29.

———. (2009b), 'From Baby Slings to Feather Bibles and From Star Utensils to Jaguar Stones: The Multiple Ways of Being a Thing in the Yanesha Lived World', in F. Santos-Granero (ed.), *The Occult Life of Things: Native Amazonian Theories of Materiality and Personhood*, Tucson, AZ: University of Arizona Press, 105–27.

———. (2009c), *Vital Enemies: Slavery, Predation, and the Amerindian Political Economy of Life*. Austin, TX: University of Texas Press.

———. (2011), 'The Virtuous Manioc and the Horny Barbasco: Sublime and Grotesque Modes of Transformation in the Origin Of Yanesha Plant Life', *Journal of Ethnobiology*, 31(1): 44–71.

———. (2012), 'Beinghood and People-Making in Native Amazonia: a Constructional Approach with a Perspectival Coda', *HAU: Journal of Ethnographic Theory*, 2(1): 181–211.

Sarmiento Barletti, J.P. (2011), *Kametsa Asaiki: The Pursuit of the "Good Life" in an Ashaninka Village (Peruvian Amazonia)*, PhD thesis, University of St Andrews.

———. (forthcoming), '"It Makes Me Sad When They Say We Are Poor, We Are Rich!": Of Wealth and Public Wealth in Indigenous Amazonia', in F. Santos-Granero (ed.), *Images of Public Wealth in Tropical America*, Tucson, AZ: University of Arizona Press.

Sarmiento Barletti, J.P. and Ferraro, E. (n.d.), 'Wellbeing, Well-being and Being Well: Bringing the "Local" into Discussions of Well-being', Unpublished paper.

Sauer, C. (2009 [1937]), 'The Prospect for Redistribution of Population', in W.M. Denevan and K. Mathewson (eds), *Carl Sauer on Culture and Landscape: Readings and Commentaries*, Baton Rouge, LA: Louisiana State University Press, 277–91.

Schiel, J. (2004), *Tronco Velho: histórias Apurinã*, Ph.D thesis: Universidade Estadual de Campinas.

Schmidt, M.J. and Heckenberger, M.J. (2009), 'Amerindian Anthrosols: Amazonian Dark Earth Formation in the Upper Xingu', in W.G. Texeira, J. Lehmann, C. Steiner, A.M.G.A. WinklerPrins and L. Rebellato (eds), *Amazonian Dark Earths: Wim Sombroek's Vision*, New York, NY: Springer, 163–91.

Schultes, R.E. (1967a) 'The Place of Ethnobotany in the Ethnopharmacological Search for Psychotomimetic Plants', in D.H. Efron, B. Holmstedt and N.S. Kline (eds), *Ethnopharmacological Search for Psychoactive Drugs*, US Department of Health, Education and Welfare: Public Health Service Publication No. 1645, 33–57.

———. (1967b), 'The Botanical Origins of South American Snuffs', in D.H. Efron, B. Holmstedt and N.S. Kline (eds), *Ethnopharmacologal Search for Psychoactive Drugs*, US Department of Health, Education and Welfare: Public Health Service Publication No. 1645, 291–306.

———. (1973), 'Introductory Words', in H. Schleiffer (ed.), *Sacred Narcotic Plants of the New World Indians: An Anthology of Texts from the 16th Century to Date*, New York, NY: Hafner Press.

Schultes, R.E. and Raffauf, R.F. (1990), *The Healing Forest: Medicinal and Toxic Plants of the Northwest Amazonia*, Portland, OR: Dioscorides Press.

Schwartz, S.B. (1996), *Slaves, Peasants, and Rebels: Reconsidering Brazilian Slavery*, Champaign-Urbana, IL: University of Illinois Press.

Seeger, A. (1981). *Nature and Society in Central Brazil: The Suya Indians of Mato Grosso*, Cambridge, MA: Harvard University Press.

Seeger, A., da Mata, R. and Viveiros de Castro, E. (1979), 'A Construção da Pessoa Nas Sociedades Indígenas Brasileiras', *Boletim do Museu Nacional, Série Antropologia*, 32: 2–19.

Shepard, G. H. (1998), 'Psychoactive Plants and Ethnopsychiatric Medicines of the Matsigenka', *Journal of Psychoactive Drugs*, 30(4): 321–32.

——— (2004), 'A Sensory Ecology of Medicinal Plant Therapy in Two Amazonian Societies', *American Anthropologist*, 106(2): 252–66.

Sherzer, J. (2001 [1983]), *Kuna Ways of Speaking: An Ethnographic Perspective*, Tucson, AZ: Hats Off Books.

Shryock, A. and Lord Smail, D. (eds) (2011), *Deep History: The Architecture of Past and Present*, Berkeley, CA: University of California Press.

Silva Satisteban, F. (1964), *Los Obrajes en el Virreinato del Peru*, Lima: Publicaciones del Museo Nacional de Historia.

Silverwood-Cope, P. (1972), *A Contribution to the Ethnography of the Colombian Maku*, PhD thesis: University of Cambridge.

Smith, H.H. (1879), *Brazil: The Amazons and the Coast*, New York, NY: Charles Scribner's Sons.

Smith, N.J.H. (1996), *The Enchanted Amazon Rain Forest: Stories from a Vanishing World*, Gainesville, FL: University of Florida.

Stebbins, K. (2001), 'Going like Gangbusters: Transnational Tobacco Companies "Making a Killing" in South America', *Medical Anthropology Quarterly*, 15(2): 147–70.

Steere, J.B. (1901), 'Report of a Visit to Indian Tribes of the Purus River, Brazil', *Report of the National Museum*, 1: 388–93.

Steward, J.H. (ed.) (1949), *The Comparative Ethnology of South American Indians. Handbook of South American Indians*, Volume 3: The Tropical Forest Tribes, Part 3: Tribes of the Montaña and Bolivian east Andes, Washington, DC: Smithsonian Institute.

Stolze Lima, T. (1999), 'The Two and Its Many: Reflections on Perspectivism in a Tupi Cosmology', *Ethnos*, 64(1): 107–31.

———. (2000), 'Towards an Ethnographic Theory of the Nature/Culture Distinction in Juruna Cosmology', *Revista Brasileira de Ciências Sociais*, 1(Special Issue): 43–52.

Stork, W.F., Weinhold, A. and Baldwin, I.T. (2011), 'Trichomes as Dangerous Lollipops: Do Lizards Also Use Caterpillar Body and Frass Odor to Optimize Their Foraging?', *Plant Signaling and Behavior*, 6(12): 1893–6.

Strathern, M. (1988), *The Gender of the Gift: Problems with Women and Problems with Society in Melanesia*, Berkeley, Los Angeles, CA and London: University of California Press.

Sullivan, L. (1988), *Icanchu's Drum: An Orientation to Meaning in South American Religions*, New York, NY: Macmillan.

Taussig, M. (1987), *Shamanism, Colonialism and the Wild Man: A Study in Terror and Healing*. Chicago: University of Chicago Press.

Taylor, A.C. (1996), 'The Soul's Body and Its States: An Amazonian Perspective on the Nature of Being Human', *The Journal of the Royal Anthropological Institute*, 2(2): 201–15.

Tessmann, G. (1928), *Menschen ohne Gott. Ein Besuch bei den Indianern des Ucayali*. (Veröffentlichung der Harvey-Bassler-Stiftung Völkerkunde, Band I), Stuttgart: Strecker und Schröder.

———. (1930), *Die Indianer Nordost Perus: Grundlegende Forschungen für Eine Systematische Kulturkunde*, Hamburg: De Gruyter and Co.

———. (1999), *Los Indígenas del Perú Nororiental: investigaciones fundamentales para un estudio sistemático de la cultura*, Quito: Abya-Yala.

Thevet, A. (1558), *Les singularitez de la France Antarctique, autrement nommée Amerique: et de plusieurs Terres et Isles découvertes de nostre temps*, Paris: Maurice de la Porte.

———. (1575), *La Cosmographie Universelle d'André Thevet Cosmographe du Roy. Illustrée de Diverses Figures des choses plus remarquables veues par l'Autheur, et incogneues de noz Anciens et Modernes*, Paris: Guillaume Chaudière.

Thompson, D. (1945), *On Growth and Form*, Cambridge: Cambridge University Press.

Tomlinson, M. (2007), 'Everything and Its Opposite: Kava Drinking in Fiji', *Anthropological Quarterly*, 80(4): 1065–81.

Torres, C.M. (1995), 'Archaeological Evidence for the Antiquity of Psychoactive Plant Use in the Central Andes', *Annuli dei Musei Civici Roverero*, 11:291–326.

———. (1998), 'Psychoactive Substances in the Archaeology of Northern Chile and NW Argentina: A Comparative Review of the Evidence', *Chungara Volumen*, 30 (1): 49–63, Universidad de Tarapacá, Arica, Chile.

Townsley, G. (1993), 'Song Paths: The Ways and Means of Yaminahua Shamanic Knowledge', *L'Homme*, 33(2–4): 449–68.

Trewavas, A. (2003), 'Aspects of Plant Intelligence', *Annals of Botany*, 92: 1–20.

Tschopik, H. (2009 [1953]), *El Pueblo Shipibo: Men of the Montana*, DVD Video directed and edited by J. C. Odland, New York, NY: The American Museum of Natural History.

Turner, V. (1967), *The Forest of Symbols*, Ithaca, NY: Cornell University Press.

Turner, T.S. (2009), 'The Crisis of Late Structuralism. Perspectivism and Animism: Rethinking Culture, Nature, Spirit, and Bodiliness', *Tipití: Journal of the Society for the Anthropology of Lowland South America*, 7(1): 3–42.

Twigg, J. (2000), *Bathing, the Body and Community Care*, London: Routledge.

Urbina, F. (2010), *Las palabras de origen: Breve compendio de la mitología de los uitoto*, Bogotá: Ministerio de Cultura.

Uzendoski, M. and Calapucha-Tapuy, E. (2012), *The Ecology of the Spoken Word: Amazonian Storytelling and Shamanism among the Napo Runa*, Urbana, IL: University of Illinois Press.

Varese, S. (2002), *Salt of the Mountain: Campa Ashaninka History and Resistance in the Peruvian Jungle*, Norman, OK: University of Oklahoma Press.

Veber, H. (1998), 'The Salt of the Montana: Interpreting Indigenous Activism in the Rain Forest', *Cultural Anthropology*, 13(3): 382–413.

Veber, H. (2000). 'An Introduction to Eight Essays on the Structures of a Social Order in the Upper Amazon' in H. Veber (ed.), *Gendered Spaces and Interethnic Politics: The Pajonal Ashéninka Case*, Copenhagen: University of Copenhagen Press, 1–25.

———. (2010), 'Memories of Ucayali – On the Narrative Historicities of the Asháninka', Paper presented at the Edinburgh Workshop on Autobiographical and Biographical Narrative in Lowland South America.

Vidrine, J.I., Businelle, M.S., Cinciripini, P., Li, Y., Marcus, M.T., Waters, A.J., Reitzel, L.R. and Wetter, D.W. (2009), 'Associations of Mindfulness with Nicotine Dependence, Withdrawal, and Agency', *Substance Abuse*, 30(4): 318–27.

Vilaça, A. (2002), 'Making Kin Out of Others in Amazonia', *Journal of the Royal Anthropological Institute*, 8(2): 347–65.

———. (2005), 'Chronically Unstable Bodies: Reflections on Amazonian Corporalities', *Journal of the Royal Anthropological Institute*, 11(3): 445–64.

———. (2010), *Strange Enemies: Indigenous Agency and Scenes of Encounters in Amazonia*, Durham, NC: Duke University Press.

Viveiros de Castro, E. (1992), *From the Enemy's Point of View: Humanity and Divinity in an Amazonian Society*, Chicago, IL: University of Chicago Press.

———. (1998), 'Cosmological Deixis and Amerindian Perspectivism', *Journal of the Royal Anthropological Institute*, 4(3): 469–88.

———. (2001), 'GUT Feelings about Amazonia: Potential Affinity and the Construction of Sociality', in L. Rival and N. Whitehead (eds), *Beyond the Material and Visible*, Oxford: University Press, 19–43.

———. (2004), 'Exchanging Perspectives: The Transformation of Objects into Subjects in Amerindian Ontologies', *Common Knowledge*, 10(3): 463–84.

———. (2012), *Cosmological Perspectivism in Amazonia and Elsewhere (Masterclass Series 1)*, Manchester: HAU Network of Ethnographic Theory.

Voeks, R.A. (1997), *Sacred Leaves of Candomblé: African Magic, Medicine and Religion in Brazil*, Austin, TX: University of Texas Press.

Waldram, J. (2000), 'The Efficacy of Traditional Medicine: Current Theoretical and Methodological Issues', *Medical Anthropology Quarterly*, 14(4): 603–25.

Walker, H. (2009a), 'Baby Hammocks and Stone Bowls: Urarina Technologies of Companionship and Subjection', in F. Santos-Granero (ed.), *The Occult Life of Things: Native Amazonian Theories of Materiality and Personhood*, Tucson, AZ: University of Arizona Press, 89–102.

Walker, T.D. (2009b), 'Establishing Cacao Plantation Culture in the Atlantic World: Portuguese Cacao Cultivation in Brazil and West Africa, Circa 1580–1912', in L.E. Grivetti and H.Y. Shapiro (eds), *Chocolate: History, Culture, and Heritage*, Hoboken, NJ: Wiley, 543–58.

Wallace, A.R. (1895), *A Narrative of Travels on the Amazon and Rio Negro: With an Account of the Native Tribes, and Observation on the Climate, Geology, and Natural History of the Amazon Valley*, London: Ward, Lock, and Bowden.

Wassén, H. (1965), *The Use of Some Specific Kinds of South American Indian Snuff and Related Paraphernalia*, Göteborg: Etnografiska Museet.

Wassén, S.H. (1972), 'A Medicine-Man's Implements and Plants in a Tiahuanacoid Tomb in Highland Bolivia', in S. Henry Wassén et al. (eds), *Etnologiska Studier*, Volume18, Gothenburg: Göteborg Etnografiska Museum.

Wasson, R.G. (1968), *SOMA, Divine Mushroom of Immortality*, Ethno-Mycological Studies, No. 1, New York, NY: Harcourt, Brace and World.

Weiss, G. (1975), *Campa Cosmology: The World of a Forest Tribe in South America*, New York, NY: The American Museum of Natural History.

Whitehead, W.T. (2006), 'Redefining Plant Use at the Formative Site of Chiripa in the Southern Titicaca Basin', in W.H. Isbell and H. Silverman (eds), *Andean Archaeology III*, New York, NY: Springer, 258–78.

Whitehead, N. and Wright, R. (2004), 'Introduction', in N. Whitehead and R. Wright (eds), *In Darkness and Secrecy: The Anthropology of Assault Sorcery and Witchcraft in Amazonia*, Durham, NC: Duke University Press, 1–16.

WHO [World Health Organization] (2003), *Framework Convention on Tobacco Control*, Geneva: WHO.

———. (2011a), *Global Status Report on Noncommunicable Diseases 2010*, Geneva: WHO.

———. (2011b), *WHO Report on the Global Tobacco Epidemic, 2011: Warning about the Dangers of Tobacco*, Geneva: WHO.

Wilbert, J. (1972), 'Tobacco and Shamanistic Ecstasy among the Warao Indians of Venezuela', in P.T. Furst (ed.), *Flesh of the Gods: The Ritual Use of Hallucinogens*, London: George Allen and Unwin, 55–83.

———. (1987), *Tobacco and Shamanism in South America*, New Haven, CT: Yale University Press.

———. (1994), 'The Cultural Significance of Tobacco Use in South America', in G. Seaman and J.S. Day (eds), *Ancient Traditions: Shamanism in Central Asia and the Americas*, Denver, CO: University Press of Colorado and Denver Museum of Natural History, 47–76.

———. (1996), *Mindful of Famine: Religious Climatology of the Warao Indians*, Cambridge, MA: Harvard University Press.

———. (2004), 'The Order of Dark Shamans among the Warao', in N.L. Whitehead and R. Wright (eds), *In Darkness and Secrecy: The Anthropology of Assault Sorcery and Witchcraft in Amazonia*, Durham, NC: Duke University Press, 21–50.

Wilbert, J. and Simoneau, K. (eds) (1990), *Folk Literature of the Yanomami Indians*, Los Angeles, CA: UCLA Latin American Center Publications.

Winter, J.C. (2000a), 'Botanical Description of the North American Tobacco Species', in J.C. Winter (ed.), *Tobacco Use by Native North Americans: Sacred Smoke and Silent Killer*, Norman, OK: University of Oklahoma Press, 87–127.

———. (2000b), 'Traditional Use of Tobacco by Native Americans', in J.C. Winter (ed.), *Tobacco Use by Native North Americans: Sacred Smoke and Silent Killer*, Norman, OK: University of Oklahoma Press, 9–58.

———. (2000c), 'Food of the Gods: Biochemistry, Addiction, and the Development of Native American Tobacco Use', in J.C. Winter (ed.), *Tobacco Use by Native North Americans: Sacred Smoke and Silent Killer*, Norman, OK: University of Oklahoma Press, 305–28.

Wiseman, B. (1999), 'Portrait of the Therapist as a Shaman', *European Journal of Psychotherapy and Counselling*, 2(1): 41–53.

Wonnacott, S., Russell, M.A.H. and Stolerman, I.P. (eds) (1990), *Nicotine Psychopharmacology: Molecular, Cellular and Behavioural Aspects*, Oxford: Oxford Scientific Publications, Oxford University Press.

Wright, R. (1993), 'Pursuing the Spirit: Semantic Construction in Hohodene Kalidzamai Chants for Initiation', *Amerindia*, 18: 1–40.

———. (1998), *Cosmos, Self and History in Baníwa Religion: For Those Unborn*, Austin, TX: University of Texas Press.

———. (2004), 'The Wicked and Wise Men: Witches and Prophets in Baniwa', in N. Whitehead and R. Wright (eds), *In Darkness and Secrecy: The Anthropology of Assault Sorcery and Witchcraft in Amazonia*, Durham, NC: Duke University Press, 82–108.

———. (2013), *Mysteries of the Jaguar Shamans of the Northwest Amazon*, Lincoln, NE: University of Nebraska Press.

Young, D. (2005), 'The Smell of Greenness: Cultural Synaesthesia in the Western Desert', *Etnofoor*, 18(1): 61–77.

Zeder, M., Bradley, D., Emshwiller, E. and Smith, B.D. (eds) (2006), *Documenting Domestication: New Genetic and Archaeological Paradigms*, Berkeley, CA: University of California Press.

Index

Note: Locators followed by the letter "n" refer to notes

For Product Safety Concerns and Information please contact our EU representative GPSR@taylorandfrancis.com
Taylor & Francis Verlag GmbH, Kaufingerstraße 24, 80331 München, Germany

www.ingramcontent.com/pod-product-compliance
Ingram Content Group UK Ltd.
Pitfield, Milton Keynes, MK11 3LW, UK
UKHW021010180425
457613UK00019B/878

* 9 7 8 1 3 5 0 0 0 7 3 9 0 *